⊷ T H E ⊶

Sagebrush Anthology

Mark Twain and His Circle Series
Tom Quirk, Editor

THE

Sagebrush Anthology

LITERATURE FROM
THE SILVER AGE OF THE OLD WEST

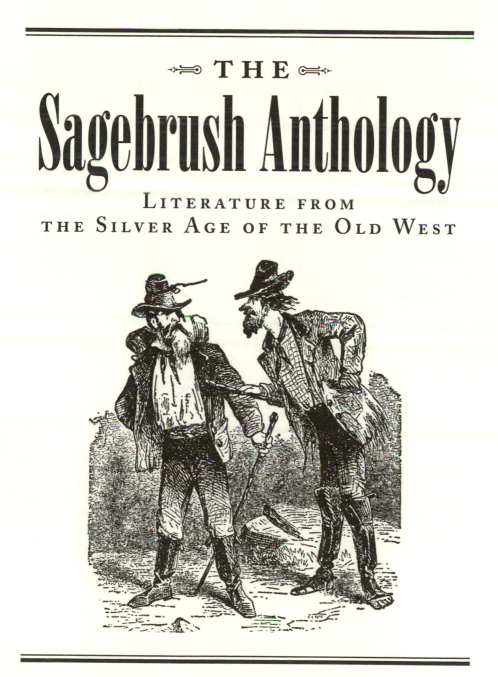

Edited by Lawrence I. Berkove

UNIVERSITY OF MISSOURI PRESS COLUMBIA AND LONDON

The Sagebrush Anthology
Copyright © 2006 by
The Curators of the University of Missouri
University of Missouri Press, Columbia, Missouri 65201
Printed and bound in the United States of America
All rights reserved
5 4 3 2 1   10 09 08 07 06

Library of Congress Cataloging-in-Publication Data

The sagebrush anthology : literature from the silver age of the Old West /
edited by Lawrence I. Berkove.
   p. cm. — (Mark Twain and his circle series)
  Summary: "Sixty-eight selections representing writers who spent their
creative years in Nevada from the 1860s to the early twentieth century and
have become known as the Sagebrush School. Features Mark Twain, Dan De
Quille, Sam Davis, Joe Goodman, and Rollin Daggett, and lesser-known writers
Arthur McEwen, Fred Hart, and others"—Provided by publisher.
  Includes bibliographical references and index.
  ISBN-13: 978-0-8262-1662-5 (hard cover : alk. paper)
  ISBN-13: 978-0-8262-1651-9 (pbk. : alk. paper)
  1. American literature—West (U.S.) 2. West (U.S.)—Literary collections.
3. West (U.S.)—Civilization. I. Berkove, Lawrence I. II. Series.
PS561.S24 2006
810.8'09793—dc22

                 2006000186

Designer: Kristie Lee
Typesetter: Crane Composition, Inc.
Printer and binder: The Maple-Vail Book Manufacturing Group
Typefaces: Adobe Caslon and Bodoni Poster Compressed

Publication of this book has been generously assisted by
a contribution from the Sprint Foundation.

For Gail

Her children rise up, and call her blessed;
Her husband also, and he praises her:
"Many daughters have done valiantly,
But thou excel them all."

Contents

⊷⊶⊷ ⊶⊷⊶

Short Fiction

Memoirs

Nonfiction

Letters

Poetry

Acknowledgments

◁═ ═▷

It is my pleasure to acknowledge a debt of gratitude for friendly assistance to: Tom Quirk, the godfather of this book, who first encouraged me to undertake it and gave me sage advice thereafter; Joe McCullough, for his enthusiastic support and welcome counsel; the Sponsored Research office of the University of Michigan–Dearborn, ably and understandingly administered by Drew Buchanan, for the various grants that over a period of years greatly aided me in conducting the research that led to the compilation of this book and in preparing the manuscript; the staff of the University of Missouri Press, who have been ideally considerate and helpful; and Connie Shelton, for carefully transcribing many texts from original manuscripts not always in the best of condition. I am deeply grateful to the late Sylvia Crowell Stoddard, who opened up the treasure-house archive of her grandfather, Sam Davis, to me; and to her heirs, Royal and Diane Crowell, who have kept it open. I acknowledge a debt beyond reckoning to the various authors represented herein, whose exceptional writings have been a constant delight and inspiration to me and made all my work a labor of love. And an infinite debt is owed to my beautiful wife, Gail, for her unfailing love, indulgence, and maintenance.

⊷ T H E ⊶
Sagebrush Anthology

Sagebrush Literature

An Introduction

I.

Few creative movements within American literature are so little known and so underestimated as the Sagebrush School. It lasted only from the early 1860s to the second decade of the twentieth century, and its high period did not extend much beyond the 1890s—but it shaped America's greatest writer, Mark Twain; it influenced Ambrose Bierce; and it nurtured some of the most talented authors of the period. Because no author develops in a vacuum, an acquaintance with the Sagebrush School is valuable for those who wish to trace the roots of Twain's artistry and attitudes. This collection serves that end by introducing representative authors and works of the school and suggesting connections and parallels to Twain. In addition, it demonstrates that the Sagebrush School is in itself worthy of attention. Its authors had diverse and interesting lives apart from their connections with Twain, pursued purposes and goals of their own, and merit recognition for having achieved literary successes independent of Twain. They did not achieve a Golden Age of literature, such as had occurred several generations earlier with the writers of the American Renaissance, but they wrote more and better than has been recognized and, in the final analysis, were worthy of the mineral that drew them to the mountains and deserts of Nevada, achieving their own Silver Age.

This collection has several purposes. One is to introduce readers to the group of writers who shaped Twain and gave him his final tempering and sharpening and thus prepared him, in personal values as well as in technique, for the career that was before him. Selected items by and about Twain during his Sagebrush years illustrate the connections that were established then and that remained with him throughout his career, growing ever deeper and more subtle. A second purpose is to give some sense to readers of how talented and

1

versatile the Sagebrushers were, and how broad their range was, far beyond the use Twain made of them. A final intention is to begin the process of resurrecting the Sagebrush School for its own sake, by demonstrating how interesting and entertaining its writings can be, and how much they can yet teach us.

Calling the Sagebrush movement a "school" implies a formal adherence to some literary creed, whereas there was only a loose association of writers with a common base in nineteenth-century Nevada. Most of these writers were men, and at least part-time or occasional journalists. All but Sarah Winnemucca were born in the East and emigrated from there to Nevada, and few lived there for as long as three or even two decades. The border between Nevada and California was especially porous, and most of the Sagebrush writers moved back and forth frequently between Nevada and San Francisco, with many eventually choosing to settle permanently in California and continue writing from there. Designating writers as Sagebrushers, therefore, may sometimes seem arbitrary, and no definition can escape some degree of looseness. The term, nevertheless, is legitimate and is the best way to describe the small but remarkable constellation of authors who were inspired by their immersion in the unique atmosphere of Nevada's first mining boom to produce excellent and memorable literature under conditions seemingly inimical to art. Ella Sterling Cummins recognized the Sagebrush School in *The Story of the Files* (1893) and applied the term to most of the authors represented herein. It is used here to further include authors whose extensive or frequent sojourns in Nevada were significant in shaping their thought and art. Discussions of individual authors below will specify the nature of their connections to Nevada.

Unlike the emigrants who settled in most parts of the West, agriculturists who homesteaded and put down roots in the areas in which they settled, most Sagebrushers were technically skilled individuals attracted to the Nevada region by the high salaries and standard of living made possible by its silver and gold mines, and they were inclined to be mobile. Mining is an exploitative enterprise, and once mines are exhausted, communities dependent upon them quickly lose viability. Mining regions are notorious for "ghost towns," communities that sprang suddenly into existence, flourished for a few years, and then were deserted with almost equal suddenness. Much of Nevada's population of this period consisted of transients who moved into and out of the state in synchrony with its fortunes. Most of the Sagebrushers were similarly transient; they happily worked in Nevada while the living was good, but when better opportunities opened up elsewhere, they moved on. As a consequence, neither the Nevada mining towns nor the Sagebrush School lasted long enough to establish an ongoing local tradition. Much Sagebrush literary productivity was not even published in books but has to be located in archives and in often incomplete files of newspapers of small or even vanished towns. But, when unearthed, as in this collection, like long-buried but still vital seeds, these writings come back to life.

In California, many of the early pioneers were prospectors who hoped to achieve wealth by locating and working deposits of loose gold as independent placer miners, using mainly pick, shovel, and pan. Some few Sagebrushers briefly shared that experience, but Nevada mining was largely industrial, a process that required enormous outlays of capital and a technological infra-structure that could drill and blast shafts and tunnels into the hard rock that contained silver and gold ore, then crush the ore, and finally extract and re-fine the valuable minerals from it. Nevada mining therefore reflected a complex culture and depended upon specialization. Prospectors might locate potentially rich deposits, but few could afford to develop them. Instead, they sold their claims to wealthy individuals or to companies put together by fi-nanciers. Professional engineers assembled and ran the component parts of the infrastructure, lawyers were hired to defend or challenge claims, and politicians were enlisted to introduce and support legislation favorable to the mining interests. Nevada mining thus had many human as well as natural complications.

Almost every feature of mining in nineteenth-century Nevada brought out the worst and the best in men. Given spectacularly rich deposits of ore in unstable rock located in remote, arid, and inhospitable country, fortunes were at stake in every phase of development: the ownership of claims, the mining and refining processes, transportation, the supplying of water and timber, and the unionization of labor. Believers in Social Darwinism could have used Nevada as a prime example of its operation. Development proceeded at such a breakneck pace and was often so far ahead of existing legislation that regu-lation lagged, when it did not simply serve the rich and powerful. It was a time of practically unrestrained capitalism and technological innovation; al-most anything could be done without regard to long-term consequences to the environment or to population centers, because the land seemed empty and communities were disposable. Nevertheless, as the Sagebrush writers chronicled what was happening, at their best they kept a tally of the human spirit in the midst of this juggernaut of "progress," recording its human cost and praising resistance to its inhumanity.

II.

Sagebrush literature has several distinct features. First, on a surface level, it manifests a fierce love of the Nevada experience. It is remarkable that most Sagebrushers, even those who were critical of aspects of the mining culture, or who were rejected by a later and more mercenary generation, were nostalgic about their experiences in the early days. In some cases, they were nostalgic even as their experiences were ongoing, as if they knew they were living in a charmed but fleeting moment of history. Their writing has a sense of high spirits, of tasting life at its most flavorful, and of a camaraderie of soul mates. It is obvious in the poetry—especially Joe Goodman's "Virginia City," Sam Davis's "The Lure of the Sagebrush," and Rollin M. Daggett's "My New Year's Guests"—and it can also be easily seen in the memoirs and in Twain's letters.

To an unusual degree, Sagebrush literature tends to favor personal narrative; many items are told from a first-person perspective or lend themselves to biographical reference. Indeed, the number of memoirs that Sagebrush writers produced is astonishing, and only a small fraction of this large corpus could be reproduced herein. But memoirs always raise the question of accuracy; even granting that a number of memoirs reinforce each other in a general way, the specificity of recollections after the passage of decades should always be taken with a grain of salt. Truth to tell, Sagebrush writers loved to embellish their recollections. Sam Davis once described Joe Goodman's chief fault as his inability to lie, but Davis did not labor under the same disability. Goodman's memoirs *are* unusually dependable, although he several times misremembered details, but many authors' and even Davis's fictions often contained more than a kernel of truth. Perhaps Davis's background as the son of an Episcopal priest left him with a taste for parable: an essential truth in a fictional vehicle. However that may be, Sagebrush authors in general were acute observers of human nature as well as recorders of incidents, and much of their fiction arose out of real-life experiences.

Sagebrush literature also tends to be thoughtfully moral. Its authors were moral not so much in their endorsement of the forms of legal justice and democracy as in their adherence to less sophisticated but perhaps deeper values: honor, virtue, and fair play. Also, they had high regard for *manliness*, a trait that some today consider old-fashioned if not downright sexist but that, as they conceived it, encompassed principle and decency as well as courage. The Comstock Sagebrushers, especially, were strongly pro-Union as the Civil War first smoldered and then ignited, and it is probable that they influenced Mark Twain in this moral inclination, as well as in other matters.

In Nevada, because they had to be prepared to literally defend their journalistic stands with their lives, writers had to decide early which values were luxuries and which were essential and worth fighting for. In the small subgenre of writings about journalism (and written by journalists), for instance, a common denominator is the wryness of the humor about editors whose idealistic but shallow notions of principles and courage were quickly moderated by practical consequences. Behind this humor is a skeptical attitude toward grown men who had not yet decided what their bedrock values were, along with an almost disdainful attitude toward cowards and equivocators.

Many of the writers probed morality to philosophical and even to theological levels. "Who is good?" depends on the prior question of "what is good?" and the Sagebrush authors had not lived in a rough-and-tumble world without having come to doubt not only the mannered and theoretical norms of civilized society but also some of its cherished beliefs. In a society where law broke down, and where order often was what was imposed by the vicious and the brutal, Fred Hart depicts fire being fought with fire, with vigilante organizations ridding society of its bullies. Due process is secondary to survival. It may be theoretically illogical and immoral to do wrong in the service of virtue, but in extreme cases the ends may justify the means. In Davis's stories, particularly "A Christmas Carol" and "The Conversion of Champagne Liz," individuals frowned on by society for not being sufficiently moral and respectable give more good to society than they take. The author's positions challenge conventional morality, but the results speak for themselves.

The Nevada mining culture was not kind to the timid and naive. "Caveat emptor all ye who enter here" might well have been posted at all Nevada border crossings. Extravagantly optimistic descriptions of mining claims and financial opportunities were commonplace; outright lies were frequent; the stock market was so routinely manipulated that it might as well have been another loaded gambling game; stockholders—a specialized category of speculators—seldom got an accurate accounting of expenditures and earnings; and contracts were often honored in the breach. But little sympathy was wasted on someone who had been cheated and was not man enough to enforce his rights by taking the law into his own hands. There were indeed sheriffs, judges, and juries, but most of them were acutely aware of the practical wisdom of putting their own well-being ahead of any abstract notion of law. The state's rich ores were temptations that brought out the worst in men of all classes. Shootings, often over trivial incidents, were commonplace; among the first provisions in a new town was a graveyard, and it seldom had to wait many days before being used. The rich and powerful subverted the law, bought votes openly (giving Nevada the nickname of "the rotten borough"), and did not refrain from using intimidation or force to achieve their ends. In the face of this practically unbridled capitalism and a pervasive working philosophy of "might makes right," most Sagebrush authors were, though not saints, personally moral. They were entertained by the human comedy playing out before their eyes, but they seldom if ever praised the unscrupulous. They did esteem those who stood up against the corruptions of the system, and sometimes they were the ones who stood up. The Sagebrushers were cynics in the original, classical sense of the term: they uncovered and examined the true agendas of individuals. Those who only posed as virtuous were exposed, and those who, even in failure or tragedy, displayed manly or heroic values were shown respect and admiration.

Last, but most important, is the Sagebrushers' mastery of style. Readers who expect Nevada journalists to have been poorly educated, unsophisticated, and only rudely talented are in for a pleasant surprise. There were, indeed, many Nevada writers who preferred vernacular in prose or poetry, but the best of the Sagebrush authors were cultured individuals (although many were self-educated) who appreciated the nuances and effects achieved by the great authors of English, American, and world literature and who took pride in being able to write well. They were masters of both formal and informal style and could not only switch back and forth between them with ease but could also wield both with the great skill of the literary artists they admired, combining irony, subtlety, and wit in their distinctive use of the literary hoax.

The Sagebrush authors did not invent the literary hoax, but they did nurture it into a high art. Immersed as they were in an environment where financial and legal hoaxes were perpetrated every day, and where the universally popular card game of poker made use of the hoax in the form of the bluff, they naturally reflected on hoaxes, described and recorded them in their writings, and ultimately incorporated them into a main characteristic of their style. Hoaxes always involve deception, but unlike the hoaxes of the real world, the literary hoax, far from harming readers, only entertains and may also instruct and protect. All literary hoaxes strive to make something impossible or improbable seem plausible, but there is almost always a clue that can give the hoax away, a loose thread that if pulled will unravel the whole scheme. These hoaxes play upon the naivete or credulity of victims who do not sufficiently analyze what is presented to them but accept what they see or hear at face value. Most often, the humor of the hoax is shared with an in-group that understands what is happening and can enjoy observing the fish being enticed, hooked, and finally reeled in. In bolder hoaxes, the hoaxer takes on the entire audience and takes a private enjoyment in outwitting everybody. The gentler kind of hoax is usually of the first variety, where readers are taken into the author's confidence and can observe and enjoy the way the target is duped. Dan De Quille (the pen name of William Wright) was a past master of this kind of hoax, but readers of his "quaints" are likely to be surprised at how subtle and ingenious they can be. The most challenging kind of hoax, on the other hand, is aimed at readers and usually jolts them once they realize how vulnerable they have been. Mark Twain is the American champion of this more aggressive variety, and Ambrose Bierce approaches Twain's level in his most famous short story, "An Occurrence at Owl Creek Bridge." Both of these authors had extensive contacts with Sagebrushers and, as Proverbs teaches, "iron sharpens iron."

Although one category of this collection is devoted to humor and hoaxes, it will be noticed that the categories of fiction and memoirs also contain humorous narratives, including ones that make pointed use of hoaxes. That these categories have a considerable degree of overlap must be conceded; nevertheless, the distinction intended is that of humor and hoaxes as ends in themselves, as opposed to means to an end. That humor and hoaxing were practically ubiquitous in Sagebrush literature is, in itself, an important clue to the pervasive and deep influence of the Sagebrush style on Mark Twain. Twain is still—and justifiably—regarded as America's greatest humorist, yet only in relatively recent years has it been recognized that moral seriousness underlies much of his humor, and that most of his greatest works incorporate subtle hoaxes at their cores.

III.

A collection such as this is a survey, not an exhaustive compendium. An effort was made by the editor to select from the best writings of the authors represented herein, but he does not claim to have picked all of the best of any author, or even to have selected all of the best authors of the Sagebrush School. Like his predecessor, Duncan Emrich, whose *Comstock Bonanza* (1950) broke trail for this book, the editor found that some selections were inevitable. A few pieces, especially those by Dan De Quille, Sam Davis, and Joe Goodman, are so outstanding that a collection of Sagebrush writings cannot call itself representative without them. Research during the past twenty-five years has, however, recovered both more Sagebrush writing than Emrich knew about and much more Sagebrush literature than can be represented in this type of anthology. Accordingly, although this collection overlaps with Emrich's, it also moves far beyond his book into new territory. Readers who wish to know more about the school and read more of its literature can turn to the bibliography and learn what is available. Should they wish to discover more on their own, the good news is that there are authors and much fine writing yet to be brought to light.

Even though the process of recovering Sagebrush literature is far from complete, it is not too soon to recognize that a literary hierarchy is in the process of evolving. Dan De Quille is certainly the most important writer of the Sagebrush School after Mark Twain. Indeed, he may be the most accomplished Western author after the long-established triumvirate of Twain, Ambrose Bierce, and Bret Harte. Samuel Post Davis is without doubt the next in line. It is too early to be confident about the relative standings of Joseph Thompson Goodman and Rollin Mallory Daggett, except to say that their days of being overlooked should be over. Because these writers are so representative of the Sagebrush School and claim a prominent place in this anthology, their biographies follow here to illustrate Sagebrush traits that have been mentioned.

Dan De Quille (1829–1898) was the pen name of William Wright. As was the case with his friend Mark Twain, the pen name came to be preferred over his real one even by people who knew him well. From his earliest years, he read widely and trained himself to write. He spent 1857–1861 in California prospecting for gold. Shortly after he arrived in Virginia City in 1861, he was hired by Joe Goodman and Denis McCarthy to work on their paper, the *Territorial Enterprise*. He quickly became, according to Goodman, the paper's ablest writer. The accuracy and fairness of his mining reports helped make the *Enterprise* the leading paper in the West. Even before he joined the paper, his contributions to *The Golden Era*, a prestigious San Francisco literary magazine cofounded by Rollin Daggett, were esteemed for their imagination and wit. After joining the *Enterprise*, in addition to publishing his stories and literary hoaxes there, he continued to freelance in periodicals across the country as well as in the West.

In 1862, the *Enterprise* hired Sam Clemens, who quickly became a friend and somewhat of a mentee of De Quille and soon adopted the pen name of Mark Twain. The two men were kindred spirits, although De Quille was six years older than Twain, and became roommates. The association was fateful for De Quille. Without intending to, Twain began to eclipse De Quille, who remained on the Comstock while Twain moved first to California and then to the East and went on to success after success. De Quille appears to have been shaken by his comrade's quick rise to fame, and he suffered both envy and a loss of self-confidence. After completing *The Big Bonanza* (1876), his now classical account of the Comstock, he took to drink and soon fell so deeply into alcoholism that his good friend Joe Goodman had to fire him from the *Enterprise*.

The shock appeared to reinvigorate him. He overcame his alcoholism, took on a weekly feature column for the *Salt Lake Daily Tribune*, owned and edited by his friend C. C. Goodwin, and earned more income by increasing his freelance productivity. He became more thoughtful, and his stories became more socially, morally, and psychologically penetrating. In the last decade of his life, as he grew frailer, he hurriedly completed several novellas but did not live long enough to publish them: "Pahnenit," *The Sorceress of Attu,* and the fine *Dives and Lazarus.* (These, and many of his stories, were published for the first time in the 1980s and 1990s.) At the time of his death, he was both a nationally and an internationally recognized author. Probably because most of his short writings were inaccessible in archives or in the files of discontinued periodicals, he was almost forgotten until interest in him revived in the 1980s, when his works began to be collected and published.

Sam Davis (1850–1918), the son of an Episcopal priest, was sent to a theological seminary but left it to become a journalist. He worked on several papers in Nebraska, Missouri, and Chicago before following his father to California, where he resumed his career as a journalist. From the beginning, Davis manifested wit and courage in his writing to such a degree that other periodicals took note of his doings. He moved to Nevada in 1875 and began working for the *Virginia City Evening Chronicle* under its outspoken and capable editor, Denis McCarthy. In 1879, he accepted an editorial position at the *Carson City Morning Appeal,* whose editor, the courageously straightforward and talented Henry Mighels, had just died. Shortly after taking over, he put an end to the vilification of Mighels begun by the dead man's enemies when he publicly announced that he, Davis, was ready to defend Mighels's reputation by deed as well as by word. Davis married Mighels's widow in 1880 and for the rest of his life enhanced both by editorial policy and by example the *Appeal*'s reputation for public-spiritedness and doggedly fearless opposition to corruption and intimidation. Davis also involved himself in state politics, contributing exceptional personal integrity and strong devotion to the commonweal. In 1906, for instance, after the San Francisco earthquake, many insurance companies attempted to default on their policies. Davis, acting unilaterally as ex officio state insurance commissioner, announced that any insurance company that did not pay 100 cents on the dollar in California would not be allowed to do business in Nevada. Soon, other states followed his lead, and solvent insurance companies yielded to this pressure.

Davis was a man of many talents. He was in great demand as a humorist; he was an avid fan of the theater, both acting in plays and writing some of his own; and throughout his life he composed poems and sketches for periodicals in Nevada and California. In 1886, reputedly encouraged by his friend Ambrose Bierce, he published his only literary anthology, *Short Stories.* It had some very good stories in it, and one of them, "The Reporter's Revenge," arguably influenced Bierce's great story, "An Occurrence at Owl Creek Bridge." Davis, however, never collected the many fine stories he continued to write over the next twenty years. Below the surface narratives of some of these are subtle and thoughtful explorations of moral issues and paradoxes. Early in the twentieth century, he wrote and copyrighted a delightful comic opera, *The Prince of Timbuctoo,* which was not published until 2006. He edited and contributed to the two-volume *History of Nevada* in 1913 and almost until his death continued to write memoirs, several of which are included herein but many of which remain uncollected.

Joe Goodman (1838–1917) was a Renaissance man. He began his career as a printer, moved to Virginia City in 1861, and with his partner Denis McCarthy bought the *Territorial Enterprise.* Both men put policies into effect that transformed the *Enterprise* from a struggling weekly into a dynamic daily that employed some of the best journalistic talent in the West. Goodman soon bought out McCarthy and ran the paper so successfully that its sales made it independent of both government and big business. Without being "reformist," the paper nevertheless stood for honest government and political principle, and Goodman set the tone. Early in his career, he forced the resignation of the entire bench of the Nevada Supreme Court because of its corruption, and as late as 1872 he wrote an editorial that destroyed the election hopes of William Sharon, one of the richest but most venal Comstock financiers. In 1874, Goodman sold his paper at a profit and moved to San Francisco, where he was a stockbroker for some years. In 1884 he founded the *San Franciscan,* a high-quality literary journal for the six months he ran it. Tiring of stockbroking and editing, Goodman next turned to raising grapes for raisins. In his later years, he moved to Alameda and became interested in Central America. From his home, he single-handedly deciphered the hieroglyphs that explained the Mayan calendar; his name today is known and respected by Meso-American anthropologists.

All the while, Goodman was an active writer with a straightforward and virile style. He wrote editorials, serious poetry, and play reviews for his own paper, few of which have been collected. In 1870 he wrote a series of outstanding travel letters from Europe, which the *Enterprise* published (and which were collected and republished in 1997). In 1872 he collaborated with Rollin Mallory Daggett, one of his editors, on a play, *The Psychoscope.* It was more than a generation ahead of its time in realism and in pioneering use of the motifs of science fiction and detectives. (The play was first published in 2006.) In San Francisco, Goodman wrote short stories, and late in his career wrote his most famous one, "The Trumpet Comes to Pickeye!" (included herein). In the last twenty-five years of his life, he wrote many memoirs, only some of which have been collected.

Goodman was a bold spirit, self-confident, exceptionally talented and able, and a paragon of integrity and courage. Among his close friends were De Quille, Daggett, Davis, Alf Doten, Thomas Fitch, Jim Townsend, and, most especially, Mark Twain. Twain looked up to Goodman for the rest of Twain's life, and Goodman unfailingly braced Twain with support and advice. Goodman personally embodied most of the virtues of the Sagebrush School and was, although unintentionally, one of its centers of inspiration.

Rollin Mallory Daggett (1831–1901) was another multitalented Renaissance man. Raised in Ohio, he crossed the Great Plains alone as a young man. After cofounding *The Golden Era* and a newspaper in San Francisco, he came to Virginia City as a stockbroker but changed jobs and worked as a reporter on the *Enterprise*. He soon was promoted to an editorial capacity and became known for both his pugnacity and his wit. He also wrote serious poetry and competed with his friend Joe Goodman for top poetic honors on the Comstock. He collaborated with Goodman on *The Psychoscope* but in his earlier years was more interested in politics than in literature. After participating in local politics, he was elected in 1879 to a two-year term in the U.S. House of Representatives, where he championed Nevada causes and fought the railroads, whose powerful grip held Nevada in a near stranglehold. He was defeated for reelection in 1881 but was appointed by President Chester Arthur as minister to the kingdom of Hawaii and served ably in that post until 1885. So close, in fact, was his friendship with King Kalakaua that when Daggett retired the two men collaborated on a book, *The Legends and Myths of Hawaii* (1888).

In 1882, Daggett published *Braxton's Bar*, a novel about miners. In his last years, he built himself a house in California and from there produced many stories, sketches, essays, poems, and memoirs. The full extent of his writing is not known, and much of it remains uncollected.

When these biographical sketches are regarded in contiguity, the first impression should be of what remarkable lives full of variety and accomplishment these authors lived. In today's world, even restricting ourselves to considering only statewide venues, how many of our leading editors, journalists, politicians, and men of affairs have lifted themselves so far from humble beginnings and in the course of their activities additionally become authors of creative literature, and distinguished ones at that? Of course, not all Sagebrushers were so outstanding, but the wonder is that so many of them, and so many of these central figures, were. They were the opposite of uninvolved recluses, and out of their confrontations with a rough and ethically challenging world they crafted a literature of character, strength, and wit that still has the vitality to entertain and engage.

A NOTE ON THE TEXT

Wherever possible, the sources of the texts used here have been indicated. In a few cases, when multiple copies of a manuscript were available but no single source could be identified, an educated guess served as an editorial choice. Because much of this collection has been gathered from newspapers and magazines whose proofreading standards were uneven, and some handwritten manuscripts were not proofread, typographical or punctuation errors unavoidably occurred. Fortunately, these were few and almost always obvious, and they have been silently emended. In a few cases, such as authorial spelling of nonstandard names or dialect words—for example, Sarah Winnemucca's use of "Bannack" for the Bannock Indians—standard spellings have been used as replacements. Sam Davis's manuscript texts were the one case where an unusual degree of editorial input was needed, but even there the problems were obvious and so were the solutions. The editor believes in a light touch and minimal intervention, and the generally high quality of Sagebrush writing has supported this position.

Humor and Hoaxes

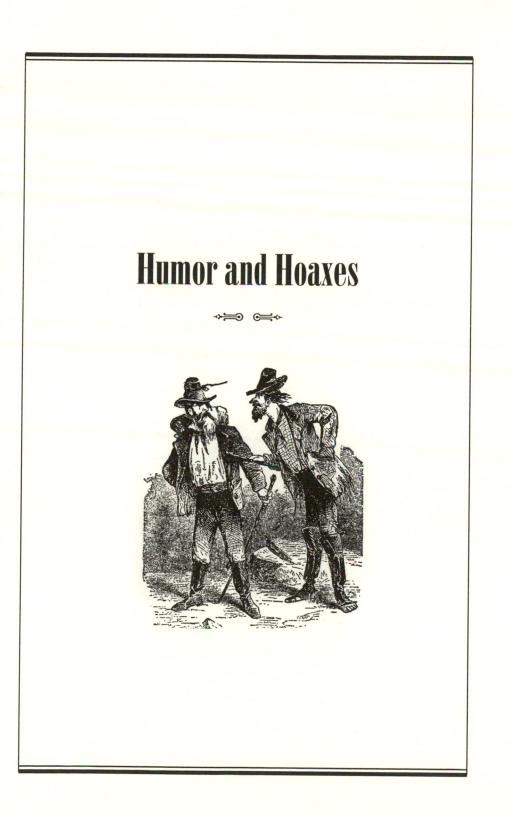

Introduction

Nevada audiences and Sagebrush writers enjoyed a good laugh, even when the joke was on themselves. The satires on journalists—by journalists—provide an excellent case in point. "Why the Gold Gulch News Suspended" is funny but not unbelievable. The "Sam Davis Newspaper Story" is an ironic recognition by an editor that the "moral high ground" of editors often is only rationalized self-interest. Although Nevada journalism had more than its share of exceptionally competent editors and writers, there were some, like Major Hoister, whose talents had been dissipated by drink, and some, like the owner Andrew Brown, whose college training had not prepared them for the real world. "The TRUMPET Comes to Pickeye!" is one of the few Sagebrush stories that has been kept current by occasional reprintings. Its ironic view of how journalistic idealism is modified by reality remains convincing. Not all editors learned as quickly as the one in "Whipping an Editor." Sam Davis's "The Typographical Howitzer" daringly mocks a number of contemporary authors, Twain and Davis himself chief among them, by ridiculing their pet stylistic mannerisms. Humor this good apparently defused retaliation by journalists whose sensibilities might have been ruffled.

In the early days of his career, while he was still absorbing influences from the Sagebrush ambience, Twain was known primarily as a humorist and not as a writer of fiction. Two early hoaxes, "Petrified Man" and "A Bloody Massacre near Carson," fooled most of their readers and demonstrated not only his fondness for hoaxes but also his talent at subtlety, because familiarity made the audience he wrote for ordinarily more alert to hoaxes, literary and everyday. "Washoe.—'Information Wanted'" reveals Twain making a special effort not to be misunderstood and also reveals his basic inclination to honesty beneath the surface funning. His tribute to Artemus Ward is biographically interesting, but "The Carson Fossil-Footprints," dating to 1884—

15

almost two decades after he left the Comstock—not only obviously originates in Twain's Comstock experience but is also one of the few pieces he ever wrote that directly suggests an influence of Artemus Ward's technique of double-talk. Joe Goodman's "That Affair at Pollard's" skillfully incorporates another one of Ward's techniques: concealing his purpose inside a superficially disorganized verbal ramble. Twain brilliantly improved and made use of this technique in his major books.

Dan De Quille's hoaxes, "A Silver Man," "Eyeless Fish That Live in Hot Water," and especially "Solar Armor," were widely popular, partly because of their ingenuity and partly because, unlike Mark Twain's more pointed spoofs, they were ultimately gentle and entertained without inflicting insult or pain. The subtlety and skill of these "quaints," as De Quille termed them, can be used as a measure of the audience for which they were intended. Unlike tall tales, the quaints were written for fairly sophisticated readers, knowledgeable about science. De Quille, however, uses his audience's knowledge against it as he moves slowly and carefully to begin with something impossible or at least improbable and gradually adds plausible details until the whole edifice topples when the weakness in the structure is at last discovered. "Frightful Catastrophe—Wonderful Escape" gives itself away at the end as a hoax, but until that point the narrative disguised as a sympathetic though sensational account of a frightening incident probably convinces most readers with its psychological plausibility.

The sheer effrontery of some of the hoaxes tickled the fancy of the Sagebrushers, and even that of their targets. It is difficult to imagine a journalist trying to pull off a hoax today like Sam Davis's "earthquake" and escaping intact. Orson Welles's notorious "War of the Worlds" radio hoax in the 1930s might have been the last time the technique was even approximated. Similarly, it is difficult to imagine today's society being sufficiently independent of considerations of "political correctness" to dare to appreciate Arthur McEwen's "One Solution." Or, as in the case of "How to Win at Faro," to imagine a group of serious gamblers appreciating their having been outwitted by an evangelist, and accepting with grace his offer of grace.

"The Tables Turned" and "Serious Trifling" use humor to sugarcoat a bitter pill for some people of influence. Usually, the rates the railroads charged were anything but funny, and the guilty superintendent of the latter story could probably have been multiplied in real life many times over. In these cases, the humor enhances the justice of the biter getting bit. Similarly, "A Libel Suit" is a prize example of a transparently insincere apology that takes more with its left hand than it gives back with its right. Under the guise of retracting an "alleged" libel, it repeats the original exposé of the fraud in

painful detail and inspiredly "praises" the swindler with fulsome exaggera-
tions. It is a model of how to circumvent the law while following it.

Davis's "Carson Poker Incident," another case of a story based on a real
hoax, is wryly humorous when its issues are considered. The "honor" of two
disreputable towns is "defended" by gamblers, men whom society looks down
upon. It is to the credit of Davis, however, that instead of leading readers to
smile condescendingly on a travesty of honor, he induces them to admire the
public spirit of Virginia City and the cool nerve of its champion as he bluffs
his way to victory.

America prides itself on its rich heritage of choice humor. The contributions of the Sagebrush writers are belatedly fresh but worthy additions to
that heritage.

Petrified Man

Mark Twain

This is one of the earliest hoaxes Twain wrote for the *Territorial Enterprise*, and it shows signs of his budding genius. The hoax is signaled by the gesture of thumbing the nose, which can be seen by replicating the positions of the hands and fingers; by the detail of the Indian supposedly having a wooden leg, an anachronism for Indians before the coming of the white man; and by the impossibility of petrifying a human body, especially one with water trickling over it. Twain intended this hoax to ridicule Judge G. T. Sewall, by making him appear foolish. Dan De Quille's later hoax, "A Silver Man" (included herein), was undoubtedly inspired by Twain's sketch.

A petrified man was found some time ago in the mountains south of Gravelly Ford. Every limb and feature of the stony mummy was perfect, not even excepting the left leg, which has evidently been a wooden one during the lifetime of the owner—which lifetime, by the way, came to a close about a century ago, in the opinion of a savan who has examined the defunct. The body was in a sitting position, and leaning against a huge mass of croppings; the attitude was pensive, the right thumb resting against the side of the nose; the left thumb partially supported the chin, the fore-finger pressing the inner corner of the left eye and drawing it partly open; the right eye was closed, and the fingers of the right hand spread apart. This strange freak of nature created a profound sensation in the vicinity, and our informant states that by request, Justice Sewell or Sowell, of Humboldt City, at once proceeded to the spot and held an inquest on the body. The verdict of the jury was that "deceased came to his death from protracted exposure," etc. The people of the neighborhood volunteered to bury the poor unfortunate, and were even anxious to do so, but it was discovered, when they attempted to remove him, that the water which had dripped upon him for ages from the crag above, had coursed down his back and deposited a limestone sediment under him which had glued him to the bed rock upon which he sat, as with a cement of adamant, and Judge S. refused to allow the charitable citizens to blast him from his position. The opinion expressed by his Honor that such a course would be little less than sacrilege was eminently just and proper. Everybody goes to see the stone man, as many as three hundred having visited the hardened creature during the past five or six weeks.

Territorial Enterprise, October 4, 1862

A Bloody Massacre near Carson

Mark Twain

Almost all readers of this hoax fell for it, and their anger and resentment at having been taken in quickly rose to such proportions that Twain felt obliged to publish the following explanatory retraction the next day:

I TAKE IT ALL BACK.

The story published in the Enterprise reciting the slaughter of a family near Empire was all a fiction. It was understood to be such by all acquainted with the locality in which the alleged affair occurred. In the first place, Empire and Dutch Nick's are one, and in the next there is no "great pine forest" nearer than the Sierra Nevada mountains. But it was necessary to publish the story in order to get the fact into the San Francisco papers that the Spring Valley Water company was "cooking" dividends by borrowing money to declare them on for its stockholders. The only way you can get a fact into a San Francisco journal is to smuggle it in through some great tragedy.

Twain might have added that a man with his throat cut from ear to ear would have been dead in less than a minute and could not have ridden any distance. (See also Joe Goodman's memoir of the hoax, included herein.)

⊶⊷ ⊶⊷

From Abram Curry, who arrived here yesterday from Carson, we have learned the following particulars concerning a bloody massacre which was committed in Ormsby county night before last. It seems that during the past six months a man named P. Hopkins, or Philip Hopkins, has been residing with his family in the old log house just at the edge of the great pine forest which lies between Empire City and Dutch Nick's. The family consisted of nine children—five girls and four boys—the oldest of the group, Mary, being nineteen years old, and the youngest, Tommy, about a year and a half. Twice in the past two months Mrs. Hopkins, while visiting in Carson, expressed fears concerning the sanity of her husband, remarking that of late he had been subject to fits of violence, and that during the prevalence of one of these he had threatened to take her life. It was Mrs. Hopkins' misfortune to be given to exaggeration, however, and but little attention was paid to what she said. About ten o'clock on Monday evening Hopkins dashed into Carson on horseback, with his throat cut from ear to ear, and bearing in his hand a reeking scalp from which the warm, smoking blood was still dripping, and fell in a dying condition in front of the Magnolia saloon. Hopkins expired in the course of five minutes, without speaking. The long red hair of the scalp he bore marked it as that of Mrs. Hopkins. A number of citizens, headed by Sheriff Gasherie, mounted at once and rode down to Hopkins' house, where a ghastly scene met their gaze. The scalpless corpse of Mrs. Hopkins lay across the threshold, with her head split open and her right hand almost severed from the wrist. Near her lay the ax with which the murderous deed had been committed. In one of the bedrooms six of the children were found, one in bed and the others scattered about the floor. They were all dead. Their brains had evidently been dashed out with a club, and every mark about them seemed to have been made with a blunt instrument. The children must have struggled hard for their lives, as articles of clothing and broken furniture were strewn about the room in the utmost confusion. Julia and Emma, aged respectively fourteen and seventeen, were found in the kitchen, bruised and insensible, but it is thought their recovery is possible. The oldest girl, Mary, must have taken refuge, in her terror, in the garret, as her body was found there, frightfully mutilated, and the knife with which her wounds had been inflicted still sticking in her side. The two girls, Julia and Emma, who had recovered sufficiently to be able to talk yesterday morning, state that their father knocked them down with a billet of wood and stamped on them. They think they were the first attacked. They further state that Hopkins had shown evidence of derangement all day, but had exhibited no violence. He flew into a passion and attempted to murder them because they advised him to go to bed and compose his mind. Curry says Hopkins was about forty-two years of age, and a native of Western Pennsylvania; he was always affable and polite, and until very recently we had never heard of his ill treating his family. He had been a heavy owner in the best mines of Virginia and Gold Hill, but when the San Francisco papers exposed the game of cooking dividends in order to bolster up our stocks he grew afraid and sold out, and invested to an immense amount in the Spring Valley Water Company of San Francisco. He was advised to do this by a relative of his; one of the editors of the San Francisco *Bulletin,* who had suffered pecuniarily by the dividend-cooking system as applied to the Daney Mining Company recently. Hopkins had not long ceased to own in the various claims on the Comstock lead, however, when several dividends were cooked on his newly acquired property, their water totally dried up, and Spring Valley stock went down to nothing. It is presumed that this misfortune drove him mad and resulted in his killing himself and the greater portion of his family. The newspapers of San Francisco permitted this water company to go on borrowing money and cooking dividends, under cover of which cunning financiers crept out of the tottering concern, leaving the crash to come upon poor and unsuspecting stockholders, without offering to expose the villainy at work. We hope the fearful massacre detailed above may prove the saddest result of their silence.

Territorial Enterprise, October 28, 1863

Washoe.—
"Information Wanted"

Mark Twain

Nevada newspapers occasionally received letters from potential immigrants asking for information. This is a satire of such letters—and of possible answers to them. Noteworthy in this piece is its admission of sarcasm and nonsense, for Twain was normally less obvious. His atypically broad humor suggests that he purposed to avoid misleading possibly naive readers. The original *Enterprise* publication of this sketch has been lost. The present text is based on its reprinting in the *San Francisco Golden Era*, May 22, 1864, and in *Early Tales & Sketches*.[1]

⋆⇒ ⇐⋆

SPRINGFIELD, Mo., April 12

"Dear Sir:—My object in writing to you is to have you give me a full history of Nevada: What is the character of its climate? What are the productions of the earth? Is it healthy? What diseases do they die of mostly? Do you think it would be advisable for a man who can make a living in Missouri to emigrate to that part of the country? There are several of us who would emigrate there in the spring if we could ascertain to a certainty that it is a much better country than this. I suppose you know Joel H. Smith? He used to live here; he lives in Nevada now; they say he owns considerable in a mine there. Hoping to hear from you soon, etc., I remain yours, truly,

WILLIAM——."

1. Mark Twain, *Early Tales & Sketches, Volume 1: 1851–1864*, ed. Edgar Marquess Branch, Robert H. Hirst, and Harriet Elinor Smith, 367–71.

DEAREST WILLIAM:—Pardon my familiarity—but that name touchingly reminds me of the loved and lost, whose name was similar. I have taken the contract to answer your letter, and although we are now strangers, I feel we shall cease to be so, if we ever become acquainted with each other. The thought is worthy of attention, William. I will now respond to your several propositions in the order in which you have fulminated them.

Your object in writing is to have me give you a full history of Nevada. The flattering confidence you repose in me, William, is only equaled by the modesty of your request. I could detail the history of Nevada in five hundred pages octavo, but as you have never done me any harm, I will spare you, though it will be apparent to everybody that I would be justified in taking advantage of you if I were a mind to do it. However, I will condense. Nevada was discovered many years ago by the Mormons, and was called Carson county. It only became Nevada in 1861, by act of Congress. There is a popular tradition that God Almighty created it; but when you come to see it, William, you will think differently. Do not let that discourage you, though. The country looks something like a singed cat, owing to the scarcity of shrubbery, and also resembles that animal in the respect that it has more merits than its personal appearance would seem to indicate. The Grosch brothers found the first silver lead here in 1857. They also founded Silver City, I believe. (Observe the subtle joke, William.) But the "history" of Nevada which you demand, properly begins with the discovery of the Comstock lead, which event happened nearly five years ago. The opinion now prevailing in the East that the Comstock is on the Gould & Curry is erroneous; on the contrary, the Gould & Curry is on the Comstock.[2] Please make the correction, William. Signify to your friends, also, that all the mines here do not pay dividends as yet; you may make this statement with the utmost unyielding inflexibility—it will not be contradicted from this quarter. The population of this Territory is about 35,000, one-half of which number reside in the united cities of Virginia and Gold Hill. However, I will discontinue this history for the present, lest I get you too deeply interested in this distant land and cause you to neglect your family or your religion. But I will address you again upon the subject next year. In the meantime, allow me to answer your inquiry as to the character of our climate.

It has no character to speak of, William, and alas! in this respect it resembles many, ah, too many chambermaids in this wretched, wretched world. Sometimes we have the seasons in their regular order, and then again we have winter all the summer and summer all winter. Consequently, we have never

2. The Gould & Curry was one of the leading Comstock mines.

yet come across an almanac that would just exactly fit this latitude. It is mighty regular about not raining, though, William. It will start in here in November and rain about four, and sometimes as much as seven days on a stretch; after that, you may loan out your umbrella for twelve months, with the serene confidence which a Christian feels in four aces. Sometimes the winter begins in November and winds up in June; and sometimes there is a bare suspicion of winter in March and April, and summer all the balance of the year. But as a general thing, William, the climate is good, what there is of it.

What are the productions of the earth? You mean in Nevada, of course. On our ranches here, anything can be raised that can be produced on the fertile fields of Missouri. But ranches are very scattering—as scattering, perhaps, as lawyers in heaven. Nevada, for the most part, is a barren waste of sand, embellished with melancholy sage-brush, and fenced in with snow-clad mountains. But these ghastly features were the salvation of the land, William, for no rightly constituted American would have ever come here if the place had been easy of access, and none of our pioneers would have staid after they got here if they had not felt satisfied that they could not find a smaller chance for making a living anywhere else. Such is man, William, as he crops out in America.

"Is it healthy?" Yes, I think it is as healthy here as it is in any part of the West. But never permit a question of that kind to vegetate in your brain, William, because as long as providence has an eye on you, you will not be likely to die until your time comes.

"What diseases do they die of mostly?" Well, they used to die of conical balls and cold steel, mostly, but here lately erysipelas and the intoxicating bowl have got the bulge on those things, as was very justly remarked by Mr. Rising last Sunday. I will observe, for your information, William, that Mr. Rising is our local Episcopal minister, and has done as much as any man among us to redeem this community from its pristine state of semi-barbarism. We are afflicted with all the diseases incident to the same latitude in the States, I believe, with one or two added and half a dozen subtracted on account of our superior altitude. However, the doctors are about as successful here, both in killing and curing, as they are anywhere.

Now, as to whether it would be advisable for a man who can make a living in Missouri to emigrate to Nevada, I confess I am somewhat mixed. If you are not content in your present condition, it naturally follows that you would be entirely satisfied if you could make either more or less than a living. You would exult in the cheerful exhilaration always produced by a change. Well, you can find your opportunity here, where, if you retain your health, and are sober and industrious, you will inevitably make more than a living, and if you don't you won't. You can rely upon this statement, William. It contemplates any line of business except the selling of tracts.[3] You cannot sell tracts here, William; the people take no interest in tracts; the very best efforts in the tract line—even with pictures in them—have met with no encouragement here. Besides, the newspapers have been interfering; a man gets his regular text or so from the Scriptures in his paper, along with the stock sales and the war news, every day, now. If you are in the tract business, William, take no chances on Washoe;[4] but you can succeed in anything else here.

"I suppose you know Joel H. Smith?" Well—the fact is—I believe I don't. Now isn't that singular? Isn't it very singular? And he owns "considerable" in a mine here, too. Happy man. Actually owns in a mine here in Nevada Territory, and I never even heard of him. Strange—strange—do you know, William, it is the strangest thing that ever happened to me? And then he not only owns in a mine, but owns "considerable," that is the strangest part about it—how a man could own considerable in a mine in Washoe and I not know anything about it. He is a lucky dog, though. But I strongly suspect that you have made a mistake in the name; I am confident you have; you mean John Smith—I know you do; I know it from the fact that he owns considerable in a mine here, because I sold him the property at a ruinous sacrifice on the very day he arrived here from over the plains. That man will be rich one of these days. I am just as well satisfied of it as I am of any precisely similar instance of the kind that has come under my notice. I said as much to him yesterday; and he said he was satisfied of it, also. But he did not say it with that air of triumphant exultation which a heart like mine so delights to behold in one to whom I have endeavored to be a benefactor in a small way. He looked pensive a while, but, finally, says he, "Do you know, I think I'd a been a rich man long ago if they'd ever found the d——d ledge?"[5] That was my idea about it. I always thought, and I still think, that if they ever do find the ledge, his chances will be better than they are now. I guess Smith will be all right one of these centuries, if he keeps up his assessments[6]—he is a young man yet. Now, William, I have taken a liking to you, and I would like to sell you "considerable" in a mine in Washoe. I think I could get you a commanding interest in

3. Religious pamphlets.
4. Washoe is now the name of the northwest Nevada county that includes Virginia City, but at the time Twain wrote this piece it referred to Nevada in general.
5. The terms *ledge, lead, vein,* and *outcropping* all referred to deposits of ore, except that outcroppings broke the surface.
6. Stock owners of mines were frequently assessed additional payments for improvements. In Nevada, these assessments were often fraudulent means for the directors to enrich themselves at the expense of the rest of the owners, and failure to pay assessments would result in a forfeit of ownership.

the "Union," Gold Hill, on easy terms. It is just the same as the "Yellow Jacket," which is one of the richest mines in the Territory. The title was in dispute between the two companies some two years ago, but that is all settled now.[7] Let me hear from you on the subject. Greenbacks at par is as good a thing as I want. But seriously, William, don't you ever invest in a mining stock which you don't know something about; beware of John Smith's experience.

You hope to hear from me soon? Very good. I shall also hope to hear from you soon, about that little matter above referred to. Now, William, ponder this epistle well; never mind the sarcasm, here and there, and the nonsense, but reflect upon the plain facts set forth, because they *are* facts, and are meant to be so understood and believed.

Remember me affectionately to your friends and relations, and especially to your venerable grand-mother, with whom I have not the pleasure to be acquainted—but that is of no consequence, you know. I have been in your town many a time, and all the towns of the neighboring counties—the hotel keepers will recollect me vividly. Remember me to them—I bear them no animosity.

Yours affectionately,
MARK TWAIN.

⇢ *Territorial Enterprise,* May 1–15, 1864

---

7. In 1862, in a notoriously corrupt lawsuit in which the witnesses, judge, and jury had all been bought off by the Yellow Jacket mine owners, a rich property owned by the Union mine was awarded to the Yellow Jacket. This made Union stock practically worthless.

A Silver Man

Dan De Quille

"A Silver Man" was almost certainly inspired by Mark Twain's "Petrified Man" (1862). The obvious similarity of subject matter makes it worthwhile to compare and contrast the two. Twain's piece is short and aims at ridiculing the public official it mentions, but it also engendered a good deal of resentment on the Comstock by readers who were taken in by it. De Quille's is longer and much more ingeniously elaborated but also more good-humored, and it was well received. Although Twain was ultimately much the better writer, De Quille was the past master of the hoax form he called the "quaint."

‹—⊙ ⊙—›

THE WONDER OF THE AGE

Dear Era:—Everybody, no doubt, has heard of the discovery of the wonderful "Silver Man," found in a mine between Esmeralda and Owen's River.

Everybody, however, has not heard the full particulars of the discovery, and many will hoot the idea of any such discovery ever having been made.

They will at once say that it is impossible for a human body to be changed to silver ore.—Let them have their say!

Although the story is almost too much for belief, yet I hope to be able to show, before finishing this account, that, startling as the assertion may appear, such a change in the substance of the human body is not only possible, but that there is on record one well authenticated instance of a similar changing of a human body into a mass of ore.

We have had all kinds of astonishing discoveries. Many things formerly classed among the impossibilities, are now familiar, every-day possibilities. We are now to acknowledge that it is not impossible for a human body to be changed—through contact in a mineral vein with solutions of certain salts, carbonic and hydrosulphuric gases, and the electrical currents induced by the reaction of said solutions upon each other—into a mass of sulphuret of silver.

As no particular account of the discovery of the Silver Man has ever been published, and as all who have heard of the wonder will be pleased to know something in regard to the finding of the body thus curiously mineralized, I will venture to give a full history.

Mr. Peter Kuhlman, a gentleman who has for some months past been engaged prospecting in a range of mountains lying to the southeast of Mono Lake, between Esmeralda and Owen's River, has kindly furnished me with the particulars given below:

The body is that of a full grown man, and was found in what is known as the Hot Springs Lead.

The body, when first found, was almost perfect, even to the fingers and toes. The features are distinctly traceable, but not wholly perfect. They present a blurred appearance.

In removing the body from its resting place, an arm was broken off. It was from observing the peculiar appearance of the fractured arm that Mr. Kuhlman—who is not only a good practical miner, but an excellent chemist and mineralogist—was induced to make a careful assay of pieces taken from the severed limb.

When it was announced to the miners that what they had looked upon as merely a most remarkable petrifaction, was a mass of sulphuret of silver, slightly mixed with copper and iron (in the shape of pyrites) they were at first incredulous. But repeated and careful tests, made before their own eyes, at length convinced them that such was the indisputable fact. The iron and copper pyrites are found lining the cavities of the bones and filling the spaces occurring between the body and the robe in which it was found partially enveloped, as these minerals often occur in holes and crevices in petrified wood. Pieces taken from the arm were tested with acids, with the blow-pipe, and in other ways; always with the same result. A small button of pure silver, extracted by means of the blow-pipe, was shown me by Mr. Kuhlman. He started for this city with part of the hand from the severed arm, with the thumb and two fingers attached and entire, but was induced to leave it with a scientific friend at Aurora, Esmeralda.

The body is supposed to be, and doubtless is, that of an Indian; but in its present changed state it is impossible to be certain on that point. The robe found about the body, part of which crumbled away on being exposed to the air, appears to have been of some kind of coarse cloth. Nothing but a few sticks of charred wood, also mineralized, was found with the body.

The lead in which the "Silver Man," as he is popularly termed, was found, was discovered last year, about the first of May, by three prospectors—Wm. R. Prescott, Oscar E. Hartman, and Patrick O'Haloran. On account of there being several hot springs on the cañon, some twenty rods above the vein, they called it the "Hot Springs Lead." The lead was discovered at a point where it was laid bare by the action of the water of the cañon passing over it. Here the cañon is very deep, the mountains rising in rugged walls on either side. Getting the course of the vein, the miners opened a cut on the side of the mountain about sixty feet above the bed of the cañon. On striking the lead, a tunnel was driven in upon it to the distance of seventy-five feet. The lead being found of rather a loose structure, it was thought best to start a shaft at the end of the tunnel and follow the lead down to where it became more solid, in the hope that the metal it contained would there be found more concentrated. While sinking this shaft, and after it had reached the depth of forty-five feet, a blow with a pick, by the man working below, was followed by a tremendous rush of air, and the terrified miner shouted lustily to his partners above to haul him up. The upward rush of air continued for some minutes after he had reached the surface, coming out with a noise like that made in blowing off a steam boiler, much to the astonishment and consternation of the three honest miners, who stood quaking in the tunnel above. Upon consultation, after the startling noise had ceased, the true cause of the singular phenomenon was conjectured. Having made up their minds that the noise was caused by the escape of a large body of air compressed in a cavern in the lead, they at once determined to cut through into it and see what it might contain. Tying the windlass rope securely about his waist, one of the men descended and with a heavy drill succeeded, after a few minutes' labor, in staving out a hole nearly the full size of the bottom of the shaft; the shell left being little more than a mass of metallic concretions of a pyritous nature. On sounding the cavern with a rope, it was found to be no more than twelve to fifteen feet deep. As a candle burned clearly at the bottom, which looked safe and solid, two of the men were let down to explore the opening. It was found to be nothing more than a huge crevice in the rock, four or five feet in width at the point where cut into by the shaft, but back in the direction of the mountain closing in till not more than ten inches in width.

The body I have been talking about was found stretched upon the ground, a few feet from where the men landed, lying face upwards.

Had the finders been any other than California or Washoe miners, there would have been a jolly stampede and some frantic climbing of the windlass rope. Although startled and greatly astonished, they stood their ground and soon sufficiently regained their composure to make a critical examination of the singular object before them.

The news of the wonderful strike soon spread through the neighborhood, and the "Petrified Man," as he was then called, was visited by all living near—that is to say, within twenty or thirty miles.

When Mr. Kuhlman first visited the "Silver Man," which was three days after the discovery—he living twenty-three miles southwest of Hot Springs—that argentiferous *homo* was still reposing, as found, in the cavern.

At his suggestion the body was loosened from the floor, where it was held by an accumulation of pyritous concretions, and hoisted out to the light of day. During this operation, one of the arms—the right one—was broken off, as has been stated. The left arm, being pressed across the body, as though in the act of clutching the robe, was saved.

Mr. Kuhlman describes the walls of the cavern as presenting the most magnificent appearance imaginable, being a complete mass of pyrites of the most perfect and brilliant description,—all as fresh as the crystals in the heart of an unbroken geode. The cavern, or crevice, widens in the direction of the cañon and is blocked up by a mass of rocks; all, however, covered, as well as the walls, with a thick and bristling incrustation of pyrites.

The opinion of Mr. Kuhlman—which is very reasonable—is that the body so singularly discovered is that of an Indian who ages ago sought shelter in this cleft in the rocks during a rain storm, and that the face of the mountain, worn perpendicularly by the water of the cañon and softened by the rain, slid down, confining the lone red man in the cavity, and leaving him to die of starvation and become mineralized—to become, in short, "Silver Man," for us in this age to wonder about.

The miners who have this great curiosity intend taking it to San Francisco, thence to New York, and expect to make fortunes by its exhibition; but Mr. Kuhlman says it is certain soon to fall to pieces and be destroyed by the action of the atmosphere,—in fact that it is already crumbling.

As I said at the outset, this story of a human body turning into silver ore will doubtless strike the majority of my readers as a thing wholly impossible and absurd in the extreme, but I will try to show that it is neither one nor the other.

In Sweden is an old mining town called Falun, situated on Lake Runn, and about fifty-four miles south-west of Gefle. This town is the capital of the Swedish laen, or province, of the same name, though sometimes called Kopparburg's-Laen, on account of its extensive copper mines. The mines, which are west of the town, are worked for copper, though the ore contains a small per cent. of gold, silver and lead. These mines have been worked hundreds of years, and are still quite productive. By the falling in of ancient galleries, a vast chasm has been formed on the surface, the opening being no less than 300 feet deep, 1,200 long, and 600 wide. Stairs now lead down the sides of this chasm to its bottom, whence, by means of ladders, the workmen descend to the pits and galleries below. The works extend for miles under ground, and far below are many vast galleries. In one of these immense chambers, magnificently illuminated for the occasion, Bernadotte and his queen once banqueted.

But with all this we have nothing to do, further than to understand that the mines are of very ancient date and that they contain many great galleries, a portion of which were once broken in and filled up, and doubtless great loss of life occasioned by the accident. In re-opening these old galleries, bodies of miners are often found, more or less preserved by the action of the copper and gases of the mine.

The particular case which I wish to quote is one mentioned by Breithaupt, who says:

"In one instance, the body of a miner was recovered from a very deep part of the mine, where it had remained no longer than sixty years, yet it was found converted into iron pyrites which had slowly and completely replaced the organic materials, retaining their forms."

Here is positive proof, on indisputable authority, that this supposed great absurdity of a "Silver Man" is not so absurd after all.

All who have the least knowledge of palæontology know that all those wonderful remains of fishes, animals, etc., found in limestone and other rocks, and about which so much is said and written, are not the creatures themselves, but merely their shapes replaced by mineral substances.

There are many instances of veins once worked out being filled afresh with mineral deposited by gases ascending from the depths of the mine, in connection, perhaps, with water holding in solution various mineral salts. Often the ore and vein stone have been found in a position so natural that but for the finding of the tools of the ancient miners embedded in the solid quartz, the fact of its being other than the primitive deposit would never have been suspected. So certain is it that many ores are thus deposited, that the operations of nature may in this respect be imitated by artificial means. M. de Senarmont has made numerous experiments with such solutions as are found in hot springs, and by ingenious combinations in vessels hermetically sealed and properly heated, has succeeded in producing not only perfect quartz crystals, but the ores of iron, copper, silver, etc.

From what I have said, it will readily be seen that what appears so very wonderful in the fact of a human body being changed into a mass of mineral, is not so very strange after all.

The place where the body was found, be it remembered, was most admirably calculated to produce such a change. Sealed up by a not uncommon accident in a cavity in the very heart of a metallic vein, and this again hermetically closed in every part by an accumulation on all its walls of pyritous concretions, while from below steamed upward gases loaded with volatilized minerals, it would have been strange if no remarkable change had been produced in the organic remains subjected to these combined influences. There is every sign that the hot springs near the mine were at one time situated as far below the lead in which the body was found as they are now above it. Hot springs are generally caused by the decomposition of pyrites in contact with water. Once this operation commences, it proceeds in pretty much the same manner as the burning of a stratum of coal, following the unburnt portions of the deposit. The course of this burning at Steamboat Springs, Washoe, is northward. Even within the memory of the present generation, certain hot springs in California have moved several rods up the ravine on which they are situated, following the bed of pyritous matter to which they owe their existence. The strong subterranean heat of the Springs I have mentioned, during the time they were passing under the lead in which the mineralized body was found, doubtless caused immense volumes of various gases to be evolved, and this, besides the production of a favorable temperature, must most assuredly have had much to do in the production of the "Silver Man."

I might say much more in proof not only of the fact of a human body so changed having been found, but of the simple and natural causes which have operated to produce a change which at the first glance appears so wonderful; however, as many would not believe, even though I should produce the body and melt it up into buttons before their very eyes, I refrain.

In conclusion, I have only to say that in my opinion the greatest wonder that Washoe has yet produced—the greatest wonder of the age—is this marvelous "Silver Man!"

Golden Era, February 5, 1865

Frightful Catastrophe— Wonderful Escape—a Man Falls over 1,000 Feet and Is Not Killed!

Dan De Quille

We have a friend living somewhere in the upper portion of this city who, although somewhat robust and slightly corpulent, is of a sanguine, nervous temperament, and particularly afraid of fire—always fearful lest any building he sleeps in might happen to take fire during the night, and he be burned to death—roasted alive. He never puts up at a hotel anywhere without first of all critically examining into all the chances for escaping in case anything should happen, and stipulates with the landlord to awake him at the first sign of an alarm of fire. He is down on the manufacturers of gunpowder and friction matches, and would with infinite pleasure assist in disemboweling the man who invented nitro-glycerine. Now, the front of the house he dwells in is of reasonable height where it is entered from the street, but owing to the abrupt slope of Mount Davidson, the rear end of the building being down hill, is very high. Our obese friend being rather of a poetical turn of mind, and fond of gazing and cogitating on the beauties of nature from an elevated stand-point of view, selected for his lodging room, the one at the rear end of the attic, where he could sit at the back window and look musingly abroad upon the sage-brush hills, sandy deserts and alkali flats, and wonder what the Lord made all that waste country for. As we said before, this window was very high from the ground, and he often used to look out of it to the depths below and calculate the chances of escape that way in case of fire, should all other means of escape be cut off. In order to provide against such a horrible emergency, he procured a long stout rope, which he could make one end of fast to anything that came handy, and by means of which he could get out of the window and slide safely to the ground. His ears when he was asleep were ever open and keen to hear the first alarm of any fire that might occur, and on the occasion of the recent great fire he was among the very first to be up and dressed and battling with the devouring element. The appalling celerity with which that fearful conflagration leaped from house to house, remorsely sweeping everything in its course, barely allowing the unfortunate inmates to escape with their lives, caused him to work all the more frantically as the thought came home to him of how he would feel were their case his. It was only a couple of nights afterwards that he retired to bed as usual, after carefully blowing out his candle, and with his wetted finger and thumb snuffing the residual spark from the wick. He lay awake awhile, thinking over the exciting scenes of that awful fire, but gradually he fell into a quiet comfortable doze. Suddenly there seemed to come to his ears the sound as of crackling flames, and a strong smell of smoke pervaded his keen nostrils. Good heavens! the house was on fire. There was not a moment to lose. He was under the impression that he sprang out of bed. Where was his rope? How came it misplaced? Louder roared the flames, and the hot smoke was coming in through every crack. His only chance for escape was by the window. Wildly he scrambled about the floor, feeling for that rope in the dark, for there was no time to light a candle, besides in his agitation he had upset the matches. Ah! here was the rope. Quickly he tied one end to the bed-post, and threw the other out of the open window. There was no time to put on his pants, for the red forked flames were already creeping through the cracks of his chamber door, and in another instant would burst through. Quickly he backed out through the window, and carefully he glided down the rope through the pitchy darkness, enveloped in clouds of thick black smoke. Suddenly he came to the end of the rope, but where was the ground? He kicked wildly about with his feet, but it was not there. He would have to let go, but how far would he fall? That was the question. Just then there was a lurid flash of light and the flames burst out from his window overhead. He looked fearfully down— and horror of horrors!—directly beneath him was a wide-mouthed open shaft, of unknown depth; one of those old abandoned shafts sunk in the early days of Washoe, and which are so often to be met with along the sides of old Mount Davidson. He closed his eyes, while his very life-blood seemed to freeze in his veins. He tried lustily to shout aloud, but he could not utter a word. He would have prayed, but he didn't know any prayer except "Now I lay me down to sleep," which was hardly appropriate in view of the prospect below. Suddenly a peculiarly singeing, crackling sensation passed down the rope. It was burning off! He gasped for breath and nervously drew up his limbs, as snap went the rope and down he went. Down into the depths;

down, down, that fearful yawning shaft; down through the close, stifling air; down he went backward, rope and all, with heels and hands flourishing wildly above; down, down, down, with a rushing sound in his ears; down thousands upon thousands of feet, until he began to fear he never would stop falling, when suddenly a most ferocious concussion assured him that he had at length "struck bottom," and poor Spikins awoke breathless, to find himself on his back on the floor beside his bed, kicking about wildly, clinging fast to the sheet which he had pulled off after him. Spikins has sold his rope for horse-halters, nailed down his window, built a railing about his bed, and takes no more such chances. He has looked carefully, too, for that huge old shaft beneath his window, but fails to see it. Spikins don't believe much in dreams, but when he goes to sit down he thinks there's something of a "stern reality" about this one, uncomfortable to dwell upon.

Territorial Enterprise, June 24, 1866

Whipping an Editor

[D. Jones?]

Editors, like other shrewd men, must live with their eyes open. A good story is told of one who started a newspaper in a Western town. The town was infested by gamblers, whose presence was a source of annoyance to the citizens, who told the editor that unless he came out against them they would not patronize his paper. He replied that he would give them a good "smasher" next day. Sure enough his next issue contained in full the promised "smasher," and on the following morning the redoubtable editor, with scissors in hand was seated in his sanctum, when in walked a large man with a club in his hand and demanded to know if the editor was in. "No, sir," was the reply; "he has just stepped out. Take a seat and read the papers; he will return in a minute." Down sat the indignant man of cards, crossed his legs, with his club between them, and commenced reading a paper. In the meantime the editor very quietly vamosed downstairs, and at the landing he met another excited man, with a cudgel in his hand, who asked if the editor was in. "Yes, sir," was the reply; "you will find him seated upstairs, reading a newspaper." The latter, on entering the room, with a fearful oath, commenced a violent assault upon the former, which was resisted with equal ferocity. The fight was continued till they had both rolled to the foot of the stairs, and had pounded each other to their hearts' content.

⇢*Pioche Daily Record,* Lincoln County, Nevada, September 17, 1872[1]

---

1. Although this sketch was unsigned, "D. Jones" was listed as the editor of the paper.

A Libel Suit

[Rollin Daggett? and] Joe Goodman

One of the most brilliant demonstrations of sardonic Sagebrush journalism appeared in the *Territorial Enterprise* in connection with its exposé of a diamond mine swindle. The exposé itself was written by Joe Goodman, who was among the first to recognize the nature of the scam. The accused, William M. Lent, was a financier, based in San Francisco, who was deeply involved in mining properties in California and on the Comstock. Even among his friends he was known to be "as sharp as the sharpest," and he was talented at involving himself in potentially profitable ventures. When Lent threatened a libel suit, this editorial, seemingly an apology but transparently the addition of insult to injury, was written by a staff member. Inasmuch as Rollin Daggett was an editorial writer for the paper, was fond of controversy, and was known for his stinging pen, we infer that he wrote the rejoinder. The suit never got to trial because the eminent geologist Clarence King, in San Francisco after having just completed his survey of the Fortieth Parallel, heard of the supposed diamond mine. He and his associate Jim Gardiner determined where the mine was located and made a special trip to the spot. They soon picked up a hundred rubies and a few diamonds that they determined had come from other locations. They reported that the imported stones had been used to salt the surface and that the diamond mine was a hoax. The suit died.

The telegraph informs us that William M. Lent has initiated a suit for libel, in a San Francisco court, against J. T. Goodman, proprietor of this paper. For referring to Mr. Lent as a swindler, in connection with the Colorado diamond operation, that gentleman asks for damages to the amount of fifteen thousand dollars—and costs of court, we presume. The alleged libel consists in the publication in the **Enterprise** of the 31st of last August, of the following article:

The Diamond Swindle

The communication of Ritter, Leverson & Co., diamond brokers, to the London *Times*, stating that a few months ago an American bought a large quantity of uncut diamonds from them, regardless of quality or weight, and strongly intimating that this same lot of stones has been made use of to promote the Arizona diamond hoax, goes far toward establishing our original theory of the swindle. If they had stated that the name of the purchaser was Wm. M. Lent the evidence would be complete. Mr. Lent visited Europe in January last, and the facts that the scheme was concocted and sprung upon the public soon after his return and that he was prominently interested in it, give color to the suspicion that he was the "American gentleman" who purchased the large lot of uncut diamonds from Ritter, Leverson & Co. Again the initiatory steps in the swindle appear to have been taken in the East, where the names of McClellan[1] and Barlow were lent to it before it received the indorsement of Latham, Genxxl [illegible], Selby, and other San Francisco notables, and the Bank of California was obtained for a show-shop. This would be the natural course of events, assuming that Mr. Lent landed in New York with his bag of purchased diamonds and thought it expedient to enlist the aid of names that would give his swindle something of sensational character. The London *Times* expresses surprise that the gentlemen mentioned should have pawned their names to such base uses. Is that journal so innocent as to suppose they may not have been deceived by crafty misrepresentation, or so guileless as to believe that for the consideration involved they could not be induced to lend their names to any fraud whatsoever? If so, London must be a paradise for rogues, or the reputation of the gentlemen in question must stand higher there than upon this slope.[2] There can be no question that the affair was a downright swindle, and until the gentlemen concerned disprove their complicity in the fraud they must all alike be regarded as swindlers. If the people of San Francisco treated them according to their deserts, they would be lubricated and plumed and ridden out of town on the narrowest of narrow gauge conveyances[3]—though their expulsion left every San Francisco bank without a president and deprived the city of the august presence of the hero of the Chickahominy. The only circumstance that pleads in mitigation of such punishment is the fact that

---

1. General George B. McClellan allowed his name to be used in the promotion of the supposed diamond mine. As a Union general during the Civil War, he beat back a Confederate attack on Union forces at the Chickahominy River, in Virginia.

2. California was often referred to as the Western, or Pacific, slope (of the Sierras); Nevada, as the Eastern slope.

3. Tarred and feathered, and ridden out of town on a rail.

their scheme failed to precipitate a ruinous rush to the alleged diamond fields. But this is attributable to the good sense of the press and people, and not to any conscientiousness on the part of the swindlers. In this connection it may not be out of place to rexxxx [reveal?] that certain parties have endeavored to practice xx [an?] extension of the fraud upon this community. Our evening contemporary received a fifth interest, in consideration of its efforts to promote the scheme. It has labored zealously for its hire but without effect, so that it is difficult to say which party has the best of the bargain. That poor specimens of minor precious stones are to be found in Arizona, we have no reason to doubt. But they are of such inferior quality and color as to render them as worthless as glass, and could they be shoveled up by the carload, the business of gathering them would not be profitable. That a diamond of any considerable value has ever been found there we do not believe, and incline of the opinion that no diamonds at all have ever been discovered either in Arizona or New Mexico. The best evidence that the whole thing is a humbug is that every reputed explorer has endeavored to convert his assumed discoveries into a stock jobbing speculation. The sooner the public turns a deaf ear and cold shoulder upon them all, the sooner the diamond fever will be allayed, and the charlatans meet with the rebuke they deserve.

Upon a careful perusal of this article we discover that there is a certain personal roughness in connection with the mention of the name of Mr. Lent, which is doubtless the incentive to the suit against the proprietor of this paper. The leading grievance of Mr. Lent probably consists in the fact that the **Enterprise** was the first journal on the coast to refer to the incorporation of the Colorado Diamond Company as a gang of swindlers. In the absence of Mr. Goodman we xxxx [deem?] it a duty to disavow, in his behalf, an intention of associating the name of Mr. Lent with any scheme in which there was a suspicion of fraud or wrongdoing. Familiar, as we are, with Mr. Goodman's habits of thought, we are satisfied that he is the victim, in this instance, of some terrible typographical blunder. It is probable that the writer intended to say that Mr. Lent was the "victim" rather than the "purchaser" of the diamonds from Ritter, Leverson & Co., for it is unreasonable that his name should have been associated in the mind of the writer with anything bearing the remotest resemblance to sharp practice or dishonesty. All acquainted with Mr. Lent know him to be incapable of a dishonest action. He is a model of virtue and integrity, and God-fearing mothers point to him as an example for their children. No mother contemplates with composure the possible death of her son upon the gallows, and in the career of Mr. Lent a means of escaping that unhappy fate is discerned, no matter how merciless may be the exactions of violated law. Mr. Lent a swindler! Wm. M. Lent a party to fraud of any kind! Bill Lent a corrupt and dishonest man! Perish the thought, and with it the recollection that it has ever been entertained. His character is as pure as the lily of the Sierras, which grows amidst perpetual snows and dies with the breath of summer.[4] Mr. Lent is well known in California and Nevada, and within the large circle of his acquaintance he is everywhere beloved and respected as a man of irreproachable integrity and self-sacrifice. His ways are ways of pleasantness, and all his paths are peace. In the article quoted we observe through the mist that will intrude between our eyes and the great injustice, that Mr. Lent is certainly referred to as a swindler, with the grosser intimation that he is little better than a thief. It is wonderful that this thing should have crept into print. And now, with the solemnity with which the resolutions of reproach were expunged from the journals of the United States Senate years ago, we deliberately draw our pencil across the obnoxious sentence referring to Mr. Lent as a swindler or the confederate of swindlers. Around it we draw the black lines of our ceaseless regret, and blot the letters with the drops of our repentance. With this explanation, if Mr. Lent still refuses to dismiss his suit, we shall be constrained to believe that he is stirred to the litigation by malice, and prepare to meet the outraged and injured gentleman with such weapons as law and public sentiment afford.

Territorial Enterprise, February 27, 1873

4. A mythical plant; hence, the compliment is sarcastic.

Solar Armor

Dan De Quille

This is one of De Quille's best "quaints"—literary hoaxes—and has been frequently reprinted. The first part of the hoax rapidly spread across the country through exchanges. The *Scientific American* reported it without comment, and it was reprinted in England, where the London *Daily Telegraph*, unsure of the story's authenticity, even though the corpse was described as having an icicle a foot long hanging from its nose in the blazing sun in the middle of summer in Death Valley, expressed the wish that more information had been supplied. An English engineer working in Nevada who received the *Telegraph* by mail brought the paper's response to De Quille's attention; he decided to supply more "information" and promptly composed the ingenious second part. This is a classic hoax: it starts with an impossible premise and seeks to make it believable through the use of specious but seemingly credible details and reasoning.

--→⊃ ⊂←--

I.

SAD FATE OF AN INVENTOR

A gentleman who has just arrived from the borax fields of the desert regions surrounding the town of Columbus, in the eastern part of this State, gives us the following account of the sad fate of Mr. Jonathan Newhouse, a man of considerable inventive genius. Mr. Newhouse had constructed what he called a "solar armor," an apparatus intended to protect the wearer from the fierce heat of the sun in crossing deserts and burning alkali plains. The armor consisted of a long, close-fitting jacket made of common sponge and a cap or hood of the same material; both jacket and hood being about an inch in thickness. Before starting across a desert this armor was to be saturated with water. Under the right arm was suspended an India rubber sack filled with water and having a small gutta percha tube leading to the top of the hood. In order to keep the armor moist, all that was necessary to be done by the traveler, as he progressed over the burning sands, was to press the sack occasionally, when a small quantity of water would be forced up and thoroughly saturate the hood and the jacket below it. Thus, by the evaporation of the moisture in the armor, it was calculated might be produced almost any degree of cold. Mr. Newhouse went down to Death Valley, determined to try the experiment of crossing that terrible place in his armor. He started out into the valley one morning from the camp nearest its borders, telling the men at the camp, as they laced his armor on his back, that he would return in two days. The next day an Indian who could speak but a few words of English came to the camp in a great state of excitement. He made the men understand that he wanted them to follow him. At the distance of about twenty miles out into the desert the Indian pointed to a human figure seated against a rock. Approaching they found it to be Newhouse still in his armor. He was dead and frozen stiff. His beard was covered with frost and—though the noonday sun poured down its fiercest rays—an icicle over a foot in length hung from his nose. There he had perished miserably, because his armor had worked but too well, and because it was laced up behind where he could not reach the fastenings.

Territorial Enterprise, July 2, 1874

II.

A MYSTERY EXPLAINED
The Sequel to the Strange Death of Jonathan Newhouse,
the Inventor of the Solar Armor.

The *Daily Telegraph,* London, England, appears to doubt the truth of the account we some time since published of the strange death of Jonathan Newhouse, in Death Valley, where he fell a victim to an apparatus of his own invention, styled a "solar armor." Under the date of August 3 the *Telegraph* says:

> A curious story reaches us from Virginia City, which, to quote transatlantic phraseology, is the "last new thing in the town line" that the young State of Nevada has produced. Virginia City is the child of the celebrated Comstock lode, which is in its immediate neighborhood. "The city," says Mr. Ross Browne, "lies on a rugged slope, and is singularly diversified in its up-risings and down-fallings. It is difficult to see upon

what principle it was laid out. My impression is, it was never laid out at all, but followed the dips, spurs and angles of the immortal Comstock." Be this as it may, the alkaline plains lying between the young Capital of Nevada and the eastern border of the State have a terrible reputation for burning heat and waterless sterility. It is not uncommon for men—and even wagons, with their teams of from eight to sixteen mules or oxen—to sink overwhelmed with heat and thirst when an effort is made to cross this desert during the height of summer. The *Virginia City Enterprise* tells us that a Mr. Jonathan Newhouse, being a man endowed with considerable inventive faculties, devised what he called a "solar armor," which he proposed to don before taking to the alkaline plains. This armor "consisted of a long, close-fitting jacket, made of common sponge, with a hood of the same material, both being saturated with water." Under the right arm its wearer had an india-rubber pouch filled with water, and connecting with the top of the hood by means of a gutta-percha tube. As the traveler proceeds and feels the sun scorching his head, he compresses his right arm and squirts water into the hood, whence it percolates through the entire jacket. Clothed in this strange outfit, Mr. Newhouse set out from Virginia City for a place called "Death Valley," which, if this story be true, has more than ever earned the name that it bears. He expected to be absent for a couple of days. The heat of the sun was torrid, and, on the second day after his departure, an Indian, in a terrible state of "scare," rushed into a camp of white men on the edge of the desert, announcing that a man was lying frozen to death, under a rock towards which he pointed his finger. Followed by his startled companions, the Indian led them to the body of poor Mr. Newhouse. It was then found that the traveler had been unable to unlace the jacket which his friends had fastened with thongs before he started, and the evaporation of moisture from the saturated sponge vestment had produced such intensity of cold that its wearer and inventor paid the penalty of his too successful ingenuity with his life. His beard is represented as having been covered with frost, and a large icicle hung from his nose and lips. The marvelous stories which come from "the plains" are apt to be received with incredulity by our transatlantic kinsmen who dwell upon the Eastern seaboard of the United States. We confess that, although the fate of Mr. Newhouse is related by the Western journal *au grand serieux*, we should require some additional confirmation before we unhesitatingly accept it. But every one who has iced a bottle of wine by wrapping a wet cloth round it and putting it in a draught, must have noticed how great is the cold that evaporation of moisture produces. For these reasons we are disposed to accept the tale from Virginia City in the same frame of mind which Herodotus, the Father of History, usually assumed when he repeated some marvel that had reached him—that is to say, we are neither prepared to disbelieve it wholly nor to credit it without question.

Had not our attention been called to the above by Mr. Duncan McKay, Superintendent of the Santiago mill, Carson River, who is in the weekly receipt of several English newspapers, we should probably never again have referred to the death of Mr. Newhouse. However, as the truth of our narration appears to be called in question, if not directly at least impliedly, by a paper which enjoys the reputation of having the largest circulation of any daily newspaper in the world, we feel that it is but right that we should make public some further particulars in regard to the strange affair—particulars which throw a flood of light upon what, we must admit, did appear almost incredible in our account of the sad occurrence as published. It seemed strange that so great a degree of cold could be produced simply by the evaporation of water, but it now appears that it was not water—at least not water alone—that was used by the unfortunate gentleman.

We are glad that the *Telegraph* has given us the opportunity, long awaited, of publishing in detail the sequel to the curious affair. [The *Telegraph* is mistaken in supposing Death Valley to be near Virginia City. It is 250 or 300 miles distant.][1]

A fortnight after our account of the sad affair was published we received a letter in regard to the matter from one David Baxter who states that he is Justice of the Peace and ex-officio Coroner, of Salt Wells, a station in Inyo County, California, situated at the head of the Sink of Amargosa River, at the north end of Death Valley. Mr. Baxter states that he held

An Inquest on the Body

Of the deceased, Newhouse, in due form, and that the verdict rendered was as follows: "We find that the name of the deceased was Jonathan Newhouse, a native of Knox County, Ohio, aged 47 years; and we further find that deceased came to his death in Death Valley, Inyo County, California, on the 27th day of June, A.D. 1874, by being frozen in a sort of coat of sponge called a 'solar armor,' of which he was the inventor and in which he was tightly laced at his own request, said 'solar armor' being moistened with some frigorific mixture, with the precise nature of which we are unacquainted."

Mr. Baxter further states in his letter that he had before him as witnesses the men stopping at the camp on the borders of Death Valley where Mr.

---

1. Brackets in the original.

Newhouse was last seen alive. These men produced what Mr. Baxter had not before heard mentioned, namely:

The Carpet-sack of Deceased,

Which he had left at their camp. In this was found, besides a few light articles of wearing apparel, several bottles and small glass jars, containing liquids and powders or salts of various kinds, with the nature of the most of which no person in the settlement was acquainted. One of the largest bottles was labeled "Ether," known to them to be a very volatile liquid and capable of producing an intense degree of cold by evaporation.

From this they were able to give a shrewd guess at the nature of the contents of the other vessels. Although it was at first stated—and generally believed until after the contents of the carpet-sack had been overhauled and the inquest held—that deceased had used water only in filling the little India-rubber sack used in supplying moisture to the armor, one of the witnesses, Mr. Robert Purcell, testified that he had observed Mr. Newhouse at a spring about fifty yards from camp, half an hour previous to his donning the armor, and recollects distinctly to have seen him handling one or two of the bottles and jars found in the carpet-sack; though at the time he thought nothing of it, and did not approach very near to deceased, as he did not wish to be thought inquisitive.

Besides the bottle containing the ether, there was another in which was a liquid labeled "Bisulphide of Carbon." There were small glass jars containing what appeared to be salts. They were labeled "Ammonic Nitrate; Sodic Nitrate; Ammonic Chloride; Sodic Sulphate, and Sodic Phosphate."

Mr. Baxter is firmly convinced that with these chemicals, either alone or diluted with water, the degree of cold was produced which caused the death of the unfortunate man. He thinks that in his attempts to reach the fastenings of his armor, on his back, when he began to experience a painful degree of cold, he unavoidably compressed the India-rubber pouch and thus constantly ejected more and more of the freezing fluid into the head-piece of his armor.

As He Stiffened

In death, his arm, under which the sack was suspended, naturally pressed more strongly upon his side and thus caused a steady flow of the fluid. Mr. Baxter is of the opinion that the frost and icicle found on the beard and depending from the nose of deceased were formed from the water mingled with the more volatile fluids comprising the frigorific mixture.

He states as a remarkable fact—and it is strange that this was not mentioned by the gentleman from Columbus, Mr. Abner Wade, who gave us our first brief and imperfect account of the affair—that the men who went out with the Indian to find the remains of Mr. Newhouse came near having their hands frozen in handling the body when trying to place it upon the back of a horse. The freezing mixture oozed out of the spongy armor upon their hands and gave them intense pain. Finally—after they found they could handle the body in no other way—they were obliged to cut the lacings to the armor; when, after an infinite deal of pain to their hands and fingers, the armor was peeled off the body and left lying in the desert, where it probably still remains.

One of the men, Alexander Martin, suffered for about three weeks from the freezing his left hand received and he came near losing the middle finger, gangrene supervening at the root of the nail.

Viewed in the flood of light which Mr. Baxter throws upon the strange death of Mr. Newhouse, we think there can be but one opinion in regard to it; which is, that he fell a victim to a rash experiment with chemicals with the nature of which he was but imperfectly acquainted.

In conclusion, it only remains for us to state that Mr. Baxter informed us that it was his intention to send the bottles and jars of chemicals to the Academy of Sciences at San Francisco; also, the solar armor, in case he could recover it. Whether or not he has done so we cannot say. For several weeks we have closely watched the reports of the proceedings of the learned body named, but as yet have seen no mention made of either the chemicals or the armor.

Territorial Enterprise, August 30, 1874

Eyeless Fish That Live in Hot Water

Dan De Quille

De Quille was at the top of his form with this tongue-in-cheek "quaint" about fish that thrived in the scalding and heavily mineralized water of the lower levels of the mines but died of chilling when placed in cool fresh water. Nevertheless, because it seemed to suggest that a huge reservoir or lake was always draining into the mines, the piece troubled some readers who feared that investors would be discouraged by De Quille's revelation. Fortunately, most Comstockers appreciated the humor of the piece. Years later, Sam Davis revived and elaborated on the hoax in his tale "The Mystery of the Savage Sump" (included herein).

⟶⟞⟐ ⟐⟝⟵

A most singular discovery was yesterday made in the Savage mine. This is the finding of living fish in the water now flooding both the Savage and Hale and Norcross mines. The fish found were five in number, and were yesterday hoisted up the incline in the large iron hoisting tank and dumped into the pump tank at the bottom of the vertical shaft. The fish are eyeless, and are only about three or four inches in length. They are blood red in color.

The temperature of the water in which they are found is 128 degrees Fahrenheit—almost scalding hot. When the fish were taken out of the hot water in which they were found, and placed in a bucket of cold water for the purpose of being brought to the surface, they died almost instantly. The cold water at once chilled their life blood.

In appearance these subterranean members of the finny tribe somewhat resemble gold fish. They seem lively and sportive enough while in their native hot water, notwithstanding the fact that they have no eyes nor even the rudiments of eyes. The water by which the mines are flooded broke in at a depth of 2,200 feet in a drift that was being pushed to the northward in the Savage. It rose in the mine—also in the Hale and Norcross, the two mines being connected—to the height of 400 feet; that is, up to the 1,800 foot level. This would seem to prove that a great subterranean reservoir or lake has been tapped, and from this lake doubtless came the fish hoisted from the mine last evening.

Eyeless fish are frequently found in the lakes of large caves, but we have never before heard of their existence in either surface or subterranean water the temperature of which was so high as in the water in the mines. The lower workings of the Savage mine are far below the bed of the Carson river, below the bottom of Washoe lake—below any water running or standing anywhere within a distance of ten miles of the mine.

Territorial Enterprise, February 19, 1876

A Carson Poker Incident

Sam Davis

This tale, though fictionally embellished, likely had its origin in a real-life poker contest between Carson City and Virginia City and captures the gambling spirit of the Comstock. It originally appeared in the *Argonaut* of March 23, 1878, under the title "Hold the Fort."

⋆⟴ ⟴⋆

Ever since civilization began to make any progress in Nevada, Carson has been considered the stamping-ground of the poker expert. While the superior dexterity of the Virginia City faro dealer is never questioned, the artistic accomplishments of the Carsonite at a little or big game of draw is often alluded to with pride or delight by residents of that metropolis. The peripatetic stranger in his wanderings through the sage-brush, would sometimes stop over night at Carson, and realize the superior mentality of the artist of that section, when telegraphing home for the funds necessary to get his baggage away from the Ormsby house. It is said that on one occasion the Chaplain of the House of Representatives lifted up his voice and prayed: "Give us this day our daily stranger."

Yet there was an occasion when Virginia City wrested the laurels of victory from Carson in a style worthy of record.

Some of the boys had been down to a picnic, and while there fell into the hands of the poker Philistines. Their absence was not noticed in Virginia City; however, until about eight o'clock in the evening, when Orndorff & Magee, of the Delta, received the following dispatch:

Send down $500 by telegraph.—Billy.

Then it was known that Billy Robinson and some of the boys were down at Carson, holding the fort for reinforcements. The Delta boys, with charac-

50

teristic promptness, sent the required sum and waited anxiously for the next hour, when they received the following:

Send $1,000 more and Joe Dixon.—Billy.

Dixon was soon found in his palatial headquarters, next the Washoe club rooms, going for the exchequer of a number of prominent citizens. The situation was at once explained. Joe rose from his seat, sent up to Mooney's for a team, and took a fat sack of coin from his safe. Jack Magee joined him in a few minutes, and Joe drove across to the Western Union.

"A friend of mine passes Reno on the Eastern-bound train. He's a lightning-striker, and if I can stop him with a dispatch, the game is ours." Joe spoke with great deliberation, and sent the following:

> To Charles Huntley, on board eastern-bound train at Reno—Get off and come to Carson by rapid conveyance. Meet me at Ormsby House before 3 o'clock. Business.   Dixon.

"He'll be there," said Joe, "if the wires don't go back on us."

In another instant the two men were flying over the Divide en route for Carson.

It was a little before midnight when the horses, drenched with foam, reached the city. There was no time to lose. They began to hunt the leading sporting resorts, and soon found Billy Robinson and his gang in the hands of a crowd, whom the new-comers recognized, at a glance, as the very flower of paste-board chivalry of Carson.

Joe is an open-up sort of a man, and, walking up to the table, remarked: "I s'pose a man with coin can take a hand here?" And he laid down his bag.

Nothing suited the Carson chaps better. Room was made for Joe and Jack and a fresh deal inaugurated as they took the places of Virginia men, who had been fighting, like the soldiers of Marathon in the pass of Thermopylae, since noon. Joe looked at his watch. It was 20 minutes past twelve, and Charley, his friend, must be on hand before 3 o'clock. Robinson stood back a little from the game and telegraphed important results.

Meanwhile the Delta Saloon, in Virginia City, was the scene of an anxious gathering, and the bulletins from the seat of war were posted up. They were as follows:

> Carson, 1 o'clock. Jack has just taken a pot of $360.—B.

Here all hands imbibed. Presently another came:

> 1:20. Joe bluffed them out of $700. Set up the wine.—B.

The wine was set up. At 2 o'clock came the intelligence, which dropped like a bombshell into the place:

We've just lost a pot of $1,500. Send down more coin.—Joe.

The answer went back at once:

We endorse your paper for $10,000.

> Orndorff & Magee.
> Grant Isrial.
> Dick Brown.

Fortified by the sinews of war, the little band still held the fight gallantly. Joe went out to raise some more money on his dispatch, and Pantling, of the Ormsby, furnished the bullion. Joe left word where to send Huntley, and was soon in the field again.

At a little after 3 o'clock Huntley stalked in. Joe and he had not met for years, and during the time had known each other only by correspondence; yet there was no gleam of recognition as Huntley slid like a phantom into the game. He showed the requisite amount of coin, and the Carsonites laughed inwardly because they had another victim. He looked like a divinity student. When he dealt, his thin hands played like lightning over the pack; his shuffle was the work of a magician, and the cards seemed alive.

After the deal, the bets began to pile up very much as if every man had a big idea of the value of his hand. They went twice around, and every body stood in with the raise.

A Carson man remarked quietly: "I see it two thousand better."

It was a stranger's turn next. He said: "I raise it five thousand," and laid down the checks. Then the Carson men, after a brief consultation, dispersed, leaving the table and looking for the door.

Virginia had won.

The morning light was stealing in just as the worsted Carson gamesters were stealing out. It was a bright, inspiring kind of morning, too, but they didn't seem to notice it. The stranger helped Joe and Jack rake the pot into a big bag, and then they all shook hands.

"What did you have?" asked Joe.

"Don't know," said Mr. Huntley. "To tell you the truth, I haven't yet looked at my hand. If a man looks at his hand, sometimes he gets confused and loses his nerve."

Sam Davis's Earthquake Hoax

Anonymous

Although corroborating information about the hoax reported in this piece has not yet been found, there is little reason to doubt its essential accuracy. From his youth, Davis had been fond of practical joking, and he indulged this proclivity for the rest of his life, becoming only more sophisticated with it in his journalism and sometimes, as in this case, more audacious. The event relating to Vallejo, California, apparently occurred in 1874, a year before Davis moved to Nevada. It obviously earned him an admiring notoriety among his fellow journalists. The humorous scheme involving a "Christian Chinaman" is not currently known.

⇥ ⇤

Sam Davis's connection with the scheme of sending a "Christian Chinaman" East to lecture on "The Chinese Question from a Chinese standpoint" recalls to one of our correspondents an exaggerated newspaper hoax perpetrated by Sam on the Vallejo public. It was at the time of the great race in 1874. Sam had a detail to report the race for one of the [San Francisco] city papers. At the race-track he met a reporter on the Vallejo *Chronicle*, who was bewailing the loss of his credentials, without which he could not gain admission to the reporter's stand. Sam, seeing an opportunity for a hoax, at once offered his services, and the Vallejo scribe, after giving Sam an order on the telegraph operator to "forward anything written by the bearer," started off to see the town. Davis took advantage of his opportunity by writing the following dispatches, which were duly forwarded to the Vallejo *Chronicle:*

"GRAND STAND, Nov. 13, 1 p.m.—At least 100,000 people on the ground. The Masonic Cemetery overlooking the track crowded with people. Eligible tombstones are selling at $5 apiece for reserved seats.

1:30 p.m.—Horses ready to start. 'Thad Stevens' has the pole.

2 p.m.—Tremendous shock of earthquake has just demolished grand stand. People, horses, etc., flying in wild confusion; will send list of killed and wounded in half an hour.

2:15 p.m.—The dead have been cleared away, and it has been decided to run the heat. 'Thad' favorite in pools.

2:30 p.m.—'Thad' won the first heat.

2:45 p.m.—Another shock of earthquake has leveled everything. Several thousand people swallowed up. Get out an extra. My life is in danger. I must go."

Sam signed the initials of the accredited reporter to all these dispatches, and on the suggestion of the last dispatch the *Chronicle* did get out an extra.

Vallejo was wild with excitement when the startling news contained in the *extra* became circulated. The next boat to San Francisco was crowded with friends of possible "killed or wounded," and all this time the unfortunate Vallejo reporter was getting himself blissfully full of beer.

As though all this was not injury enough, Davis sent the following letter to the proprietor of the Vallejo *Chronicle* the next day:

"Inclosed you will please find bill for services rendered at the great race on Saturday. You will observe that I succeeded in getting an exclusive account of the earthquake to you, thereby beating every other paper on the coast. I only succeeded in this sublime piece of journalistic enterprise by the sleepless vigilance which is the invariable price of good items. Immediately after sending your dispatches I hired a small boy to cut the wires, thereby preventing the San Francisco *Chronicle* from sending similar ones, and the *Post* and *Alta* from stealing them. Any further orders for exclusive items will be filed on application at the shortest notice.

Yours fraternally,   SAM DAVIS."

For earthquake item—two shocks at $5 per shock $10.00
Paid boy to cut wire 2.50

Received payment. $12.50

Argonaut, March 22, 1879

[A Sam Davis Newspaper Story]

[Sam Davis]

In the days before syndication became standard, newspapers all over the country exchanged subscriptions and reprinted items of interest, commonly known as exchanges, from each other's columns. Usually, as a courtesy, they acknowledged the source of each piece. Items about such popular individuals as Mark Twain and Jim Townsend, or by such popular writers as Dan De Quille and Sam Davis, were especially in demand. The *Argonaut* appears to have reprinted this ironic sketch by Davis from Davis's own newspaper, the *Carson Appeal*.

⊷⟞⟊ ⟊⟝⊶

Sam Davis, in the Carson *Appeal*, gives an excellent specimen of country newspaper business management. The editor sees in the rival paper a political announcement which, after careful search, he fails to find in his own sheet. Thereupon he seats himself and writes:

A NICE PILL.—Bill Wiggins is out with an announcement that he is a candidate for sheriff. Who is Wiggins? A hundred persons have asked us that question within the past few days, and we have taken pains to hunt up his record. Wiggins is a man who has bummed in this community for the past ten years, seeking office and finding none. He has bucked like an old mule, stiff-legged, at every ticket that he has not been on, and tried to bust every combination that was not made in his interest. He is a political parasite, that the voters of the town should put their foot on for the last time. He needs a final quietus, and the next ——

Just then Mr. Wiggins entered and laid down five dollars for his announcement, explaining that he had intended to bring it earlier, but it had slipped his mind. He was hardly around the corner before the editor had thrown his article in the waste-basket, and wrote as follows:

55

A Representative Man.—We are glad to announce the fact that Colonel William Wiggins, well and favorably known in these parts, announces himself as a candidate for sheriff. Mr. Wiggins has always been a consistent man, and never identified with the bolters and soreheads who have made themselves so odious to the country for the past ten years. He has stood by the party in the darkest hours of its history. Mr. Wiggins's name will be a tower of strength for the ticket, and will lead us to a glorious victory. His name, heading the county ticket, makes it folly for the opposition to nominate a man to run against him.

→*Argonaut* 7:15 (October 9, 1880): 3

The Tables Turned

A Hackman Robs Steve Gage and Stanford

He Runs His Hack on the Principles of the Science of Transportation—
$15 to Golden Gate Park, $5 to the Cliff House,
and $500 for the Return Trip

[Denis E. McCarthy?]

Although the authorship of this piece is uncertain, and it may have been written by Arthur McEwen, circumstantial evidence suggests Denis E. McCarthy, who at the time was the *Virginia City Evening Chronicle*'s editor and publisher and was known for taking strong stands. McCarthy was a famous and respected Comstock journalist and had been the coowner and publisher, along with Joe Goodman, of the *Virginia City Territorial Enterprise* in that paper's early years. As so often happened with good stories that appeared anonymously in Nevada and California, this one was taken up and modified; it was recast, anonymously, as "The Tale of a Tug" for the *San Franciscan*.[1] Instead of a cab and driver, that version uses a tugboat and its captain, and instead of Leland Stanford and Steve Gage, it focuses on Charles Crocker and Frank Pixley, the former an organizer of the Central Pacific Railroad and the latter a San Francisco publisher. Except for those details, the general plot and the antirailroad thrust of the rewritten tale are the same as in "The Tables Turned."

⋆⇒ ⇐⋆

A communistic person[2] identified with the dangerous classes of the Comstock and notorious for his disregard of truth and contempt for vested

---

1. *San Franciscan*, April 19, 1884, p. 12.
2. Terms such as *communistic, Nihilist,* and *Socialist* are used generically and ironically in this tale

rights, has just returned from a visit to San Francisco. This morning he endangered the good name of the CHRONICLE by entering its editorial rooms. The Nihilist declared that he had "a good thing on Stanford and Steve Gage,"[3] but he supposed the CHRONICLE, like the rest of the corrupt and time-serving press, would be afraid to publish it.

"Tell your story," said the editor with dignity, and gazing inquiringly at the boot of the Socialist which was resting upon the editorial table. The boot remained there, however, while the following ridiculous narrative was delivered:

It's fine weather at the Bay and everybody who can afford it takes a spin occasionally out of the dust and heat. Last Saturday Stanford and Gage were walking along Kearny street, and when they got to the corner of Bush the Governor took off his hat, wiped his brow and remarked:

"Steve, it's too hot for anything. What do you say to a breath of fresh air?"

"Have we time?" inquired Mr. Gage, pulling out his watch. So did the Governor, who replied:

"There isn't anything very pressing for a couple of hours, I guess, and we may as well take a spin out to the park. It isn't worth while to have out my horses. Let's take a hack, and then we can enjoy a walk when we get there. It'll be better than riding around the drives."

So they got into a coupe and were driven out to Golden Gate Park. At the entrance the Governor and Gage alighted.

"What's the fare?" asked the Governor.

The driver, a retired prize fighter, replied:

"On'y fifteen dollars, Guv'nur."

"What!" yelled Stanford and Gage in the same breath.

"Fifteen dollars," repeated cabby, unbuttoning his coat and spitting on his hands.

"But my good man," protested the Governor, "such a charge is exorbitant. The law confines you to a certain price for your services, and you can be arrested and punished for such a violation of the ordinances."

"Hang the law!" growled cabby. "My money bought and paid for this hack an' hosses, and the essence of ownership is control."

---

to refer to opponents of the unrestrained and freewheeling capitalism that led to the monopolistic practices described.

3. Leland Stanford (1824–1893) was a wealthy financier involved in the formation and operation of the Central Pacific Railroad, which ran across the middle of Nevada. Stanford served as governor of California in 1862–1863 and was later president of the railroad and then a U.S. senator from 1885 until his death. Steve Gage was the owner of a sawmill in Nevada but later moved to California, where he associated with the Southern Pacific Railroad as a lobbyist and tax specialist.

"Hem!" coughed the Governor, looking slyly at Steve, who began to grin. "That's all well enough when applied to my railroads; but—but—er—— Now if you charge us fifteen dollars to bring us to the park, what on earth would you charge us to take us to the Cliff House?"

"Five dollars."

"From here?"

"No; from the city."

"But it's twice the distance!"

"Yes, but it's a competitive point. Fifteen to the park, five to the Cliff. No hoggin' about it. Through rate to the Cliff, local rate back to park added— just as you fellows do when you charge $300 for drawing a car-load of stuff from New York to Frisco, and make it $800 if you drop the car at Elko, about 500 miles nearer New York."[4]

It was Steve's turn to cough and the Governor's to grin.

"Well," said the Governor with a sigh, "take us to the Cliff."

At the Cliff House the Governor and Stephen drank their beer and smoked a cigar and listened to the barking of the seals, and filled their lungs with the sea breeze. Suddenly Steve clapped himself on the leg and cried out:

"By Jove, Governor! I forgot that lot of coal of Smith's that the Sheriff is to sell at 3 o'clock. It's 2 now. If we miss that a chance to save at least a thousand dollars will be gone."

"Good heavens!" cried the Governor snatching out his watch, "let's hurry back at once. Driver! Oh, driver!"

"Here, sir," answered cabby, who had been leaning over the balcony parapet within ear-shot, "here, sir."

"We want to return to town immediately," cried Mr. Gage.

"Ya-as, I s'pose so," said cabby, slowly chewing a straw, "but I'll take my pay in advance, if it's all the same to you gents."

The Governor growled something between his teeth and tendered $5.

"'Tain't enough," said cabby, contemptuously.

"In heaven's name, how far will your extortion go?" snorted the Governor. "How much do you want?"

"Five hundred more," calmly replied the hackman.

"Hey?" shrieked Steve and the Governor.

"Five hundred, an' not a cent less," repeated cabby.

"How sir—er—damme sir! how do you dare ask such a price for driving two gentlemen four or five miles?" sputtered the Governor.

---

4. The cabman's description of extortionate railroad freight charges was accurate. Nevadans (and Californians) were deeply resentful of those monopolistic rates.

"I bases my charge on what the traffic will bear," replied the hackman with a grin. "If taters is sellin' in Los Angeles for 50 cents a bushel and at $3 a bushel in Tucson, you fellers charge the poor devil of a rancher $2.50 a bushel to pack his taters to Tucson an' gobble all the profit. Now I ain't as hoggish as that. I heerd Mr. Gage say if he could get into town by 3 o'clock he could make a thousand dollars. As there ain't no other hack here, I'm as good a monopoly for the wunst as any blasted railroad on earth; but I ain't so greedy. I don't want all you can make by usin' my hack. I'm willin' to get along with half."

With a dismal groan the Governor and Steve emptied their pockets and counted out the money.

"Now, see here," said cabby, as he closed the door of the hack on his victims, "I've done for wunst what you roosters do day in an' day out an' have been doin' for years, an' made yer millions by it. I happen to be able to give you a small dose of yer own medicine for wunst, an' I don't want you to do no kickin'. I know you kin send me to jail for runnin' my business on your principles; but if you jails me, I'll have yer blood when I get out, an' don't yer forgit it."

Hereupon the hackman clapped the door to with a bang, and climbing to his seat drove at a rattling pace to the place where the Sheriff was about to sell out poor Smith. Smith was a coal dealer who didn't have special rates.

When the Nihilist had finished this absurd and libelous tale, he took his foot off the editorial desk, laughed hoarsely, and departed for the nearest saloon.

Virginia City Evening Chronicle, May 10, 1881

The Carson Fossil-Footprints

Mark Twain

In the early 1880s, a scientific disagreement developed over the origin and nature of locally famous tracks in the sandstone quarry of the Nevada State Prison at Carson City. Although now a resident of Hartford, Connecticut, Twain alluded to this dispute in a humorous look back to his Sagebrush days that he provided in response to an appeal for copy from Joe Goodman, who was about to launch a literary journal, the *San Franciscan*. Twain's piece, probably a long-range echo of Artemus Ward's double-talk and subliminal humor, is as ingenious as it is delightful in its creation of the persona of an old-timer whose rambling memory and shaky grasp of scientific terminology result in a semi-coherent recollection rich in nonsensical explanation, non sequiturs, and faulty logic, with hints of a proto-Faulknerian style. Despite its skill, this sketch is little known. It has been reprinted several times, most recently in 1980, when it was edited by Everett Emerson, but has not previously been anthologized.

⊷⊜ ⊜⊶

It may be all very well for Professor Marsh and Professor Harkness[1] to talk their scientific talk about the Carson Footprints, and try to saddle them onto the Primeval Man, the Irish Elk and others who are gone and cannot now defend themselves; it may be all very well, I say, and entertaining, and within the just limits of scientific slander and research, but it is not *moral*. For I know the cold facts about the Footprints, and I know they were not made by the Primeval Man, or the Irish Elk, or any of that sect: they were made by the first Nevada Territorial Legislature, and I was there when it was done. It

---

1. Othniel Marsh, a Yale professor of paleontology, maintained that the tracks were made by some ancient quadruped, perhaps a mylodon; Albert Harkness, a scientist associated with the California Academy of Sciences, believed that prehistoric humans might have made the tracks.

was done at the time of the *sine die* adjournment. It had rained all the evening outside, and it had rained whisky all the evening inside—inside the fence, I mean, for there were no buildings in that early day—and neither you nor a much older man could have told on which side of the fence the weather was the most inclement. I was on both sides of it, and sometimes on it, for a brief uncertain season, and I couldn't tell. The Footprint quarry, where that legislature sat—stood, while they could, I mean—was a dry alkali flat with a fence around it, when the rain began: just a dry alkali flat, containing a fence-full of dry honorable alkalied flats from all over the Territory; and in three hours that first mentioned flat was absolutely soaked, to a depth of three inches; and the others all the way through. I make no exceptions; I say all. I was there, and I know. So the place was become just a regular marsh, full of irregular marshes, so to speak—meaning the legislature. Meaning the legislature, but intending no disrespect. And when the weather moderated so that one could venture outside—outside the fence—these latter adjourned. They adjourned, in the usual form—form used by territorial legislatures of the day—the Speaker bringing down his gavel on the head of the member mistaken by these scientists for the Irish Elk—which he, the Speaker, mistook for a fence-post—and thus, as you see, is the gloom and sorrow of a double error spread over this moldering historic incident—and said—common time, four beats to the measure, that is to say four hiccoughs to the sentence: "The modder having weatherated," and so on, in a similar strain, till he got through. I remember it as if it were but yesterday. Thus dissolved, they departed thence.

It was then they made the tracks. They couldn't help making them; for the place was a marsh, as I was telling you. I saw it done; for I was there. I was there, and I shall now cast upon this pale dim void of scientific conjecture the lurid glare of history. I was there, and I saw them march. The Primeval Man was absent; the Irish Elk did not arrive; the Cave Bear responded not to the summons; the Old Silurian Ass got left. The menagerie was wholly local. Part of it I saw, and the rest of it I was. This is history; this is cold history; and history cannot lie.

The Speaker went first. He made the large tracks—the ones that are eight inches broad and eighteen inches long, and resemble the footprint of a champagne basket. He was a prime man in two or three ways, and evil in forty; but he was not the Primeval Man, just the same: reflect upon this. I was there; I was there all the time; and I knew him well. He made the large tracks. And he did it without an effort. He could have done it with one hand tied behind him. He said so himself; he didn't tell me so, though I knew him well. His name was Welsh; either Welsh or Sanders, I don't remember which; but it was a name that sounded like those. He was a rancher; kept a ranch; cattle ranch; and did not wear shoes, such not being his custom, though a praying man from his mother's knee. And always when he went forth ranching with all his might into the pasture amongst the cattle, there was much hay and straw lying scattered about, and with it much other material—material of a plastic nature; mud, to wit; acres of it; and this material and the straw did of a truth and by custom combine and form unto him uncreated sandals, as you may say—uncreated, because not projected by volition nor wrought by art— nay they were but the cumulative achievement of time, that is to say time and patient neglect. And as the prosperous years rolled on, his sandals waxed, and gathered grace and style, and also magnitude and majesty; insomuch that the footprint of him was like to the footprint of a hogshead which is up-ended in the snow. And he became a legislator, and also Speaker. But there was jealousy because of the splendor of his attainments in the field, there was rancor because of the sublimity of his sandals. And besides, there was not room; for the alkali flat was circumscribed in area, and he unjustly occupied space proper and sufficient for the representation of several counties; also, he trod upon the feet of distant members. Those near at hand could see the danger, and avoid it; but those who were further removed, having no warning, his step being noiseless, like to that of the stealthy and cushioned cat, suffered. Yet his intentions were pure, he did these things inadvertently—usually while absorbed in thought concerning the national debt.

So, charges were brought against him, and he was indicted, tried, and condemned, as an obstructionist. The verdict was confirmed by the appellate courts in succession, by Congress also, and finally by the United States Supreme Court, sitting in bank, or chambers, or somewhere, and this latter condemned him to cut his sandals down to eight inches broad and eighteen inches long, with costs, and thus it was with these reduced powers, these diminished capacities, that he made the now world-renowned Footprints for the Primeval Man. But suppose he had had a chance to do some fossil tracks for the benefit of science before they trimmed his golden slippers? Which one of the late lamented would they have laid *them* on? But that is not vital to my theme—they'd have found a fossil to fit them, I judge.

Such is history; and thus is the Primeval Man vindicated, struck down from the roster, and dismissed from further service in this conflict. I now proceed to dispose of the rest of those myths. If I were gone, and the treasury of history with me, they yet could not stand; for even the scientific theory that gave them being would be also their destruction. Because it locates them back in the Old Red Sandstone Period. There were no Irish in the Old Red Sandstone Period. The Irish are a comparatively recent formation. They belong in the Old Blue Grindstone Tertiary, and are there confined to the stratified rocks of the post-pliocene alluvium and upper pentamerous lime-stone. The assertion of Hugh Miller and other early observers, that traces of them are discovered in the Jurassic deposits of the Carboniferous Chalks, be-tween the median layer of old basaltic gneiss and the marsupial crinoids of the Paleozoic Conglomerate, was regarded with suspicion at the time, and is now known to have been wholly bituminous. Now then, we come to the point. If these footprints belong to the Old Red Sandstone Period, what be-comes of your Irish Elk? What was he doing there, when there weren't any Irish yet? Answer me that. Crack me that nut, Messieurs Marsh and Harkness—and pray let us have no scientific folderol about it. Let us have a square deal just this once. The case is simple: I see your geological blunder, and go you a geological *fact* better—now you call me, if you can. Then we'll draw three apiece and double the pot. I think nobody can offer fairer than that.

And so I have disposed of the Irish Elk—as I look at it. Now we come to the Cave Bear. What is his period? He belongs among the talcose horn-blendes of the Post-Tertiary Devonian,[2] along with the thecodont saurians, cryptogamous batrachians, and other gold-bearing rocks of the Azoic age; and there isn't a trace of him to be found anywhere else for money. Then what is he doing out there among the Old Red Sandstone schist? Why, hon-ored sirs, when he died out of the world for good and all, there wasn't enough Old Red Sandstone in it to make a whetstone out of. It hadn't begun to de-posit, yet. And another thing: the Cave Bear couldn't have lived in Nevada, any way, for there isn't a cave in it, from one end of it to the other—except the comparatively recent ones in the mines, and perhaps here and there in the mining stocks.[3] Too recent to do *him* any good, or hardly anybody else.

This disposes of the Cave Bear, as I look at it. Now the same arguments that dispose of the Irish Elk and the Cave Bear, dispose also of the Old Silurian Ass; for they trained together. They were of the same general breed of mammals, and were the only mollusks that were able to hold their own against the Megatherium, the Ichthyosaurus, and other flesh-eating birds of the birdo-reptilian period, and did it then only through that vigilance which is the price of liberty, and that union in which is strength. All honor to the brave!

Now then—enough of that. Let conjecture stand aside, and history go to the bat. For I was there myself, and I know. The tracks which have been at-tributed to the Irish Elk were not made by an Irish Elk at all; they were made

2. Hornblende is bluish green or black rock with no silver in it.
3. In this sentence, *cave* is used both in its familiar sense, as a hollow in a hill or the ground, and also to mean a "cave-in."

by an Irish bricklayer—named Stephen McGinniss. Member of the legislature. I knew him perfectly well. He had a hoof; hoof like a cow's. It was a birth-mark. He was a high tempered man, and very handy with his birth-mark. And is even now at this minute after the scientists—and they will see. Even the elect may not call Stephen McGinniss an Irish Elk with impunity, nor misinterpret his hoof-prints in a spirit of scientific wantonness. These are truths, these are facts; in a word, history. For I was there.

Little remains to be said. Only this: The Cave Bear tracks were made by Mr. R. M. Daggett,[4] now grown honorably famous in other walks in life, but still depositing the same identical track to this day, let us freely believe, when he goeth unshod—as was the sternly simple custom of the pioneer legislator of the Territory of Nevada, in a day when virtuous endeavor was held above the comfort of the body, and godliness above meretricious gauds of fashion.

The tracks attributed to the Old Silurian Ass, were not made by the Old Silurian Ass. I made them myself. I made them myself, and I am not an Old Silurian Ass. I may be some kind of an ass, and some observers have held the theory that I was and am; but I am not an Old Silurian Ass. I made those tracks; and I make the same track now; and it appears that even an expert cannot tell it from an Old Silurian Ass's track, and neither can I, for that matter; but it is not an Old Silurian Ass's track, just the same, any more than I am an Old Silurian Ass; yet the person who calls the track out yonder an Old Silurian's Ass's track, does in effect call me an Old Silurian Ass, by reason that I made that track. And it must not be repeated. For I have my feelings, as well as another; and the man that calls me an Old Silurian Ass, and proves it, shall not go out of this world alive. I have said it. The language may be intemperate, but the provocation is great.

These scientists are in an ill-concealed sweat because they cannot tell *why* there are so many tracks, and all going one way, all going north. It was a large legislature, dear sirs; and the saloon was north. This is history, not conjecture. For I was there—in person.

And they cannot divine why the Primeval Man took such short steps, yet with so little lateral spread. Think of the feet he carried; also remember his condition: of course a person could not spread laterally, in his condition, as deftly as he could formerly, when sober; necessarily he would spread laterally, formerly, but not laterally, the conditions being reverse, you see. This seems simple. Also unanswerable.

And they are perturbed because they cannot tell why the tracks are so

---

4. Rollin Mallory Daggett, a Sagebrush author represented in this volume, had been Twain's colleague on the *Territorial Enterprise,* and the two friends were still in contact.

confused, and move in such subtly sinuous curves. Listen, then; I will explain this also. It is a law of nature that whisky cannot be conveyed in straight lines by a legislature, except in buckets. A legislature never uses buckets, man.

I am done.

Such is history. Such are the Carson Footprints. They are not fossiliferous, they are legislative; they are uniform, they are identical with the tracks deposited by all adjourning legislatures. In the West, I mean. Let us have peace.

San Franciscan, February 16, 1884

Why the Gold Gulch News Suspended

Arthur McEwen

Arthur McEwen (1851–1907) began a distinguished journalistic career with the *Virginia City Evening Chronicle* in the 1870s, at a time when it was attacking corrupt city officials. He later moved to the *Gold Hill News* and from there to San Francisco, subsequently becoming managing editor of William Randolph Hearst's *San Francisco Examiner*. In 1894 and 1895 he published his own newspaper, *Arthur McEwen's Letter*, which was especially critical of moneyed interests that manipulated government. He eventually went east to assist John Wanamaker in his attacks on political machines. In his western years, McEwen also contributed works of fiction, such as this story, to a variety of local periodicals. This tale is one of a small subgenre of fictional accounts by Western journalists of the difficulties and hazards of Western journalism. Other familiar works in the subgenre include Mark Twain's "Journalism in Tennessee" (1869), Ambrose Bierce's "Why I Am Not Editing the 'Stinger'" (1874), and Joseph T. Goodman's "The TRUMPET Comes to Pickeye!" (n.d.).

◦⇒ ⇐◦

Gold Gulch, Nev., July 10, 1876.

MY DEAR MCNABB: I have bought out the *Daily News,* as I contemplated when I saw you. The camp is rough, but lively, and I think I shall make money. I have written the editorials for the past week myself, being obliged to discharge the former editor, Colonel Hasbyn. I always thought it was an easy thing to write for a paper, but I find I have run out of ideas already. Besides, the business, which is all new to me, requires my attention. Please go to some of the newspaper offices and get me an editor—a sober one, if there are any. I'll pay a good salary. Yours in haste, ANDREW BROWN

Gold Gulch, Nev., July 22.

My Dear McNabb: Major Hoister arrived a week ago and took editorial charge to-day. We have seen very little of each other. He explained, when I found him at his desk this morning, that he had been making the acquaintance of the leading citizens. In the course of half an hour he handed me an article. He wrote it with a speed that astonished me. It was really an excellent article, the language being elegant as well as forcible, and the points were made with great vigor. The only fault to be found with it was that it was strongly Democratic. I explained to him a fact which he had forgotten—that the *News* is a Republican organ. He seemed neither surprised nor annoyed—not even amused—by his funny blunder, but taking back the manuscript, went coolly to work, and in exactly four minutes handed it back to me again. What this extraordinary man had done was just to put in the word Republican for Democratic, and *vice versa,* throughout. The article is highly spoken of by the leaders of the party here, and they stop me on the street to congratulate me on my new editor. Evidently he is a genius. His strange manner confirms in this belief. To-day when he had filled the editorial space—which he did with marvelous rapidity—he leaned back in his chair, with his hands clasped behind his head, and stared at vacancy. He murmured to himself repeatedly, but returned no answer to several remarks which I addressed to him. I could see that he did not hear me. Much of his unoccupied time to-day he spent spearing flies on his desk with his pen. There is a bold originality about the man that I cannot help admiring. How different he is from that odious old nuisance, Colonel Hasbyn, whom I was forced to discharge on account of his intemperate habits. He made the office a camping-ground for the whole tribe of Forty-niners,[1] and spent his time in talk about the early days, and in going out for drinks with his friends. The *News,* as you know, is one of the oldest papers in the state. It was founded by Colonel Hasbyn, but he drank himself out of the proprietorship years ago. Somehow he seemed to regard the purchase of the paper by a young man like me as an outrage upon himself, and frequently talked at me over the shoulders of his cronies in the most insulting and exasperating way. On several occasions, when he was drunker than usual, I was really afraid he would strike me with the crook cane which he always carries—not for anything in particular, but on general principles. I found out that the old humbug was in the habit of copying articles bodily from Eastern journals and palming them off on me as his own. The only faculty of his mind that has not been drowned out with whisky is his memory.

---

1. Immigrants to California following the discovery of gold there in 1849 were known as "forty-niners."

That remains in astonishing vigor. Forty-nine is as clear to him as yesterday is to me.

I write so much as this about the Colonel because he has become the chief annoyance of my life. Having learned that I am a Berkeley graduate,[2] the old wretch has been going around the saloons of the Gulch roaring out the fact, as if the mere statement of it ought to lastingly disgrace me in the eyes of everybody. He is the only man in the camp, so far as I know, who does not admire Major Hoister's editorials in to-day's *News*. He (the Colonel) is, as I write, reading one of them aloud to a crowd on the sidewalk in front of the office, and pretending to be vastly tickled over the faults which he professes to find in them. This roaring aloud to a crowd of Gulchers is one of the fixed habits of the Colonel. He used to treat them to his own articles in the same way. Of late it has given him great satisfaction to pull from his pockets notices of himself, clipped from other Nevada newspapers, and roar them out to the idlers on the main street, who always gather to hear him. It is very exasperating to see how the press speak of this absolutely empty-headed relic of other days. To read these panegyrics on Colonel Hasbyn one would suppose that the earth never before supported on its surface so much intellect, learning, wisdom and wit combined in one man. Incorporated in these fulsome and ridiculous compliments are the most unwarrantable and brutal attacks upon me. I am referred to variously as the "unfeathered snipe," the "fresh young tenderfoot," and the "callow Johnny-come-lately" who has had the temerity to invest his money in a Nevada newspaper, and the criminal audacity to discharge the incomparable Colonel Hasbyn.

Thank you and Heaven for Major Hoister. He is a jewel.

Yours gratefully,   ANDREW BROWN.

Gold Gulch, Nev., July 24.

MY DEAR MCNABB: As I write I am locked in my private office, refusing to see any visitors, though scores of the leaders of the party and other prominent Gulchers are demanding an audience. After being nearly talked to death I rebelled and hid myself. Great excitement prevails throughout the Gulch, and even in this seclusion I can hear the voice of Colonel Hasbyn as he harangues the crowd.

While I sat in the editorial room this morning going over some proofs, my attention was attracted to Major Hoister. It was not that he was muttering to

---

2. The University of California at Berkeley. Most journalists learned their trade through on-the-job training, so Brown was vulnerable to the charge that he depended on book knowledge and did not have a practical understanding of journalism or of mining communities. In this story, the validity of that charge is borne out.

himself, for I had grown used to that strange peculiarity, but as he wrote he kept constantly plucking at his tongue, and then jerking his fingers towards the floor, as if casting something down. I asked him if anything was the matter. I got only a wild sort of stare in answer; and he went on with his writing and plucking. Presently he rose and came toward me, grasping his tongue with his left thumb and forefinger, while in his right hand he held the large editorial shears. These he extended, handle toward me, and said, as well as his tightly held tongue would permit him:

"Pleathe cut thith in two, will you?"

I thought he was joking, though he had impressed me as being a solemn sort of man. When I laughed he gave a terrible scream, threw both arms up and fell backward into the big clothes-basket into which the exchanges are thrown. His face was purple, his eyes protruded, and he foamed at the mouth. I tore open his collar, yelled for the printers, sent for a doctor, and emptied the water pitcher over him. When the physician came he instantly opened a vein in the Major's arm—which flooded the floor of the editorial room for a yard square with blood—and ordered the insensible patient to be carried to bed at once. This was done, and I asked the doctor, in natural agitation, what was the matter with my editor.

"Delirium tremens," he said, wiping his lancet on his sleeve as calmly as if it was an everyday occurrence that had happened.[3]

But this shocking business of the Major was a trifle compared with the awful disaster which has come from it. After the excitement into which the office was thrown, there was a call from the printers for copy. I was out, and the "devil" picked up the manuscript written by the delirious Major and slapped it on the hook.[4] I didn't see the paper until the whole edition had been run off and the carriers were out on their routes. What do you think, McNabb, that monstrous lunatic had done? Nothing less than to write a vicious assault on the Miners' Union, and to call on the owners of the mines to reduce wages from $4 to $2 a day; and import Chinamen if a strike ensued![5]

---

3. Delirium tremens was certainly seen frequently, if not daily, by doctors in mining camps. Bleeding was a very old, standard treatment for many maladies.

4. Printer's devils were apprentices in print shops who, while learning the trade, did most of the menial work. Reporters and editors hung finished articles on hooks, and printer's devils took those articles to the printers.

5. Reducing wages and replacing white workers with cheap Chinese labor were two topics certain to enrage most miners. Nevertheless, once the profitability of Comstock mines began to drop by the late 1870s, mine owners who did not dare to lower wages directly did shorten the workweek, in effect reducing wages. And Chinese labor was extensively used on the railroads, and in most towns of any size, for work that white men were reluctant to do.

I do not know what the result will be on my business. It is as if a religious journal should come out with a denial of the divinity of the Savior and hail Bob Ingersoll[6] as the true Messiah.

I still hear the voice of Colonel Hasbyn haranguing the crowd.

Yours distractedly,   ANDREW BROWN.

[Telegram.]

RENO, Nev., July 24—Midnight.

To PETER McNABB, San Francisco: Have just arrived here on horseback after a terrible ride of thirty miles. The mob, led by Colonel Hasbyn, wrecked the office. I am ruined, but thank God I am alive. Expect me tomorrow. ANDREW BROWN.

[34—Collect.]

San Franciscan, February 16, 1884, p. 15

6. Robert Ingersoll (1833–1899) was a controversial American lecturer famous for attacking the Bible and Christianity. Religious leaders detested him, but freethinkers and skeptics regarded him as a hero.

The Typographical Howitzer

Sam Davis

This completely fictitious sketch, an involved series of in-jokes and spoofs on contemporary personalities, is one of Davis's best-known and most-reprinted pieces. Every detail in it is either made up or deliberately warped. For instance, De Quille and Twain never set out to establish their own newspaper, in Mendocino County or anywhere else. Also, in real life, it was De Quille, not Twain, who was noted for having found and brought back to Carson City an abandoned mountain howitzer (a small, light cannon). Although all of the names mentioned (including, of course, Twain's and De Quille's) are of popular writers, journalists, or politicians of the time, the works ascribed to them are either real works being ridiculed or imaginary works whose titles are ironically inappropriate. The narrative is presented in the style of "Cannibalism in the Cars" (1868), Twain's short story in which he also gave fictitious characters the names of friends or nationally known personages, for ironic purposes. Twain was not fond of having his name used without his permission, so the fact that Davis took such liberties without suffering some sort of repercussion is testimony to their close friendship and Twain's acceptance of Davis's bold humor.

⋆⇒   ⇐⋆

It was nearly twenty years ago when Dan De Quille and Mark Twain attempted to start a paper in Mendocino County. They took the type and material of their recently defunct newspaper establishment in San Francisco, and, loading the stuff on a big wagon, struck out into the country to retrieve their fortune. They packed their type just as it stood in the forms, tied up the articles with stout cords by a process well known to printers, and packing them closely in boxes, vowed to establish a newspaper somewhere which would be the leading exponent of politics and history for the Pacific Coast. Had not an unfortunate circumstance taken place it is evident that the news-

72

paper which they contemplated founding would have been alive to-day. Their journey over the mountains was utterly uneventful until they reached Simpson's station, a spot well known to old travelers on that route. Here they met a party of emigrants making for Lower California, and the latter had with them a small mountain howitzer which they had brought with them across the plains.

Twain took a great fancy to this gun, and offered fifty dollars for it, with two kegs of powder. The emigrants were glad enough to part with it, as they concluded the time for its use had passed. Dan thought the purchase of the artillery and military supplies was a reckless piece of extravagance, and said as much, but Mark replied:

"When we start our paper we must fire a salute. A newspaper office with artillery has a big bulge on the business. No well-regulated office in California should be without a howitzer. If a man comes in for a retraction we can blow him into the next county. The howitzer goes."

This silenced the argument, and the next day the two journalists took the road with their printing outfit and artillery.

The next night they camped in a mountain ravine, fifteen miles from Simpson's, and after building the usual camp-fire, fell asleep. About eleven o'clock the horses wakened them by prancing about, and the two journalists were led to the conclusion that a party of Indians was making arrangements for a night attack. In the clear moonlight human forms could be distinguished about half a mile away at the foot of the ravine. The idea of encountering Indians had never entered the heads of the two fortune-seekers, and they had no arms. Suddenly Twain brightened up, remarking:

"The howitzer?"

"We've got nothing but powder," said Dan.

"Well, powder'll scare 'em; and we'll load her up."

The piece was immediately loaded with a good big charge, and the two men felt quite certain that the Indians, hearing the roar of the gun, would beat an unconditional retreat. The piece was hardly loaded and placed in position when about forty of the red-skins came charging up the ravine.

Twain seized a brand from the camp-fire and was about to lay it on the touch-hole, when Dan yelled "Hold on!" as he rammed something into the mouth of the piece and remarked:

"Turn 'er loose."

The roar of the howitzer echoed through the lonely forest, and the savages, with frantic cries of pain, reeled down the ravine in wild confusion.

"What in h— did you put in?" asked Mark.

"A column of solid nonpareil[1] and a couple of sticks of young spring poetry."

"The poetry did the business, Dan. Get one of your geological articles ready for the next charge, and I guess it'll let the red devils out for the present campaign."

The savages again advanced. Mark attended to the powder, and Dan assorted the shot, so to speak.

"Jeems Pipe's song, 'My Mountain Home.'"

"Good for three Indians—sock'er in."

"An acrostic by John B. Ridge, in long primer."

"It'll paralyze 'em."

"Frank Pixley on the Constitution,—half a column of leaded brevier."[2]

"If it hits 'em, the day is won."

"Your leader on 'Law and Order.'"[3]

"Save it as a last resort."

Dan pulled the type out of the boxes, and stuffed column after column in the howitzer's mouth as the savages came charging on. Another round from the gun, and the red-skins rolled over and over each other like boulders swept away by a mountain cloud-burst. Mark, in an ecstasy of delight, pulled an American flag out of his effects, nailed it to the tail-board of the wagon, and was about to make a speech, when the dusky figures of the foes were once more seen moving to the attack.

The piece was again loaded, and this time with a double charge. Mark's leader on "Law and Order"; the puff of an auction house, by Fred. McCrellish, "as a sickener," Dan said; Frank Gross' verses on "The Rebel Yell"; an agricultural article by Sam Seabaugh, showing the chemical properties of corn-juice as an educational lever; a maiden poetical effort by Olive Harper, and some verses by Col. Cremony and Frank Soulé, completed the load.

"That poetry reaching 'em first will throw 'em into confusion, and my editorial coming up on the heels of the rest will result in a lasting demoralization. It will be like the last cavalry charge of the French troopers at the battle of Austerlitz."[4]

For the third and last time the faithful howitzer belched its typographical compliments to the advancing foe. The havoc was terrible. There was a wild

1. Nonpareil, in printing, is six-point type.
2. Brevier is a slightly smaller type than nonpareil.
3. In printing terminology, a leader is the main editorial in a newspaper.
4. The battle of Austerlitz (December 2, 1805) was regarded as Napoleon's greatest victory. Brilliant charges by French cavalry forced back the allied Austrian and Russian armies and set the stage for the final maneuvers that resulted in a French victory.

yell from a score of savage throats, and then the low groans of the dying floated up the ravine on the gentle wind. The two men walked over the field of slaughter and counted fifty-six aboriginals lying in heaps. The bodies were horribly mutilated with nonpareil, bourgeois, "caps," misery dashes, and un-assorted pi.[5]

"My leader cooked that man's goose," said Mark, pointing to a savage hanging over the limb of a cedar.

"My geological article did the business for him," rejoined Dan, nodding carelessly at an Indian whose head was lying twenty yards away.

"The pen is mightier than the sword."

"You bet. Hurrah for Faust and Gutenberg!"[6]

"Is there any type left?"

"Not a pound."

Ten days later the two journalistic tramps reached Virginia City, weary, discouraged, and footsore, and secured places on the *Enterprise*.

A few days ago Dan received the following from his former partner:

> HARTFORD, Connecticut, January 1, 1880.
> Dear Dan: —I send you the congratulations of the New Year. Do you recollect the time we exterminated the tribe of unlettered (?) savages in Mendocino County? If you can spare the time I wish you would make a pilgrimage to that historic spot, gather the ghostly relics together, and plant a tablet (not too expensive, and at your own expense) to the memory of the departed. Have a shooting-stick lying across a long bow, with our monogram and coat-of-arms entwined, and some appropriate epitaph carved on the stone; an extract from Carl Schurz's views on the "Peace Policy" might do.[7] Enclosed is a dollar and a half for your incidental expenses; you can deadhead traveling expenses.
>
> Yours,   Mark Twain.
> P. S. —Send a thigh-bone of the fallen chief by next express.
>
> M.T.

Dan will attend to the matter in the spring. The old howitzer used on the occasion is still in his possession.

⇢*Short Stories* (1886), 127–31

---

5. Technical printing terminology for different sizes, fonts, punctuation marks, and mixed pieces of type.

6. Johannes Gutenberg and Johann Fust (often confused, as in this instance, with Faust) were famous fifteenth-century German printers.

7. Carl Schurz (1829–1906), an immigrant to America from Germany, became a general, political figure, and editor.

One Solution

Arthur McEwen

"Pshaw!"

Martin Smith lighted his pipe and pulled at it fretfully after this exclamation of impatience, which had been provoked by a letter that went floating from his tossing hand to the other side of the room. It was a very nice room, sumptuously furnished, as all the apartments in the Argonaut Club's fine building are. Only men of means can afford to occupy them. Martin Smith was a man of means, but neither that fact nor his handsome quarters gave him any pleasure at the moment. He gazed with eyes that saw nothing of his luxurious furniture, the pictures and weapons on the walls and the tapestry and couches and curios that helped to make an opulent and harmonious interior. The fortunate young man was thinking of the letter he had so impulsively thrown from him and felt very old, though he was only twenty-nine—a good, long, healthy, athletic fellow, with the look of a man about him, though his brown mustache was curled, his hair parted in the middle and his dress as dandified as a maturing taste would permit.

"That fellow Youngson will never be anything but a school boy," he thought.

"It's eight years since we emerged, and here he's writing about 'our jolly days at Harvard' with a zest that shows he'd like to live them over again."

And he pondered in retrospective, unsympathetic wonder over rude merry-makings that had seemed to him, and still seemed to Youngson, revels of rare delight, and freaks of amateur ruffianism, sidesplitting at the time, but now powerless to call up a smile.

"Well, I suppose those four years of irresponsibility and devil-may-care companionship will always be the poetry of Youngson's life, poor wretch. He's tied for good to that New England woolen mill. He'll be rich and a deacon, fearing the Lord much and the opinions of his neighbors more, and live and die a 'prominent citizen.' Moses, what an existence!"

76

Then it struck Martin Smith, as it had been striking him very often and hard of late, that his own existence was far from satisfactory. He rose and reached for a decanter on the oak sideboard, and put it down again with a half-angry emphasis.

"No more of that, anyhow," he said. "Misery and a bottle are but a sum in multiplication. I've found that out."

Snatching the evening paper he ran his restless eye over the advertisements.

"There's nothing at the theatres; there never is any more. It's enough to drive a man to crime to sit out an evening in them."

He read the news. The reports of the races didn't interest him. He had sold his stable. The arrival of Lord Lynnpurse in his yacht from Sydney only gave him a disgustful qualm, for it brought back his own last cruise with that gang of guzzling, noisy, brainless fellows whom he had taken along. In the club they had seemed intelligent and amusing enough. The stock list charmed him not, for he had found that and cards stupid, since it neither excited him to win nor depressed him to lose. The gambler's instinct had been denied him, and he had all the money he cared for.

It will be seen that Martin Smith was to be pitied. The one child of his mother, he had come in at twenty-two for that father's substantial fortune. Though not a millionaire quite, he was beyond all need of work.

He complained to himself of this—not to others, for the young man had a rather sensitive dignity and kept his feelings and his affairs to himself usually. "If I'd been poor," he growled more than once a day, "I'd have had to struggle and I dare say I'd have managed to make something of myself—not anything remarkable, but something respectable. As it is—"

As it was he had tried. Among the magazines on his book shelves were a few in which reposed short stories and a serious paper or two of his authorship. On the merits of these performances his good sense had long ago passed final judgment. That they were fair he knew, but he had frequently read better, as well as worse. "No doubt," he decided, "I could make a sort of living as a writer if I had to, but any hack with education and average brains can do that. What's the use of my wasting my time in adding to the intolerable mass of commonplace print!" So he wrote no more, even though in his reading he was stirred by the power of some pages to try again. It seems so easy to be a genius when under the spell of one. He read a great deal, but without system. Once he had heard a clever man say that anybody who read to improve his mind hadn't a mind worth improving, and the light remark impressed him.

"I'm a useless, floating chip on life's stream," said Martin Smith, scowling

and striding over to where lay the cordial, foolish letter of poor Youngson, arrested in his development by an environment of New England wool. Martin
was orderly. He folded the letter, penciled a line on its back, and added it to a
neat pile in a pigeon-hole of his desk.

This done, he drove his hands into his trousers pockets, stood with his
long legs wide apart, frowned at the fire, next at the clock, and giving utterance to an unseemly ejaculation grabbed his hat and went downstairs.

He looked into the club's dining-room, faintly hoping for some bearable
face. The great hall, gloomy in its machine-made grandeur, contained only a
few men. Old Grubleigh, purple of visage and congested of eye, seemed the
happiest there as he packed away that impossible quantity of provisions for
which he was renowned, and chuckled fatly as Judge Tankton told his little
story in the precise, self-conscious and deliberate fashion becoming to one
who knew that when he chose to unbend he could hold his own with any
professional raconteur—Judge Tankton who drank a whole bottle of brandy
every night of his life and was regularly assisted in drunken dignity to his bed
upstairs, and so far from being ashamed was rather proud of it. Distinguished
men always have these little private weaknesses. Judge Tankton was not dis-
pleased to have it known that so eminent an authority on maritime law had
his human side.

Hard by, that side-whiskered prig of a Caseby, junior member of the solid
firm of Nail & Keepit, lawyers, was dining with his man-of-the-world air, relating the circumstances of a will case involving the customary California il-
legitimate heir that had just come into his hands, and Inkerton, the
managing editor of the *Daily Dredger,* was listening to him respectfully but
uneasily. Inkerton did not enjoy himself at the Argonaut Club. He came
there because it gave him tone, though nothing made him more uncomfortable than tone in others. It was always with a great explosive puff of comfort
that he threw off his coat on returning to the *Dredger* office and became natural. The reporters knew when he had been at the Argonauts by the peculiar
indecency and violence of his oaths.

In a far corner three lads with flowers in their buttonholes, their eyes shining and their young faces inflamed, were laughing and talking too loud over
their wine, but the dining-room was so very long and wide and high that
their voices sounded quite faint and thin to Martin at the door, and likewise
to the head waiter standing near, looking surprisingly like an elder brother of
the side-whiskered Caseby. But the lads might have laughed and talked
much louder had they chosen ere the head waiter would have taken notice.
They were sons of rich men and came to the club only when they had no
money. Their bills went to their fathers monthly.

It was dreary, very, and Martin sauntered away into the reading-room. His face lighted, for there by the fire, as ever, sat Jim Marshall—an old, old man, tall and gaunt and bent, reading a newspaper held far from him, with head thrown back, eyeglasses on nose and his mouth open in the intensity of the effort. This was one of the men of the club whom Martin liked heartily, though he was not wise or witty or well-informed. Only a simple, unaffected, kindly old soul, with an odd touch of stateliness in his bearing. The young-sters called him a "hold-over"—and such he was, from the pioneer days. His guilelessness, his inability to comprehend a joke, his fatherly amiability, his sudden bursts of indignation when the newspaper that was seldom out of his hand disclosed some new instance of official villainy; his piety, which was revealed to strangers by a grave word of rebuke when conversation be-came too modern—Martin knew him for one of the best, the purest-minded, and most upright men living. He also knew that Jim Marshall, once rich and now poor, had for thirty years lived with a woman who was not his wife, and followed the business of a stockbroker. Like himself, the easy going, familiar "Jim" was a hold-over from younger days, rollicking days. It was absurdly out of place, but everybody called him Jim. It had specialized itself into a title of honor.

Martin seated himself beside Jim Marshall, who was glad to see him. He beamed upon all manly young men and gave them sympathetic and often useful advice in their scrapes, toward which he was charitable, though he deemed it his duty to wind up with bits of quaint reproof that might have been taken from a prayer or copy book.

"Well, Mr. Smith"—Jim never failed to confer the Mr. upon his friends, young and old, though none bestowed it on him—"well, Mr. Smith, you are not looking cheerful, sir."

No, Martin was not cheerful, and he grumbled out that he wished he was at the devil, for life bored him.

"You should travel, sir," advised Jim.

Travel! Martin had traveled, and he was tired of it. "When the mere out-side of things ceases to be an interesting show, Jim," he said, "you want to go deeper, but if you don't know anything about art or architecture, and have read enough of history to comprehend that life is too short to post yourself minutely about the past, why you get discouraged and don't try, but just drift and yawn. Besides when a fellow has gone about a good deal in various coun-tries he learns that the world is inhabited by the average man, and the aver-age man is a dense pig of selfishness and conceit, a dullard and a nuisance. If he isn't being oppressed he's oppressing, if not robbing, robbed, and on the whole, the less one sees of the world the more highly he is disposed to think of it. A thousand men and women and little children have to drudge and suffer in order that one brute may be rich and comfortable. There's nothing in life. It's a skin game."

"Mr. Smith," said old Jim Marshall seriously, and looking over his eye glasses, with friendly concern, "you ought to go to work."

"I don't have to," said Martin, staring disconsolately at the fire.

"Then take to drink," advised the pioneer. "It'll stir you up and give you new ideas and make you feel more natural like. I wouldn't recommend it if you hadn't good leather in you, but you're not the kind to go to hell. You're too respectable by nature."

An hour later Martin was pacing up and down a Pacific avenue drawing-room—a drawing-room with everything about it indicating inhabitation and a knowledge of how grace and elegance and comfort could be combined into a whole that made a rich and entrancing setting for dainty women. It was the drawing-room of the home of Brownson Briggs, the well-known agricultural implement dealer, President of the Chamber of Commerce, ex-Mayor and chief mover in the new overland railroad enterprise—a Yale man, who, instead of choosing a profession had invested his capital of mediocre brains in business and been rewarded for his good sense with a fortune. With financial came social eminence, of course.

The daughter of the deserving Brownson Briggs swished softly into the half-light of the drawing-room. She was a sweet girl, tall, oval-faced, with large dark eyes so calm and deep that a man in love could read in their dusky quietude whatever was best in his own desires. Her dress was of a creamy white, and where it did not cling to her lithe young body, fell away in sweeping lines. The picture was beautiful as she halted and looked at Martin, with her firm but rounded chin lifted a little and a smile on her parted lips, which were not full, though prettily arched. He felt her beauty, rather than saw it, for his action of advance was instinctive. Both his hands went out to hers, and hers met his. He looked down fondly into the dark eyes, and murmured under his breath, "Lucy." Lovers love their ladies' names.

"There, there, Martin, that will do," she laughed, twisting herself from his arms with the sinuous skill which nature gives tall women, when he would have kissed her again. "Once is quite enough, you foolish fellow. Sit down and be sensible. What have you been doing all day?"

And she talked to him of himself, a theme which will get pleased echoes from any man, no matter how low his spirits—yea, though his hanging were fixed for the morning.

Lucy believed in Martin, and she scoffed at his discontent. What! A young man with a Harvard training, perfect health and unburdened leisure not strive for distinction? She was educated herself, and her Wellesley sheep-skin, framed in her virgin chamber, was dear to her. She believed in Martin, and loved him, too.

Bored? Nonsense. There was work in the world for all who were born into it. He had but to persevere in order to make a name in literature. That paper of his in the *Arena* on the "Social Problem" showed profound thought. Everybody said so. And that story, "Darby and Jean," was charming really, though too sentimental for her own taste. But if he was tired of writing why shouldn't he enter public life? Wouldn't he like to be a Congressman?

Martin, adoring her animated countenance, watching wistfully the slim, shapely white hands as they gave the emphasis of gesture to her strenuous speech, asked her, out of sheer emptiness, if she had read Rudyard Kipling's new book.

"The one with the drunken soldiers in it?"

"Yes."

"I suppose it's fine and powerful and all that," said Lucy doubtfully, "but I can't help feeling, you know, that it's gross and rough."

"It's awfully human," ventured Martin.

"Yes, yes; I dare say, but the finer side of life is better worth writing about. Art should deal with delicacies. Oh, by the way, Martin, there's a new piece of music—a thing of Stewart's—I want you to hear."

She went to the piano and Martin's eyes embraced her. Had she been a duke's instead of an American business man's daughter, she could not have been more distinctly the product of care, of cultivation—more removed in purpose and result from nature's first intention in making woman. For the business man is the republic's noble. He accepts his civic primacy unquestion-ingly, and Lady Clara of the line of Vere de Vere does not have in more con-trolling measure than his womankind the instinct, the saving pride of caste.

There were years on years of practice in Lucy's touch, and natural apti-tude, too. She awoke in the atmosphere of music. The soul of her, in this one field of free expression, found full voice. Surely in those clear, unrestrained, dulcet tones of song, in that tender tremble and gentle, almost sobbing ca-dence, the heart of a woman throbbed and comprehended.

Martin, his eyes moist, his breast full, laid his hand in light caress upon her hair, lifted her chin and kissed her.

She smiled up at him and yielded to the impulse that bade her wind her arm about his neck. But as he would have drawn her closer to him she slipped away, not in conscious coyness, for she was above the common arts of sex, but—well, because she did.

In her chair again, she talked, brightly and with sense.

He sat, his elbow on his knee, his chin on the heel of his hand, and regarded her long in her cool, cheerful, chaste girlhood—ladyhood. It was a lovely face, with more possibilities of reserve than of ardor. To be worthy of her—to mate with this girl truly! Could he do it? It meant being at his highest always.

Martin's eyes fed upon her with baffled yearning. "She does not love me," his constricted heart said, "but loves what I am—me, plus what I import socially and materially. She doesn't know it, for she is what they have made her—and it is well. But if I transplanted her from the little hothouse she thinks the world, the fresh air of reality would kill her. Would I transplant her if I could?"

"Why do you look at me so, Martin?" she asked, suddenly fixing her clear, calm eyes upon his troubled face.

"Was I looking at you, dear?"

"Yes, and very strangely."

"Well, you are good to look at, Lucy."

She gave him a moonbeam of a smile.

Then they talked of the fine new house he was building on the Green-street bluff, which was being hurried, for when it should be finished they were to live in it. Her finger traced the lines of the plan here and there, and she was insistent on an alteration that would considerably enlarge the music-room.

The moon was shining on the Pacific and a gentle breeze blew from the south that filled the sails of the lumber schooner Palo Alto, bound from San Francisco to Huddy's Cove. Everything was snug on deck and aloft, and the crew of one at the wheel had all he could do to keep awake, so steady was the easy progress of the vessel and so useless did it seem for him to perform his mechanical function of doing nothing save to hold the rudder rigid.

Caption Huddy was below. Captain Huddy owned the schooner and owned the cove whither he was heading. Captain Huddy was an owner of things by nature. He began it by owning a wagon and oxen that brought him from Indiana across the plains in '51. When other men dug for gold, he owned a store and sold canned meats and whisky. When other men rioted on their earnings he invested his profits in land. Land became his dissipation. It was cheap everywhere, but cheapest on the wind-swept coast two hundred miles or more from San Francisco. Nobody else wanted it, and it could be had for next to nothing. Acres were valued in cents, and Captain Huddy bought thousands of them. Hill and valley, fruitless plain and tree-choked canyon were all one to him. He just wanted land. The estate to which his schooner was sailing in the moonlight embraced 8,000 acres. It descended over sloping pastures from wooded hills on which the pine and redwood, the manzanita, the laurel and madrona grew, and poked its nose out into the Pacific. Under the lee of this nose, known as Huddy's Headland, Greek fishermen had spread their nets, and in season gone out in their boats to shoot the seals swimming down from the North to breed. But Captain Huddy had changed that. The rent he demanded inflamed the Greeks and they departed. Indeed, Captain Huddy possessed a talent for compelling departures and preventing arrivals. In 1891 his domain was as free from settlers as it had been in 1851, when he built his house at the Cove and erected an adobe hotel there with a cottage flanking it. This hotel he let to a miner who had left an arm and an eye in his claim in testimony to the obduracy of a blue-rock bowlder that called for blasting. The miner had a wife, who made abalone soup, which was consumed by occasional visitors that for the sake of the sea breeze and the view drove over from a summer resort that had grown up beyond the confines of the sterile and primeval Huddy estate. Captain Huddy might have had half a dozen summer resorts in his canyons and on his beaches but for the peculiarity which impelled him always to set an impossible rental value upon anything that anybody else wanted.

The miner's wife, besides preparing abalone soup, bore children with a fecundity that alarmed Captain Huddy; she threatened to populate the estate in spite of him—and children paid no rent. Captain Huddy had a wife himself and also a family. In the pure air and dry sunshine of the Cove, his own and the miner's children throve and made a settlement. The county, in obedience to the Captain's request—being a man of property he had influence—built a schoolhouse near the adobe hotel and bestowed a salary on the Captain's eldest daughter for herding and teaching therein her brothers and sisters and the miner's swarming offspring. She made her monthly report in conformity with law and signed it "Emeline Huddy, Principal." Life at the Cove was as lonely and remote and as windy as on a ship at sea.

"Tom," said Captain Huddy, thrusting his tousled head up into the moonlight out of the cabin hatch.

"Aye, aye, sir," answered a figure that had been lying at ease, its head pillowed on a coil of rope, in the shadow of the bulwark. The call brought the figure to its feet.

"Come down and have a smoke," said the Captain, disappearing.

It was a small cabin, grimy but snug. The Captain's bunk left just room enough for a little table, on which a bottle and two glasses were set. Above the table swung a lantern that gave out an equal proportion of smoke and illumination. Tom took one of the two chairs and stretched his long legs lazily. He luxuriated in the dirty comfort of the cabin.

"Fill your glass, Mr. Mate," said the Captain, given to being a trifle formal and official when the Palo Alto was under sail. He filled his own glass.

Tom obeyed the order with alacrity. Indeed, Captain Huddy's face, which, in its weather-beaten corrugations, was brother to an oak knot, wrinkled itself with some extra anxiety as he glanced at the tremendous tumbler Tom had poured.

But Tom was at ease and unconscious. A moment like this set the crown on life. His hand that enfolded the tumbler and the other that held his pipe were brown and hard, telling of much rope-pulling and freight handling. All the work of the schooner fell upon him and the crew, now manning the wheel. Together they had shot down the long chute from Huddy's Headland the cargo of firewood, sole merchantable product of the Cove; together they had unloaded the same at the wharf in San Francisco, and taken on board the return cargo of canned meats and vegetables to be sold to the intelligent farmers who tilled the soil contiguous to the Huddy estate. In these operations Captain Huddy assisted by standing around and swearing. Tom and the crew bore the Captain's profanity and ill-nature with the philosophy of sailors, recognizing that it is a Captain's privilege to be a brute. The Captain on his part understood what was expected of him, and did his duty. But away from shore he relaxed. The greatest of mankind feels need at times for the companionship of his species.

"Tom," asked the Captain, laying down his glass after a judicious swig and eyeing his stalwart and good-looking young mate shrewdly, "How much you got?"

"Well, sir, not very much."

"You been with me close on a year; how much you saved outen your thirty a month?"

"Fifteen, Captain, for eleven months."

"That makes one hundred and sixty-five. What you done with the rest?"

"Oh, besides keeping up my dunnage I've blown in a dollar or two ashore with the boys. I lost twenty on the race at the Cove on Fourth of July, you remember. We drank a great deal at the hotel that day, too, of course."

"You're keerless, Tom, but you ain't shiftless. I've kep' my eye on you while you have been with me, and I think you're the makin's of a man. Now, why have I been watchin' you?"

"I don't know, sir."

"Yes, you do; don't you lie. You been makin' up to my Becky."

Tom was thrown into confusion. He reddened under his sunburn, hitched his broad shoulders, took his pipe from between his teeth, spat irresolutely on the cabin floor, and then turned with sudden resolution and met the Captain's keen gaze boldly.

"Well, what of it?"

"Nothin'," said the Captain, "if y' mean business."

"That's what I mean," said Tom, with relief, and compensating himself from the tumbler for the shock.

"Gimme your hand," growled the Captain, stretching his own over the table and grasping his mate's. "You're a decent young chap and a hard worker, and I'll build you up. Quit bettin' on races, dodge the bottle and you can have Becky. The day you're married you get a half interest in the Palo Alto."

The Captain threw himself back, glass in hand, with a thumb in each armpit, to observe the effect of this cloudburst of good fortune.

Tom was affected. Tears came into his eyes.

"Captain," he said, huskily, "I'll try to deserve her."

The two shook hands again and emptied their glasses with the grave manner of men performing a ceremony.

It was morning, the sun glancing and dancing on the water, when the Palo Alto came to anchor under Huddy's Headland, the nose of the estate. Up at the top of the chute—hung swinging from great piles bedded on the rocks among the swaying, swirling seaweed, the mussels and the starfish—stood a girl. She held her straw hat in place with one hand and the ocean breeze blew her dress of useful gingham flutteringly. On the side toward the sea the outline of her figure was as frank and as graceful as a sculptor could have made it. From shoulder to ankle her form stood out as nature had given it to her, and nature had been generous.

Tom, the mate, as he climbed the bluff, admired. The puffing Captain, being a parent, was not so appreciative.

"How d' do, Mr. Fowler?" cried the girl, with blushes and smiles, nodding as the mate toiled up over the edge of the precipice, a dozen feet from her.

"It's all right, Becky," called out Tom, joyously, and marching straight to her he took her in his arms.

"But Lord, Tom, pa's coming!"

"He's fixed, Becky. We've settled everything between us."

Becky laughed with gladness and her plump arms flew up and clasped the mate's neck. The kiss she gave him startled a raucous cry from a bright-eyed, observant seagull circling overhead.

"That's all right, young folks!" shouted the empurpled Captain, whose hat at the moment rose above the line of the Headland's edge, and the wrinkles of his sea-buffeted visage amiably smoothed themselves as well as they could into a benevolent and approving God-bless-you-my-children expression.

Becky was good to look at as she walked away from the chute with the mate's arm about her waist—which knew no corset. A great armful of girl she was, with a round fresh face and laughing blue eyes, subdued now and dewy as she glanced up at her stalwart, rejoicing lover. With the ardor of sixteen she hugged him when a turn of the road hid them from the Captain, and the mate fondly gave her hug for hug. Her gaze was adoring, for Tom was to her the handsomest, strongest, cleverest among men. And to that worship he responded by feeling large and noble and able and deserving. Dear, simple, trustful, admiring, plump little Becky! How he loved her, to be sure, and how satisfying it was to be with her! What a fine fellow he was too!

It was all settled as Tom had said. They were to be married, and live in the cottage flanking the hotel until they should build a better one of their own.

Mate Tom discovered he had business in the city and took stage next day. He brought back a fine engagement ring for blushing, worshiping Becky—and great news besides. An elder half-brother had died away off in San Bernardino and left him a bit of a ranch and a band of sheep there. It made him quite rich, he said, but he wouldn't think of taking his wife to such a lonely, desert place. No; they should live at the Cove, and he would stick by the schooner and the sea—a life he liked far better than ranching and sheep herding. He would put the ranch and sheep in charge of some one and run down and take a look at it now and again. It was agreed between the Captain and the ecstatic mate that he must go there at once and put his property in order.

"You won't be gone longer than you can help, will you, Tom?" tearfully whispered Becky, in his arms.

"No, darling, you can bet your bottom dollar on that," the mate whispered back, with his whole soul in his voice. He had been taking a farewell tumbler or two with the Captain.

Martin Smith sat in his room at the Argonaut Club gazing intently at two objects on the table before him.

In the great, depressing dining-room below young Caseby, the rising attorney, had fingered one of his stiff little side whiskers and said to the florid Inkerton of the *Dredger:*

"Oh, by the way, I dropped into the University Club this afternoon after court and there was a young fellow there just out from Harvard—a New Yorker with plenty of money I believe—and he's a connection of Martin Smith's and was asking me about him. What's become of Smith, lately? He isn't often here now, I notice."

"No," answered Inkerton, "and small loss. He's an offish, stuck-up young dude. And on what, I'd like to know? Has he any brains? Has he ever done anything? One would think the old man—a cursed money-grubber that I always wanted to roast—had left him money enough. But no. The youngster's a chip off the old block, and is for making more. He's up to his eyes in Idaho mines, I'm told, and puts in most of his time superintending them. That's what takes him away."

"Gad," agreed Caseby, who himself was never known needlessly to spend a dollar or to lend one to anybody who needed it, "Gad, he *must* be a money-pig. I never liked Smith myself much. He's a glum, discontented, conceited fellow, with no soul or imagination. If you or I had his money we'd make things hum, eh Inkerton?"

And these two expansive roysterers exchanged winks and smiles over their glasses of club claret.

"But, to do him justice," added Mr. Inkerton, reluctantly, "he did take his fling when he was over in London and Paris—went it strong, I've heard, and was mixed up in an awful scandal, and had a duel with a Frenchman about an actress and that sort of thing, too. I've been trying for a long time to get the particulars. May come in handy for the *Dredger* some time, you understand. Nothing would please me better than to give that supercilious young rooster a roast."

Martin, happily unconscious of the good opinions of his friends beneath, sat and gazed at the two objects on the table before him. Then with a sigh he laid them in the drawer and locked it. Rising, he threw off the great ulster that enfolded him from neck to heels, and gave a short, sharp laugh as he surveyed himself in the glass.

For Martin Smith was looking at the reflection of Tom Fowler, the mate of the Palo Alto.

It was very late when he returned to his rooms dressed as a gentleman, and feeling like one. Lucy had been kind if not ardent, and had exclaimed with pleasure at his brown face and bright eyes and general air of health, vitality and high spirits.

"Mining agrees with you, sir," she said, letting him kiss her flushed cheek as he held both her hands.

She turned the palms of his upward and remarked with surprise on the hardness.

Yes, he liked to turn to with pick and sledge in his mines. It gave him an appetite and killed the blues. "Those mines, Lucy, will make me a millionaire I hope, but they will take me away from you a good deal for a few years, darling. I must attend to them personally, you know, if they are to be rightly managed."

Well, that would be hard, of course, sensible Lucy thought, but then it was worth some sacrifices to make Martin a millionaire.

She played for him and sang, and talked in her intelligent, forceful way and charmed her lover. He sunned himself in her brightness and feasted on her delicate beauty. Even the opulence of her surroundings was sweet to him. He felt lifted and refreshed, and possessed of a swelling desire to be the worthy mate of so much intellect, refinement and loveliness.

The fine new house was all but finished, and at parting Martin, overbearing that instinctive shrinking which ever assailed her as he became passionate, pressed her in a masculine embrace. She checked a little fluttering sigh, and, escaping with her sinuous twist, held him off with an outstretched hand, and, laughing softly, let him set the day for their marriage.

"She's an angel," Martin cried inwardly as he marched clubward. "A pure, high-minded angel, and I'm a villain and a blackguard and a gross beast, I suppose. Whatever is best in me that girl appeals to. And I respond with all my heart when I am with her—no, with half my heart. There's two of me, and each of me has his turn. If she knew both of me she'd turn away in horror—and small blame to her, though there's good in my other self, too. I can't make myself over, God help me! My feet are on the earth, and my head in the skies where Lucy dwells. Starving one self will kill the other, too. I've tried, and know. God help me, God help us all."

He was in his room again and at the table with the two objects before him. One was a large and beautiful photograph of Lucy, the other a little tintype of Becky. In turn he raised them to his lips and kissed them.

Then he fell back in his chair, a picture in either hand, and his eyes looked beyond the wall and beyond the night.

Martin smiled presently, and his brown, handsome face wore a look of restful happiness, given back by the visions he beheld beyond the wall and the night.

He married them both.

San Francisco Examiner, March 19, 1893, p. 19

Serious Trifling

Sam Davis

It was a common thing in Virginia City in the early days, for a number of people to get together and present some public man with a testimonial, in the shape of a gold watch or a silver service. As a rule, the testimonials were presented to people who could well afford to buy such luxuries, by impecunious persons who could ill afford to pay even a fractional part of the value. The poor giving to the rich!

Some years ago the Superintendent of —— mine became very popular, and a number of his friends concluded that it would be the correct thing to present him with a gold watch and chain. They raised $350 among the miners who worked under him. The miners did not receive the idea of a testimonial with acclamation, but somehow thought it unwise to refuse to subscribe. The friends of the Superintendent thought it would be well to make the affair as much of a surprise as possible. It was to come off in the office of the mining company, and in order to make the surprise more complete, it was determined to make the presentation as much as possible like an investigation of official corruption up to the moment that the watch should be flashed in sight.

The following note was accordingly sent to the Superintendent by the jokers:

Mr. ——: Sir—You are ordered to appear in person this evening at the office of the —— Mining Company, at 7:30 o'clock, to answer to certain grave charges which have been made against your official conduct in connection with the superintendency of the mine. Promptness upon your part will greatly facilitate business.

Yours, etc.,

THE TRUSTEES.

At seven o'clock about a hundred of the Superintendent's friends were on hand to take part in the festivities. Several baskets of wine were in sight, and the party selected to make the presentation speech had a funny one learned by heart. At half-past seven, however, there was no superintendent. Eight o'clock came, and he was not there. Half an hour later some friends went to room to see if he had received the note.

He had received it, and JUMPED THE TOWN.

→San Francisco *Midwinter Appeal,* March 3, 1894

How to Win at Faro

Rev. E. M. Reynolds Will Show You How

W. H. Marshall

This sketch appeared in the exhibition newspaper Sam Davis published in San Francisco for the city's 1894 Midwinter Fair, the *Midwinter Appeal and Journal of Forty-Nine,* and was signed W. H. Marshall. It was reprinted, without authorial identification, in the exhibition newspaper Davis published in San Francisco for the Panama-Pacific Exposition, the *Forty-Nine Camp Appeal* (March 17, 1915).

⊷═◌   ◌═⊶

In 1878 Bodie was the wickedest town in all the world. It had been a mining camp in 1861, had been worked out, rediscovered by George Story in 1877, and by August 1878 contained 15,000 inhabitants.[1]

The daily accounts of the day's doings at Creede, Colorado, are commonplace compared with a recital of the feverish existence at Bodie during the boom. The "Bad Man from Bodie" acquired a world-wide fame. The hurdy-gurdies never closed and were crowded at all hours.[2] Magnificent saloons cropped up with plate-glass mirrors and furnishings in solid woods and marbles. Dave Nagle, the slayer of David S. Terry; Bill Withrow, since famous as a shotgun messenger; John Wagner, who spent $18,000 in furnishing his barroom, were the principal saloonkeepers and consequently the leading citizens.

---

1. Bodie, California, now a ghost town and state historical park about five miles west of the Nevada border and less than ten miles north of Mono Lake, fitfully existed through short periods of mining booms and long periods of "borrasca" (busts) from the 1860s to the 1950s. This population claim is probably excessive. Although its population fluctuated, according to the 1880 census Bodie then had approximately seven thousand inhabitants.

2. Hurdy-gurdies were dance halls with unsavory reputations that, for a fee, supplied women as dance partners.

The camp had its daily paper, the Standard, edited by Frank Kenyon, who afterward died in Guatemala, and managed by John M. Dormer, subsequently Secretary of the State of Nevada. All the miners and workingmen were well paid, and gambling was the principal diversion. Every saloon had its faro bank.[3] But up to the time the place contained 12,000 people there was no church in town, and worse than that, no sermon had been preached there. Bodie had been given over to the Evil One.

On Tuesday, August 26, 1878, a memorable event happened in the history of the camp. The boom was at its height. A few days prior Russian Pete had made a big strike in the northern end of the Sigourney, the Booker on Booker Flat was looking up, and everything about the camp even to the hurdy-gurdy girls, wore a roseate hue.

It was early in the afternoon when a stranger entered the office of the Standard and presented his card to Mr. Dormer. It read:

REV. E. M. REYNOLDS,
Of the M. E. Church

The new arrival was a stout built man of medium height, florid complexion, and a determined look about his large mouth. He was attired in a loosely-fitting suit of gray stuff badly worn.

"Glad to see you," said Mr. Dormer, pleasantly. "One of the crying needs of this camp is a pastor. The Standard since it started has done its best to reform the camp, but its efforts have been futile. No use trying. What Bodie wants is a spiritual awakening. Its people want to be aroused to the imminent danger they are in. It is a dreadfully immoral place."

"I have heard so," replied Mr. Reynolds, quietly. "For the past few weeks I have been laboring for the Master in Aurora."

"What success?"

"Not as great as I could desire. People seem to be careless of their soul's salvation. There are a great many families at Aurora, but I found few devout Christians."

"Are you going to preach here?"

"Yes. I have seen a member of the Executive Committee of the Miners' Union and they have kindly consented to my using their hall on next Sunday. The object of my call was to see you about getting out some dodgers calling attention to the meeting."[4]

"What do you wish on the dodgers?"

---

3. Faro was a popular card game of the period, in which bets were placed on the top card of the dealer's deck. Faro phraseology is used frequently in this story.

4. "Dodgers" were publicity handbills.

Mr. Reynolds thought a moment and wrote:

RELIGIOUS SERVICE

At Miners' Union Hall, Sunday Evening, August 31, 1878.
Rev. E. M. Reynolds, of the Methodist Church,
will preach at 7:30 o'clock.
Subject—"And He said unto them,
follow me and I will make you fishers of men."

SINNERS AND CHRISTIANS
CORDIALLY INVITED

"That subject won't draw," said Mr. Dormer, promptly and emphatically. "Why you won't have a corporal's guard there. You must preach on some live subject—something in touch with the people; something that appeals to their sympathies—to their every-day life. The text from St. Matthew is all right in its place, but it is not the thing here."

"Can you give me a subject, then?" asked the minister.

"Stocks and faro are what interest people here. Few people can beat either game. Why not preach on 'How to Beat Faro'?"

Mr. Reynolds knitted his brows a moment. He evidently was weighing the matter in his mind, and it took him a very few moments to decide.

"I'll do it," he said earnestly.

Then he took his pencil again and wrote.

"This is what I'll have on those dodgers," he remarked, as he handed over what he had written:

HOW TO WIN AT FARO!

At Miners' Union Hall on Sunday Evening,
August 31, 1878, at 7:30 o'clock.

REV. E. M. REYNOLDS,

Of the Methodist Church will address the Citizens of Bodie on
"How to Win at Faro."
How to Bar Splits and not Get Whip-Sawed on the Last Turn.
If You Strike a King Deal,
Don't be Afraid to Set your Checks In.

"I think you are right," he said to Dormer. "The ordinary layman may not understand this. I do not. I merely use the catch phrases which I have heard on the street. But every miner in Bodie will know what it means."

Rev. Mr. Reynolds had an immense crowd to hear him. His application of How to Win at Faro to the gospel of St. Matthew had a thrilling and beneficial effect. He wound up his address as follows:

"My friends, I have been in your camp but a few days. During the short time I have resided here I have been deeply impressed with the wealth of your mines and the enormity of your wickedness. Crime, in all of its shades and stages, instead of being frowned upon and discountenanced, is encouraged. The chief amusements of the people of Bodie are gambling, drinking and carousing.

"What a precarious living is afforded a gambler! Perhaps you never have thought of this before. Pass your saloons at any hour of the day or night and see the poor wretches who have lost all at the gambling tables, surreptitiously trying to appease their hunger at the lunch counter! Young men of good families have lost all hope and hang about these places in their despair.

"I have advertised that I would tell you how to win at faro. I mean in a spiritual way. Let us assume, my hearers, that the World is the Layout and the Church is the Case-keeper. The King represents our Lord and the Jack the Devil. Do you want everlasting happiness? Do you want eternal life? If you do, copper[5] the Jack on the heel and play the King to win. Boundless and infinite will be your joy when the last turn is made and the Case-keeper makes it Jack-King, for you have called the turn and won a crown in the heavenly kingdom.

"But many of you, in fact nearly all of you, copper the King and play the Jack to win. It is a terrible wager, for at the last turn you will find that you have lost eternally!

"My friends, let me entreat you, by everything that is dear in the transitory life and sacred in the everlasting life, to come and change your system! Copper the Jack's heel and play the King open. And when the Last Great Turn is made there will be no splits, no whip-saws, and you won't be afraid to set your chips in. It will be a King Deal."

Seven gamblers confessed their sins there and then, and enough money was taken in to build a church without mortgaging the property. Russian Pete passed the hat.

Rev. E. M. Reynolds has been engaged to preach in the El Dorado Gambling Hall in the '49 Camp whenever he can secure an audience on Sunday evening. Public invited. Jake Wallace, the banjo player, will pass the hat.

         ⇢*Midwinter Appeal and Journal of Forty-Nine*, March 31, 1894, p. 2

---

5. To "copper" was a slang term meaning to bet against.

That Affair at Pollard's

Joseph T. Goodman

Sam Davis participated in the California Midwinter Fair of 1894 by agreeing for its duration to print an old-style newspaper in the Mining Camp of '49 exhibit. The *Midwinter Appeal* was the result, a short-lived and humorous version of his real newspaper, the *Carson Appeal*. The *Midwinter Appeal* was a medley of imaginary and real news, some old items and some new, most of it with a comic twist. Davis persuaded many of his friends to contribute something to the paper. Joe Goodman contributed the following item. Like Artemus Ward's "The Babes in the Wood" lecture, which rambled everywhere but never got to its announced topic, this piece also delightfully avoids saying anything about its supposed subject, a lurid Washington, D.C., sexual scandal between Rep. W. C. P. Breckinridge and Madeline Pollard, a woman thirty years younger. Goodman, who enjoyed a reputation for truthfulness, is ribbing his good friend Davis about his reputation as a hoaxer and good-humoredly insulting their common friends Sam Wright and Jim Townsend. But Davis, as the editor of the *Appeal*, manages to get the last word by wittily turning Goodman's argument to his own advantage.

⊶⊜ ⊜⊰

I am going to try to state the true facts in the case. That appears easy enough to you probably, but it isn't as easy as you think. I doubt if any one can tell the absolute truth. There is a warp in the candidest intellect that twists things. The most conscientious man I know—Sam Davis of Carson, Nev.—has staggered under this disability all his life. He desires to tell the truth on all occasions, but is simply incapable of doing it. An approximate reach toward facts—always largely on the side of error—is the nearest point to which he can ever arrive. This fault or infirmity—or whatever you choose to call it—became at one time a burning international—but here I am wandering away from the facts—because, I say, a State question, and is embalmed in the statutes of Nevada. He has mulcted the commonwealth to a large amount through advertising in the Carson *Appeal,* but was incompetent to recover owing to his inability to take the ordinary oath. But his genius rose to the occasion. With the help of Sam Wright he lobbied an act through the legislature empowering him not to tell the truth but to come as near to it as he could, and under this statute he sued and collected from the State an amount that left it permanently bankrupt.[1] I told this to Bill Nye, but he didn't see fit to avail himself of it and has gone on twaddling irrelevant bosh ever since.[2]

As I said, however, I am going to try to state the facts in the Pollard affair—but again it isn't as easy as you think. I have a case of hereditary, persistent and perpetual prevarication in my mind. I know Mr. James Townsend, better known as Lying Jim Townsend. He walked into the old Golden Era office in 1859—a slim, clipper-built lad, who had boxed the compass in his cruises—and proclaimed that he was then forty-six years old.[3] By dead log reckoning he must now be 81, yet he is still a boy, and has never been known to tell the truth from that day till now. Hence his reputation.

But to get down to the facts of the case which, as I have said, isn't as easy as you think. For, without heredity or strain for reputation, I find it difficult to tell the truth myself. Things round themselves up in one's imagination so much better than they really occur. You, my Christian friend, have undoubtedly often added or suppressed a little to make a statement more dramatic and complete.

And so, upon full consideration, lest my biases should pervert the actual facts, I shall not attempt to give an account of that affair at Pollard's.

J. T. GOODMAN

[When a man of Joe Goodman's veracity doubts his ability to tell the truth, none of the rest of us need be blamed for lying.—ED. APPEAL]

⇢*Midwinter Appeal,* January 21, 1894, p. 1

---

1. Samuel Wright was an early settler of Carson City. He started as an undertaker, soon became politically influential, and eventually was appointed superintendent of the U.S. Mint in Carson City.

2. Bill Nye was a justice of the peace and nationally syndicated popular journalist in Laramie, Wyoming. Newspapers around the country, including the *San Francisco Examiner,* for years printed weekly his columns of humorous narratives.

3. Jim Townsend claimed to have been a sailor on a clipper ship, gave wildly improbable accounts of his adventures around the world, and pretended to a much greater age than was possible. *The Golden Era* had been an early literary magazine in San Francisco.

The TRUMPET Comes to Pickeye!

Joseph T. Goodman

There is no more telling how population will drift than which way a frog will jump.

In '50 we all were dead sure that Ragtown would be the emporium of the Southern Mines.

With the perspicacity of the early bird I rushed some type and an old press there, and started the *Ragtown Trumpet*.

But within three months the Pickeye diggings were discovered, and the course of empire turned that way.

It required little observation to satisfy me that Time's latest offspring was his best, and that to be in the swim at all I must go with the tide.

If I had called my sheet the *Eagle* or *Mud Turtle*—or anything else locomotive—it mightn't have been so difficult to get a move on it.

But the *Trumpet* had blared for Ragtown until the citizens of that place felt that they had a vested right in it. It is only fair to state that most of them had.

In consequence, when I announced my intention of removing to the new metropolis, a qualified but very effective embargo was proclaimed—that is, I might go to Pickeye or to Tophet, if I liked, but the *Trumpet* office should remain in Ragtown.

I considered this an open assault on the freedom of the press, and resented it as became the sole representative and champion of the noble Fourth Estate in that region.

When a Coriolanus is turned down at home what recourse has he but to go to the Volscians?[1] I went to Pickeye, and told my wrongs. The response was what first revealed to me the loftiness of its public spirit.

---

1. The narrator, in justifying himself with an allusion to Shakespeare's *Coriolanus*, is seemingly unaware that Coriolanus is not a completely admirable figure when he deserts Rome for its Volscian enemy, and that the public Shakespeare depicts is fickle.

Business was suspended in the town; work ceased in the surrounding camps; and three thousand armed men, with seven prairie schooners carrying their blankets and commissary stores, moved against Ragtown.

There were no Roman matrons to supplicate me and save the town. Powerless to defend itself, Ragtown passed under the yoke, and the *Trumpet* office was borne off to Pickeye.

Then and there I vowed to dedicate my talent and my fortune to Pickeye. It would be immodest to speak of my own achievements. I will only say that the *Trumpet* became a power in the land.

But now that the flower of manhood which flourished there has almost passed away, and I am but a last leaf,[2] I feel it incumbent on me to perform my final votive duty.

It took me ten days to get things to rights and issue the first number.

I met with unexpected literary assistance at the very outset. One day I was busy at work when an overgrown boy, or a retarded young man, came shambling diffidently into the office. He wore a gray flannel shirt, canvas trousers, and heavy boots. His hair was long and tow hued, and his inexpressive face was covered with a fuzzy growth of a yet more colorless shade. He was as out-and-out a Nazarite as I ever saw.[3]

"I write poetry, Mr. Editor," he said modestly, "and I thought you might like some of it for your paper."

"Indeed I should, if it's the right sort. Have you any samples with you?"

"Only a few lines I've wrote about your paper coming to town."

"Will you let me see them, please?"

He fished out of his shirt-pocket a folded piece of wrapping-paper and handed it to me. The gem was this:

ON THE COMING OF THE PRESS TO PICKEYE

Two things there be which make a State
Or mining camp supremely great:
The orator who talks to men,
The scribe who does it with his pen.

This town has had since it was young
A superfluity of tongue,

2. If this figure of speech has any autobiographical value, it suggests that Goodman wrote this story late in his life. Like his poem "Virginia City," which also makes explicit reference to the writer's age, this story has been frequently reprinted, but the circumstances of the original publication are not known.

3. In the Old Testament, a Nazarite was a man (such as Samson) who took certain vows, including that of never allowing his hair or beard to be cut.

But it was short on literature
Till now we've got the simon-pure.

Pickeye stands pat and waits the dare
Of fate behind her bully pair,
And if the times keep up their rush
She'll maybe pull a royal flush.

"Capital!" I cried: "just the kind of poetry I want. What name shall I put to it?"

"My full name is Charles Augustus Dinkey," replied the youth, his dull countenance suddenly becoming transfigured by pleasure, "but I think it would look more poetical to sign it C. Augustus Dinkey. And, if it's all the same to you, I'd like to have the 'Foothill Bard' follow it. Sounds kind of pretty, don't it?"

"Your taste is admirable, Mr. Dinkey. Everything shall be as you wish."

Thus came about the acquaintance and life-long friendship between me and that gifted genius, the young Foothill Bard.

The name of Pickeye hasn't figured in history to any great extent up to date, but future historiographers may discover in the annals of that place a veritable mine. The map and the whole earth might be searched in vain for the town now. Time set a dele mark against it, as it did against Troy and Carthage. The melancholy epitaph "Pickoculus fuit" or "Delevitus est Pickoculus" might be inscribed upon its site.[4] But the stirring events and heroic deeds of its palmy days still live in story, and will continue to live while memory holds a seat within the book and volume of many an old-timer's brain.

It was one of those mining camps which sprang up like mushrooms in the early days of California, just a medley of houses, cabins, and tents, on the bank of the Tuolumne, where the river had formed a long flat. Its population was only a few thousand, but that was no measure of the town's importance. When the surrounding mining camps poured in their additional thousands it became a theater where unrestrained human nature exhibited itself in every phase of comedy and tragedy, as mood or occasion prompted, and it was recognized as the metropolis of the Southern Mines.

Its modest name was derived, like so many others in those days, from a trivial circumstance.[5] The supposed discoverers of the place found the shank,

4. Pickoculus is made-up Latin for Pickeye; thus, "Pickoculus fuit" is Latin for "Pickeye was." "Delevitus est Pickoculus" is probably mock-Latin for "Pickeye is exterminated" and is intended to be reminiscent of Cato's famous oratorical demand, "Delenda est Carthago" (Carthage must be destroyed).

5. One of those communities whose name owed to a trivial circumstance was Virginia City, so

or eye, of a rusted pick embedded in the gravel many feet below the surface. The incident gave rise to many conjectures and to the name of the locality. The former died away in futile discussion, but the name survived. It was a homely and foolish name, but to the archeologist it may become in course of time as pregnant with meaning as Palenque or Persepolis.[6] And, after all, what's in a name? We have it on high authority that a rose by any other name would smell as sweet.[7] The persons and events that give pomp and circumstance to history are what consecrate the name of a city, and in this respect Pickeye will ever be as famous as if it had borne the most high-sounding appellation in the world.

If, mindful of the unhonored dead and striving in these artless tales to relate some of their intrepid doings, I fail to impress the reader with a sense of their illustriousness, let the failure be imputed to my lack of skill, not to a want of grandeur in the deeds themselves. The greatest actions dwindle in importance if poorly told. The Trojan War would seem a tedious affair but for Homer. Except for Xenophon the retreat of the Ten Thousand would be an uninteresting occurrence.[8] I am neither a poet nor a historian, but I have done my best. Should the glory of Pickeye sink into oblivion it will be because I am not gifted enough to depict it properly, and the true genius never arises to write its Iliad or Anabasis.

The files of the old *Pickeye Trumpet* (the only possession I have managed to retain during a lifetime now fast yellowing) have been of great use to me in verifying names and dates, but in little else; for doing the editing, composition, and presswork all by myself was not favorable to extended reports of events, even if there had been no other restriction.

But those were times that tried the editor's nerve as well as his brain. He had to run the gauntlet, as it were, with every issue of his paper, and he learned to be circumspect.

But if there be no full reports in these faded old files, I find something better in them—the lavender fragrance of a time that is vanished. In turning them over I breathe again the aura of my youth, and the glory of those days and of Pickeye rises like a beautiful apparition from their tattered leaves.

Of no less service has been the manuscript collection of the late C. Augus-

---

important to Goodman. According to story, one of the earliest discoverers of the Comstock fell while drunk and broke a bottle of whisky. Unwilling to completely waste good liquor, he baptized the spot Virginia.

6. Ruined and abandoned but once-great ancient cities, rediscovered and studied by archaeologists. Palenque is in Mexico, Persepolis in Iran (formerly Persia).

7. See Shakespeare's *Romeo and Juliet* 2.2.43–44.

8. Xenophon's *Anabasis* narrates the successful retreat of a Greek army in Turkey to a Black Sea port whence it could be safely evacuated.

tus Dinkey, bequeathed to me as literary executor of the lamented Foothill Bard. So far I have been unable to find a publisher willing to exploit the poems. But I trust the specimen that appears in this sketch will awaken the world to a sense of what it is losing by their suppression.

The day of the advent of the *Trumpet* was a red-letter one in the annals of Pickeye.

We who have grubbed all our lives behind the scenes, and know how tawdry and squalid everything is there, can appreciate the halo that surrounds the "press" in the sight of the uninitiated only by the plaudits from the auditorium.

When the long procession of armed men who had captured the handful of printing material from Ragtown returned to Pickeye, the triumphal nature of their entrance would have caused one unacquainted with the facts to suppose they were escorting the ark of the covenant, or that a palladium[9] dropped direct from heaven was being exultantly borne to their citadel.

The outfit was housed in a cabin tendered me by the municipality, and then the entire population gave itself up to an afternoon and night of celebration and rejoicing. There was marching, with a brass band; there were bonfires and salutes and speeches, and so much noise generally that you might have fancied the *Trumpet* had become animated and was blowing itself to death.

So grand a demonstration naturally inspired me, and I resolved they should see that the mountain hadn't labored to bring forth only a mouse.

Expectation had been wrought to a high pitch, and the day the paper was to appear the streets in the neighborhood of the office were crowded.

It is the custom of journalists to complain that the public isn't responsive—or, as they phrase it, that they hear no echoes from their work. They should have lived in Pickeye.

For an hour or more I sold papers at fifty cents a copy as fast as I could turn them off the press. Then explanation began to interfere with presswork.

"See here, young fellow," said a flushed citizen, "do you think it the square thing, after what we've done for you, to speak of Pickeye as 'reeking with slums'?"

"It's only a reference to the condition of the back streets," I replied.

"Well, don't you refer to our streets, d'ye hear? If they don't suit you, there's a trail leading straight out of town which maybe will."

I had no opportunity to make a rejoinder, for another citizen, equally flushed, was flourishing a copy of the paper in my face and shouting:

"What do you mean by giving such a send-off to French Bar? Have we

9. A holy object that supposedly confers security and preserves whoever holds it.

brought your picayune thumb-sheet here to make us play second fiddle to every wickiup settlement within a hundred miles?"

"It was intended only as a pleasant allusion to a neighboring camp," I answered.

"Well, just a few more 'pleasant allusions' of that kind, young man, and you'll land in a neighboring camp, if you land at all."

Again I was deprived of the chance of retorting. A yet more frenzied man was shaking his fist at me and exclaiming:

"How dare you try to make fun of me, you featherless gosling?"

"I assure you that I haven't, for I don't know you."

"You'll get acquainted with me almighty quick, if you don't apologize."

"What is wrong, pray?"

"You say here that Gooseberry Sam's girl has barred kissing until he shucks his prickles."

"That's just a skit to lighten up the columns—a mere fancy."

"But that's my name, you pin-feathered snipe; and if you ever use it again you'll find that my prickles haven't been shucked."

My materialized fancy was crowded aside by a new arrival, whose eyes fairly glared.

"You infernal smooth-faced ghoul! to traduce the memory of my old friend Jim Bangs!"

"In what way?"

"You say a whisky-bottle was found beside his body."

"Well, wasn't that the fact?"

"Yes, but you could have suppressed it, couldn't you? It isn't necessary to tell every fact you know. There's more than forty thousand whisky-bottles up around Jim's cabin, but I'd like to see the jack-legged editor who dares state that fact in his paper."

The friend of the late Mr. Bangs gave place to an individual dressed in black, whose quiet demeanor inspired me with an expectation of clerical approval.

"My name is Cross," he said, in a low and pleasant tone. "I see myself mentioned here as a gambler."

"Isn't the statement true?"

"It is true, but it isn't agreeable. We of the sporting fraternity pride ourselves on being gentlemen. I request you to bear that in mind. I have never descended to kindergarten work yet, and I should hate number eleven to be a chicken."[10]

_____

10. This sentence has resisted interpretation.

A gentleman of the same fraternity succeeded Mr. Cross, but he wasn't as polite in his tone and manner.

"See here, young chap," he said, "why are you so fresh as to apply the term 'outcast' and other opprobrious epithets to Gentle Annie?"

"What other language could fitly describe her outrageous conduct on the street?"

"I observe you have a dictionary there, my young undergraduate friend. You will find in it the word 'lady,' and many others with which to gracefully and respectfully qualify it. I advise you to study your dictionary well. Annie is a friend of mine."

The thing was getting to be very monotonous and tiresome. A lull, however, encouraged me to hope that the remaining contents of the paper were blameless. But it was only a respite. In rushed a pompous person, just swelling with indignation.

"Curse your impudence, you little whiffet!" he exploded, "don't you know how to treat a man with common decency?"

"I try to treat every one respectfully. How have I offended you?"

"You've put only 'captain' to my name, while you've be-majored and be-coloneled and be-generaled almost every other man in the camp."

"What is your title? I'll make a note of it."

"I haven't any title. But when you're giving me one I want it to be as big as anybody else's—and don't you forget it."

"Thank you; I won't."

My mis-titled friend was hardly gone before a plethoric citizen came stamping in, steaming with rage.

"Now this has got to stop right here, my fine lad," he puffed, "or this town will be too hot for your comfort!"

"What thing?" I asked, almost desperate.

"This booming the Northern Mines. You've given them a boost that may put them on top of us for the rest of our days."

"I only spoke of a reported rich strike in Shasta County."

"Don't speak of them at all, or only to write them down. We're not going to stand it. If you can't crow for your own section we'll see that you light out of it."

A small man came bolting in next. He was red faced and red haired, but the most fiery thing about him was the blaze in his eyes.

"Ye puny little blackguard, what d'ye mean by putting me name 'michael mcCarty,' without big m's?"

"I ran out of sorts; I hadn't any capital m's left."

"Ye'll run out of something else if ye ever do it again. The next time ye print me name, if ye haven't big m's, carve 'em out of wood, or I'll carve 'em out of yer heart."

"I'll do so, I assure you, Mr. McCarty."

"It's yerself who'll need insuring if ye don't."

It was a relief to see the portly form of one of Pickeye's most substantial citizens enter. I thought that at last I was about to hear something commendatory. But his cool exterior concealed more hot stuff than I could have imagined possible.

"You've made a pestiferous little jackanapes of yourself," he blurted out. "If there's anything strong in Pickeye it's the Whig sentiment, and you've butted in with an endorsement of McDougall for governor."

"I simply state that he will probably be the next Democratic nominee for that office."

"Just keep on making such statements, my pretty stripling, and see where you'll bring up. We didn't fetch your tuppenny sheet here to have it betray our political interests. If we find we've brought a wooden horse within our gates, it won't take long to dump it into the river."

The irate Whig had scarce crossed the sill when an equally prominent Democrat tore in.

"How came you to make such an ass of yourself as to cast your lot with the Whigs?" he demanded.

"What do you mean?"

"Mean? Why, this article about Clay."[11]

"There's nothing political in that; it's only an anecdote concerning him."

"Well, a few more such anecdotes will cook your goose. If Pickeye is one thing more than another, she's intensely Democratic. The *Trumpet* was brought from Ragtown by Democrats. If we find that we've warmed a viper in our bosoms, it won't take us long to scotch it."

I had just seated myself wearily on a candle-box, sighing, "O that Grouchy or night would come!" when a tall, weather-seasoned stranger entered. He looked around and around, as if in search of some particular object. At length he approached me and asked:

"Is the editor in?"

"Yes; I am he."

The stranger stood and gazed at me so long that I thought he had forgotten his purpose. I was about to recall him, when he said:

11. Probably Cassius Marcellus Clay (1810–1903) or Henry Clay (1777–1852). Both men were politicians who had associations with the Whig Party. The Democrat who assailed the narrator was vehemently opposed to the Whigs.

"I mean the responsible editor, the fighter."

"Well, I'm not much of a fighter," I answered, "but I'm the only editor there is."

There was another protracted inspection of me. Then the stranger said, very deliberately:

"That being so, we may as well proceed to business. I happened to be in town today and see in your paper an account of the killing of Dooney Sullivan down at Split Rock, in which you indulge in some moralizing about the homicide and cast some aspersions on his slayer. Now, I happen to be the man who killed Dooney Sullivan, and I take issue with your account."

"Were there any misstatements?" I asked, shaking in my boots.

"No, none worth mentioning. You got the facts about straight. What I object to is the general view you take of the affair. The coroner's jury down at Split Rock were disposed to take a similar view, but I supplied them with a verdict which by a little persuasion they were kind enough to render: 'Came to his death by a just dispensation of providence.' I should like you to say the same thing in the next number of your paper, if you please."

"With the greatest pleasure. I'm only too glad to correct any mistakes I may have made."

"Thank you. It is so easy to do business with reasonable people. I never have any trouble with them. Dooney Sullivan's failing was that he wasn't reasonable. Good day, sir."

My nerves couldn't stand another jolt. I closed the office and put in the rest of the afternoon writing out a set of rules which ever afterward remained posted over the nail-keg that served me for a desk:

The *Trumpet's* Eleven Commandments

1. Don't try to be funny.
2. Say only pleasant things of Pickeye.
3. Say nothing pleasant of any other camp.
4. Don't speak of a live man except to praise him.
5. Don't speak of a dead one till you know if he left any friends.
6. Give every man the biggest title you can without it appearing too raw.
7. Always refer to gamblers as "gentlemen of the sporting fraternity."
8. Always speak of their companions as among "the leading ladies of the town."
9. Abuse and belittle the Northern Mines ad lib., but always exalt the Southern ones.

10. Don't moralize or censure; ascribe everything that happens to the will of providence.
11. Eschew politics, further than declaring that the interests of Pickeye are above party and that the *Trumpet* stands for them.

Possibly larger and more modern journals may have had to steer their course by similar charts. I am not qualified to speak as to that; I only know how it was in Pickeye.

⊶"The TRUMPET Comes to Pickeye!" [San Francisco:]
Book Club of California, 1939

Short Fiction

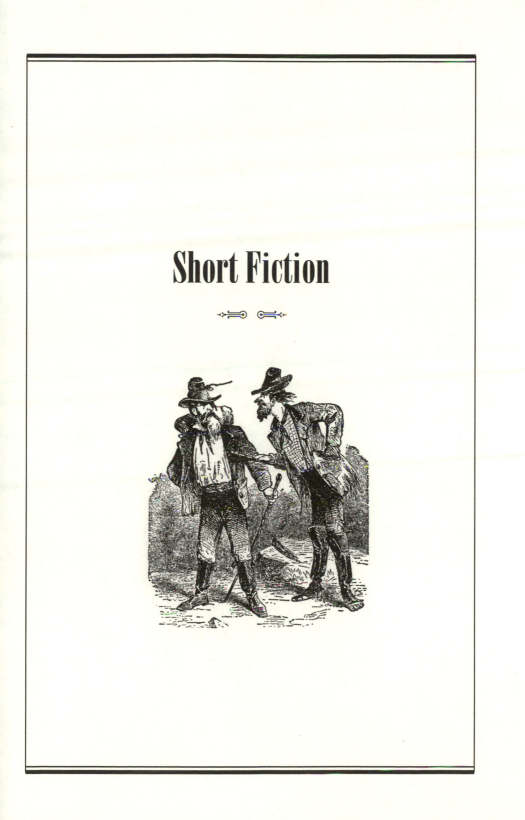

Introduction

꘎꘎꘎

The need of Nevada newspapers for feature material to entertain readers provided journalists considering venturing into creative writing with the inducement of a ready-made market. This was not only a Nevada phenomenon, it operated everywhere in the country; what was unusual in Nevada's case was the high quality of the writing that resulted, possibly due to the fact that so many Sagebrush journalists were uncommonly talented.

Alfred Doten's "The Living Hinge" is one of the earliest full short stories of the Sagebrush School. The "gotcha!" hoax of the cryptogram at its end is a bit sensational, a sly carryover from coded reports Doten was in the habit of entering into his journal about his illicit amours, but the germ of the story is a psychological insight into a man normal in most respects but in the grip of a delusion of increasing strength.

James W. Gally's "Big Jack Small," another early work, is not a simple glorification of an American type. The protagonist does not rest on inherent, natural virtues but instead improves on them with a healthy and measured skepticism of religion. He has thought his own thoughts and retains a keen sense of beauty and awe in regard to a Creator, but judges men by their deeds rather than by their creeds. He is a symbol of wholesomeness and imparts that quality generously to those who are open to it.

Hoaxes appear in many of Sam Davis's stories, but they are subordinated to more serious issues. "A Christmas Carol" is an early demonstration of Davis's impressive literary powers and moral inclination. Carefully considered, the story is a study in moral paradox. How could a man of such sensitivity deceive a man who showed him kindness? Why does not a "good upbringing" protect against temptation? Despite the deception, did the saloon patrons gain more or lose more by their evening's illusion? Eugene O'Neill explored some of the same issues in *The Iceman Cometh* (1946).

"My Friend, the Editor" was based, as are many of Davis's fictions, on a true story of a scam perpetrated by con men who hired an editor to revive a defunct newspaper and devote it to creating a mythical town and reporting on the imaginary activities of its imaginary mines. The editor was Davis's friend "Lying Jim" Townsend, himself a man of great talent devoted, as his nickname indicates, to concocting gorgeous lies. Nevertheless, the depth of the story is in its contemplation of the whole man, a devoted father and generous host, balanced against the part of him that deceives. "When Booth Was Not Booth" could be a refutation of Emerson's famous dictum that "imitation is suicide." In this case, not only does imitation fulfill the actor and lift him to a higher level of achievement, but it paradoxically has the same effect on Booth as he imitates the actor imitating him. "The Conversion of Champagne Liz," published here for the first time, takes readers into a tangle of judgment. Granted that Liz's life was largely used up in hedonistic activities, did she not do more good in the world than did many of her more religious neighbors? The poem at the end is a clever, but also thoughtful, inversion of the conventional sentiments favoring the soul over the body memorably represented in Anne Bradstreet's famous poem "The Flesh and the Spirit" (1666?).

"The Loco Weed" is a story of almost naturalistic power as it practically equates men and horses by showing, by means of the same effect of locoweed on both, nature's indifference to their "status." The story reflects a skepticism in Davis that ran deep. "The Mystery of the Savage Sump" combines Davis's use of Dan De Quille's earlier hoax, his interest in the new genre of detective fiction, and his relentless campaign to expose James Fair as a murderer. The story also contemplates the phenomenon of the wealthy never feeling wealthy enough, and going even to the extreme length of murder to satisfy the irrational passions that rule them.

De Quille, in "The Eagles' Nest," explores a similar issue, the fact that men will risk life itself, their most precious and irreplaceable possession, for gain, and sometimes only a little gain. This issue is at the heart of the phenomena of gold and silver rushes, and perhaps only longtime and thoughtful observers like De Quille and Davis (and Mark Twain) could reflect on the truth of "radix malorum cupiditas est" (the root of evil is greed) and the seeming inability of most human beings to resist the temptation of gain.

"Sister Celeste," by C. C. Goodwin, refutes its author's reputation of crusty, cranky conservatism. On the contrary, like some of the other stories, it reveals a deep vein of honest sentiment in the supposedly hardened Sagebrush writers. Beyond that, however, it is psychologically astute in tracing the origin of Sister Celeste's vocation and the purposeful effort she devotes to constructively turning adversity into blessing.

Rollin M. Daggett, in "Looking Down upon the Suisun Marsh Tules," and Thomas Fitch, in "A Heart Flush," both seem to tap into real-life antecedents of their stories. The issue of justice is a vexed topic in both narratives, from both legal and ethical perspectives. In authentic Sagebrush style, the authors recognize the appeal, and perhaps the validity, of a "rightness" beyond legal justice and not just in opposition to it.

In the psychological and moral acumen of most of these stories and their focus on wealth, it is possible to discern a family similarity to stories such as Mark Twain's "The Man That Corrupted Hadleyburg" (1899) and "The $30,000 Bequest" (1904). Indeed, the context of the rich legacy of these Sagebrush tales ought to enhance the reading and appreciation of Twain's stories. When he left Nevada he took some of the state's lessons with him.

The Living Hinge; Or, The Seventeen Pots of Amalgam

Alfred Doten

Alfred Doten (1829–1903) was an eminent Comstock journalist who eventually became owner as well as editor of the *Gold Hills News*. He is best known for the extraordinarily complete and frank journal of daily events that he kept faithfully from 1849 until his death and that is now an indispensable source of information about the Comstock. Doten also wrote several short stories—this one was originally published on July 21, 1867, in the *Territorial Enterprise*—and a number of valuable historical essays.

⋆⊷═ ═⊶⋆

CHAPTER I.—PROSPECTIVE

Some four or five miles east of the town of Como, Palmyra District, is a small lake which looks very pretty at a distance, but does not amount to much on close inspection. It is a couple of hundred yards or so in diameter, is very shallow, and contains no fish or anything of the sort, except a few sullen, disconsolate frogs, who merely stay there out of pure reckless desperation, because they can go nowhere else, there not being another drop of water for miles around.

What that pond was put there for, unless it might be for the accommodation of the few mountain sheep which sometimes stray over in its vicinity, no one could ever say. It is away from any mines, and the low, rolling hills on either side are completely barren of all vegetation except a very inferior article of sage brush, interspersed with here and there a solitary tuft of bunch grass. Even if there was a large population dwelling around the rocky margin, the

112

water would be of little use as a beverage, as in the winter it freezes solid, and in the summer it is too warm and disagreeable for anything but an emetic.

Captain Henry C. Smith, one of the first projectors of Como, for some reason or other took a notion to dub this ridiculous scrub of a lake "Como" also. He must have been in a very imaginative mood, to thus transfer the pretty little name of that lovely lake in Italy, so often sung of by enamored poets, to this horribly unromantic locality. The name, however, recoiled back in judgment upon him, and he was ever afterwards known as "Como" Smith.

A little over three years ago I was a resident citizen of Como, a very remarkable town in many respects, when one takes into consideration the remarkable character of its population. There was more real fun enjoyed and real hard work done up there than could be realized by any one unacquainted with the place; others may have their own opinion, but I will say for Palmyra District, abandoned as it is, that it can show more deep shafts, tunnels and extensive thorough prospecting work than any other district of like character in the State of Nevada.

One day I resolved myself into a grand exploring expedition, and, with a shot-gun on my shoulder and a small hammer stuck in my belt, took a tour of observation and prospective inspection throughout the land away to the northward and eastward.

I found no rich ledges, although I cracked open every suspicious looking quartz stone I came across, neither did I see any game, except a little cotton-tailed rabbit which sprang up some two hundred yards ahead of me.

Now any old sportsman will agree with me that two hundred yards was a pretty long range for a shot-gun, and when I fired I had no expectations of hitting that rabbit. Sure enough I didn't.

Along in the afternoon I came around to Lake Como, and just as I came in sight of it my attention was attracted by the strange actions of a man standing on the shore of the lake.

He was standing sideways towards me, bowing vigorously at the lake, sometimes bringing his head nearly to the ground in the vehemence of his adulation. Occasionally he would pause, and after reaching behind him with something I could not at first distinguish, he would go on working himself up and down as before.

He ceased as soon as he noticed my near approach, and when I came up to him he bade me "good evening" in response to my salutation, remarking, smilingly, "Well, I presume you must have thought a little strange of my actions just now, but I assure you it was unavoidable on my part. I have a peculiar requirement, consequent upon my condition in life, and although I rather dislike being detected in this as a general thing, yet on the present occasion I am heartily glad to see you, for I am in a small bit of a difficulty. Will you please do me the favor to oil me?"

As he made this odd request, he handed me, with all imaginable gravity, an oil feeder, such as is used in oiling machinery, and bent over with his back towards me.

"Squirt it right here," said he motioning towards the small of his back. "That's the only place what needs it."[1]

As might well be supposed, I was more or less wonderstruck by this very queer little episode, and hardly knew at first what to make of it, but quickly arriving at the conclusion that the man was a little luny, I resolved to humor the poor devil. So I took the feeder and attempted to squirt with it, but it failed. It was empty.

"Why, look here, my dear fellow," said I, "you haven't got any oil in this thing. What do you mean? how do you expect me to oil you without oil?"

"Oh, you're very much mistaken," laughed he, "for it's over half full; try it now; let me hear the bottom snap in and out."

I did so, and although no oil came forth, he exclaimed:

"That's it! good! that feels all right."

Then he swayed his body up and down at a great rate for about a minute, and straightened up, saying with a long drawn breath of relief:

"There now. I'm all right once more, thanks to your kindness. I tried it mighty hard before you came, but somehow couldn't reach the right spot."

CHAPTER II.—A DEMENTED CHRISTIAN.

"I ain't nobody's fool, as you already perceive. I'm an educated man and used to be a Universalist minister once. I found myself too much naturally inclined to be a regular built sinner, so I just turned preacher in self defense and as a matter of precaution, for I didn't want to land in Tophet after shuffling off this mortal coil.

"And then, too, Universalist ministers are much better than those of other denominations, because believing as they do in sure and inevitable present punishment here on earth for all sins committed, either morally, physically, or any other way, they act in accordance with such belief, striving to avoid the consequent punishment, while others who preach up the doctrine that all punishment for sin committed is reserved for the great hereafter—punishment of the hell fire and brimstone order—are disposed to take chances on

---

1. This is an interesting, if coincidental, anticipation of the Tin Man in L. Frank Baum's famous book, *The Wizard of Oz* (1900).

its remoteness, intangibility, and possible non-existence—also on repenting in time to get around it.

"Come, now—you know yourself that it's much easier and pleasanter to travel in the path of sin and iniquity than in the straight-laced, unsociable ways of those who feel that they have got a sure thing on being punished for any sin they may commit, and punished, too, just in proportion to the enormity of the sin or crime committed."

He was a small, lightly built man of about fifty-five, with dark hair, whiskers, and mustache, considerably mixed with gray. He had high cheekbones, narrow forehead, and a pair of the queerest little brown eyes anybody ever saw, set closely on each side of a thin, wedge-like nose, which projected out from his face like the figure-head of a down-east fishing schooner. He was dressed in a well worn suit of grey, with a little old brown felt hat on his head; his boots conformed with his general appearance, in being rather dilapidated; and from the old leather haversack which lay on the ground with a hammer beside it, I judged that he also was a quartz prospector.

And such a little rattle-head to talk as the old fellow was! He hardly allowed me to get in a word edgeways, but kept right on chatting freely like an old acquaintance.

"Now I think of it," continued he, "you must think me rather a strange chap—eccentric, maybe. Everyone else thinks me so; why shouldn't you? But then I ain't strange; I ain't eccentric at all. Everything has its own proper peculiarities; why shouldn't I? Now this little peculiarity of mine is simply: I've got to be oiled or I can't work; and right where you squirted that oil is the grand working joint of my organism. Great God! if I should ever allow that to get disabled with rust so it couldn't work, I'd be stiff as a wagon tongue forever afterwards, and fit for nothing except old iron.

"I may say I wasn't successful as a preacher. I drew mighty poor houses. Even when I tried street preaching I couldn't make the thing win. No crowd would stay by me any length of time, unless some fools or other would get to hooting at me and mocking me, when I'd get more or less wrathy, and the excitement would draw a good big audience for a short time.

"You oughter seen the huge audience I raised one Sunday evening in San Francisco. It was my last. I felt mightily pregnant with the spirit of truth, and I let myself out. I don't remember now just all what I said. I only know I was full of burning, fervid eloquence; but the boorish rabble before me only laughed and jeered at my excited, earnest words, which, alas! fell as pearls before swine.

"Then I told them in the sad bitterness of my soul that they were no better than the Jewish rabble who made themselves so disagreeable at the crucifixion of Christ. I said I was poor, and anyone stealing my purse would steal trash, but I was a proud-hearted man. Pride and poverty was the downfall of old Cole's dog, but I was willing that such, too, should be my downfall. Then I became fiercely angry and sprang down from the steps on which I was standing, in order to drive the whole crowd off into the bay, even as the devil did the herd of swine into the sea of Galilee, when a couple of stout men with stars on their breasts laid violent hands on me and hurried me along the street so fast that the houses and all passing objects reeled into chaos, and I into a thick black night.

"It was a long, long, strange night, and when I was conscious it was daylight once more. I found myself—don't laugh at me, please—I found myself transformed into a hinge, a real living iron hinge, on the front door of the Insane Asylum at Stockton.

"I was none of your common, insignificant hinges, but a large, handsome, portly, well oiled hinge, bending my jointed back gracefully whenever the door was swung back for the admission of talent and respectability. The humbler degrees of society always have to pass in and out at side doors.

"Should you ever become a hinge, be a first class upper one, like I was; don't ever be a common butt, but a genuine high-toned wrought-iron strap hinge. There's honor in it.

"The honor in my case, however, was not sufficient to induce me to stay long, and although envied by all the other hinges in the house, I had a realizing sense that I was something besides a hinge, so one night I contrived to unscrew myself from the door and took quiet leave of the Asylum.

"Whatever happens to you in life, don't you ever allow yourself to be taken to Stockton. No one can be put to baser uses than they put folks to at that Asylum. I am told that the big soup-kettle in the kitchen was formerly a City Alderman, and the cook-stove itself used to be a member of Congress; all the hinges on the doors once swung round in the most respectable circles, and God knows what the shovels, mops and brooms used to be.

"The devil take Stockton! the devil take the Asylum! the devil fly away with everybody who's fool enough to be there! Whoop! Damnation!" and away the little fellow flew off the handle, as crazy as a Dayton bed-bug in May.

He was red in the face with passion, and wrung his hands about with great energy of gesticulation as he trotted vehemently back and forward; but his little crazy fit only lasted a minute or so, for directly the anger-flushed expression of his countenance gave way to one of pain, and he backed up to me saying, earnestly:

"Do, please, oil me again, sir; that's what's the matter with me; I was getting a little too dry and squeaky. Ah! there we are again all right, thank you, sir. You hit exactly the right spot."

He worked himself up and down with great satisfaction a few times, and then continued:

"You must think I'm a little wandering in my upper story; crazy, maybe, but I ain't; not a bit of it. I'm as sound as a saw-log, all except the small of my back, where the great joint of me is. If 'twasn't for that joint, I shouldn't know I was a hinge at all. I keep that a secret from everybody, and only oil up when I do so unobserved. But what are we doing here? It's getting late, and we'd better be traveling."

I agreed to this proposition, and being much amused with my novel companion, invited him home with me.

On our way we examined several quartz ledges which we came across, and I found the old man really quite a good judge of rock, as well as intelligent in mining matters generally.

He told me of vast amounts of copper ore which he had found existing only a few miles distant, and in the neighborhood of Walker River, which he said would some day be very valuable, when railroads should make transportation to San Francisco cheaper; also of gold and silver mines on the forks of Walker River, and about that section of the country, showing that he had been prospecting around pretty extensively for some time past.

We slept together that night at my cabin, and next day started out on a prospecting trip over to Walker River. The old man showed me all the copper, gold and silver discoveries he had made; but the richest gold quartz we saw was between the east and west forks of the river. We did not think it worth while at that time to locate any claims, leaving that for some future time, when perhaps we might go there to work and develop whatever riches there might be.

We were absent from Como about three weeks, and on my part I must say I enjoyed the companionship of that queer little rattle-brained old man very highly. He was often rather flighty in his ideas, but I knew how to manage and appreciate him, and keep him oiled up properly; so we got along finely, and he became more and more attached to me.

Sitting at our camp-fire during evenings, the old man was the best hand I ever saw at telling stories—and right interesting ones, too—generally of his traveling experiences and observations among mankind, and in me he never failed to find an attentive as well as instructed audience.

CHAPTER III. —WONDERFUL IDEAS.

One evening, after being apparently in a brown study for an hour, the old man said to me:

"Alf., my son, come sit down on this rock side of me, and I'll tell you something."

I complied, and, after gazing thoughtfully for about ten minutes at the kettle of beans cooking over the fire, he turned towards me with an unusually serious countenance, saying, as he passed me the oil feeder:

"Oil me up once more, and I'll tell you a story nobody ever heard."

I went through the imaginary process of squirting oil on the small of his back, as usual, and he proceeded:

"I never told you about what a great thief I was, but really I have stolen more gold and silver, and have been more successful in concealing it and avoiding all manner of suspicion than any one single man in the State of Nevada. Yes, that's so; I concealed it so effectually that I have never been able to get at it since; neither do I much think I ever will. I'm going to tell you all about it, and without fear—for now I have perfect confidence in you; and the secret I am about to impart to you may make you a rich man; yes, a rich man; richer than you dreamed of. You never laughed at me, but always oiled me right and good when I needed it; you are my friend, and you shall find that hinges are not all ungrateful. I am a machinist by trade; that is to say, I learned the business when I was a boy, but I have never followed it regularly since. I wish I had. Nobody ever had a more inventive head than mine, and being, as I said, a machinist, there's no telling what valuable and important inventions I might have developed, had it not been for my extreme poverty. I was always studying out something new and wonderful. Among scores of other schemes which would have startled the world as with an electric shock, had they been properly brought out, was this, my best one, the vast intrinsic merits and feasibility of which will strike you at once. It is simply a plan by which the broad deserts of Arabia, or the vast plains of the continent can be traveled with a common steamboat, with perfect comfort and safety, and in any chosen direction, even ascending and descending slight elevations, the steamer sailing along smoothly at the rate of fifteen or twenty miles an hour, with the same facility as she would on the Mississippi.

"This is the way I propose to accomplish this important project: I would take a light draught, flat-bottomed steamer, and under her and over her I will build an endless track with low sides to it. This track will be of a flexible nature, passing up under the stern and over across a series of wheels, carrying it length wise of the boat and down under the bow again.

"The track being filled with water, so that the boat floats, the wheels are set in motion by the machinery of the boat, same as the paddle-wheels are worked, and operating by means of cogs above and below, the track is set in motion and the steamboat driven ahead at the same time.

"Thus you will perceive, the passengers can travel with luxuriant comfort even in the most sweltering clime, the track passing continually overhead creating a strong current of air, as well as shading them completely from the fierce rays of the sun, while they recline at ease on the sofas of the hurricane deck, smoking their cigars, drinking sherry coblers, and all that sort of thing. Ah! it is one of the grandest projects of the nineteenth century, and had I only been properly supported and encouraged, thousands of my style of land steamboats would have been now traversing the vast prairies and broad alkali deserts of the American continent, as well as all other parts of the world. I should have made my mark, and been the richest and most prominent man in existence.

"With such a steamer, rivers, snow, ice, in fact all similar obstacles would prove no obstruction, and with sufficient provision and fuel I might traverse away into the far regions of the north, across the illimitable fields of ice, and embark upon that great open polar sea discovered and described by the more recent Arctic explorers.

"The water floating my steamer within my endless track being constantly in motion could not freeze, which circumstance, combined with the heat from the boilers, would have the effect to preserve the temperature immediately surrounding at a comfortable summer-like warmth, even in the highest latitudes.

"And then again my mind expands with the idea of what great and sensationally startling discoveries would be made in sailing still farther north on that open polar sea—for let me tell you there's *something beyond.* The explorers who stood on the margin of that great unknown sea had passed the broad frozen zone, and had arrived at where a warmer belt of climate was just commencing, and with ships at their command they might have sailed north until they had again passed through temperate and tropical zones similar to this part of the world, and to another frozen polar region beyond.

"This world is not, as is generally supposed, round like a ball, but like an immense, eternal cylinder, which has neither beginning nor end, the tropical and frozen zones succeeding each other at regular intervals and in endless series, each being similarly inhabited, and possessing the same general conformation. But then, dear me, how I am rattling along and digressing entirely from what I started in to tell you.

"As I said before, notwithstanding all my efforts and representations, I never could interest any people in my behalf who were possessed of the requisite wealth to assist me in the development of either this or any of my other schemes; in fact, many ridiculed me as a demented dealer in wild impracticabilities.

"My father was a poor Universalist preacher in Illinois, and, following in his footsteps, I, too, occasionally took to preaching by way of variety, for 'variety is the spice of life,' you know.

"When I did preach, it was with all sincerity, but I never could make it pay; after all, I was cut out more for a mechanic than a preacher. The most I ever received as a reward for my labors in the Lord's vineyard was a bare subsistence. At length after years of wandering service in that line throughout the Western States, I strayed down into Texas, Mexico, and finally found myself in California.

"After I got away from the Asylum at Stockton, I came across the Sierra Nevada to this State, and sought employment, carefully always concealing my real character, and oiling myself only when no one could see me. The first job I got was tending battery in a quartz mill, not over a thousand miles from Gold Hill, and it was not long before being promoted, step by step I became head amalgamator. This was just about two years ago.

"Now here we come to the points of interest—the secrets—in what I am going to impart to you. Oil me up once more, please. There, that's it; good!

CHAPTER IV. —THE HIDDEN TREASURE.

"I had the handling of all the amalgam[2]—and it was rich amalgam, too—rich in gold. I used to steal that amalgam. There, now, don't look that way at me, I'm only telling you the truth. Yes, I used to steal it, just a little at a time.

"The owner of the mill was a fine man, an excellent good man in pretty much all respects, except one. He was a little too avaricious, and in an evil hour was induced to enter into an arrangement with a certain mining superintendent, by which first class ore was supplied to the mill from the mine, and rated as second or third class ore, the returns being made to correspond as such, thus defaulting the mining company, while the wicked superintendent and my employer pocketed a very desirable amount of extra cash by the operation. Ha! ha! they didn't pocket quite so much after I became cognizant of their iniquity.

"'The wages of sin is death'—so the good book tells us—and as a true Christian I believed it to be my plain duty, pointed out by the Lord, to allow them as little of those sinful wages to atone for as possible, so every day I quietly abstracted of this amalgam all I could conveniently carry off, taking it to my little cabin and dropping it through a knot hole in the floor.

---

2. Amalgam is a mixture of different ores. In the Comstock Lode, much of the ore was an amalgam of silver and gold, with silver predominating. The ore had to be treated with different processes in order to extract the profitable minerals from the worthless rock and to separate the gold and silver from each other.

"Another object, too, which I had in view, was the accumulation of wealth sufficient to allow me to carry out some of my great schemes, especially the wonderful land steamboat arrangement I have described to you. I considered the Lord in this matter was now assisting me in supplying the means required, as well as making me an adjuster of sin in this amalgam arrangement.

"For months I followed up this practice. The ore paid far richer than any one dreamed of except myself, and although our naughty superintendent and mill-man evidently seemed disappointed somewhat in the yield of the amalgam, yet, strange to say, I remained unsuspected.

"At length this arrangement between them ceased from some cause or other, which I never cared to inquire into. Perhaps first-class ore was found less plenty in the mine, or fear of detection, or the stings of guilty conscience may have interfered in the matter: I can't say; be that as it may, however, we soon came down to working nothing but regular third-class ore, so I threw up my position and quit the concern. It was astonishing how fast that amalgam had accumulated. Along latterly, whenever I deposited a fresh lot, I had to take a stick and poke it away from the knothole. All underneath the floor seemed full of the precious stuff.

"Next thing was, how to dispose of it. I went to work and built me a small furnace, and retorting a few pounds at a time, I soon had quite a nice little lot of crude bullion, sufficient to furnish me with all the money I might want for present purposes, as it contained so much gold combined with the silver, that it was worth from four to eight dollars an ounce when refined.

"Becoming fearful lest my amalgam deposit might be discovered, by some unforeseen accident or other, I resolved to remove it to a more secure place, and after some little time spent in search of a safe locality, I decided on an old, abandoned tunnel, which I examined and thought would answer my purpose.

"This tunnel had been run at an early date by persevering prospectors, after some anticipated rich ledge supposed to exist at that particular point; in which, however, they were doomed to disappointment. The tunnel was about three hundred feet in length, and had several little drifts or branches to it, running in various directions. Into one of these branches I carried all my amalgam one dark, stormy night, in iron pots which I had procured for the purpose—such as are used on a cook stove—and placing them at the extreme end, with flat stones laid over them as covers, I carefully caved down all the loose rock and earth I could over them with a pick, and came away as soon as possible, for now a singular and unforeseen danger developed itself.

"The tunnel was not timbered at all, and although firm enough originally, the action of the atmosphere, and natural dampness, had caused that peculiar swelling and slacking of the stiff clayey earth and rock, so well understood by

miners, and in many places the sides and roof of the tunnel were already beginning to fall in large scales.

"It was well that I got out of that drift as soon as I did, for my picking had
started a cave, and for some moments heavy masses continued falling in from
both roof and sides, completely filling it up nearly to the main tunnel in
which I stood. I left, for the indications were, now that it had got started, no
one could tell where the cave would stop. One thing was pretty morally certain; my treasure was secure, and if I never got at it again, probably no one
else would.

"A day or so afterwards I put my crude bullion in sacks, and with an old
wagon and two horses which I had purchased for the purpose I drove to Sacramento, taking the bullion with me in that way to avoid the possible suspicion consequent on shipping it by coach.

"In San Francisco I found no difficulty in converting it into cash, representing myself as running an arastra in Washoe,[3] and returned here with over
$15,000 in greenbacks in my possession.

"I have been wearing out fast lately, and something seems to tell me that in
a few short months my great joint will give out entirely, in spite of oiling and
attention, and I shall be tossed aside among the worthless things of the past.
For of what use is a hinge when its gudgeon-pin and bearings are worn out?
Oil me again, please. Ah! capital! Thank you; your complaisant kindness I
ne'er shall forget.

"I am going home now to Illinois, and have got money enough to carry me
through all right the rest of my life. I will tell you all about the precise locality of my old cabin (or rather where it stood, for it has since been destroyed
by fire), and also exactly where to find that amalgam deposit. That is the
grand secret I wish to impart to you; but not here, not here," said the little old
man, looking apprehensively around. "Not here, for bushes have ears, and
even the tattling winds whisper what is uttered in their presence. I'll write
out full directions in a very few words, so that you cannot fail to understand,
and find that hidden store of rich amalgam. There are seventeen pots of it,
and the whole is worth over $50,000. The last time I was there—three or four
months ago—the tunnel was caved and filled in nearly to its mouth, but you
can get at the treasure by running a new tunnel for it, and you will be a rich
man. But wait till tomorrow, when we arrive at Como."

I was considerably excited over what he had been telling me, for surely
such a prospect of sudden wealth is agreeable for any poor miner or carpenter to contemplate, and I would have questioned him more particularly re-

---

3. An arastra was a crude device used for crushing ore. It consisted of a round, flat bed of rock
upon which large chunks of ore were placed and crushed by dragging or rolling heavy stones over
them.

garding it, but he totally repudiated anything further on that point, simply saying, "wait till we get to Como; just wait. I'll write it out for you. I'll write it in cipher, so nobody but you and I can read or understand it, and we'll be safe."

CHAPTER V.—THE MYSTERIOUS CIPHER.

"I have," said he, "an arrangement of letters studied out and perfected by myself the like of which no man ever saw or dreamed of before. It is a cipher arranged on a very simple but perfectly undiscoverable principle, yet in less than five minutes I can learn you the key to it so that you can read it with almost the same facility as common print, and we can communicate together in any part of the world by telegraph or letter, on the most private or important subjects, freely and openly, without the least fear of being detected or understood by outsiders. I will write out full directions for finding the treasure deposit, by means of this cipher, and learn you the key. Oil me once more and we'll go to sleep. Good; again; that's it; God bless you! I'll write it out for you in cipher. Wait till we get to Como."

We arrived at Como about sunset the next day, and after a hearty supper the old man left me, saying, "I'm going up-stairs a while. I'll meet you in an hour, at McCumber's saloon."

At the time appointed I was at the saloon, which was well-filled with men engaged in drinking, playing cards, billiards, etc., amusing themselves after the style usual at such places, when the old man entered hastily, with an expression of trouble on his countenance, which I had well learned to comprehend, and placing a slip of paper within my hand, said, "come out quick and oil me; I need it mighty bad; then I'll learn you the key to the cipher I just gave you. Quick! Oh, my God! There, I knew it!—listen how I squeak!"

The poor, demented old fellow stood in the middle of the floor, with his hands on his hips, painfully swaying backward and forward without bending his back, while the bystanders, attracted by his queer exclamations and appearance, gathered around. I felt in his pocket for the oil feeder, but it was not there.

"No," said he sadly, "I left it in my room, curse the luck, but what the devil are you all gaping at, you d—d baboons you; git!" This forcible remark with its accompanying gestures, brought forth peals of laughter from those around, and one tipsy fellow stepped up to him saying:

"Take a drink old toppy, suck down a little beverage; never mind the ile. Don't jerk around that way, it's bad."

The old man's face was blazing with passion, and foreseeing trouble, I left him and ran for the oil feeder. I was gone only a moment, but when I returned, there he stood in the middle of the floor with his shirt off looking crazy as could be desired, swinging his fists wildly about and apparently oblivious of either friend or foe, while in a high old key and strain he was thus addressing the crowd:

"Yes, gentlemen, by h—l! you've jumped up a peaceable man. Don't talk to *me! Be calm?* Ain't I calm? What d—d man presumes to tell me I'm excited? Yes, d—n you all, you've jumped up the peaceablest man in the world. A peaceabler man never existed; but you've jumped me up, and d—n the first son of a gun of you that dares to speak or look cross at me! You're a set of miserable cur dogs, and for two bits I'd just waltz through you like a dose of strychnine through a lot of hound pups! *You'll* jump up a peaceable man, will you? Whoop! take that! you blasted scrub," and with a wild attempt to strike the nearest man to him, the poor little old fellow gave a whirl half round and fell flat on his back upon the floor, stiff and motionless.

From that time forward he never moved or spoke a word. He had received a paralytic stroke from which he could not recover. The poor old hinge was worn out at last; broken past all mending.

I removed him to Dayton the next day, and in the course of a couple of weeks to San Francisco, where he had the benefit of the best medical attendance which could be procured, but all was of no avail. He lingered along, still speechless and motionless, for two months, when he died without a struggle.

His secret died with him, for although evidently conscious at times of what was going on around him, yet he could never divulge the key to that remarkable cipher, although he gazed into my eyes with peculiar earnestness on various occasions, as though he longed to tell me something.

Sewed into various parts of his clothing were found over twelve thousand dollars in greenbacks, and after all the expenses of the funeral, medical attendance, etc., were paid, the balance was forwarded to his relatives in Illinois.

As for myself, three months after my return to Como, I removed to Virginia, where I have been ever since. I have studied over the mysterious cipher for hours and hours at a time, and can read it just as well now as I could when I first received it. The majority of the old man's other stories, aside from his peculiar theories and idiosyncrasies, proved so correct, that I have often been inclined to believe there might be something in his amalgam treasure story, and the more so from the fact that in my perambulations I have found the ruins of a burnt cabin, with the remnants of what was evidently a small furnace and retort, but where is the old tunnel containing those seventeen pots of rich amalgam? I have searched for it all I am going to. I give it up. It is a riddle I cannot solve, but perhaps some one else can.

It must be within a mile of Virginia or Gold Hill, otherwise he could not well have carried those heavy pots of amalgam to it from his cabin all in the course of one night.

The American people are fonder of being humbugged than any other on the face of the globe, and I partake of the general characteristics of my countrymen; but how much humbug there may be in this matter, I leave the reader to judge.

Here is the mysterious cipher precisely as I received it from the old man. It is well worthy the study of the curious, and those skilled in deciphering puzzles. As to myself, I feel so much interested in it that I will gladly pay a good round sum, or even share whatever profits may be developed, with any person who will furnish me a manifestly correct solution or translation and full explanation of this lettered mystery, together with the key which unlocks it:

S	R	X	H	L	L	S	R	S	J	D	L	N	R	N
Z	H	D	W	S	S	H	Q	Z	H	B	S	T	X	J
J	I	Z	S	B	Z	D	D	C	D	Z	T	J	I	H
H	P	X	R	B	J	D	L	R	Z	D	Y	N	V	J
Z	Y	Z	D	Z	C	D	S	M	Z	Z	Z	L	L	G
R	X	Z	I	H	X	G	S	X	Z	F	R	I	I	V
L	G	D	H	L	S	T	N	J	Y	B	J	I	V	I
H	S	D	Z	S	Z	L	S	L	V	N	C	G	J	J
Y	N	H	Z	R	L	F	I	G	D	G	Z	E	N	D
Z	H	L	Z	W	O	I	L	J	J	N	J	F	E	L
T	H	J	S	Z	Z	X	I	N	J	Z	C	I	Z	I
X	Z	S	S	D	I	L	U	L	G	V	S	H	T	R
D	Z	T	L	Z	N	S	I	K	D	X	Z	X	D	J
X	H	H	V	I	D	Z	T	H	X	S	I	H	P	C
I	Z	Z	R	J	J	X	I	J	D	S	S	I	D	J[4]

⇒The Journals of Alfred Doten, 1849–1903, 3:2205–18

4. When decoded, the cipher has this message: "Leather-headed fool is he whose talents in his heels doth lie. Yet greater jackass still is he who believing all the foolish tales he reads goes about hunting up stray pots of gold or even wastes his time puzzling over this queer lot of letters. He will

find pots of gold in a horn." The cryptogram can be decoded by using the following key: There are nine pairs of letters that are always interchanged: A-X, B-P, C-U, D-T, E-Z, F-V, I-L, J-O, W-Y. All other letters (G, H, K, M, N, Q, R, S) keep their value and are read the normal way. Figure 1 presents the decoded letters capitalized and the unchanged letters lowercased.

s	r	A	h	I	I	s	r	s	O	T	I	n	r	n
E	h	T	Y	s	s	h	q	E	h	P	s	D	A	O
O	L	E	s	P	E	T	T	U	T	E	D	O	L	h
h	B	A	r	P	O	T	I	r	E	T	W	n	F	O
E	W	E	T	E	U	T	s	m	E	E	E	I	I	g
r	A	E	L	h	A	g	s	A	E	V	r	L	L	F
I	g '	T	h	I	s	D	n	O	W	P	O	L	F	L
h	s	T	E	s	E	I	s	I	F	n	U	g	O	O
W	n	h	E	r	I	V	L	g	T	g	E	Z	n	T
E	h	I	E	Y	J	L	I	O	O	n	O	V	Z	I
D	h	O	s	E	E	A	L	n	O	E	U	L	E	L
A	E	s	s	T	L	I	C	I	g	F	s	h	D	r
T	E	D	I	E	n	s	L	k	T	A	E	A	T	O
A	h	h	F	L	T	E	D	h	A	s	L	h	B	U
L	E	E	r	O	O	A	L	O	T	s	s	L	T	O

The resulting cryptogram is then read, starting in the lower left corner, according to the following pattern: one space to the right, then diagonally up and left to the margin; up one space, then diagonally down and right to the bottom; one space to the right, then diagonally up and left to the margin; up one space, then diagonally down and right to the bottom; one space to the right, then diagonally up and right to the margin; and so on through the entire square.

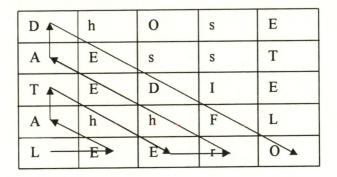

For help in solving this cryptogram, I wish to thank the late Walter Van Tilburg Clark, who as editor of Doten's *Journal* (1973) revealed the key to Doten's use of ciphers in those pages; and my son, Ethan J. Berkove, of the Mathematics Department of Lafayette College, for completing the solution. The last line's phrase "in a horn" has two meanings: (1) a horn spoon or scoop was used in detecting fine flakes of gold in the process of washing placer deposits or crushed ore, and (2) the phrase was also the slang equivalent of "in a pig's eye," that is, it implied the reverse of what had just been said.

Big Jack Small

James W. Gally

James W. Gally (1828–1891) lived in Nevada for at least ten years during the 1860s and 1870s, during which time he both ranched and mined and was also a justice of the peace. At the same time he contributed feature articles to the *Territorial Enterprise* under the pen name of Singleline. Around 1875 Gally moved to California, where he published stories in various magazines. "Big Jack Small" first appeared in the *Overland Monthly* in May 1875 and was republished in 1880 with the novel *Sand*.

⋗═⃯ ⃰═⋖

You do not know Big Jack Small? That is a bad omen; because if you did know Big Jack Small, you would know many things which, as I think, you do not now know—for Jack would be sure to talk to you, if you met him, and in his talk he would be quite as sure to tell you something about teaming with six or eight or ten yokes of oxen, and two or three or four great red wagons, over the hills, across the valleys, and through the bare, rock-walled canyons of the State of Nevada.

That is his profession—ox-teamster; or, as he calls it, "bull-puncher." Not one of your common farmer boys who can drive one yoke, or two or even four yokes, of oxen, with a long, limber fishing-pole stock, and a lash that hangs down like a dead garter-snake speared through the eyes; but a regular graduate of the science of ox—a bovine persuader—with a billiard-cue whip-stock, and a lash on it like a young boa-constrictor, and a little steel spike in the lash end of the stock about as big as a carpet-tack when it stands on its head on the point of a walking-cane. With the yellow leather lash wound round the stock, the great square braids shining like scales, as of the brazen serpent

Moses set up,[1] and the glittering steel tongue sparkling in the sunlight out of the serpent's head—with this awful wand in his hand, and elevated diagonally above his head, Big Jack Small will stand in the highway of the desert, the chief of the ox-magi; while his meek-eyed and clicking-footed company draw slowly round him, at the proper distance and with regular step, straining the great red creaking wains after them in a true circle. "Come row-a-d, boys! You, Turk!" sharply to the near-side wheel-ox, because an ox-teamster always turns on a haw-pull[2] unless compelled to do otherwise—"Come row-a-d, boys! Steady, now—like a Freemason funeral!" and he elevates or depresses the glittering tongue of the serpent above his head. The oxen know what that means, and the whole long procession winds about him with mathematical precision.

That is the way Big Jack Small does it. He is an artist. Why does not some brother artist go forth and canvas him? He is worth preserving as the picture of a true American, void of European or classic taint—a strong American, calm and humorous in the hardest struggles, through the very thrill and tickle of abundant life and pure mountain air. Tall?—no; he is not so very tall. About six feet, or half an inch less than that. Head well set upon his shoulders, with an inclination to one side, as if to give room for the big whip on the other shoulder; while his soft, slouched hat inclines just in the opposite direction, as if to equalize things and maintain a perpendicular outline. No coat on. Woolen shirt—in winter three of them, one inside the other; heavy vest buttoned to the chin, or to somewhere hidden under the long flow of the lion-colored beard. Legs clad externally in thick white ducking or buckskin, terminating in coarse boots drawn over the trouser's bottoms. Hands cased in rough buckskin gloves. So dressed, Big Jack Small may not be a very large man, but he looks large. When he walks from you, you are impressed with a broadness of shoulders and strength of neck and loin. When he walks toward you, you are made conscious of the coming of great thigh muscles, and fists, and a lion-like front; and you would not have any rash impulse to rush upon him for the fun of a little combat. Then he has a curious long springing stride—a sort of dropping and rising upon his thigh muscles with every step—that suggests power; though I suppose it is mere force of habit, caught in walking across plowed ground in early life, and maintained by striding over the sage-brush and loose rocks in Nevada.

Big Jack Small has a head under his slouched hat, and a face that shows between his hat-brim and his beard. If you are not in the habit of looking at

1. See Numbers 21:9.
2. "Haw" indicates the left, or near, side of whatever oxen or horses are pulling. "Gee" directs the animals to the right.

heads and faces for the purpose of forming your own estimate of men, it would not be worth while to look at Jack. You might as well pass on. He is of no interest to you. But if you want to look into a face where the good-natured shrewdness of Abraham Lincoln shines out, smoothed of its rough-carved homeliness, you can accost Jack when you meet him walking beside his winding train down the rough canyon or across the dusty valley, and ask him how the road is over which he has come. This interrogation requiring some length of answer, he will shout, "Whoa-ooa-ah, ba-a-ck!," then, drawing down the great iron handle or lever of the brake on his first wagon, his team will gradually stop. Now he steps out into the sage-brush in front of you, sets the point of his whip-stock carefully in the fork of a bush, builds his arms one on top of the other upon the butt of the stock, shoves his hat to the back of his head, and says:

"We-e-ll, the road's nuther good nur bad. Hit's about from tol'able to middlin'. Seen wuss an' seen better."

"How's the alkali flat?"

"Well, yer know thar's two alkali flats 'tween yer'n Austin. The first one's a little waxy, an' t'other'n 's a little waxy too."

"Will our horses sink down in the flats so as to impede—that is, so that we cannot get through?"

"Oh, hell, no. Only hard pullin' an' slow, hot work—sockin' through the stiff mud. I hed to uncouple an' drop all my trail-wagons, an' pull an' holler an' punch round at both o' them flats fer two days, till my cattle looks like the devil; but you kin go right along, only slow, though—very slow. The rest o' the road's all right—no trouble."

"Thank you."

"You're welcome. But, I say, tell me—I'm out now about two weeks—what's the news? Hev they caught them stage robbers?"

"No, they were not caught when we left Hamilton."

"Damn 'em! Hev ye any newspapers? I'd like to hev somethin' to read when I'm campin' out on the road—a feller gits mons'ous lonesome."

By this time you have hunted out of your traps all the newspapers and parts of newspapers, and passed them over to him.

"Thank ye. Git up, Brigham! Gee, Beecher!"[3] The loosened lever of the brake clanks back in its ratchet, the oxen slowly strain to the yokes, the great wagons groan to the tightening chains.

"Good-by."

---

3. Almost certainly humorous allusions to Brigham Young (1801–1877), the Mormon leader, and Henry Ward Beecher (1813–1887), a prominent American clergyman, abolitionist, and editor.

"So long."

And the slow dust-cloud moves onward, musical with the strong voice encouraging "Beecher" and "Brigham," on the lead, to stiffen their necks under the yoke, as a bright example to the entire train.

You, passing on your way, say to yourself, or companion, "What a fine face and head that rough fellow has; with what a relish that full, wide forehead must take in a good story, or survey a good dinner; what a love for the sublime and the ridiculous there must be in the broad high crown of that skull which is so full at the base! Why, the fellow has a head like Shakespeare, and a front like Jove! What a pity to waste so grand a man in ignorance among rocks and oxen!" All of which may be a good and true regret; but you must not forget that nature knows how to summer-fallow for her own rare products.

You will please to understand that Mr. Small is his own master, as well as master and owner of that long string of wagons and oxen; and that train, which slowly passes you, is laden with perhaps every conceivable variety of valuable articles, worth in the aggregate thousands of dollars, for the safe conveyance whereof, over a road hundreds of miles long, the owners have no security but a receipt signed "John Small." It is safe to say that nothing but the "act of God or the public enemy" will prevent the sure delivery of the entire cargo—a little slowly, but very surely.

I do not think you will get a just idea of Big Jack Small and the men of his profession, who are very numerous in Nevada, without I tell you that the sage-brush ox-teamster seldom sleeps in a house—does not often sleep near a house—but under his great wagon, wherever it may halt, near the valley spring or the mountain stream. His team is simply unyoked and left to feed itself until gathered up again to move on, the average journey being at the rate of eight miles per day—some days more than that, some less.

Twice a day the teamster cooks for himself and eats by himself, in the shadow cast by the box of his wagon. Each evening he climbs the side of his high wagon—very high it sometimes is—heaves his roll of dusty bedding to the earth, tumbles it under the wagon, unbinds it, unrolls it, crawls around over it on his hands and knees to find the uneven places and punch them a little with his knuckles or boot-heel, and—and—well, his room is ready and his bed is aired. If it is not yet dark when all this is done, he gets an old newspaper or ancient magazine, and, lighting his pipe, lies upon his back, with feet up, and laboriously absorbs its meaning. Perhaps he may have one or more teams in company. In that case, the leisure time is spent smoking around the fire and talking ox,[4] or in playing with greasy cards a game for

4. Talking *about* oxen, similar to "talking cars."

fun. But generally the ox-teamster is alone, or accompanied by a Shoshone Indian, whose business it is to pull sage-brush for a fire where pinewood is scarce, and drive up the cattle to be yoked.

In Jack Small's train there is usually an Indian, though you may not always see him, as sometimes, when the team is in motion, he is off hunting rats or away up on top of the wagon asleep; but at meal-time he is visible, sitting about the fire or standing with his legs crossed, leaning against a wagon-wheel.

The early training of Mr. John Small, having been received while following the fortunes of his father in that truly Western quest—the search after cheap, rich land—had been carried forward under various commonwealths as his parents moved from State to State of our Union—out of Ohio and into and out of the intermediate States of Indiana, Illinois, Iowa—until his father dragged into the grave and ended his pilgrimage in Nebraska, while waiting for the locomotive of that great railway which was to make him rich. A training so obtained has made Mr. Small something of a politician, with a keen ear for distinguishing the points in the reading of a State statute, and a high appreciation of the importance of State lines; while the attempts at teaching and the example of his worn-out, pious mother have turned his attention to the consistencies and inconsistencies of religious forms: so that Mr. Small's heaviest and highest thought dwells upon the present State where he resides, and the future state where he is promised a residence. His greatest intellectual joy he finds in talking to a politician or a preacher. Of course, he has smaller joys of the intellect in talking ox with the other teamsters, or in "joshing" over a game of cards; but he does not find solid comfort until he strikes a master in politics or a teacher in religion.

"What I'd like to be shore of," said he, one day, "is this yere: Kin a American citizen die, when his time comes, satisfied that he leaves a republic behind what'll continue as it was laid out to; an' that he's goin' to sech a country as his mother thought she was goin' to. Now, them's two o' the biggest pints in Ameriky. And dern my skin ef I haint got doubts about 'em both! Now, yere's a letter from my sister in Iowa, an' she says she's sick an' goin' to die; but that she's happy because she's goin' where mother's gone, to be happy ferivver and iver. An' yere's her husband—he's a lawyer, an' he's rejoicin', in his part o' this letter, over Grant's election, because, he says, that puts the Republikin party onto a sure foundation, an' secures that support o' Republikin principles fer iver and iver in Ameriky. Now, you see I've knocked round a heap—yes, sir, knocked round a heap, an' seen a good deal, an' seems to me some people knows a mighty sight for certain, on powerful slim proof. An' yere, my sister wants me to be a good Christian, an' my brother-in-law wants me to be a good Republikin, when, ef you pan me all out, I'm only a bull-puncher, an' haint more'n half learned the science o' that!"

It will be surmised from this hint of Mr. Small's character, taste, and disposition, that he was highly satisfied when the Rev. L. F. Sighal requested the privilege of a trip with the ox-team for the purpose of roughing it against the dyspepsia. Mr. Sighal said he had been recommended to come to Mr. Small as a humane and intelligent person, and having heard that Mr. Small's wagons were loaded for a long trip to the south-eastward, he would very much like to accompany him as an assistant, being willing to rough it as much as his constitution would stand.

"All right!" said Jack. "Heave yer beddin' right up thar on top o' the wagon, an' come ahead. But, I say, did y'ever play billiards?"

"I have—yes, occasionally, at the house of a friend; never in any public place. Yes, sir."

"Did y'ever play bull-billiards, I mean—with this kind of a cue, with a brad into it? Make a run on the nigh-wheeler and carom on the off-leader, yer know?"

"Ah! You mean, have I ever driven oxen? Well, no, sir, not in that way—though I was brought up on a farm in Pennsylvania, and have drawn logs with one yoke."

"All right. I'll teach yer how to punch bulls, an' you kin convert me an' the Injin. I've been wantin' that Injin converted ever since I hed him. He's heerd a little about Christ, in a left-handed way, but we'll go fer him, on this trip!"

Mr. Small, while making these remarks, was striding, with long strong strides, up and down the road on either side of his wagons, with whip on shoulder, making all ready for a start; looping up a heavy chain here, taking up a link there, and inspecting—shortening or lengthening—the draw of brakes, etc.; while his long team, strung out and hitched in the order of march, were standing and some lying down under the yoke, on the hard shard-rock road beneath the hot summer sun. His Indian, ycleped Gov. Nye,[5] was standing with his legs crossed near the ankle, stoically watching the preparations, well satisfied for the present in the comfort of a full stomach and the gorgeous outfit of a battered black-silk "plug" hat, a corporal's military coat with chevrons on the sleeves and buttoned to the chin, a pair of red drawers for pantaloons, a red blanket hanging gracefully from his arm, and a pair of dilapidated boots on his feet.

Gazing bashfully upon this scene, and striving to catch a word with Mr.

5. A humorous allusion to Governor James W. Nye of Nevada. "Ycleped," an antiquated word meaning "called" or "named," is self-consciously used here for a mock-formal effect.

Small, the Rev. Mr. Sighal turned his hands each uneasily over the other, and said:

"Mr. Small, I can not heave my bedding up there."

"Can't! Well, give it yere to me; I'll heave it fer you."

"But I have not brought it yet. It is just here, almost at hand, where I lodge."

"Well, well, rustle round an' fetch it! Biz is biz with me now. I must git up an' dust. Yere, Gov, you go him—all same me—he talk. Take this Injin with yer—he'll help yer carry what you've got."

"Thank you. You are very kind, indeed," said the reverend, as he marched off, followed by the gorgeous red man, down the steep street of the mining town.

While he was gone, Mr. Small, having all things in readiness, proceeded to straighten his team so as to tighten the chains and couplings whereby the great wagons are made to follow each other, in order that he might be sure that everything should draw even, strong, and true. Presently, Mr. Sighal and Gov came panting and trotting round the corner, out of the street into the road, each having hold of the end of a roll of bedding; the reverend carrying a black overcoat and purple scarf on his right arm, and Gov having his royal red blanket on his left arm.

Mr. Small, taking the roll poised on end on his right palm, steadied it with his left, and shot it to the top of the high wagon-box as if it had been a bag of feathers.

"Thar, Gov, heap jump up—heap fix 'em—little rope—no fall off. You sabe?"

"Yash—me heap sabe!" said Gov, tossing his precious blanket to the wagon-top and slowly climbing up after it, over the wheel and side.

"All ready, Parson?" said Mr. Small, interrogatively, as he picked up his baton of command.

"Yes," timidly, "I—I—believe I am."

Rapidly Mr. Small strode forward, drawling out in the indescribable rhetoric of his profession, "You Ro-w-dy! Turk! Dave! Gee, Brigham!" Then suddenly, "Who-o-ah—ba-a-ack!"

"See yere, Parson! Got anything to eat aboard?"

"No, sir. I have presumed I could buy provisions at the houses where we stop."

"Houses, hell! Oh, excuse me, Parson. Thar hain't no houses to speak of, an' ef thar was, bull-teams don't hev nothin' to do with houses, 'thout they're whisky-mills." Then, shoving up his hat and scratching his head with a vigorous rake or two of his hard fingernails, he pulled the hat down on his nose, and leaning back, looked at the Reverend Mr. Sighal, and said, "S'yere, Parson, I'll grub ye, but my grub's lightnin'—beans, bread, bacon, coffee, an' cantruck. You go into camp an' buy—le'me see—well, buy a small sack o' oatmeal, two papers o' pinoly,[6] a pound o' black tea, an' half a dozen cans o' condensed milk. That'll pull ye through. Yer kin easy ketch up to the team. Gee, Brigham! Git up, Dave! You, Roany! Bally! Haw thar! Roll out! Roll out!" And the slow line moves over the rocky road at a snail's pace, the wheels grinding, almost imperceptibly, to the top of the not large stones, and then dropping off at the other side with a sudden fall and a jar which, though the fall be but an inch or two, makes the loading talk in various voices as it settles more firmly to its place.

Up, slowly—ah, so slowly, so dustily!—up and up the mountain, by the canyon road, pausing at intervals to breathe the panting herd, Mr. Small grinds and crushes out a solid shining line, with his many wheels, in the porphyry and granite dust. The dry mountain summits rise on either hand, capped with the undaunted rocks which have defied the artillery of heaven before man in any color stood to witness the shock—the rays of the sun converging upon the head of Big Jack Small, as he marches up the side of his team, to pause for its clicking step, then up another march, and then pausing again, lifting the serpent-coiled baton above his head, shouting anon the name of some throbbing toiler of the yoke. Thus he gains the summit and halts to draw the rearward brakes.

"Ah, Parson! H'ist them things up thar to Gov. Gov, you fix 'em. Now we're off. Plenty time, though, Parson, to look at the scenery. You see that round peak yonder—way off? That's jest eighty-two miles from yere. Can't see that-a-way in Pennsylvania, kin ye? Gee, Brigham! Git a-a-up!"

More rapidly, and with much clinking and clanking of yoke-rings, hooks, and chains, and the loud braying and howling of the friction of wheel-tire and brake-block, the team winds down the canyon of the opposite side of the mountain, the big wains rocking, reeling, and groaning as they crowd each other round the curves of the declivity; and, above all, the driver's voice echoing along the canyon the drawling words of command and encouragement.

Mr. Sighal is behind, out of sight; pausing mayhap upon some bold outcrop of earth's foundation-stone, to gaze far around and across the uplifts of the grand furrows where the forgotten forces have plowed the field that now lies fallow in the wisdom of a plan wise beyond all that is yet written or revealed. Oh, servant of the faith, look well! It is the aristocracy of Nature upon

6. Probably two paper bags of pinole, a meal, of Mexican origin, composed of ground corn or wheat and mesquite beans.

which you gaze. Sublime it is in the reposeful grandeur of its indifference to commerce, agriculture, or the petty avenues of human thrift. Locked in the coffers of the rocks are the wages of its early days of labor. Stern and forbidding is the giant land, sad and unsocial; but rich in the abundance of that which renders even man unsocial, stern, and forbidding.

At the foot of the mountain the team halts where the water sinks and the dry valley begins. It is but short work for Big Jack Small to draw out the bow-pins, release his cattle, and drop his eight yokes in a line, with the bright, heavy chains linking them together in the gravel and dust.

Meantime, Mr. Sighal arrives in camp with each hand full of fragments of varicolored stone, he having tried his wits at prospecting for silver.

"Hullo, Parson! Hev you struck it rich?" interrogated Big Jack, as he let down the grub-box and cooking utensils from the wagon top to Gov Nye. "That's a bad beginning, Parson!"

"Why so, Mr. Small?"

" 'Cause," said Jack, jumping down from the wagon and coming up to take a look at the rocks in the parson's hands—" 'cause ef you ever get quartz on the brain, you're a goner! That ar meetin'-house in Pennsylvany'll put crape on the doorknob—shore![7] an' 'dvertiz fer a new parson. But ye'll not get quartz on the brain—not much—s'long's yer don't find no better stones than these yere," said he, after examining the collection.

"Ah! I was merely guessing at the stones to amuse myself. Are they not quartz fragments?"

"No, sir-ee," said Jack, as, driving his ax into a pine log, he made the wood fly in splits and splinters—"not much. Them's iron-stained porphyry, greenstone, black tap an' white carb'nates of lime. Hold on till we git across the valley an' git a-goin' up the next mountain, 'n I'll show yer some good quartz. Some bully float-rock[8] over thar, but nobody hain't found no mine yit—never will, I reckon; I've hunted fer the darned thing twenty times. Yere, Gov, git a bucket o' water. Parson, d'ye feel wolfish?" added Mr. Small, after he had his fire lighted and was proceeding culinarily.

"Wolfish!" exclaimed Mr. Sighal with some surprise.

"Yes—hungry," explained Jack, as he sawed with a full knife at the tough rind of a side of bacon, cutting down one fat slice after the other upon the lid of the grub-box near the fire.

"Not unusually so."

"Hain't et nothin' sence mornin', hev ye?"

---

7. In other words, "if you ever get obsessed with hunting for gold (in quartz), your church back in Pennsylvania will for sure have to give up on your returning."

8. Loose surface rock whose mineral content may suggest the presence of nearby ore veins.

"No, not since early morning."

"Must do better'n that!" said Jack, putting the frying-pan upon the fire.

"I usually eat but little, for fear of eating too much."

"Well, s'pose yer heave away them rocks, an' run this fryin'-pan—jest fer appertite. Nothin' like facin' an inemey, ef yer want to git over bein' afraid of him!"

Mr. Sighal immediately complied, and, squatting by the fire, poised the frying-pan upon the uneven heap of burning sticks in his first lesson at camp life.

"I don't allow yer kin eat much this evenin', as we've only traveled half a day, but tomorrer we've got to cross the valley through the alkali dust, an' make a long drive. Git a lot o' that alkali into ye, an' you'll hanker after fat bacon!"

"Ah?" said Mr. Sighal, carefully balancing the pan on the fire.

"Yes, sir"—with great emphasis on the sir. "Alkali an' fat bacon goes together like a match yoke o' leaders. Does that seem to be any coals a-makin' in that fire, Parson?"

"The wood seems to burn; I infer there will be coals."

"Inferrin' won't do, Parson! We've got to hev 'em, 'cause I must bake this bread after supper, fer tomorrer. Allus keep one bakin' ahead," ejaculated Mr. Small, as he finished kneading bread in the pan, and quickly grasped the ax, proceeding to break up some more wood. "Yer see, Parson, a bull-puncher hes to be up to a little of every sort o' work in the mountains. Gov, you look out fer that coffee-pot, while I put this wood on the fire. Drink coffee, Parson? No? Well, then, make yer some tea in an empty oyster-can—hain't got only one pot fer tea an' coffee."

"No, Mr. Small, do not make any trouble for me, in that way. I drink water at the evening meal."

"All right, then; this hash is ready fer bizness!"

The Reverend Mr. Sighal, sitting cross-legged on the ground, received the tin plate and rusty steel knife and fork into his lap from the hand of Mr. Small, and then Mr. Small sat down cross-legged opposite him, with the hard loaf of yellow yeast-powder bread and the sizzling frying-pan between them, surrounded by small cotton sacks containing, respectively, salt, pepper, and sugar.

"Now, Parson," said Mr. Small, "pitch in!"

"One moment, Mr. Small," said the parson, removing the hat from his own head, "will you not permit me to ask the blessing of God upon this frugal repast?"

"Certainly!" assented Mr. Small, snatching off his hat and slapping it on the ground beside him. Then, happening to note quickly the Indian sitting listlessly on the other side of the fire, he said, "Yere, you Injin, take off yer hat; quick."

"Yash—heap take 'em off," said the obeying Indian.

"Now, Parson, roll on!"

The reverend, turning his closed eyes skyward, where the wide red glory of the setting sun was returning the eternal thanks, offered the usual mild and measured form of thanksgiving and prayer for the Most High's blessing upon the creature comforts, at the end of which he replaced his hat; but Mr. Small, being too busy with his supper and with cogitation upon the new style of etiquette, and being careless about his head-covering in camp, neglected, or omitted, the replacement of his hat; which state of the case bothered the "untutored savage" as to his own proper behavior, whereupon, lifting his cherished "plug" from the earth, he held it in his hand brim up, and grunted interrogatively:

"Uh, Jack, put um hat on? No put um hat on?—me no sabe!"

"Yes, put um hat on."

"Uh! yash, me heap put um hat on. All right—all same modisum (medicine) White-a-man. Heap sabe!" and relapsed into silent observation.

The parson did not enjoy his supper. His day had been one of tiresome, nervous preparation for a new kind of life; but Mr. Small was in hearty sympathy with all Nature, which includes a good appetite (if it is not founded upon a good appetite), and he ate with a rapid action and a keen relish, talking as he ate, in a way to provoke appetite, or if not to provoke, at least raise a sigh of regret for its absence.

"Thar!" said Mr. Small, with sighing emphasis, "that lets me out on creature comforts in the grub line till tomorrer. Yer don't waltz in very hearty on this grub, Parson. All right; I'll bake yer an oatmeal cake soon's I git done with my bread, an' mix yer a canteen o' milk fer tomorrer's lunch."

"Thank you, indeed, Mr. Small."

"Yere, Gov," said Mr. Small, as he piled the greased frying-pan full of broken bread, and poured out a tin cup of coffee, "yere's yer hash!"—to which Gov responded silently by carrying the pan and cup to the fire, and then sitting down between them on the ground, to eat and drink in his own fashion.

"These yere Injins is curious," said Mr. Small, in his running commentary on things in general, as he actively passed from one point in his culinary duties to another; "they wun't eat bacon, but they'll eat bacon grease an' bread, or beef an' bacon grease; an' they won't eat cheese, but they'll eat dead hoss. I b'lieve the way to conquer Injins would be to load cannons with Limburg cheese an' blaze away at 'em!"

"As the Chinese shoot their enemies in war with pots of abominable smells."

"Yes, I've heerd before o' the Chinee way o' makin' war, but reckon 'tain't the smell Injins keer fer—it's mighty hard to knock an Injin with a smell! Injins, leastway this yere tribe, hain't got no nose fer posies. They got some kind o' superstition about milk an' cheese, though I reckon they must hev drinked milk when they's little." And Mr. Small chuckled at the delicacy of his own allusion to the font of aboriginal maternity.

"Don't yer smoke, Parson?"

"Not of late years," replied Mr. Sighal; and paced up and down meditatively past the fire, gazing up at the darkening sky. "I formerly enjoyed a cigar, occasionally, but my dyspepsia has cut me off from that vice."

"Well, I've got this bread bakin', an' reckon I'll take a smoke. Yere, Gov, done yer supper? Scoot up thar an' throw down them beds, so we kin have a seat." The silent and ready compliance of the Indian enabled Mr. Small, as he tossed the rolls of bedding over by the fire, to remark, "Yere, Parson, take a seat. This yere's high style—front settin' room, fust floor. You'll want yer legs tomorrer, though yer kin ride if yer want to; but it's powerful tejus, ridin' a bull-wagon." And he sat down on his roll of bedding to cut his plug tobacco, fill his short pipe, and watch the process of bread-baking while he enjoyed his smoke.

The reverend also sat down on his bed.

The Indian sat on the ground at the opposite side of the fire, humming the low, buzzing, dismal ditty of his remote ancestors.

The stars came quietly out in the clear sky, and the dry still air seemed to listen to the coming on of the innumerable host. So still,—O, so crystalline still—is the summer night in Nevada!

"Yer see, Parson," began Mr. Small, after a short, quiet consultation with his pipe, "they say 'at bull-punchin's slow business, but they don't know. People kin tell what they don't know powerful slick-like. Let some o' them talkin' fellers what knows all about this business in three squints from a stage-coach winder—let 'em try it on. Let 'em stand in once, an' chop wood, build a fire, cut bacon, make bread an' coffee, an' so on, all in the same minute—an' do it faster'n they kin write it down in a letter, an' they wun't talk so much with their mouth!"

"Yes, I was just, in the moment you began to speak, reflecting on the multiplicity of your duties and the rapid execution of them. Does not your life wear upon you terribly?"

"No, sir. Hit's head work does it. Seems to me when a feller hes a big idee in his head, an' is jest a-boomin' with the futur, an' lookin' forward, that work doesn't hurt him a darned bit. Hit's hangin' back on the yoke 'at wears a feller out—an' a ox, too. When I used to foller a plow, by the day's work fer wages, an' havin' no pint ahead to steer to—no place to unload at—I wasn't no more account than a cripple in a county poor-house!"

"What is your great aim at this time?—if I may be so impolite as to make such an inquiry on so short acquaintance," queried Mr. Sighal, in a soft voice and balmy manner.

"Oh, no; nothin' imperlite about it. Open out on me, Parson, when you feel like it. I hain't got no secrets. My great aim is to play my game up to the handle. Every feller's got a game. Some's politics, some's religion, some's big money, some's land, some's keards, some's wimmin an' good clo'es, some's good, some's bad," said Mr. Small, rapidly, and punctuating his remarks with puffs of tobacco smoke; "an' my game is to hev the best eight-yoke o' cattle, an' the best wagons, an' pull the biggest load to yoke, in these yere mountains; an' then," he added, laughing and stroking his long bronze beard, "I kinder think there's a solid square-built gal some'rs what I ain't jest seen yet, that's a-waitin' in her daddy's front porch fer a feller like me—an' the old man he's gittin' too old, an' hain't got no other children, an' he's just a-walkin' up an' down under the shade trees, expectin' a feller about my size an' build, what kin sling ink in the Bank o' Californy[9] for about ten thousan' cash, honest money. How's that fer high, Parson?" And Mr. Small roared with his loudest laugh, until the parson and Gov joined sympathetically.

"A very laudable endeavor, Mr. Small; and let me say that I heartily wish you God-speed."

"Amen, Parson! I don't know ef I kin make it. But that's my game; an' ef I can't make it—well, hit's better to hev a game an' lose it than never to play at all. Hain't it, Parson?"

"It surely is. No good endeavor is ever entirely lost. God, in His great providence, gives germinating power to the minute seed of the plant which grew and died last year, though the seed may have been blown miles away."

"Do you b'lieve," said Mr. Small, after a long pause in which he raised the bake-kettle lid with the point of a stick and piled more hot coals upon the top—"do you b'lieve, fer certain—dead sure—that God looks after all these little things?"

"Surely, Mr. Small. Have we not the blessed promises in the Good Book?"

"I don't jest reck'lect what we've got in the Good Book. But do you, as yer mammy's son—not as a parson—do you b'lieve it?"

"If I at all know my own thoughts and convictions, Mr. Small, I do."

---

9. The Bank of California was the largest and most respected bank in Nevada.

After another long pause and strict attention to the baking bread: "Parson, gittin' sleepy?"

"Not at all, Mr. Small."

"Thinkin' 'bout somethin', p'r'aps?"

"I was reflecting whether I had done my whole duty and had answered your question as fully as it should be answered."

"Well, whenever you feel sleepy, jest spread yer lay-out where you choose, an' turn in. Needn't mind me. I'll fuss round yere an' smoke a good while yit. Thar hain't no ceremony at this ho-tel—the rooms is all fust-class 'part-ments."

"Thank you, Mr. Small," said Mr. Sighal; and then, after some pause, resuming audibly the thread of his own thought, he asked, "Mr. Small, do not you believe in the overruling providence of God?"

"Which God?"

"There is but one God."

"I don't see it, Parson. On this yere Pacific Coast, gods is numerous— Chinee gods, Mormon gods, Injin gods, Christian gods, and the Bank o' Californy."

"Perhaps so, Mr. Small—it is written there be gods many; but there is one only true God, Jesus Christ the righteous."

"Don't see it, Parson."

The Reverend Mr. Sighal rose quickly to his feet and pulled down his vest at the waistband, like a warrior unconsciously feeling for the girding of his armor.

"Do you deny the truth of the sacred Scriptures, Mr. Small?"

"I don't deny nothin', 'cept what kin come before me to be reco'nized. What I says is, I don't see it."

"You don't see it?"

"No, sir!"—emphasis on the sir.

"Perhaps not, with the natural eyesight, but with the eye of faith, Mr. Small, you can see it, if you humbly and honestly make the effort."

"I hain't got but two eyes—no extra eye fer Sunday use. What I can't see, nor year, nor taste, nor smell, nor feel, nor make up out o' reck'lection an' hitch together, hain't nothin' to me. That's my meanin' when I say, 'I don't see it.'"

"I am deeply grieved to hear you speak so, Mr. Small."

"Now, look yere, Parson," replied Mr. Small, as he got up to bustle about his work, "fellers like me, livin' out o' doors, has got a God what couldn't git into one of your meetin'-houses."

"Mr. Small—pardon me—there is a glimmer of what seems to be meaning in your remark, but really I fail to comprehend you."

"That's hit"—it will be observed as a peculiarity in Mr. Small's language (a peculiarity common to unlettered Western-born Americans) that he sounds the emphatic form of the pronoun *it* with an aspirate *h*—"that's hit! That's the high-larnt way to say, 'I don't see it.' Now we're even, Parson—only you've got a million o' meetin'-house bells to do the 'plaudin' fer you, an' I hain't got nary one. But these ere mountains, an' them bright stars, an' yonder moon pullin' bright over the summit, would 'plaud me ef I knowed how to talk fer what made 'em. Hush—listen!" said Small, suddenly pausing, and pointing under the moonlight across the dim valley. "That's a coyote; I wonder which of us he's laughin' at."

"Yash; kiotee. He heap talk. Mebbe so tabbit ketch um," said the Indian, rising and gathering up his blanket to retire. "Me heap shneep."

"Throw down another stick o' wood off the wagon, Gov, before yer go to bed."

"Yash; me heap shneepy," replied the Indian, stretching and yawning with uplifted hands from one of which his red blanket draped down for a moment over his shoulder, gorgeous in the dancing campfire light.

While the Indian climbed the wagon-side for the stick of wood, Mr. Sighal remarked, "Mr. Small, before we retire, may I not ask the privilege of a few words of audible prayer to God for His preservation through the night hours?"

"Yes, sir. Yere, Gov, come yere. I want the Injin to year one prayer, ef he never years another. I've paid money when I was a boy to hev Injins prayed fer,[10] an' now I'm goin' to see some of it done. Come yere, Gov."

The Indian came to the fireside.

"Yere, Gov—you sabe? This-a-way; all same me"—and Mr. Small dropped upon his own knees at the side of his roll of bedding.

"All-a-same—Injin all-a-same—little stand-up?" asked Gov, dropping his blanket and placing his hands upon his knees.

"Yes! Little stand-up—all same me!"

"Yash!" assented Gov, on the opposite side of the roll, settling gradually upon his knees.

It happened that the parson kneeled facing the Indian, so that the Indian had him in full view with the fire-light shining on the parson's face, and, not being accustomed to family worship, nor having had the matter fully explained to him, he conceived the idea of doing as others did; so that when the parson turned his face to the stars and shut his eyes, the Indian did so, too, and began repeating in very bad English, word for word, the parson's prayer—

10. Small is referring to his Sunday school contributions to missions to convert the Indians.

which piece of volunteer assistance not comporting with Mr. Small's impression of domestic decorum, caused that stout gentleman to place his two hands upon the Indian's shoulders and jerk him, face down, upon the bedding, with the fiercely whispered ejaculation, "Dry up!"

The Reverend Mr. Sighal prayed for the persons present, in their various conditions, and their safety through the night; acknowledging that he knew God's hand was, in these vast solitudes, guiding as of old the swoop of the raven's wing and marking the death-bed of the sparrow.[11] There was much in the prayer that was fervent and fitting, but nothing that could be fairly called original.

When the party arose to their feet, Mr. Sighal sat down, burying his face in his hands supported by his knees; Mr. Small changed an unbaked for a baked loaf with the bake-kettle; and the Indian, taking up his "plug" hat and red blanket, merely remarked, "Me heap shneep!" and retired behind a sagebrush.

"Parson!" said Mr. Small, after refilling his pipe and resuming his seat, and as the Reverend Mr. Sighal sat gazing reflectively into the fire.

"Sir," responded Mr. Sighal, with a slight start from his reverie.

"I'm a-thinkin' over your prayer."

"Well, Mr. Small, I hope God will make my humble effort of some slight use in opening to you the door of His great mercy."

"I wasn't thinkin' about it jest that-a-way. I was tryin' the sense of it on."

"I wish, Mr. Small, that God had vouchsafed to me the power of making its meaning plain."

"Oh, you made it plain enough accordin' to—to—well, ef my mother'd been yere, she'd ha' thought that was a Number 1 prayer, an' she'd ha' hollered 'Amen!' every time yer went fer me an' the Injin; but what I was thinkin' about was your callin' on Jesus Christ as the Giver of all good, the Creator of all things. Now—you excuse me, Parson!—right thar is jest whar' I can't quite go with ye."

"It is written, 'the Word was made flesh and dwelt among us, and by it were all things made which are made.' "

"Yes, I've read it. I know hit's written, an' hit's printed. But written things hain't no deader'n some things what hain't been wrote yit."

"Deader! Deader!" repeated Mr. Sighal.

"Yes, dead sure—certiner."

"Ah! I understand it now."

"An' as fer printed things," continued Mr. Small, "they crawl"—then, ob-

11. See *Hamlet* 5.2.230ff.

serving the look of perplexity in the parson's face—"Yes! They crawl!—wun't stay put. Allers changin' with new translatin' an' new lights."

Here Mr. Small had occasion to look after his baking. Resuming his seat, he said:

"Parson, ever been to Yosemite?"

"I have not."

"Ever see the Grand Canyon o' the Colorado River?"

"I have not."

"Well, Parson, I've seen both them places. I resked my skelp, me an' two other fellers—bully fellers them was too!—a-packin' my blankets fer three weeks in an' out an' aroun' the Canyon o' the Colorado, jest to see it. I b'lieve I could stay there feriver an' climb an' look!"

"I have read of the great works of God made manifest in the desert places."

"Parson, that remark don't touch the spot! Ef ever yer see that canyon, yer'll jest think any printed book yer ever opened, or any words yer ever heard, hain't got no power in 'em."

"I have no doubt it is magnificently grand."

"Parson," slowly queried Mr. Small, "do yer think Jesus Christ made the Canyon o' the Colorado, an' the world hit runs through, an' the sky hit opens under, an' the ocean 'at takes hits waters?"

"I do."

"Well, I don't know! Seems to me thar was never nothin' born in Judear that hed hands that kin lay over Ameriky—an' nothin' was never born in Ameriky that hed hands that kin build a ten-cent sideshow fer that ar canyon! Parson, them's things that can't be wiped out, nor wrong-printed in no book!—nor no new light can't make 'em more'n they jest are! Whatever made sech things as them, an' these yere mountains, that's my God. But He hain't got no hands in the image o' these yere!" extending his thorny, black-ened palms, and adding as a climax, "ye kin bet yer sweet life on that."

"Oh, Mr. Small!" cried Mr. Sighal, rising to his feet. "My dear sir, do you wish to deny, and throw away as naught, all that the good Lord Jesus, our Divine Saviour, has taught, and fall back into heathenism?"

"I don't want to deny nothin' nor fall back nowhar. Ef Jesus Christ teaches men to do honest an' fair, one to another, that's all right, an' I'm with Him, in my style, sech as it is; but when you, or anybody else, asks me to jump from that p'int into the idea that He made an' rules creation—that lets me out! . . . Thar now, Parson! I kinder understood you, because you was a parson; but you wasn't likely to understand me, because I'm a bull-puncher. Now we un-derstand each other. I've hed my say, an' I'll listen to anything you've got to say on the whole trip, as well as I know how."

"Well, Mr. Small," said the Reverend Mr. Sighal, taking Big Jack's extended hand, "whatever may be my regrets, I can but respect the opinions of a man who respectfully states them. And I shall only pray to God to give you a clearer light."

"That's all right, Parson! An' now, as I've got your oatmeal cake baked an' everything done up brown, what do yer say ef we roll out the blankets, go to sleep, an' forgit it all till mornin'?"

"I shall be pleased to retire at any time."

"Well, hit's a fine night," said Jack, proceeding to untie the roll of his bedding, "an' we needn't go under the wagon, but jest spread down in the evenest places we kin find."

The Reverend Mr. Sighal made his first bed in the wilderness and, as the mountain phrase goes, "crawled in."

"Parson," said Mr. Small, as he sat in his bed straightening the blankets about his feet, "Got plenty blankets?—I kin spare ye a pair."

"Plenty, thank you."

"Good night, Parson."

"Good night, and God bless you, Mr. Small."

The bright moon and stars moved on their long-appointed courses through the wide and cloudless sky, the sage-brush of the valley stretched far away, the mountain rose ragged to the serrated summit, the cattle browsed along the slope, the shadows of the great wagons fell square and dark upon the dry desert earth, and nature's old, old silence closed down upon the wilderness.

In the morning, Mr. Sighal awakened early, after a sweet and refreshing sleep, his lungs and whole inner man toned up with the dry, dewless, fresh air, to find Mr. Small far forward in the preparation of breakfast.

"Good mornin', Parson! Didn't anybody disturb yer last night, walkin' on the upstairs floor, did thar?"

"Good morning, Mr. Small! No; I've had a fine sleep"—drawing on his wearing apparel.

"When ye sleep out nights yere, whar there's never no dew fallin', hit's better'n any ho-tel."

"Yes, sir; the air is very refreshing and invigorating," said Mr. Sighal, stamping his feet into his boots and shaking the creases out of his pantaloons.

"Thar's soap an' a sort o' towel on the wheel hub, an' ye kin take 'em an' go right over thar to them willer bushes an' hev a wash, an' then hash'll be ready."

While Mr. Sighal and Mr. Small were taking breakfast after the customary petition for grace, the first gold rim of the sun, with the distant trees painted in its halo, rose into view on the top of the far-off eastern mountains, and Gov Nye, with his red blanket about his shoulders, came softly across the nearer hills, the scattered cattle moving zigzag through the sage-brush in front of him.

"Now, Parson," said Mr. Small, when they had finished breakfast, "we'll roll up, tie up, an' h'ist up our beddin'; then hitch up the bulls while Gov eats his grub, an' roll out."

While Mr. Small, taking each heavy yoke in its turn upon his shoulder and holding one bow in his right hand, walked up to each off-side ox successively, dropped the end of the yoke gently upon his neck, slipped the bow upward and secured it to its place with the key, then, removing the other bow, rested that end of the yoke upon the ground, led the nigh-side ox to his place with the bow, and thus arranged each twain in their proper yoke, Mr. Sighal, with outspread arms and extended hands, rendered amiable assistance in keeping the herd together.

"Done eatin', Gov?" said Mr. Small, when he had stationed his horned troop in marching order.

"Yash. Heap eat um all up."

"All right," approved Mr. Small, tumbling the cooking utensils into the box. "No time to wash dishes this mornin'. Yere, Gov, snail hold o' this box. Now tumble up there an' take it." And, heaving the box up after the Indian, he drew his terrible whip from its place between the wheel spokes, stepped to the side of his team, and, letting go the lash, swung it about in the air at arm's length in front of him, and then suddenly bringing it toward him with a pe-culiar jerk, causing the buckskin snapper to go off like a revolver, shouted, "Gee, Brigham—ro-o-al out!" and the "desert schooners" slowly sailed away into the valley.

Mr. Sighal marched afoot, pausing to pick up a peculiar pebble and carry it a while, then to find a pebble more peculiar, and drop the first to take the second; now to hunker down and study the spikes upon a sleeping horned toad, then to pluck some flower so tiny small that it seemed but a speck among the pulpy, dry gravel and loose earth; now turning face about to take in the rugged outline of the mountain under whose shadow he had passed the night, and then lower his vision to note the saucy, swaggering strut of that black "prospector," the raven, walking down the road in the distant track of the wagons, not failing at the time to watch the lizards flash across his path; now again trudging along, like Bunyan's Christian,[12] with eyes survey-ing the to him unknown land in front—the Delectable Mountains, where, according to Mr. Small, he might see some "bully float-quartz." To him the

12. John Bunyan's *Pilgrim's Progress* (1678) was a familiar classic in the nineteenth century. Its main character, Christian, encounters the Delectable Mountains in one of the book's episodes.

sameness of the land was a newness; no green and gold of leaves that grow and leaves that die, no babbling streams through valleys grown with grass, no heaving fields with squares of "thine and mine"; but one wide waste of ashen gray, one cloudless sun, one wagon-road across the scene, and mountains all about.

Thus the time passed. Driving all day in the hot sun, with unhitching, cooking, eating, talking, praying, cooking, eating, and re-hitching during the cool evening and morning, and sweetly sleeping through the night. Dustily across valley after valley; slowly up this side and noisily down the other side of mountain after mountain, Mr. Small pausing on the summit of each to point out to the parson the prominent peaks as they appeared plainly to the eye in a range of one hundred miles—showing, here and there, far away, their huge sides, where man, with all his might and genius, is boring mere gimlet-holes, from which to draw the bright, white wealth that makes the yellow glitter in the city's halls.[13]

In the long, slow journey, Mr. Sighal sought by easy lessons to draw—round the consciousness of Big Jack Small—the subtle and intricate simplicity of his own faith in a personal God with feelings of humanity and feeling for humanity, yet powerful to the utmost limit of all the mighty magnitudes of power. All of which Mr. Small refused to see, and stoutly clung to his own crude materialism, overshadowed by a wide Gothic spirituality, born perhaps of the tribal tinge in the blood which gave him his fair skin, high-bridged nose, bold gray eye, and long tawny beard. It was again the old subtleties born of a southern sun endeavoring to bring the wild Norse blood upon its knees at the foot of a Roman cross.

The conversion of the Indian, which was Mr. Small's special desire, did not proceed satisfactorily. It is comparatively easy, I opine, to build religion upon civilization; but the labor must be thorough and the effort exhaustive where there is only the love of food, of passion, and of existence to start on. Yet the Indian was not without curiosity, nor, being a better specimen of his race, was he totally without the spirit of inquiry into unsubstantial things. On several occasions during the trip, he sought to discover the object of prayer.

"Uh, Jack," queried he, "what for modisum-man"—he would call the parson a medicine-man—"what for modisum-man all'er time little-stand-up, shut um eye, heap up-talk? Injin no sabe."

"Thar, now, Parson," said Mr. Small, "this Injin wants to know why yer kneel down, shet yer eyes, an' talk up at the sky. He says he don't understand it."

"I wished that I possessed a knowledge of his language, and could be the

---

13. Silver is the bright, white wealth that purchases the yellow gold and lights that glitter in cities.

means, under God, of opening to him and his people the way to life everlasting."

"Well, Parson, yere's a big game fer yer to play. Thar's hundreds o' his kind in these mountains, an' their lingo hain't hard to learn an' they hain't hard to teach about religion. Anyhow, they learn to swear an' cuss, an' nobody kin do that till he's been among people of a Christian country!"

"Mr. Small," answered the parson, who, now that he was growing stronger in body, was more aggressive in mind, "there is a sneering levity in your manner when you speak of serious things which pains me to hear."

"Excuse me, Parson. That's only style, an' style hain't nothin' in this country. The p'int is how we're goin' to git light into this Injin—that's the p'int."

"I grieve to say, Mr. Small, that I am as yet utterly unable to converse with him in the broken jargon of English which he seems to comprehend when you speak to him."

"All right, then. Come yere, Injin. I'll try my hand on him. My mother allers wanted me to be a preacher an' help convert the heathen."

The Indian came up smiling.

"Yer sabe little-stand-up?"

"Yash, heap sabe—too much."

"Yer sabe heap talk-up?"

"Yash. Heap sabe modisum-man."

"Now, Injin, me talk—Big Jack talk."

"Waynyo" (good).

"When waynyo man heap little-stand-up, heap talk-up aller time, by um by, long time, he heap old man, heap die. Yer sabe?"

"Yash. Heap sabe die. Aller same Injin yakwe."

"Yes, by um by, die," repeated Mr. Small, scratching his head through a pause, in his doubt as to how to proceed. "Then pretty soon, by um by, after while, waynyo man go up—up"—pointing to the sky—"way, way up yonder, an'—an' no come back."

"No come back!" echoed the Indian, apparently deeply interested in the revelation.

"No; no come back."

"Where he go? No ketch um wick-i-up?"

"Yes; fine house—waynyo wick-i-up."

"Heap work?"

"No; no work."

"Waynyo!" approved the Indian. "Me no like um work."

"No; no work. Heap sing—all time sing."

"Aller time sing?" repeated Gov.

"Yes; all time sing, in one big wick-i-up. No coat ketch um; no pantaloons."

"No pantaroon?"

"No; no pantaloons. One big gown—all same shirt. All time sing; no come
night. Yer sabe?"

"Yash; me heap sabe. Heap ticcup?" (food) earnestly interrogated the
Indian.

"No; no ticcup."

"Heap sequaw?"

"No; no squaws."

"What yer call um?"

"Heaven."

"Ka-waynyo hebben—no good! No pantaroon, no ticcup, no sequaw—ka-
waynyo hebben! Me no like um."

Notwithstanding the solemnity of the subject, the Reverend Mr. Sighal
found himself shaking with restrained laughter at Mr. Small's first missionary effort among the Shoshones.

"Thar," said Mr. Small, with great emphasis, "as a missionary I'm a failure.
Gov, go git some brush fer the fire. But I'll not give the Injin up! I'll go fer
him agin when I hain't got nothin' else to do," added he, going about his
usual camp work.

Mr. Sighal took a walk around the camp, apparently giving the whole
matter up as being beyond his present influence.

The camp to which Big Jack Small's freight was consigned was a new one,
and, of course, the last days of the trip led the team over newly broken roads,
which fact increased the labor of Mr. Small, and gave to his face and language a somewhat serious impression. During the last day's drive before
coming to camp, the road was particularly uneven, and on the down grade
caused the long, high wagon-boxes to reel to and fro like boats at sea. Often
the wagons, despite the strong friction of the howling brakes, pressed upon
the cattle and crowded them upon each other *en masse*. Then again, the hind-
most wagons, in making a turn, encroached so far upon the inner side of the
circle that the brake must be let up to avoid sliding farther and overturning,
as a rolling wheel slides less than a wheel which is locked.

On one of these sidelong turns, on the brink of a shallow, dry water-wash,
Mr. Small was compelled to stop his team to prevent the overthrow of the
rear wagon. As he proceeded to release the brake, which on this particular
wagon had its lever low down and between the forward and hind wheel, the
wheels, from the slight move they made after being released, settled the wagon
just a little, but far enough in its nearly poised position to turn it over suddenly, before Mr. Small could fly for safety.

Mr. Sighal had been anxiously and prayerfully observing, from the rear of the train, the attitude of things. He heard a sudden shout, a crash, and then all was silent, and Jack Small invisible. The unconscious cattle stood quietly in the yoke; Mr. Sighal ran wildly from one side of the wagon to the other, endeavoring to discover some clue to Mr. Small; while the Indian walked gravely up from the head of the team, where he had been stationed to keep it in check, and stolidly observed, pointing to the prostrate wagon, "Uh! One um wagon heap ketch um Big Jack."

Mr. Sighal looked in the imperturbable face of the Indian, the Indian looked into the face of Mr. Sighal, and they both looked at the wagon. Then the Indian sat down upon the hillside, and Mr. Sighal stood pale and sad, turning his hands nervously through each other, vainly trying to determine what to do next. Suddenly he called the Indian, and began actively unloading the unfortunate wagon, with the intention, as he afterward explained, of lifting it back by hand; which feat, considering its great size and weight, was nearly as far beyond the available power there present to lift the whole load.

While thus fiercely engaged, and urging the Indian to increased exertion in the same direction, he heard a voice as of one crying from the depths:

"Hullo, Parson!"

"Oh, thank God, my dear Mr. Small, you still live!"

"Yes, sir. I hain't dead yit."

"Are you seriously injured?—and do tell me what to do, Mr. Small."

"Guess not. I'm down yere in the holler, but it's mighty close quarters— like a fishin' worm under a board. Ef the wagon-box don't settle down on me, I reckon I'm 'bout all right. What're yer doin', Parson?"

"Unloading the wagon, Mr. Small."

"Hell! That hain't no use. Git the couplin' chains from the other wagons— but chock the wheels fust!—pass 'em roun' the box from end to end, 'bout quarter-way down from the top; then bring the ends together on the side o' the box. Sabe?"

"I hope I do, Mr. Small."

"Then take five yoke o' cattle an' another chain—an extry chain, more'n what would do to hitch up fer common with—drive the cattle roun' to the other side o' the wagon, an' p'int 'em straight across from the road; hitch that extry chain into the chain on the wagons, then hitch the cattle's chain to that extry chain. Sabe?"

"I think I do, Mr. Small."

"When yer got that done, holler to me. Don't hurry. Work right ahead as though thar wasn't nothin' wrong."

The parson conscientiously, yet with much misgiving, went about his task, and when he had all ready, and the cattle strung out at right angles with the road, he stepped up to the prostrate wagon, and, turning as one who listens down a well, he shouted:

"Mr. Small!"

"Hullo-o!"

"I believe I have done as you told me."

"Got everything hitched strong?—don't want no slips in this game, yer know!—'cause ef this wagon-box slides much, you'll have a mighty flat corpse to preach a funeral on!"

"Oh dear! dear! Mr. Small!" exclaimed the parson, vexed and horrified. "What shall I do next?"

"Give Gov a strong bar'l, ef you kin git one, or git a big stone ef yer can't git no bar'l, an' place it to the edge o' the wagon-box, so 'at he kin put it under when the cattle lift it. Sabe?"

"Yes, sir. . . . All done, Mr. Small."

"Now then, start up the cattle, an' keep 'em to it when they start. An' Gov, you look out an' heap fix up."

"Yash, me sabe," said the Indian, taking his position, while Mr. Sighal gathered to himself the terrible whip, and proceeded to try his powers in a role in which he had faint hopes of success. He swung the whip round his head, bringing the heavy lash with a rake like that of a dull rasp across his own neck, and shouted at the cattle. Slowly they tightened the chains, and then stood in the pulling attitude, but pulling not one pound more than just enough to stretch the chains.

Oxen which will pull true enough in the beaten track have doubts about pulling across country through the brush.

"Get up! Gee!" shouted the Reverend Mr. Sighal at the top of his voice, and trying in vain to jerk an explosion out of the great whip as he had seen Mr. Small do. "Get up! Gee! Go 'long!" And then seeing himself unsuccessful, and becoming heated with the exertion, he added by way of terror to the cattle, "Con*found* you! Get up!" Still the wagon-box lay flat on the top of Mr. Small.

Hearing a continued rattling of chains, and much shouting with no apparent result, Mr. Small called:

"Hullo! Parson!"

"Sir."

"What's the matter?"

"The cattle can't draw it, Mr. Small," replied the parson sadly.

"Can't draw it, be damned! Go fer 'em with the brad, an' cuss 'em! They kin pull it easy enough."

"Curse them, Mr. Small!" cried the parson, in a voice of impressive solemnity.

"Yes, cuss 'em!" shouted Mr. Small. "I wish I was out there, damn 'em!"

"Mr. Small, don't swear needlessly. This is an occasion of life and death," said the parson, desisting from his efforts at urging the cattle, whereat he had grown hot and red, excited and vexed.

"Well, well! never don't fret, Parson! Better men than me ha' died in a better cause. Write a note an' send it down to camp by the Injin—the boys'll come up an' git me out, alive or dead."

"Do not think me weak or impractical, Mr. Small," replied Mr. Sighal, with a determined ring in his voice. "Tell me what to do and I will do it, God being judge of my intentions."

"Can you cuss, Parson?"

"It is many years since I have uttered an oath of profanity, what is it I am to do?" asked the parson sternly.

"Go round to them cattle, commence on the leaders, an' brad 'em all with that steel in the end o' the whip-stock—the way you've seen me do it; then raise the whip above yer head, start 'em on the gee pull, an' jest lay your head back an' cuss as loud an' as strong as you kin holler."

The Reverend Mr. Sighal went round to "them cattle." There was audible to Mr. Small's ears a hustling of ox-feet upon the earth, a creaking of ox-bows, mixed with an occasional short bawl; then the sound of the parson's voice elevated with great vehemence—and the wagon slowly arose enough to permit Mr. Small to crawl out into the free air. The parson was still shouting at the straining cattle, when Mr. Small limped quickly to where he stood, and, taking the whip from him with one hand, extended his other, which Mr. Sighal grasped in both of his, and, turning his eyes, now full of tears, toward heaven, eloquently thanked God for His great mercy in the preservation of a life which he hoped might yet be dedicated to good and holy works.

"Thank ye, Parson," said Big Jack, as he dropped his hand and turned to the cattle; "you're a good one—thar ain't no go back to you!" And then, easing the cattle back from the pull, he said, "Parson, when I marry that solid, square-built gal, you shall do the ceremony, ef it costs me a thousand dollars to fetch yer where I am!"

"Ah! Mr. Small, this lesson should teach us that we know not what a day may bring forth."

"Well, we'll take the chances, anyway, Parson!"

What language the Reverend Mr. Sighal used to the cattle is not reported by Mr. Small; the Indian, being accustomed to much that he does not fully understand, made no note of it; and the wide, gray silence of the desert is no babbler.

Once free, though somewhat bruised in the lower limbs, Big Jack Small made short work of drawing his wagon back upon its wheels and into the road, and slowly rolled on toward his destination.

In town, and his cattle corralled, he said, "Now, Parson, ef yer don't want to go to one of these yere lodgin'-houses, you jest pile in with me under the wagons, an' wait till I unload, an' then we'll roll out agin somewhere's else fer another trip."

"Thank you, Mr. Small. I will, God willing, remain in this town and go about the work of my Master. How much am I in your debt, Mr. Small?"

"In my debt! See yere, Parson, that's too thin. You don't owe me nary cent. An' ef ever you git stuck an' can't pull out, you jest drop a line to John Small, ——, Nevada; an' ef I don't double up the hill with you, then jest write across a piece o' paper, 'Big Jack Small's dead broke an' can't borer a cent.'"

"Thank you, Mr. Small," said the reverend, shaking Big Jack's hand. "I will pray for your well-being daily, and if at any time I can assist you, do not fail to summon me. Good night."

"Good-by, Parson! An' don't fergit about me an' my gal!—that's goin' to be a whack—shore!"

--⊸*Sand, and Big Jack Small* (1880)

A Christmas Carol

Samuel Davis

Sometimes known as "The First Piano in Camp," this story was originally pub-lished in the *Virginia City Chronicle* under its present title and was also collected by that title in *Short Stories*, whose text is followed here. Probably dating from the 1870s, when Davis worked for the *Chronicle*, this is one of his best-known tales, and one of the few Sagebrush stories to have occasionally been republished.

◦──◦ ◦──◦

In 1858—it might have been five years earlier or later, this is not history for the public schools—there was a little camp about ten miles from Pioche, occupied by upwards of three hundred miners, every one of whom might have packed his prospecting implements and left for more inviting fields any time before sunset. When the day was over, these men did not rest from their labors, like the honest New England agriculturist, but sang, danced, gam-bled, and shot each other, as the mood seized them.

One evening the report spread along the main street (which was the only street) that three men had been killed at Silver Reef, and that the bodies were coming in. Presently a lumbering old conveyance labored up the hill, drawn by a couple of horses, well worn out with their pull. The cart contained a good-sized box, and no sooner did its outlines become visible through the glimmer of a stray light here and there, than it began to affect the idlers. Death always enforces respect, and even though no one had caught sight of the remains, the crowd gradually became subdued, and when the horses came to a stand-still, the cart was immediately surrounded. The driver, however, was not in the least impressed with the solemnity of his commission.

"All there?" asked one.

"Haven't examined. Guess so."

The driver filled his pipe and lit it as he continued:

"Wish the bones and load had gone over the grade."

A man who had been looking on stepped up to the man at once.

"I don't know who you have in that box, but if they happen to be any friends of mine, I'll lay you alongside."

"We can mighty soon see," said the teamster, coolly. "Just burst the lid off, and if they happen to be the men you want, I'm here."

The two looked at each other for a moment, and the crowd gathered a little closer, anticipating trouble.

"I believe that dead men are entitled to good treatment, and when you talk about hoping to see corpses go over a bank, all I have to say is, that it will be better for you if the late lamented ain't my friends."

"We'll open the box. I don't take back what I've said, and if my language don't suit your ways of thinking, I guess I can stand it."

With these words the teamster began to pry up the lid. He got a board off, and then pulled out some old rags. A strip of something dark, like rosewood, presented itself.

"Eastern coffins, by thunder!" said several, and the crowd looked quite astonished.

Some more boards flew up, and the man who was ready to defend his friend's memory shifted his weapon a little. The cool manner of the teamster had so irritated him that he had made up his mind to pull his weapon at the first sight of the dead, even if the deceased was his worst and oldest enemy. Presently the whole of the box cover was off, and the teamster, clearing away the packing, revealed to the astonished group the top of something which puzzled all alike.

"Boys," said he, "this is a pianner."

A general shout of laughter went up, and the man who had been so anxious to enforce respect for the dead muttered something about feeling dry, and the keeper of the nearest bar was several ounces[1] better off by the time the boys had given the joke all the attention it called for.

Had a dozen dead men been in the box, their presence in the camp could not have occasioned half the excitement that the arrival of that lovely piano caused. By the next morning it was known that the instrument was to grace a hurdy-gurdy saloon, owned by Tom Goskin, the leading gambler in the place. It took nearly a week to get this wonder on its legs, and the owner was the proudest individual in the State. It rose gradually from a recumbent to an

---

1. Several ounces of gold dust. In mining communities, commodities—including liquor—were often bought and sold by ounces of gold dust rather than by coin or greenbacks.

upright position, amid a confusion of tongues, after the manner of the tower of Babel.

Of course everybody knew just how such an instrument should be put up. One knew where the "off hind leg" should go, and another was posted on the "front piece."

Scores of men came to the place every day to assist.

"I'll put the bones in good order."

"If you want the wires tuned up, I'm the boy."

"I've got music to feed it for a month."

Another brought a pair of blankets for a cover, and all took the liveliest interest in it. It was at last in a condition for business.

"It's been showin' its teeth all the week. We'd like to have it spit out something."

Alas! There wasn't a man to be found who could play upon the instrument. Goskin began to realize that he had a losing speculation on his hands. He had a fiddler, and a Mexican who thrummed a guitar. A pianist would have made his orchestra complete. One day a three-card monte player told a friend confidentially that he could "knock any amount of music out of the piano, if he only had it alone a few hours to get his hand in." This report spread about the camp, but on being questioned he vowed that he didn't know a note of music. It was noted, however, as a suspicious circumstance, that he often hung about the instrument, and looked upon it longingly, like a hungry man gloating over a beefsteak in a restaurant window. There was no doubt but that this man had music in his soul, perhaps in his fingers'-ends, but did not dare to make trial of his strength after the rules of harmony had suffered so many years of neglect. So the fiddler kept on with his jigs, and the greasy Mexican pawed his discordant guitar, but no man had the nerve to touch that piano. There were, doubtless, scores of men in the camp who would have given ten ounces of gold-dust to have been half an hour alone with it, but every man's nerve shrank from the jeers which the crowd would shower upon him should his first attempt prove a failure. It got to be generally understood that the hand which first essayed to draw music from the keys must not slouch its work.

*   *   *   *   *

It was Christmas Eve, and Goskin, according to his custom, had decorated his gambling hall with sprigs of mountain cedar and a shrub whose crimson berries did not seem a bad imitation of English holly. The piano was covered with evergreens, and all that was wanting to completely fill the cup of Goskin's contentment was a man to play that piano.

"Christmas night, and no piano-pounder," he said. "This is a nice country for a Christian to live in."

Getting a piece of paper, he scrawled the words:

$20 Reward
To a compitant Pianer Player.

This he stuck up on the music-rack, and, though the inscription glared at the frequenters of the room until midnight, it failed to draw any musician from his shell.

So the merry-making went on; the hilarity grew apace. Men danced and sang to the music of the squeaky fiddle and worn-out guitar, as the jolly crowd within tried to drown the howling of the storm without. Suddenly, they became aware of the presence of a white-haired man, crouching near the fire-place. His garments—such as were left—were wet with melting snow, and he had a half-starved, half-crazed expression. He held his thin, trembling hands toward the fire, and the light of the blazing wood made them almost transparent. He looked about him once in a while, as if in search of something, and his presence cast such a chill over the place that gradually the sound of the revelry was hushed, and it seemed that this waif of the storm had brought in with it all of the gloom and coldness of the warring elements. Goskin, mixing up a cup of hot egg-nogg, advanced and remarked cheerily:

"Here, stranger, brace up! This is the real stuff."

The man drained the cup, smacked his lips, and seemed more at home.

"Been prospecting, eh? Out in the mountains—caught in the storm? Lively night, this!"

"Pretty bad," said the man.

"Must feel pretty dry?"

The man looked at his streaming clothes and laughed, as if Goskin's remark was a sarcasm.

"How long out?"

"Four days."

"Hungry?"

The man rose up, and walking over to the lunch counter, fell to work upon some roast bear, devouring it like any wild animal would have done. As meat and drink and warmth began to permeate the stranger, he seemed to expand and lighten up. His features lost their pallor, and he grew more and more content with the idea that he was not in the grave. As he underwent these changes, the people about him got merrier and happier, and threw off the temporary feeling of depression which he had laid upon them.

"Do you always have your place decorated like this?" he finally asked of Goskin.

"This is Christmas Eve," was the reply.

The stranger was startled.

"December twenty-fourth, sure enough."

"That's the way I put it up, pard."

"When I was in England I always kept Christmas. But I had forgotten that this was the night. I've been wandering about in the mountains until I've lost track of the feasts of the church."

Presently his eye fell upon the piano.

"Where's the player?" he asked.

"Never had any," said Goskin, blushing at the expression.

"I used to play when I was young."

Goskin almost fainted at the admission.

"Stranger, do tackle it, and give us a tune! Nary man in this camp ever had the nerve to wrestle with that music-box." His pulse beat faster, for he feared that the man would refuse.

"I'll do the best I can," he said.

There was no stool, but seizing a candle-box, he drew it up and seated himself before the instrument. It only required a few seconds for a hush to come over the room.

"That old coon is going to give the thing a rattle."

The sight of a man at the piano was something so unusual that even the faro-dealer, who was about to take in a fifty-dollar bet on the tray, paused, and did not reach for the money. Men stopped drinking, with the glasses at their lips. Conversation appeared to have been struck with a sort of paralysis, and cards were no longer shuffled.

The old man brushed back his long, white locks, looked up to the ceiling, half closed his eyes, and in a mystic sort of reverie passed his fingers over the keys. He touched but a single note, yet the sound thrilled the room. It was the key to his improvisation, and as he wove his chords together the music laid its spell upon every ear and heart. He felt his way along the keys, like a man treading uncertain paths; but he gained confidence as he progressed, and presently bent to his work like a master. The instrument was not in exact tune, but the ears of his audience, through long disuse, did not detect anything radically wrong. They heard a succession of grand chords, a suggestion of paradise, melodies here and there, and it was enough.

"See him counter with his left!" said an old rough, enraptured.

"He calls the turn every time on the upper end of the board," responded a man with a stack of chips in his hand.

The player wandered off into the old ballads they had heard at home. All the sad and melancholy, and touching songs that came up like dreams of childhood, this unknown player drew from the keys. His hands kneaded their hearts like dough, and squeezed out the tears as from a wet sponge. As the strains flowed one upon the other, they saw their homes of the long ago reared again; they were playing once more where the apple blossoms sank through the soft air to join the violets on the green turf of the old New England States; they saw the glories of the Wisconsin maples and the haze of the Indian summer, blending their hues together; they recalled the heather of Scottish hills, the white cliffs of Britain, and heard the sullen roar of the sea, as it beat upon their memories, vaguely. Then came all the old Christmas carols, such as they had sung in church thirty years before; the subtle music that brings up the glimmer of wax tapers, the solemn shrines, the evergreen, holly, mistletoe, and surpliced choirs. Then the remorseless performer planted his final stab in every heart with "Home, Sweet Home."

When the player ceased, the crowd slunk away from him. There was no more revelry and devilment left in his audience. Each man wanted to sneak off to his cabin and write the old folks a letter. The day was breaking as the last man left the place, and the player, laying his head down on the piano, fell asleep.

"I say, pard," said Goskin, "don't you want a little rest?"

"I feel tired," the old man said. "Perhaps you'll let me rest here for the matter of a day or so."

He walked behind the bar where some old blankets were lying, and stretched himself upon them.

"I feel pretty sick. I guess I won't last long. I've got a brother down in the ravine—his name's Driscoll. He don't know I'm here. Can you get him before morning. I'd like to see his face once before I die."

Goskin started up at the mention of the name. He knew Driscoll well.

"He your brother? I'll have him here in half an hour."

As he dashed out into the storm the musician pressed his hand to his side and groaned. Goskin heard the word "Hurry!" and sped down the ravine to Driscoll's cabin. It was quite light in the room when the two men returned. Driscoll was pale as death.

"My God! I hope he's alive! I wronged him when we lived in England, twenty years ago."

They saw the old man had drawn the blankets over his face. The two stood a moment, awed by the thought that he might be dead. Goskin lifted the blanket, and pulled it down astonished. There was no one there!

"Gone!" cried Driscoll, wildly.

"Gone!" echoed Goskin, pulling out his cash-drawer. "Ten thousand dollars in the sack, and the Lord knows how much loose change in the drawer!"

The next day the boys got out, followed a horse's tracks through the snow, and lost them in the trail leading toward Pioche.

There was a man missing from the camp. It was the three-card monte man, who used to deny point-blank that he could play the scale. One day they found a wig of white hair, and called to mind when the "stranger" had pushed those locks back when he looked toward the ceiling for inspiration, on the night of December 24, 1861.[2]

⇒*Short Stories* (1886), 1–9

2. This date is at variance with the date of 1858 in the first line. In some later printings of this story, the final date is emended to 1858 to remove the inconsistency. This "correction," however, has a problem of its own; Pioche did not exist before 1864. It grew rapidly and by 1873 its population was about six thousand. Both 1858 and 1861 are therefore unsatisfactory as dates. Possibly, a date of 1868 would be more satisfactory, but without Davis's authority to make that change, the editor is allowing the original dates to stand and the errors to remain as minor flaws in a story whose beauty and power transcend them.

Sister Celeste

C. C. Goodwin

Charles Carroll Goodwin (1832–1917) arrived on the Comstock early in the 1860s after varied experiences as a schoolteacher, lawyer, rancher, and miner. He served as a probate and district judge for several years and was thereafter known as "Judge." An attempt to enter politics was unsuccessful, but in 1874, after Joe Goodman sold the *Territorial Enterprise* to his arch-foe, William Sharon, Goodwin was given editorial duties on the paper by Sharon. Later, he was made editor. In 1880, Goodwin moved to Salt Lake City, Utah, to edit the *Salt Lake Daily Tribune*, which he subsequently purchased and managed outspokenly for most of the rest of his life. Goodwin was a loyal friend, even though his loyalty sometimes caused him to excessively downplay the actions of erring "captains of industry," and he retained a lifelong fondness for the Comstock. "Sister Celeste" appeared by itself in the *Tribune* and was subsequently incorporated into chapter 13 of his novel, *The Comstock Club* (1891).

In one of the mountain towns of Northern California, a good many years ago, while yet good women, compared to the number of the men, were so disproportionately few, suddenly one day upon the street, clad in the unattractive garb of a Sister of Charity, appeared a woman whose marvelous loveliness the coarse garments and uncouth hood peculiar to the order could not conceal. There was a Sisters' Hospital in the place, and this nun was one of the devoted women who had come to minister to the sick in that Hospital. She was of medium size and height, and despite her shapeless garments, it was easy to see that her form was beautiful. The hand that carried a basket was a delicate one; under her unsightly hood glimpses of a brow as white as a planet's light could be caught; the coarse shoes upon her feet were three sizes too large. When she raised her eyes, from the inner depths a light like that of kindly stars shone out, and, though a Sister of Charity, there was something about her lips which seemed to say that of all famines, a famine of kisses was hardest to endure. There was a

STATELY, KINDLY DIGNITY

In her mien, but in all her ways there was a dainty grace, which, upon the hungry eyes of the miners of that mountain town, shone like enchantment. She could not have been more than twenty years of age.

It was told that she was known as "Sister Celeste," that she had recently come to the Western Coast, it was believed from France, and that was all that was known of her. When the Mother Superior at the Hospital was questioned about the new Sister, she simply answered: "Sister Celeste is a Sister now, she will be a glorified saint by and by." The first public appearance of Sister Celeste in the town was one Sunday afternoon, when she emerged from the Hospital and started to carry some delicacy to a poor, sick woman— a Mrs. De Lacy, who lived at the opposite end of the town from the Hospital; so to visit her the Nun was obliged to walk almost the whole length of the one long, crooked street which, in the narrow canyon, included all the business portion of the town. When the Nun started out from the Hospital, the town was full of miners, as was the habit in those days on Sunday afternoons, and as the Sister passed along the street

HUNDREDS OF EYES

Were bent upon her. She seemed unconscious of the attention she was attracting; had she been walking in her sleep she could not have been more composed.

Many were the comments made as she passed out of the hearing of different groups of men. One big, rough miner, who had just accepted an invitation to drink, caught sight of the vision, watched the Sister as she passed, and then said to the companion who had asked him: "Excuse me, Bob; I have a feeling as though my soul had just partaken of the Sacrament; no more gin for me today." Said another: "It is a fearful pity. That woman was born to be loved, and to love somebody better than nine hundred and ninety out of every thousand could. Her occupation is, in her case, a sin against nature. Every hour her heart must protest against the starvation which it feels; every day she must feel upon her robes the clasp of little hands which are not to be." One boisterous miner, a little in his cups, watched until the Sister disappeared around a bend in the crooked street, and then cried out: "Did you see her, boys? That is the style of a woman that a man could die for, and smile while dying, Oh! Oh!" Then drawing from his belt a buckskin purse, he held it aloft and shouted: "Here are eighty ounces of the cleanest dust ever mined in Bear Gulch; it's all I have in the world, but I will

GIVE THE LAST GRAIN

To any bruiser in this camp who will look crooked at that Sister when she comes back this way, and let me see him do it. In just a minute and a half there would not be enough left of him for the Coroner to gather in a sack and sit on." After that, daily, for all the following week, Sister Celeste was seen going to and returning from the sick woman's house. It suddenly grew to be a habit with everybody to uncover their heads as Sister Celeste came by.

Sunday came around again, and it was noticed that on that morning the Nun went early to visit her charge, and remained longer than usual. On her return, when just about opposite the main saloon of the place, a kindly, elderly gentleman, who was universally known and respected, ventured to cross the path of the Sister, and addressed her as follows:

"I beg pardon, good Sister, but you are attending upon a sick person. We understand that it is a woman; may I not ask if we can not in some way assist you and your patient?" A faint flush swept over the glorious face of Sister Celeste as she raised her eyes, but simply and frankly, and with a slight French accent, she answered:

"The lady, kind sir, is very ill. Unless, in some way, we can manage to remove her to the Hospital, where she can have an evenly warmed room, and close nursing, I fear she will not live; but she is penniless, and we are very poor, and, moreover, I do not see how she can be moved, for there are no carriages."

She spoke with perfect distinctness, notwithstanding the slight foreign accent. The accent was no impediment; rather, from her lips, it gave her words a rhythm like music.

The man raised his voice, "Boys," he shouted, "there is a suffering woman up the street; she is

VERY DESTITUTE AND VERY ILL,

And must be removed to the Hospital. The first thing required is some money." Then taking off his hat with one hand, with the other he took from his pocket a twenty dollar piece; he put the money in the hat, then he sprang upon a low stump that was standing by the trail, and added: "I start the subscription; those who have a trifle that they can spare, will please pass around this way and drop the trifle, as they pass, into the hat." Then Sister Celeste had a new experience. In an instant she was surrounded by a shouting, surging, struggling crowd, all eager to contribute. There was a babel of voices, but for once a California crowd was awakened to full roar without an oath being heard. The boys could not swear in the presence of Sister Celeste. In a few minutes between seven and eight hundred dollars was raised. It was poured out of the hat into a buckskin purse; the purse was tied, and handed by the man who first addressed her, to Sister Celeste, with the remark that it was for her poor, and that when she needed more the boys would "stand in."

Again the Nun raised her eyes and in a low voice which trembled a little she said: "Please salute the gentlemen, and say to them, that God will keep the account." The man turned around and with an awkward laugh said: "Boys! I am authorized, by one of His angels, to say that, for your contribution, God has taken down your names, and given you credit."

Then a wild fellow cried out from the crowd:

"Three cheers for the angel!"

The cheers rang out like the braying of a thousand trumpets in accord. Then, in hoarse under-tones, a voice shouted "Tiger," and the deep-toned old-day California "Tiger" rolled up the hillsides like an ocean roar.[1] It would have startled an ordinary woman, but Sister Celeste was looking at the purse, and it is doubtful if she heard it at all. Then, the first speaker called from the crowd eight men by name, and said:

"You were all married men in the States, and for all that I know to the contrary, were decent, respectable gentlemen. As

MASTER OF CEREMONIES,

I delegate you, as there are no carriages in this camp, to go to the sick woman's house, and carry her to the Hospital, while the good Sister proceeds in advance, and makes a place for her." This was agreed to, and the Sister was told that in half an hour she might expect her patient.

Then she turned away, the crowd watching her, and remarking that her usual stately step seemed greatly quickened. Long after, the Mother Superior related that when Sister Celeste reached the Hospital on that day she fell sobbing into the Mother's arms, and when she could command her voice, said: "Those shaggy men, that I thought were all tigers, are all angels disguised. Oh Mother! I have seen them as Moses and Elias were when the Master was transfigured."

The eight men held a brief consultation in the street; then going to a store, they bought a pair of heavy white blankets, an umbrella, and four pick-handles. Borrowing a packer's needle and some twine, they proceeded to sew the pick-handles into the sides of the blankets, first rolling the handles

---

1. "Tiger" was a special cheer.

around once or twice in the edges of the blanket. They then proceeded to the sick woman's house; one went in first, and told the woman, gently, what they had come to do, and bade her have no fears: that she was to be moved so gently that, if she would close her eyes, she would not know anything about it. The others were called in; the blanket was laid upon the floor; the bed was lifted with its burden from the bedstead and laid on the blankets, the covers were neatly tucked under the mattress; four men seized the pick-handles at the sides,

LIFTED THE BED,

Woman and all from the floor; a fifth man stepped outside, raised the umbrella, and held it above the woman's face, and so, as gently as ever a mother rocked her babe to sleep, the sick woman was carried the whole length of the street to the Hospital, where Sister Celeste and the Mother Superior received her.

Then all hands went up town and talked the matter over, and I am afraid that some of them drank a little, but the burden of all the talk, and all the toasts, was Sister Celeste.

After that the Nun was often seen going on her errands of mercy, and it is true that some men who had been rough, and who had drank hard for months previous to the coming of the Sister, grew quiet in their lives, and ceased going to the saloons.

One day a most laughable event transpired. Two men got quarreling in the street, which in a moment culminated in a fight. The friends of the respective men joined in, and soon there was a general fight in which perhaps thirty men were engaged. When it was at its height (and such a fight meant something), Sister Celeste suddenly turned the sharp bend of the street, and came into full view not sixty yards from where the melee was raging in full fury. One of the fighters saw her, and made a sound between a hiss and a low whistle, a peculiar sound of alarm and warning, so significant that all looked up.

In an instant the men clapped their hands into their side pockets, and commenced moving away, some of them whistling low, and dancing as they went, as though the whole thing was but

A JOVIAL LARK.

When Sister Celeste reached the spot, a moment afterward, the street was entirely clear. The men washed their faces; some wag began to describe the comical scene which they made when they concluded that the street under certain circumstances was no good place for a fight; good humor was restored, the chief contestants shook hands with perfect cordiality, a drink of reconciliation was ordered all around, and when the glasses were emptied a man cried out: "Fill up once more boys. I want you to drink with me the health of the only capable peace officer that we have ever had in town—'Sister Celeste.' " The health was drunk with enthusiasm.

The winter came on at length, and there was much sickness. Sister Celeste redoubled her exertions; she was seen at all hours of the day, and was met sometimes, as late as midnight, returning from her watch beside a sick bed.

The town was full of rough men; some of them would cut or shoot at a word; but Sister Celeste never felt afraid. Indeed since that Sabbath when the subscription was taken up in the street, she had felt that nothing sinister could ever happen to her in that place. Once, however, she met a jolly miner who had been in town too long, and who had started for home a good deal the worse for liquor. She met him in a lonely place, where the houses had been a few days previous burned down on both sides of the street. Emboldened by rum, the man stepped directly in front of the nun, and said:

"My pretty Sister, I will give your Hospital a thousand dollars for one kiss."

The Sister never wavered; she raised her calm, undaunted eyes to the face of the man; an incandescent whiteness warmed upon her cheek, giving to her striking face unwonted splendor; for a moment she held the man under the spell of her eyes, then stretching her right arm out toward the sky, slowly and with infinite sadness in her tones, said:

"If your mother is watching from there, what will she think of her son?" The man fell on his knees, crying, "Pardon!" and Sister Celeste, with her accustomed stately step, passed slowly on her way.

Next day, an envelope directed to Sister Celeste was received at the Hospital. Within there was nothing but a certificate of deposit from a local bank for

ONE THOUSAND DOLLARS,

made to the credit of the Hospital.

On another occasion the Nun had a still harder trial to bear. A young man was stricken with typhoid fever, and sent to the Hospital. He was a rich and handsome man. He had come from the East only a few weeks before he was taken down. His business in California was to settle the estate of an uncle who had died some months previous, leaving a large property.

When carried to the Hospital, Sister Celeste was appointed his nurse. The fever ran twenty-one days, and when it left him, finally, he lay helpless as a child and hovering on the very threshold of the grave for days.

With a sick man's whim, no one could do anything for him but Sister

Celeste. She had to move him on his pillows, give him his medicines, and such food as he could bear. In lifting him, her arms were often around him, and her bosom was so near his breast that she could feel the throbbing of his heart.

As health slowly returned the young man watched the nurse, with steadily increasing interest. At length the time came when the physician said that the patient would require no further attention, but that he ought, so soon as possible, to go to the seaside, where the salt air would furnish him the tonic that he needed most.

When the physician went away, the young man said: "Sister Celeste, sit down, and let us talk." She obeyed. "Let me hold your hand," he said. "I want to tell you of my mother and my home, and with your hand in mine it will seem as though the dear ones there were by my side." She gave him her hand in silence. Then he told her of his beautiful home in the east, of the love that had always been a benediction in that home; of his mother and little sister, of their daily life, and their unbroken happiness. Insidiously,

THE STORY FLOWED ON,

Until at length he said, with returning health, his business being nearly all arranged, he should return to those who awaited, anxiously, his coming; and before Sister Celeste had any time for preparation or remonstrance, the young man added: "You have been my guardian angel; you have saved my life; the world will be all dark without you; you can serve God and humanity better as my wife, than as a lowly and poor Sister here; some women have higher destinies and nobler spheres to fill on earth than as Sisters of Charity; you were never meant to be a Nun, but a loving wife. Be mine. If it is the poor you wish to serve, a thousand shall bless you where one blesses you here; but come with me, filling my mother's heart with joy, and taking your rightful place as my wife, be my guardian angel forever."

The face of Sister Celeste was white as the pillow on which her hand lay; for a moment she seemed choking, while about her lips and eyes there was a tremulousness as though she was about to break into a storm of uncontrollable sobs. But she rallied under a tremendous effort of self-control, gently disengaged her hand from the hand that held it, rose to her feet and said:

"I ought not to have permitted this—ought not to have heard what you said. However, we must bear our cross. I do not belong to the world; but do not misjudge me. I have not always been as you see me. I can only tell you this. To a woman, now and then there comes a time when either her heart must break, or she must give it to God. I have given mine to Him. I cannot take it back. I would not if I could.

"If you suffer a little now, you will forget it with returning strength. I only ask that when you are strong and well, and far away—you will sometimes remember. The world is full of heart-aches. Comfort as many as you can. And now, God bless you, and fare well." She laid her hand a moment on his brow, then drew it down upon his cheek, where it lingered for a moment like a caress, and then she was gone. After that the Mother Superior became the young man's nurse until he left the Hospital. He tried hard, but he never saw Sister Celeste again. While he remained in the place she ceased to appear on the street.

ANOTHER YEAR PASSED BY

And Sister Celeste grew steadily in the love of the people. With the winter months small pox broke out in the village. The country was new, the people careless and no particular alarm was felt until the breaking out of ten cases in a single day awakened the people to the fact that a contagion was upon them.

Sister Celeste, almost without rest, labored night and day until the violence of the epidemic had passed; then she was stricken. She recovered, but was shockingly pitted by the disease.

She was in a darkened room, and how to break to her the news of her disfigurement was a matter of sore distress to her sister nuns. But one day to a Sister who was watching by her bed side, she suddenly said:

"I am almost well now, Sister; throw back the blinds and bring me a mirror!" and with a gentle gaiety that never forsook her when with her sister nuns, she added: "It is time that I began to admire myself."

The nun opened the blinds, brought the glass, laid it upon the bed, and sat down trembling.

Sister Celeste, without glancing at the mirror, laid one hand upon it, and shading her eyes with the other hand, for a moment was absorbed in silent prayer. Then she picked up the glass and held it before her face. The watching nun, in an agony of suspense and hardly breathing, waited.

After a long, earnest look, without a shade passing over her face, Sister Celeste laid down the glass, clasped her hands and said:

"God be praised! now all is peace; never, never again will my face bring sorrow to my heart."

The watching nun sank sobbing to her knees, but as she did so, she saw, on the face of the stricken woman, a smile which she declared was radiant as an angel's robes.

With the return of health Sister Celeste again took up the work of mercy, and for a few months more her presence

WAS A BENEDICTION

To the place. At last, however, it began to be noticed that her presence on the street was less frequent than formerly, and soon an unwelcome rumor began to circulate that she was ill. The truth of this was soon confirmed. Then, day by day for several weeks, the report was that she was growing weaker and weaker, and finally one morning it was known that she was dead.

A lady of the place who was a beneficiary of the hospital, and to whom Sister Celeste was greatly attached, was permitted to watch by the dying couch of the glorified Nun. Of the closing moment she gave the following account:

For an hour the dying woman had been motionless as though hushed in peaceful sleep. When the first rays of the morning sun struck on the window, a lark lighted on a tree near the window and in a full voice caroled his greeting to the new born day. Then the Sister opened her eyes, already fringed by the death-frost, and in faint and broken sentences said:

"A delicious vision has been sent me, *Deo Gratias!* In the vision, every act meant in kindness that I have ever performed had become a flower giving off an incense ineffable. These had been woven into a diadem for me. Every word said in comfort or sympathy that I have ever spoken had been set to marvelously sweet music which voices and harps, not of this world, were singing and playing while I was being crowned; every tear of mine shed in pity had become a flashing gem. These were woven into the robes of light that they drew around me. A glass was brought and held before me; from face and bosom the cruel scars were all gone; to eye and brow and cheek the luster and enchantment of youth had come back, and near, all radiant"—

The eyes, with a look of inexpressibly joyous surprise and happiness in them, grew fixed, and all was still save that the lark outside the casement once more warbled his morning song.

Among the few effects left by Sister Celeste was found a package addressed to the lady who had watched through the closing hours of her life. This was brought to her by the Mother Superior. On being opened, there was found within it another package tied with a ribbon of black. This, in turn, was opened, and a large double locket was revealed. On one side was the picture of a young man in the uniform of

A FRENCH COLONEL.

From the other side a picture had evidently been removed, for there were scratches on the case, which seemed as though made by a too impetuous use of some sharp instrument. On the outer edge of the case was a half round hole, such as bullets make, and there were dark stains on one side of the locket. Below the picture, in the delicate hand-writing of a woman, were the words: "Henri. Died at Magenta."

The lady showed the locket to the Mother Superior. Tears came to the faded eyes of the devoted woman.

"Now God be praised!" said she. "Three nights since, as I watched the poor child, I heard her murmur that name in her fevered sleep, and I was troubled, for I feared she was dreaming of the youth she nursed back to life in the hospital. It was not so; her work was finished on earth; she was nearing the sphere where love never brings sorrow; her soul was already outstretching its wings to join"—the poor nun stopped, breathed short and hard, and incoherently began to tell her beads.

The lady, on pretense of looking for the last time on the face of Celeste, slipped the locket beneath the folds of the winding sheet and left it concealed upon the pulseless breast.

The whole population of the place were sorrowing mourners at the obsequies of Sister Celeste, and for years afterward, every morning, in summer and winter, upon her grave a dressing of fresh flowers could be seen.

On the day of the funeral the miners made up a purse and gave it to Mrs. De Lacy, the consideration being that every day for a year the grave of the Sister should be flower-dressed. The contract was renewed yearly until Mrs. De Lacy herself died. In the mean time, a wild rose and a cypress had been planted at the head and foot of the grave, and they keep watch there still, and shield the lowly couch from storm and sun. One who passed there last year heard, from under the rose bush at the head of the grave, a mourning dove calling her mate, and the answer came back, from where the trees grew dense a little way off, and the call and the answer were low and sweet and plaintive, as though there lingered still around the spot a tender sorrow for the beautiful dead.

Salt Lake City Daily Tribune, April 5, 1884

My Friend, the Editor

Sam P. Davis

There is a kernel of truth to this story, although Davis took many liberties with the facts and added fictional details of his own. It is based on the participation of James W. E. Townsend, one of the Comstock's most accomplished liars, in a scam to sell worthless mining properties to unsuspecting investors in England. Townsend, aka "Truthful James," aka "Lying Jim," single-handedly operated an abandoned press near a deserted mining town and out of his imagination created a mythical town with active mines, peopled it with imaginary citizens, and wrote advertisements for imaginary businesses that appeared in a paper he regularly sent to his sponsors in England. Townsend and his sponsors were eventually arrested, but Townsend—already famous and admired for his talent at creating ingenious lies—somehow escaped punishment.[1] This tale also belongs to the small subgenre of stories about the difficulty of publishing newspapers in the West. The complete fictionality of the *Index* explains both the rash "candor" of the editor and why he was not "mobbed or murdered."

⊷⊷ ⊶⊶

The most extraordinary newspaper publication I have ever had any knowledge of was a paper published up in the Sierra range about fifteen years ago called the Manganetus Index.

The publication alluded to had mysteriously fallen into my mailbox in San Francisco for over a year, and it was always a welcome arrival.

It was neatly printed, carried several columns of live advertisements and had a bright, bustling air about it that always gave me a very favorable impression of the little town of Manganetus, as well as of the man who edited the paper.

1. See Richard A. Dwyer and Richard E. Lingenfelter's account of Townsend in their edited volume, *Lying on the Eastern Slope: James Townsend's Comic Journalism on the Mining Frontier*, 107–19.

He took a decided stand on all the current topics of the day, and on every-thing transpiring in the town where his paper was published he carried candor to the verge of rashness.

I never saw a paper edited with such absolute fearlessness, and I often wondered why it was that the editor was not some time mobbed or murdered.

At last my business took me in the vicinity of Manganetus and I decided to make the editor a call.

It was fast coming on nightfall as I neared the spot where the town was located, and I spurred my horse up the steep mountain, thinking of the warm bed and excellent supper I should soon be enjoying.

My mind was full of the Slavin House, a hotel of very superior accommodations, which advertised liberally in the Index, and whose royal provender and home comforts the little paper was never weary of describing.

"Only a mile more," I said to myself, as I thumped my weary beast with a good sized stick, and after another mile I repeated my observations, and so the poor horse went on checking off miles and miles, while I kept trying to persuade myself that each mile was the last.

Strange, I thought, that I could see no lights ahead. I strained my eyes for the welcome twinkle from the cottage windows that in the darkness tell the traveler of the town, but the night crept on, a little faster perhaps than the horse, and still I was alone.

Presently I came to a log cabin and my heart rose as I saw the light gleaming through the chinks. Dismounting I walked, stiff and lame, to the cabin and hammered on the door.

A little, bent-up man, with a wrinkled, leathery face, came to answer and as he opened the door cautiously, I noticed that he had a cocked pistol in his hand. Seeing the pistol I said to myself: "Here is civilization."

After the little man with the big pistol had surveyed my famished face and tired horse, he opened the door a little wider, and then, swinging it back, with a smile somewhat apologetic in its character, invited me in.

"How far to Manganetus?" I asked.

He looked at me in a rather queer way, and then bit his under lip, as if nipping a smile in the bud.

"Is it far from here? Can I reach it to-night?"

"Hardly think you can make it to-night," he replied with a tone that puzzled me somewhat; "can't you stay all night?" he added. "Better stay; you can't possibly make Manganetus to-night."

I accepted the invitation with alacrity. My horse being provided for I was soon absorbing the heat of a cheery fire and listening to the conversation of my new acquaintance. He was a man of very fluent expression, and possessed a wonderful fund of information on scores of topics not ordinarily discussed by men who occupied log cabins in the mountains.

While wondering who this odd character could be I heard a monotonous noise in the next room, and certainly thought I heard the familiar sound of some one rapidly folding newspapers.

My ear did not deceive me, for in a few moments a pleasant-faced little girl appeared and handed my companion a paper, which he at once passed over to me. It was damp from the press, and as I opened it I read the title.

"The Manganetus Index. By industry we thrive. Devoted to the material interests of Manganetus. Subscription $5.00 per annum, payable in advance."

My host smiled as he handed me the paper.

"Then the town is here," I said. "Let me go to the hotel. I do not desire to trespass upon the hospitality of a stranger."

"You will remain here, sir," he replied. "I blush to confess it, but this is the town of Manganetus, and the cabin you now occupy is the only habitation for twenty miles."

I stared at the man in astonishment.

"You may well be puzzled," he continued. "But I will explain. There is a group of mines near here which certain capitalists of San Francisco are anxious to place upon the London market. They have hired me to advocate these mines, and it is part of my bargain to run my paper in such a way that the London readers will think that a large town is flourishing in the mountains. See?"

I nodded vaguely and he went on:

"My imagination is not sluggish, and so I manufacture all I write. I leave no stone unturned to make the mythical city of Manganetus a live, bustling town. You will find in this issue a public meeting called to discuss the question of a new bridge across a stream that exists only in the columns of the Index. Here is the wife of a prominent mining superintendent eloping with a member of the city council; here is a runaway team, knocking the smithereens out of a cigar store. You will note the advertisement of the cigar store in another column.

"Here is the killing of 'Texas Pete' and the investigation of his death by a coroner's jury. The cause of the shooting was a dispute relative to the ownership of a mining location of fabulous richness. There is also in another portion of the paper a legal summons advertised, calling on a co-owner (one of the principals in the affray) to do his assessment work or lose his interest. All my work dovetails nicely in, has a plausible look and shows no flaw, yet it is all absolutely made from whole cloth."

"This is the most extraordinary thing I ever heard of."

"This country is full of extraordinary things," he replied quietly.

"Where does this edition go?" I asked.

"Clara, bring me the mailing list," he said to the child.

I glanced over the list and saw that it embraced the leading banking houses of London and New York, as well as the centres of finance and mining. My own name was oddly enough on the list. About a hundred copies were mailed, and every one went where it would do the most good.

I found that my friend edited the paper and did the typesetting, and his daughter was learning the typographic art.

"I have no companions except my little daughter—and the town of Manganetus," he added with a smile.

I passed a very comfortable night. The roar of the wind through the pines and the rocking of the cabin in the blast had a deliciously soothing effect, and I lay in the warm bed thinking and resting until almost morning before I slept.

My friend, the editor, was very talkative at breakfast. He never alluded to his name, but he told me more of the paper and the enjoyment he had in building up a town in the clouds from a purely imaginative basis.

"To-morrow," said he, "I will ride my horse to the nearest mail station, which is the hollow of a dead tree ten miles from here, and there I will deposit my bundle of papers until the mail buckboard comes along and takes them. In a few weeks they are being read in London and New York, and the parties in each of these cities who are handling the sale of these mining properties are backed up handsomely by my editorial statements."

Next day he set out with his bundle of papers tied behind him. He said it was only ten miles and he would come back soon, and that he would leave me and the little girl to run the office.

In about an hour the sky had a lowering aspect and snow began to fall. It came lightly and gently at first and melted away as it touched the rocks and chaparral, but in a little while it commenced to stay where it fell, and the full grey and brown of the landscape changed to a dead white.

Alice, the little girl who was sweeping out the office, ceased her work and a look of uneasiness came over her face as she gazed out of the window.

The snow thickened in the air and the specks of black, made by dead branches and rocks protruding through the white, were soon obliterated, and as the day waned the eye fell on nothing but an expanse of white which was everywhere. We built a fire when the night fell and Alice cooked a supper which we ate in silence.

I felt a strange sensation, being alone in the mountains with this child, and a snowstorm hemming us in every hour.

She said she had no idea of going to bed until her father returned, and so we sat by the fire until after midnight.

Her face was pale and anxious—a weary, worn-out face it was—and then the tears came into her eyes—eyes that could hardly remain open from weariness.

I could think of nothing to do, and my efforts to assure her that all was well were only met by a look sadder than the last, and so the hours dragged along until nearly two, when she started up as her quick ear caught the muffled fall of a horse's footsteps in the snow as it stumbled on some firewood in front of the cabin.

She bounded to the door with a glad look in her face, and flinging it open, held the candle over her head, and giving forth a little cry, reeled back, and then sinking to the floor, fainted.

I looked out and saw the horse standing there riderless, and, what puzzled me considerably, another horse, tied behind it. There was but a light fall of snow upon the saddle of the first horse, while on the other there was much more, and this I took to mean that the rider had but recently fallen. I lifted the girl on to a bed, and, lighting a lantern, went out. I brushed the snow off the saddle of the leading horse, and started, as I found marks of blood upon it.

I followed the trail back, and not 200 yards from the house I stumbled on to a man in the snow. He groaned with pain as I lifted him on my shoulder, but after a hard pull I got him to the cabin, struggling most of the way in the darkness, for the lantern went out soon after I started. When I laid him on the floor Alice came to herself again, and we spread some blankets and bear skins before the fire and stretched the wounded man upon them.

He was soon able to speak, and said he had become benumbed with the cold and while in this condition had fallen off his horse upon a jagged rock, which had caused him severe injuries. His daughter listened in silence to his story, and I, remembering the blood stains on the saddle, was silent also.

His arm was terribly swollen, and when we cut away the bloody sleeve of his coat, there was discovered the track of a pistol ball. There was no mistaking it, and warming up under the influence of meat and hot brandy, he made a cleaner breast of his adventure. He said that he had been belated by the storm and a few miles from his cabin a highwayman had stopped him in the road. After receiving the ball in his arm he had returned the fire and his man dropped dead in the snow.

He took the horse and kept on his way home, when at last, faint from the loss of blood, he had fallen from his horse and remained in the snow until rescued.

We managed to make him quite comfortable, and the next morning he asked me to take the horses back of the cabin and feed them. Under his direction I went down a path about a hundred yards behind the house, making it only after considerable difficulty, for I had to clear away the snow, and there, behind some great rocks, was a good-sized barn well filled with hay, and, what struck me as stranger still, five very fine looking horses in the stalls. A few yards from the door was a bubbling spring.

After feeding and watering the animals I returned to the cabin and noticed that the barn was entirely hidden from sight.

This circumstance, and the presence of the fine horses in such a locality, struck me as rather odd, but I did not give the matter much thought at the time.

He invited me to spend a few weeks with him, and asked me to edit his paper for him while his wound was healing. I was unable to resist the fascination of such a novelty, and under his direction I wrote enough for the next week's issue.

The copy accumulated on the hook, when it suddenly dawned upon me that there was no one setting it up, and so it was that being a printer myself, I fell heir to the typographical department also.

Between editing the paper and setting the type I had my hands full. We had a good stock of provisions and although the snow was so deep that we could not get our papers to the mails, we went right ahead with the edition of one hundred each week, for the wounded publisher said if they reached London by spring all would be well.

"Give the mining managers particular fits about not running the bullion product up to its full capacity," were his directions one day. "Charge them with covering up bonanzas; also speak of the charming weather and throw in a few quartz-mill accidents. All these things help to paint the scene red. Have a four-in-hand run over a child, and print some obituary poetry and then pack them into the Catholic Church to suffocate during the funeral. Have the organist play one of Mozart's requiems—that looks civilized—and also give the report of a vestry meeting of St. Peter's Episcopal Church, with the superintendent of a railroad company as the Senior Warden."

I wrote up these items as the editor lay there nursing his wound and making suggestions, and so the winter was soon whiled away. The spring came in February, and by that time he was up and doing his own typesetting.

"We must write up a big Washington's birthday celebration, with civic parade, grand ball, and all that, and I guess I'll put you down as delivering the oration." We worked on the article until evening, filling up the line of march and exercises with all the prominent people in California and Nevada that we could think of.

Each night before Alice went to bed she knelt down at a chair, with her face to the fire, and said her prayers.

She had just knelt and bowed her head when the door opened and two men came in silently, and in an instant they had my editorial friend covered with six-shooters.

They made no sound, and the child, unconscious of what had happened, still remained on her knees, her head bowed in prayer.

"Gentlemen," said the editor in a whisper, "I am your prisoner, but don't take me until after she goes to bed."

He advanced to the two men and looked into the pistol barrels without a tremor. Pitching his voice still lower, he continued:

"Don't let her witness this scene. Put up your weapons until she leaves the room."

The two men, lowering their revolvers, put them out of sight sheepishly, and then the editor motioned to them to take off their hats. Both did so and there was nothing heard for a few moments but the child's whisperings to heaven.

When she rose she turned and started with surprise as she faced the two men, who were still standing, with half-bowed, uncovered heads.

"Good night my child," said the editor, as he leaned over so that her arms might clasp his neck as he kissed her. At this, one of the men, the elder of the two, stepped forward and asked the same privilege.

The father led the child forward and the man kissed its forehead very tenderly, while the other stood there motionless.

The father led the child to the door of its room, kissed it again, and closed the door softly.

Then, like a flash, he bounded in to the center of the room, and had both the visitors covered with a six-shooter.

We all stood transfixed at his appearance.

There was a look of fiery determination in his face that made his captors of a few moments ago shrink back, but the one nearest the door suddenly sprang through it, and then my friend the editor knew that the fight had opened.

"Drop your gun quick," he said to the remaining man. "Throw it to this man. But, hold on, let him take it from your pocket."

The man's hand that had moved toward his weapon fell away.

"Hurry up," he said to me impatiently, "we've no time to lose."

I stepped over to the man and took his weapon from his pocket, and I had hardly done so when the window of the cabin was broken in and the man outside sent in one hurriedly aimed shot.

My friend the editor opened a lively fire and I covered the strange man in the cabin, but did not shoot. In fact I was puzzled in trying to figure out just what to do, as these men seemed officers of the law.

After firing three shots through the window uselessly he sprang through the back door and beckoned me to follow. I did so mechanically, in response to his impatient gesture, and he said hurriedly:

"Keep these hounds off me a few moments till I can mount a horse and you be with Alice at the —————— hotel in Sacramento in one week from to-day."

He dashed down the trail to the barn, and for a moment I heard the clatter of hoofs as his horse started and that was the last I ever saw of him.

I stood for a moment where he left me, with the weapon still in my hand, and then went back to the cabin. Alice stood in her nightclothes by the fire shivering and frightened, and the smoke of the pistol shots still rose lazily among the rafters. The man who had fired the shots through the window came in, and, covering me, asked me to throw up my hands.

I cast the weapon I held on the floor and invited him to sit down.

He declined to talk until he had induced Alice to retire again, and after she had done so we could hear her sobbing in her room. Then the two men and myself sat by the fire and talked matters over. They said that my friend the editor was a noted desperado and horse-thief, and that he was publishing a paper in the mountains to cover up his real business. They also had learned that there was some sort of a mining syndicate in San Francisco backing the man, but they were satisfied that the San Francisco people knew nothing of his real character. He had been a newspaper writer and traveled under many aliases.

Early in the winter he had shot the Sheriff of Alpine County on the highway, when resisting arrest, and taken his horse. I, of course, remembered the night in question, but I had been so well housed by the queer character during the winter that I kept my own counsel. The sheriff and his deputy were at first disposed to hold me as accessory, but after I had told my story and established my identity by letters, etc., they dropped the matter.

Next day we all started for the nearest town, twenty miles away, with the horses and Alice, leaving the newspaper office and cloud-reared town of Manganetus. On the day specified by my friend, the editor, when he left so hurriedly, I was at the hotel in Sacramento. When I registered my name, the clerk handed me a letter. It read as follows:

My Dear Sir: Leave Alice in charge of the clerk. Her room has been waiting her for several days. Do not stop here at all and never expect to see me again, although I long to see you. As you read this I am in San

Francisco. Accept my thanks for all you have done for me. I know that you are too much of a gentleman to throw a straw in the way of my liberty. Alice does not know of my past and I hope you will forget what has happened.

I had a passion for horses which I could not overcome, and it came near ruining me. But I am done with horses and newspapers forever.

Your friend,

THE EDITOR.

I folded the letter, bade Alice good-by, and the clerk led her away.

A few days afterwards in San Francisco I met a man who wanted to sell me a promising mine.

He showed me a map of it, and then taking a newspaper clipping from his pocket, asked me to read it, as it was a good description of the property.

It was from the Index. I recognized the type at once. As for the article, I had written it myself.

Nevada Magazine 1:1 (August 1899): 23–31
[San Francisco Examiner, July 21, 1889]

The Eagles' Nest

Dan De Quille

Few readers of this remarkable story are left unaffected by its gripping drama. De Quille was psychologically astute and wrote a number of memorable tales and sketches that reflect a sympathetic understanding of individuals suffering from aberrant impulses or delusions. With a mastery of verisimilitude approaching that of Poe, in this story he not only creates a believable account of reckless derring-do followed by repentance but also induces the reader into experiencing vertigo and a range of emotions along with the narrator. De Quille was also one of the very few Comstock authors who seriously questioned the acquisition of wealth as a goal.

⋆⊷⊷⊷ ⊶⊶⊶⋆

In the upper part of its course the South Yuba River dashes and boils down through a tremendous cañon for a distance of many miles. Everywhere from the town of Washington upward the mountains on both sides of the river, north and south, rise to such a height that one must "look twice" to see their tops. But down near Washington the inclosing mountains are not vertical, as are the walls of rock up where the river breaks down from the main range of the high Sierras. Up there the waters of the river thunder strong between perpendicular walls hundreds of feet in height.

It is above this mighty cañon that the waters of the river were, in the early days, turned into what was then known as Kidd's Ditch,—I suppose the same that is now called the South Yuba Canal. In constructing this ditch it was necessary to carry through the cañon a large flume. This flume had to be carried along the vertical south wall of the cañon for a great distance, at a height, in places, of from three hundred to five hundred feet above the bed of the river, and from two hundred to three hundred feet below the top of the wall, from which at several points lumber and timber were lowered by means of ropes.

The flume was supported on iron brackets, holes for which were drilled in the face of the cliff by men suspended on platforms like those used by house-painters. These platforms were lowered from above by means of a strongly anchored windlass. To construct a flume thus in mid-air was a costly and perilous work, but for gold men will venture all things,—even life.

The men working on the flume in time became accustomed to the dizzy height, and indifferent to the dangers that beset them. In the whole work only two or three lives were lost. Though the men employed upon the flume seemed to move fearlessly about in their work, one not hardened to such business could with difficulty nerve himself to venture near enough to the awful chasm to look down to where the river boiled along its bottom.

Owing to the swiftness of the current through the cañon, and to the many jutting ledges of rock, bowlders, rapids, whirls, swirls, and swashes, the water was everywhere churned into foam. Seen from the top of the cliff, the water in the channel of the river looked as white as milk.

One experienced very peculiar sensations while looking down upon the boiling and foaming waters,—a very creepy, unpleasant feeling. In looking into space above one feels all right, but on gazing into space below all is wrong; one's head seems turning upside down.

Besides this there was in the scene something weird and unnatural. But what was it? Presently it occurred to one that what made the scene uncanny was the silence,—the absence of the roar that should accompany waters so tumultuously tossed and agitated. Instead of the deafening roar and swash natural to such a scene, we only caught now and again, as brought near or wafted afar by the shifting winds, a faint and monotonous murmur,—the one note into which was merged and blended all the pouring, plunging, splashing, and dashing, so far away below.

To stand on the brink of the chasm and look down upon the wild whirl of waters at its bottom gave a man about the same uncanny feeling he would experience were he to see walls and buildings falling on all sides of him, without producing more sound than if they were walls and buildings of air,—the structures of dreamland.

It required great nerve to move to the brink of the precipice, and look down upon the white line that marked the windings of the river. No beginner could endure to stand so for many moments. Then came on a feeling that his legs were preparing for a leap into the abyss, and in spite of all the resistance his head could make, would soon plunge his body into the chasm, unless he at once turned away. This feeling begins with a sort of lifting and throbbing motion in the ground, apparently, and a tickling sensation in the soles of the feet that is very unpleasant.

One Sunday while the work of carrying the big flume through the cañon was in progress, I went with a party of half a dozen miners and others from the town of Omega to see it. We had heard so many wonderful stories about the great undertaking, the difficulties that were being overcome, and so on, that we were all anxious to see with our own eyes what was being done.

Some of us obtained on the trip such a surcharge of the peculiar sort of sensations which I have tried to describe above, that we have never since had any hankering after a repetition of them.

In going to the point where the flume-building was in progress, we procured horses and took to the main ridge above the town, where we had for nearly the whole distance a wagon road,—the Bear Valley road, I believe it was called. When opposite where the flume was going in we left the road, and taking to the forest, zigzagged down the face of the mountain to the camp of the workmen. There was not another dwelling of any kind within ten miles of the spot.

Being all young and full of fun we charged down upon the quiet camp like a band of wild Indians, and soon had the place in a considerable state of commotion, for we were received in about the same spirit as we exhibited by all who were visible about the camp. Then an irruption of visitors was not an every day occurrence.

With our party went a Mr. Van Vranken, the hotel-keeper of the town of Omega. He was the hero of our first adventure, as he came near being plunged head first into the abyss. On our arrival at the camp we had dismounted and tied our horses to some trees near the boarding-house; that is, all except Van Vranken, who being older than any other of the party, and more careful of his bones, had lagged behind executing numerous elaborate zigzags on the face of the mountain.

When Van arrived we were all out near the verge of the chasm. Seeing with us a carpenter who was an old acquaintance, Van rode directly up to our party. Shaking hands with his friend he dismounted, and stood talking with his bridle on his arm.

Van had a shepherd dog he highly prized, and this dog had come with him on the trip, as he and the horse Van rode were inseparable companions. Had the dog been left at home, he would have cried his heart out.

Now, it so happened that there were two or three cows kept at the camp, and one of these had a calf that was kept in a pen near the lodging house. As soon as Van halted and dismounted, his dog began prospecting the camp. About the first thing that attracted his attention was the calf, and he went to the pen to see it.

No sooner, however, had he reached the pen than he was discovered by the mother of the calf. The cow charged with a snort of wrath, and the dog turned tail and fled toward his friend the horse.

Seeing the yelping dog coming with the cow in full chase, the horse was startled, and throwing his head up began backing directly toward the brink of the precipice. The more Van pulled the higher the horse threw his head and the faster he backed. In running backward the horse pulled Van with him, who with feet braced was sliding along on the carpet of pine needles, quite unaware of the near proximity of the precipice.

"Look out!" "Let go the horse!" "Look out for the cañon!" cried a dozen voices, yet Van held on. Having been engaged in conversation from the moment of his arrival, he had not looked about him, and little thought he was so near a vertical precipice over seven hundred feet high.

Not heeding the babel of voices roaring at him, Van still pulled at his horse, which caused the animal to pull back all the more stubbornly, going squarely to the edge of the chasm.

"Let go the horse for Christ's sake!" yelled the carpenter, at the same time making a rush for Van and grabbing him by the coat-tails. At the very instant he did so the horse went over the brow of the cliff, the bridle luckily slipping out of Van's hands.

The horse seemed to cling to the brink a fraction of a second by his fore feet, and then disappeared. No sooner had the horse tumbled into the abyss than the dog ran to the verge and without an instant's hesitation leaped over after him.

All was over so quickly that Van hardly realized what had happened, and would have run to the brink of the chasm to look after his horse and dog had not his friend the carpenter held him, and told him of the danger. Van said afterward he thought all the time the fuss was all about some little gulley.

The next moment after saving Van the carpenter was again all excitement. "My God!" cried he, "My God! The men below! The men on the flume are all killed!" and he ran to the railing by the windlass and looked over. After a glance he turned to us and said, "Thank God, they are all right!"

We afterwards ascertained by calling down to the men that the falling horse had passed only about ten feet in front of the end of the flume where they were at work.

One of the men said: "We thought old Satan was coming with one of his imps after him!" Another said that they all very plainly "felt the wind" of the falling horse.

Looking down from the railing by the windlass we could see a black spot—the horse was black—at the edge of the milky stream. We could see nothing of the dog. We called down to the men, three hundred feet below; they said the horse was motionless, but a speck that was probably the dog seemed to show some motion at times.

As the horse was in a place that could not be reached except by a tramp of five miles up the river to where a descent into the cañon might be made, Van left ten dollars to be given to any one among the workmen who would bring out his bridle and saddle, and send them to Nevada City at the first opportunity. The man was also to bring out the dog, if he were not hurt beyond hope of recovery.

I may say right here that the man who the next day descended into the cañon found the dog with his back and both hind legs broken. The poor brute had dragged himself to the head of the dead horse, beside which he lay. He greeted the workman with glad barks. In order to give the dog a last gratification the man gave him all the water he could drink, and then put a bullet through his head.

The windlass and railing of which I have spoken were on a platform of timbers of large size and about seventy-five feet in length. The ends—there were a dozen logs—had been pushed out five or six feet over the brink of the precipice, while the "inshore" ends were anchored far back from the bank, and weighted with cribs of stone. When we had been shown this place, we could in safety stand and look down into the chasm.

As we were about starting for home, the men at the flume camp told us that about a mile and a half down the river was to be seen the nest of a pair of eagles, in which were twin eaglets. They said we might return that way and see the nest, which was on a scrub cedar growing on the verge of the precipice, and projecting over the abyss.

"But," said the man, "we do not feel afraid of your carrying off our pets. The nest is over a part of the cañon that is about one thousand feet deep, and out on the branches of a nearly horizontal tree. Not a man in the State has the nerve to climb out along the trunk of that cedar and bring in the young eagles!"

We concluded to ride by the eagles' nest in returning, as it was not out of our way.

As we rode along down the river all the talk was of the eagles. "Evidently no one working on the flume dare try to get the young eagles," said Van, who had made a bargain with one of our party to go home on foot and let him ride.

So much talk was made about the feat of going after the eagles, that I at last said I was not afraid to go out after them. I had gazed down into the cañon so long from the windlass platform that I imagined I had cured myself of dread of mere depth, and had gained such control of my head that I could trust it; besides, I would not look down into the cañon. I would follow the rule of the rope-dancers, and see nothing but the trunk of the tree and the eaglets.

I was dared, hooted, and scouted. Two or three were ready to put up fifty dollars to fifty cents, and as many more one hundred dollars to one dollar, that I would not dare go out after the young eagles. I said I would consider the bets when I had seen the situation of the nest.

When we came to the nest it was seen at a glance that it could not possibly have been so placed as to be more difficult of access. The cedar grew on the very brink of a precipice, rooted in a large cleft that contained some soil. It was only about eight inches in diameter, and extended almost horizontally from the brow of the precipice, which was vertical. Out about ten feet the tree put forth several branches, which spread out like a fan. The boughs of the tree formed a sort of platform on which was the nest and the young eagles, with naught below for a distance of a thousand feet more substantial than thin air.

The eaglets seemed to be pretty well feathered, and after a critical examination of them and the situation I told my companions I would take all their bets and go out after the birds, but would not agree to bring them in, as they might perhaps fly away.

All held to their offers.

I stripped to shirt and drawers. Then even such as before had been doubters began to believe me in earnest. Bob Paxton, a brother "Buckeye," earnestly labored to dissuade me from the undertaking. He had a real brotherly regard for me, not alone on that occasion, but to the last day of his life. Poor Bob! his bones now lie in the land of the Mormon.[1]

An eagle that had been wheeling about at a height of some hundreds of feet above us—probably the mother bird—began to grow uneasy at sight of our party so near its young. It uttered several shrill shrieks as it circled above our heads. Its cry was presently answered, and we saw coming from the north, as from the top of the great pineclad mountain on the opposite side of the river toward Eureka, the mate that had been called. The two shrieking birds swooped in a manner so threatening that Bob Paxton said they would surely attack me if I ventured out near their young. He made me belt to my side a long "Arkansaw toothpick," which he always carried, and which he informed me would "cut like a razor."

The belting on of the big knife completed my preparations for the perilous

1. "Buckeye" is the nickname of someone from Ohio. This is one of several incidental autobiographical touches in this story. De Quille was from Ohio. Paxton was his father's name, and one of De Quille's brothers did immigrate to Utah, "the land of the Mormon," and die there.

adventure. My determination was to see nothing except the tree and the eaglets. By persisting in that I thought I should easily succeed in the venture. Had the tree been out on level ground, any one of our party could have climbed out to the nest in three minutes. All I had to do was to keep out of my head the awful space below. I might look upward into space, for that I was accustomed to.

I was barefooted and stripped to undershirt and drawers. A silk handkerchief was bound tightly around my head. Amid a silence that was almost breathless I advanced to the verge of the cliff, and dropping to the ground crawled astride the trunk of the little projecting cedar. I fixed my eyes on the young eagles and would see nothing else.

It was only ten feet out to the nest. Soon I was out to where the branches put forth from the trunk, and spreading fan-like formed the platform on which was the nest. I could almost reach it. The old eagles screamed nearer and nearer, and I could hear the whistling of the feathers in their wings as they swooped to and fro above my head.

The young eagles soon became alarmed. They reared up, spread their wings, and opening their great mouths began to make a hissing noise. This appeared to enrage the parent birds, and one of them came so low as to brush my head.

Thus far I had not ventured to look up toward the birds. Seated astride a pole only eight inches in diameter, I was not in a position to look aloft. Let any one make the experiment in a safe place on level ground, and he will at once discover that it is difficult to retain his balance,—to escape toppling over.

After being touched by one of the old birds I saw that it was absolutely necessary to pay some attention to them, or I should be struck on the head and knocked off my slender perch. Reaching out with my left hand to where the limbs put forth, I grasped one that was about two inches in diameter. Thus anchored I was at liberty to make some use of my right hand. I must finish the fight with the old eagles before touching the young ones.

Drawing my bowie knife, I held it above my head, and when next one of the old eagles swooped down at me I struck it somewhere on the body, cutting out a little shower of small feathers.

Either the glitter of the knife or the upward motion of my arm frightened the young eagles. Both hopped out of the nest and went fluttering downward and away. Down, down they went, their wings but half supporting them in a feeble flight that carried them toward the opposite side of the cañon, with the old birds dashing after them.

I turned my eyes to watch the course of the eaglets, and in doing so for the first time caught sight of the milky water of the river and the rock-strewn earth toward which the birds were half falling,—the earth and the stream dimly seen far, far below.

In that downward glance of a moment my eyes had taken in the awful depth that lay below me. In an instant, terror—the terror of the awful space beneath—seized and overwhelmed me. I felt impelled to pitch headlong downward into the chasm, and at once terminate the torture which knowledge of the great gulf below me inflicted upon every nerve and muscle of my frame.

The knife dropped from my hand into the abyss, and the self-command that I still retained was barely sufficient to give me such control of my senses and use of my muscles as to permit of my tightly closing my eyes, and bending forward until my breast rested upon the solid substance of the spreading branches of the tree.

That last half instinctive action was all that saved me. Had I remained upright astride of the tree trunk another moment open-eyed, I should have ended the torture that throbbed through every nerve of my body and brain, by throwing myself at once into the space below that so thrilled me.

With my breast upon the boughs and each hand firmly grasping a thick branch I lay with closed eyes, determined not to make another move until I had become composed, and regained sufficient self-possession to do what remained to be done in order to escape with my life.

The eaglets being gone, it only remained for me to make my way back to the brow of the cliff and to the firm rock. Without moving, I mentally glanced over the route. That which immediately occurred to me was that I was faced the wrong way. I could not well go backward and make a safe landing upon the brow of the cliff; I must turn and get my face toward the top of the wall.

I studied over the maneuver that would be necessary to place me in the desired position. I saw that it would involve my having for a short time both legs on one side of the trunk of the tree; that for a moment I should be seated sidewise upon it, as a woman sits upon a horse. It would be no trick at all performed on a pole in a gymnasium. It was wholly in the thousand feet of space below me that the trouble lay. I therefore determined to perform the feat of reversing my position with my eyes shut. The branches which my hands grasped were about two feet apart, which would give me a good deal of purchase.

When I felt myself thoroughly nerved for my maneuver of facing about, I accomplished it almost in an instant, that I might have not time in which to think of the perilous position it involved.

Not until I had again firmly clasped the trunk of the cedar with both hands did I venture to open my eyes, and then I directed them in advance so that they would rest upon the edge of the cliff at the root of the tree.

As I completed my reversal feat I had heard a sort of tumultuous cry from my friends on the cliff,—the first sound I had yet heard from them,—which I took to be a sort of spontaneous outburst of applause, but when I opened my eyes I saw at once that it must have been a cry of horror.

My tree was rapidly sinking,—was giving way at the roots. Now that my attention was directed to what was occurring, I could hear the cracking of small roots as the tree settled down and swung in toward the wall. I could no longer see any one on top of the cliff, for I was already several feet below its brow. I could see the earth crumbling and dropping from the brow of the cliff as the roots of the tree stretched to the ground.

Each moment I expected the tree to tear loose and carry me with it to the bottom of the abyss. Strange as it may seem, I did not in this situation experience any such feeling of terror and horror as that which for a moment overwhelmed me when I looked down after the falling eaglets. The calmness of desperation now took possession of me. There was no more of the horrible tingling and thrilling of the nerves. All would doubtless be over in a few seconds, and I was braced for the shock. I knew the worst and was prepared to endure it. I even looked down to the rocky floor of the cañon a thousand feet below without a tremor. Space gaping beneath no longer had any terrors for me. I was already no better than a dead man.

But the roots of the tree did not tear loose as I had expected to see them do. When the top of the tree had turned directly downward the roots still held, and I clung to it ten feet below the verge of the cliff. I was astride the trunk just at the point where the main boughs, spreading out like the ribs of a fan, supported the whole weight of my body; indeed, the trunk of the tree being about eight inches in diameter, I could not clasp it except with my arms as to sustain any weight.

The tree did not hang flat against the vertical face of the cliff. There were projecting branches that kept it about three feet away from the wall. In this position it stopped; and as the roots still held, I began to hope that they would continue to hold until I could be rescued; however, with the least motion or agitation it might give way at any moment.

Finding that I was not to be instantly hurled down to death, I presently ventured to lift my eyes to the brow of the cliff. I could see no one, nor could I hear the voices of my late companions. I began to fear that I was deserted. Having seen the tree sink down out of sight, they probably believed it had fallen and carried me with it to the bottom of the cañon. Not one of them would have the nerve, in view of the happenings of the day, to come to the brink and peer over in search of me.

I looked upward along the trunk of the tree, meditating as to whether an attempt to climb it would be likely to prove successful. I saw at once that to escape in that way would be impossible.

Even though I should be able to climb the trunk, I could do nothing when I came to the brow of the precipice. I also feared making even the slightest motion,—the least jar might cause the tree to give way.

My thoughts then again turned to my friends. My soul sickened at the thought that they might have gone away,—gone up to the flume camp to report the latest accident.

I was scanning the line of the cliff as far as my eyes could follow it, in the hope of seeing one of my party out at some curve, when I heard a voice far above me, in the sky, as it sounded to me, "Are you still alive and safe?" it said.

Was I "still safe?" It seemed a cruel joke.

I turned my face upward to answer, but for a short time I hesitated. I feared that my mere exertion in shouting would so agitate the small tree as to tear loose its roots. At last, however, using my voice carefully, I cried, "Can you hear me?"

"Yes, plainly," was the reply.

"Well, then, I am still alive and on the tree, but not safe!"

"Hang on," came back. "Hang on, and we will try to save you!"

I looked up. No one was visible on the verge of the wall. They were afraid to approach it; afraid to stand where I would have given worlds to have been placed. What to them seemed a place of peril would have been to me as the Rock of Ages.

Again I was left to my thoughts and fears. I did not like this seeming desertion. It appeared to me to be very cowardly in them not to show themselves and stand by me. In such a situation, even the sound of the voice of a fellow man is a comfort.

At last another voice—one that seemed almost by my side—called to me. I looked up and saw peering down at me over the brink of the precipice a face that I recognized as that of a young man named Peter Bowers.

"Hold on, as you are," said young Bowers. "My brother John has gone back to the flume camp on the best horse for a long rope. He will soon be back."

Good God! "Soon be back!" It was a mile and a half to the camp. I must wait until a man had ridden three miles. Here was a wet blanket for me.

Somehow, when I saw a face within ten feet of mine, I had felt as though I was saved. I would be up on the cliff at once. Now they were going to make me wait until a man could ride three miles before trying to try to save me. It was rascally! Why not help me at once?

"Can't you drop me the end of a lariat?" cried I.

"No. We've only got one lariat. That's tied around me and the men are holding the other end."

"What is all that for?" cried I, in astonishment.

"Why, to keep me from falling over into the cañon."

"To keep you from falling! God Lord! Why, aren't you safe enough any-where up there on the solid rock?" sneered I.

"No. I can hardly stay here with the lariat fast to my waist. My head wants to go down and my heels feel like they'd fly right up into the air in spite of all I can do!"

"What a cowardly set!" thought I. "All up there is so solid and safe, yet every man there is afraid to come near enough to give me the end of that lar-iat!"

But I was in no position to fight any one, therefore I softly said, "Surely they can come near enough to drop me the end of the lariat!"

"Yes, but who is to come to the edge to drop it to you if he is not held fast?—and we've got but one lariat."

I groaned.

After a moment's thought I said: "Where is Bob Paxton?"

Pete turned his head and looked.

"Out holding your horse," said he.

"Ah," said I, "he is always thoughtful. Bob is determined that I shall not go home on foot."

I was so mad that I did not much care whether the tree held or pulled up by the roots.

"Wait a bit and hold fast. Do have patience!" said Pete. "John will soon be here with the rope."

"Well, if I am to wait till then I wish you'd send me down a lunch. I saw Bob Paxton slipping some biscuits and cold meat into his pockets just before we left the flume boarding-house."

Pete's head disappeared. It may to some appear very unlikely that I talked and felt in my situation as I have reported. My situation was in truth so des-perate that I also became utterly desperate; and coolly so. The brink of the precipice, which an hour before would have turned my head, was now as nothing. I could have danced along it from end to end. I could now gaze down into the chasm without a qualm. My greater danger, my imminent peril, had killed all the smaller dangers. To paraphrase Pope—

> Small dangers intoxicate the brain,
> But great ones sober us again.

My danger was so great that I was perfectly sobered by it. It was about the same as lost. There was, however, a chance of a rope's coming before the tree gave way, and I would make the best fight I could for that chance.

Again I was left alone, suspended between heaven and earth. To add to the terrors of the situation, gusts of wind began to sweep through the cañon and sway me and my tree. I was still keenly alive to whatever threatened the stability of my tree,—if stability could be said to pertain to such a thing. Occasionally I could hear a root snap, and at times dirt fell from the edge of the cliff; as if the tree were slowly but surely giving way. All these things gave me very keen little starts and pangs, but had no power to overwhelm me,—to upset my brain.

To find all drawing back from me and keeping out of sight disturbed me not a little. I thought they should have appeared to be doing something,— might at least have given me the comfort of their presence. I have since seen how eagerly a man that is about to have the hangman's noose placed about his neck catches at a kind word or even a nod of recognition, and know that the word and nod filled a yearning vacancy.

Finally, after, as it seemed to me, I had been hanging over my grave a month, I heard a great—a mighty cheer.

"John Bowers has come with the rope!" thought I.

Soon Pete Bowers again peered down at me and said: "They have got a long rope. They are going to tie one end to a tree, and will then make a noose in the other end and let it down to you. Hold on a little longer and we'll get you."

"I can hold on a month," said I: "I am well enough fixed for holding on, but what is the good of my holding on if the tree gives way? You fellows seem to think all depends upon me and my holding on. This tree is giving way all the time."

Pete withdrew to impart this information.

It seemed an hour before he again crawled to the brink,—for he came by crawling on his belly. "I've got the end of the rope," said he, "but I'm afraid to come square over you to drop it. I'm afraid to go near the roots of the tree. The ground there is all cracked and loose."

"For God's sake, keep away from there!" cried I. Then, "Can't you throw the rope so that the loop will pass beyond the trunk, and slide along down to me as it slacks in drawing back?"

Pete threw the rope, but it fell short. Again and again he tried. Once it came near me and I reached out and clutched at it. As I did so there was an ominous cracking above, and small clods of earth fell and rattled down through the branches of the tree that rested against the wall.

I clutched the tree, afraid to wink or breathe for some moments. Then I said to Pete: "What is the matter with you?—why can't you fling the rope as I told you?"

"I can't throw so hard."

"Why not?"

"If I do my heels will fly up and I'll go head first into the cañon!"

"What! With a lariat around you and a dozen men holding you?"

"Only four, and they'll let go and run if they see me go over. They say we've lost too many men already today to take any more chances."

"O yes, I see!" said I, again beginning to forget that I was not on terra firma.

I thought a moment, and then said: "Tell the men to cut a long, slender pole; sharpen the upper end of it, then twist the strands of the rope at the noose backward and thrust in between them the point of the pole; then you can pass the noose down into my hands. Do you understand?"

"Yes, I'll have it fixed," and Pete withdrew.

In about ten minutes—it seemed to me as many hours—Pete was back with the pole and rope.

I wrapped my legs tightly about the trunk of the tree in order to have free use of both hands.

Down, down came the noose at the end of the pole. I never saw a thing move more slowly. At last I clutched it, and with a death grip. I soon had the noose over my shoulders and about my waist. I then told Pete to haul up the slack. As soon as the noose tightened I felt that I was safe.

With my left hand I took a vise-like grip on the rope above the noose and prepared to emerge.

"How many men are now holding you?" I asked Pete.

"Only three now."

"Can they hold you while you give orders?"

"I guess so."

"Well, don't let your heels fly up. How many men are holding me?"

"Four or five."

"And is the end of the rope still fast to the tree?"

"Yes, sir, still fast."

"Well, then, I may as well make a move and get out of here. However, now I think of it,—where is Bob Paxton?"

"On the rope, sir."

"My rope or yours?"

"Yours, sir."

"Tell him that I'm hungry, and ask him to please to save for me the lunch he has in his coat pocket."

Pete opened his eyes in astonishment, but turned his head and gave the order. Though I felt almost as safe as if out on the brow of the cliff, I knew that the "space fright" still held Pete in its power, and I did all this talking to try his steadiness before giving him my real business orders.

The first thing was to taut the rope in line; for Pete was still holding it. I told him to let go of it and tell the men to haul gently on it until I cried halt.

Pete did as directed, and repeated my order when I called a halt. The rope did not lie directly in a line with the trunk of the tree, and I made him veer the men by motioning with his hand till it was right.

I had studied out the whole programme while waiting for the rope. I wanted to steady myself by the trunk of the tree in going up, instead of swinging in against the wall and banging about, as the butt and roots of the tree would be of assistance in getting up to the crest of the cliff.

I explained this to Pete after the rope was in line and taut. Then I said to him: "Now, Pete, if you feel quite safe we'll start up."

"I am ready, sir."

"Very well. Now repeat my orders to the men instantly and exactly as I give them."

"Yes, sir."

"Haul away steadily!" cried I.

The order was repeated and acted upon. Up I went, calling out as I went: "Steady, steady!—not so fast!—so—steady, so!"

I made but one halt. That was when my head was on a level with the brink and at the point where I had partly to support my weight upon the butt of the tree in order to mount over the roots. After that a steady haul brought me upon the brink, when I lost no time in making a few rapid steps inland, where I tumbled down all of a heap.

I was weak as an infant.

"Water, water!" I murmured. "I'm so faint!" and I came near fainting in reality.

Water was brought from a rill, and with it was mingled some brandy, which Van Vranken had remaining in his flask. Next I took a shivering fit,— I began to feel the cold,—and was helped into my clothes. I was still too weak to stand alone, so sat on the ground for a time and rested. When helped to my feet, I rose the biggest coward in the crowd. A yoke of oxen could not have drawn me to the brink of the cliff over which Pete Bowers had thrust his head while helping me. Pete went out and got for me a piece of cedar root, to show me that it was almost as tough as a buckskin string. I thought it was very hardy of him to brave so much for so little.

At last I was able to mount my horse with some help, and we started for home, sending the rope back by some men that had come down from the flume camp. In about an hour I was all right, the motion of the horse starting my blood again through all my veins.

It was not until we were almost in sight of Omega that any one ventured to speak of the bets I had won. I said that I wished never again to hear them mentioned,—that I would hold the man to be my enemy that ever again said a word about the bets; and I felt and meant it. Strange as it may seem, while I was hanging in the tree and vexed with my friends for not doing more for me, I said to myself over and over again that if I ever got out alive I would exact from those fellows the last cent of every bet I had made.

My performance was not one that I was proud of, and for years it was not mentioned in my presence by any one who cared to be my friend.

As long as I remained in the town of Omega,—even till the year 1860,— when I saw myself pointed out and eyes following me, I thought it was being said: "There goes the blamed fool that went after the eagles' nest."

Also, even to this day, the adventure often interferes with my sleep. Just when I am on the point of quietly entering the realms of dreamland I find myself out on the cedar, see the young eagles falling fluttering down, down into the awful abyss, and again I am thrilled in every nerve with the old "fright of space" yawning beneath me. It is true that I have discovered the cure for this fright, but it is "big medicine" and I don't hanker after it.

Overland Monthly, May 1891

Looking Down upon the Suisun Marsh Tules

Lights of a Passing Stockton Steamer Revive an Incident of Thrilling Interest

Rollin M. Daggett

Daggett retired in San Francisco after his term as minister to Hawaii ended in 1885. From then until his death in 1901 he wrote stories, essays, and poems for Western periodicals. This story most likely dates from those years. Despite some similarities to Joseph Conrad's "The Secret Sharer" (1909), the possibility of influence appears to be extremely remote; it is more probable that both authors coincidentally but independently were attracted to the idea of a prisoner being allowed to escape and create a new life for himself.

❖⇒ ⇐❖

HOLLYMOUNT. It is a modest mountain home, in the midst of some acres of vines and fruit trees, and surrounded on three sides by high, rolling hills slashed with ravines and covered with dense thickets of oak, bay and manzanita. The oaks are small, but their limbs are heavy with acorns. The sweet bay, or laurel, grows to a height of twenty feet, and is comely in shape. It very closely resembles the Mesopotamian laurel, and I am not sure that they are not identical. It has rather large shining leaves, lanceolate in shape and thick and fibrous in structure, and exceedingly fragrant when macerated. Its fruit is of the size of a large olive, and is oily and quite as fragrant as the leaves. Here and there the manzanita mingles its varnished bark with the duller hues of oak and wild currant and the redberry, which is the holly of California, paints the jungle with the white of its clustering blossoms, and in the autumn strug-

194

gles to lift into the sunshine its wealth of ruddy fruit. Among the branches of all the wild ivy weaves its tangled web, and along the margins of the ravines the morning-glory furtively climbs to the tops of flowerless shrubs and pins to their stems its large and creamy blooms. Among the rocks of the ravines the raccoon and badger find a home, and fox and owl keep rabbit and squirrel on the alert for their lives in the sunless recesses of the chaparral, where all seek refuge from the eye of man. The piping of the quail, the scream of the bluejay and twitter of the linnet come with the cessation of the winter rains, and tarry till long after the hollies ripen red, and the eagle, whose nest is in the westward crags, soars o'er the slopes of green on quiet wing, fearless of all that flies.

These are the outlines of the immediate surroundings of Hollymount. Its acres are in a spur of the Coast range, locally referred to as the Blue mountains, and are seven or eight miles from Vacaville. They are reached by ascending Vaca valley four or five miles and then turning abruptly into a rocky canyon and mounting the westward hills. The grade is rather steep in places, but the road is by no means insurmountable, and after slowly toiling upward to an altitude of 1000 feet above the valley, the terraces of Hollymount greet the eye. There is not a rood of naturally level land within a mile of the place. Its lands are spread around and across an amphitheater at the head of a ravine, and over some rolling hills to the northward. Such of the houses as are not perched upon terraces occupy walled excavations, and the roads through it, as well as the most of the margins of the ravines in the vicinity of tillage are walled and terraced. An abundance of stone on the grounds cleared for the plow rendered the task of terracing comparatively inexpensive, and a stone boundary wall of three-fourths of a mile in length was constructed at less than the cost of a wooden fence.

Westward from Hollymount the hills continue to rise for a mile or more with gentle ascent to the boundary line of Napa county, but to the eastward the view is incomparably grand and inspiring. From the front verandas of the family residence may be seen in a single picture two or three hundred miles of the Sacramento valley, dotted with villages, farm houses and green fields, while far beyond the river, the course of which may be traced by its wooded margins and shimmering sloughs, stretch hundreds of unbroken miles of the Sierra Nevada, its main ridges capped with snow, and its foothills and timbered slopes plainly marked. The Capitol building at Sacramento, less than forty miles distant, can be seen by the unaided eye, and the course of the overland trains across the valley may be followed by the smoke of their locomotives or the flashes of their moving headlights. At night a luminous haze rises to view above the electric lights of Sacramento, and the locations of the villages along the line of the railroad may be readily discerned. The extreme southern side of the picture includes the San Joaquin river and its stretches of tule-lined sloughs, and at night the lights of the San Francisco and Stockton steamers may be seen as they wind in and out of their tortuous channels.

It has taken some time to get around to the Stockton steamer that I know by its lights was on its way up the river last night. I could see nothing more than the lights, of course, but it was not difficult to imagine the rest. A small side-wheel boat slowly forging its way against the current; seventy-five tons of freight and twenty-eight passengers, dinner over and most of the passengers sitting out on deck in the moonlight picking their teeth. That is about what I imagined in connection with the lights. Then the lights, with the kind of vessel and cargo of which I conceived them to be a necessary appurtenance, recalled the trip of another steamer down the San Joaquin river some years ago, with which is associated a strange little story. It will not be entirely new to a few of the old residents of Stockton. Perhaps my reference to Hollymount is somewhat more elaborate than is necessary to establish the fact that the lights of the Stockton steamer can be seen from its front verandas, but the reader will not be apt to object to a modest description of a bit of mountain scenery more or less characteristic of long stretches of the western slopes of the Coast range, which will soon be covered with vineyards and picturesque homes.

For a number of years following the establishment of a State government in Nevada the insane of that State were by contract provided for in a private asylum at Stockton, Cal. It having been reported that the patients were improperly cared for, and in some cases retained in the asylum after recovery, about twenty years ago Dr. White and the writer were commissioned by Governor Bradley to visit Stockton and ascertain how much truth there was in these accusations.

While in discharge of this duty, for the purpose of comparison we made two or three calls at the two neighboring asylums for a part of the insane of California.

It was during our final visit to one of these institutions, to which males alone were admitted as patients, that two ladies made their appearance from a closed carriage at the main entrance. One of them was a sad-faced elderly woman, with streaks of gray in her thin hair, combed smoothly down over the temples. The other was her daughter, a girl of 18 or 20, and uncommonly comely in form and feature. Although plainly clad, their dress and general appearance indicated the possession of at least moderate means. Entering the reception-room, they requested an interview with the superintendent. As that gentleman was present, the request was complied with at once.

"Have you had a patient here during the past year of the name of Wilson Barry?" inquired the elderly lady in a tremulous voice.

"I think we have, madam," replied the superintendent, "but I will examine the register to be sure. Please be seated. I will return in a moment."

The lady bowed her thanks as he left the room, which he re-entered a few minutes later with the information that Wilson Barry, a young man born in Newark, N.J., had been committed to the asylum from Sacramento more than two years before.

"I understand that he is no longer living," said the lady hesitatingly.

"He died about three months ago," replied the superintendent in a softened tone, "and his grave may be found in the plat where we bury deceased patients whose bodies are not called for by friends or relatives."

"Did he leave any effects?" inquired the lady. "I do not refer to money, but to articles that might be preserved as keepsakes by his family."

"I believe not, madam. He had been insane for some time before he was committed, and when he was brought here nothing was found on his person—not even a ring, pencil or pocketknife. I now remember, since I recall his case, that he had a mania for pictures of female faces, such as are frequently used in advertising, and that a number were found in his pockets. We permitted him to retain them, but it is hardly probable that they were preserved after his death. However, I will speak to my clerk and see if anything belonging to him can be found."

Leaving the room, the superintendent returned after an absence of ten minutes bringing with him a photograph, and remarking, with a smile, as he handed it to the young lady: "I think you may be able to recognize this. He brought it to the asylum, and by chance it has not been destroyed."

The girl gazed at the picture for a moment, and then, handing it to her mother, burst into tears. It was the photograph she had sent her brother on her sixteenth birthday.

This seemed to remove all doubt concerning the identity of the deceased, and the mother then informed the superintendent that she was a widow and the mother of Wilson Barry; that he came to California from Newark in 1869; that two years before his death he ceased to write to her, nor could she discover his address; that she was about to advertise in some of the California papers for information concerning him, when she read the announcement of his death in a San Francisco journal mailed to her by a friend in New York; and, finally, that she and her daughter had come alone by steamer from the East to take back the body of her unfortunate and only son for interment beside his father.

It was a sad story that the mother told, with her eyes brimming with tears

and her arm around the neck of her weeping child. The superintendent prof-
fered every assistance within his power, and late in the afternoon of the third
day following, the plain pine coffin containing the remains of the deceased
lunatic, incased in zinc and otherwise protected, was placed aboard the Stockton steamer bound for San Francisco, the mother and daughter taking passage with it.

Down the river with the current speeded the steamer with its dead and living freight. Dinner was served, and the passengers strolled out on deck to observe the sunset in a sea of waving tules, and catch a breath of the cool breeze
that came with the twilight. Then a coarse, but ample meal, was taken into an
upper-deck stateroom well aft, and a young man with manacled hands ate it,
while a deputy sheriff from Tuolumne county walked leisurely to and fro
with a short beat in front of the door. He was conveying a prisoner to San
Quentin, who had been sentenced to a year of confinement there for shooting off the right arm of a man of substance in Sonora, who had betrayed his
confidence and assisted in swindling him out of a valuable interest in a mining claim. The case was twice tried before a conviction was secured, and although the jury probably could not do otherwise than find the prisoner
guilty, the popular verdict was the victim well deserved the punishment he
received. A petition was in circulation and an early pardon was expected. The
prisoner was a resolute looking young man of good personal appearance, and
the handcuffs seemed to be out of place on his wrists.

He was sitting on deck with his hat drawn down over his eyes and his
manacled hands covered with the folds of a linen duster when the mother
and daughter came aboard with their dead. He peered at them from under
the brim of his slouch hat, and his cramped hands grew cold and the blood
seemed to stagnate in his heart. And he saw them again through his stateroom window as they passed it, and learned from sentences dropped by passengers that they were returning to Newark with the body of Wilson Barry,
who died, insane, three months before.

As he thought of his manacles and the guard in front of his door the cold
perspiration poured from his face, and his limbs stiffened under the stress of
a measureless agony. He felt that his sufferings were dethroning his reason,
and with a cry of despair he fell to the floor. The door was opened by the
watchful guard, letting in a stream of light from the deck lamps.

"What's the matter, Barry?" he inquired, discovering the situation of the
prisoner.

"Perhaps I am insane," replied Barry, rising to his feet and staring wildly at
the officer. "Is there a corpse aboard?"

"Yes, but what of that?"

"Is it the body of a man who died insane?"

"So I have been told."

"Now, one question more. Is it in charge of an elderly lady and her daughter?"

"I believe it is."

"Then I am not insane—am not dreaming," moaned the prisoner. "They are my mother and sister, who are taking back to Newark the body of Wilson Barry in the belief that it is mine."

"Was his name Wilson Barry?" inquired the officer.

"No, not Wilson Barry, but Wilson Berry. We were both born in Newark, and through a strange coincidence were both christened Wilson. I first met him at Columbia about three years ago, and we afterward mined and cabined together on Maxwell's creek. After remaining with him for three or four months he finally deserted me one day while I was out prospecting, taking with him a suit of clothes belonging to me, in the pockets of which were a number of family keepsakes, including photographs of my mother and sister. He was in the insane asylum when I next heard of him, and the body on board is his beyond a doubt. Our names, so nearly alike, have been confounded by misprint and careless pronunciation, and my poor, heart-broken mother is bearing back to Newark a body which she believes to be that of her son. I dare not meet her with these fettered hands—dare not tell her that her son is alive and on his way to the penitentiary. My God! My God! What shall I do?"

For some moments the officer made no reply, but his face showed that he was profoundly moved. At length he said: "Are you sure the elderly lady is your mother?"

"Yes," replied Barry, confidently.

"Take another and better look, in order that there may be no mistake," said the officer. "She is in the saloon. Throw your duster over your shoulders, hiding your hands, and pass through the room with me. You will not be particularly noticed."

Barry followed the officer as directed, and returned to his stateroom satisfied that he had seen the sad face of his mother.

"See here, Barry," said the officer, as if suddenly grappling with a desperate resolution. "Your mother must not take that body back to Newark. I would be a party to the fraud if she did, and her face would haunt me."

"Would it be better to tell her that her son is a convict?" was the gloomy suggestion of the prisoner.

"I do not regard you as a criminal," continued the officer. "You simply broke the arm of a rascal whose neck should have been stretched long ago. For the sake of your mother, I intend to do something better becoming a man than an officer of the law. Can you swim?"

"Yes, if I can have the use of my hands."

"Well, I'll attend to that." And producing a key, the officer relieved the prisoner of his handcuffs and threw them into the river. "Do you see that light to the left, about a mile below?" he inquired.

"Yes, very plainly."

"Well, when the boat reaches a point a little above it I shall be in the saloon. Then go to the stem of the steamer and jump overboard. Do it quietly and you will probably not be observed. You can easily make a landing. I know the place well. There is quite a settlement in the neighborhood. Find your way to Suisun to-morrow, or some other point near the railroad, and take the evening train for San Francisco. I will report that you jumped overboard, heavily ironed, in Suisun bay, and no one will doubt that you were drowned. I know you have money enough to meet your expenses. When you arrive in the city drop me a note at the Russ House, telling me where you may be found. I will shadow your mother and sister, and bring you together. Have a plausible story ready for the occasion, and you will be able to get off on the next Panama steamer, leaving in Lone Mountain[1] the body your mother found in Stockton. How does the scheme strike you?"

"It is perfect in all its details. I will follow your directions to the letter," said Barry, seizing the hand of the officer. "But I do not know how to express my gratitude for an act of friendship so supreme and unselfish."

"Don't try to do it. The papers will have you comfortably located at the bottom of Suisun bay to-morrow under a name that will not betray you to your mother, and from the dead nothing but silence is becoming. But we are nearly opposite the light."

The officer, significantly pointing to the stem of the steamer, rose and strolled forward. Soon after there was a light splash in the water, and the prisoner had escaped. There was not a slip in the ingenious programme arranged by the officer. The events that immediately followed were the happy reunion of all that remained of the Barry family and their early return to Newark, preceded by the unceremonious burial of the body of Berry at Lone Mountain. It is believed by most of the friends of Barry in Tuolumne county that he leaped to his death in Suisun bay, but a certain old-time deputy sheriff, whose name has been withheld, knows better, and he sometimes receives letters from Newark which he does not show to his neighbors.

And this is the little story recalled last night by the lights of a San Francisco and Stockton steamer seen from the terraces of Hollymount.

⊷⇒Unidentified clipping in the Daggett file,
Nevada Historical Society, Reno

---

1. The Lone Mountain cemetery, near San Francisco.

When Booth Was Not Booth

A Startling Reminiscence

Sam P. Davis

It is a toss-up whether to call this a memoir or fiction. Inasmuch as some of the individuals named as theater critics were alive and living in San Francisco at the time this piece was published, there is possibly a substantial element of truth in it. On the other hand, Davis, though truthful in essentials, was wont to embellish and modify details of his narratives in order to make a good story.

⋯⇒◦ ◦⇐⋯

There is a small and cheap restaurant on Merchant Street where I make a point to go once a day, at least, when in San Francisco. In the old days when Clay Street was the newspaper center of the town I spent many a pleasant hour there, mingling with comrades who have passed away. The same waiter is there now who served frugal Bohemian meals twenty years ago, and the same proprietor is behind the counter. For many years not a single familiar face of the past has greeted me except when I invite some of the old boys to come and dine. It may be the cooking or the loneliness of the spot or the surroundings that affect my guests, I know not which of the three causes, but I have noticed that I find it hard to get even my closest friends there twice. They generally insist upon it that I shall dine with them, in order, I imagine, to escape dining with me at that old restaurant. They always accept my invitation until we edge down toward that particular establishment and then cook up some flimsy excuse to dine elsewhere.

These people are evidently persons who regard restaurants merely as places in which to eat. With me it is different. The food and service may deteriorate in quality, as in this case, and the proprietor grow old and crabbed, but if the spot has associations and memories dear to me, the cuisine, if such an expression is permissible in connection with so plain a place, can go to the devil, and I am still content. The pleasant hours I have spent there all come up again, and every bubble on the surface of the cheap wine has a face and memory in it. But I am spending too much time. I wish to tell a story that I don't expect any one to believe after I have told it.

I used frequently to meet there a man named Johnson, who was introduced to me by Harry Larkyns. Poor Harry, who lived long enough to excuse himself to some ladies after a bullet went through his heart, to step out of doors to die.[1]

This always struck me as more polite and thoughtful than was Chesterfield, who, with his last breath asked an attendant to give a visitor a chair.

Larkyns, after his death wound in Calistoga, bowed politely to three ladies, asked to be excused, and stepping from the room was a corpse. How I miss Harry's face when I dine at the little Merchant Street restaurant.

One night Larkyns, Johnson and I were there. Johnson was an actor, one of those talented geniuses who for some reason or another never seem to succeed. The queer thing about him was that he resembled Booth[2] both in face and figure, and could mimic him to the life. We would often take a little room by ourselves and after dinner Johnson would give us scenes from Shakespeare, and for the time he seemed Booth himself.[3] Larkyns was "very solid," as they say, with the theatrical people, and he made many vain attempts to secure an opening for Johnson, but the managers all said that Johnson wanted to fly his kite too high at the start, instead of taking subordinate parts, etc.

Larkyns was considerably incensed at the treatment his friend received and the managers were in constant fear that his sharp pen would manifest his displeasure in his theatrical criticisms, for he was an all around contributor to the papers and very happy at theatrical work. But he was too broad a man and good-natured and forgiving to take such a petty revenge.

One evening when we three were dining together, Larkyns unfolded a plan by which Johnson was to play Hamlet at the California.

1. Davis recounts this story in full in his anonymous contribution to the "By-the-Bye" column in the *Nevada Mining News*, November 26, 1908, p. 5. The story occurs as the "Harry Larkyns" item. Although this particular detail—of excusing himself to ladies after being shot—appears to be mistaken, the rest of the account is probably accurate in the main.

2. Edwin T. Booth (1833–1893), a renowned actor, especially famous for his interpretation of Hamlet.

3. The theater was a great passion of Davis's, and he counted many actors and actresses as his personal friends. He was an avid theatergoer and a theater critic for newspapers, and he also acted in some plays. In addition, he wrote several plays that were performed on the Comstock. One of them, *The Prince of Timbuctoo*, is published in *The Old West in the Old World: Lost Plays by Bret Harte and Sam Davis*.

"Be all ready," he said to his friend, "to play Hamlet next October at the California. I'll fix it."

"Why Booth plays there in October. You talk nonsense," was the reply.

"But I'll have Booth give you a night."

"Pshaw!"

"But, by Jove, old boy, I'll *make* him give you a night."

Johnson merely removed the wine bottle from Harry's reach and grinned.

"Now listen, both of you," said Harry. "I know Booth well. Met him years ago in New York. He will play Hamlet three nights the second week he is here. I got the whole programme from Barton Hill. The last is on a Saturday evening, and on that particular night, October 16, you be ready to play. You are, as you know, the dead image of Booth. I will have Booth out to dine in the afternoon, and if I ever get my hands on him he will never show up at the theater that night. You occupy his dressing room and go ahead. You attend to the stage work, Sam will help you in the dressing room and I'll attend to the outside business."

The audacity of the idea staggered us not a little at first, but Larkyns had a persuasive tongue and soon convinced us that the only thing that really detracted from the plan was its utter simplicity, and we soon began to work on the details with feverish enthusiasm; but after Booth arrived and the town went wild over his work I began to wonder if my friend Johnson would be equal to the task we had imposed upon him.

It seemed an awful thing, this practical joke we were about to perpetrate, and I began to wish myself well out of it. I suggested to Larkyns the propriety of calling the whole business off, but he brushed aside my misgivings, insisted that I had concocted most of the job and invariably wound up by charging me with treachery to Johnson—who, he said, would surely commit suicide if cheated out of his chance to play Hamlet—or a lack of nerve.

A man, especially a young man, hates to be taxed with treachery or a lack of nerve, and I finally assured Larkyns that if it became necessary to cut Booth's throat to keep him off the stage I would allow him to do it, and never mention the matter to either Crowley or Lees.

The time drew near for the event, Johnson was working like a beaver at study and rehearsal, and every day was taking a fencing lesson of a good instructor. What astonished us most was Johnson's nerve and determination. He had no thought of failure. All he wanted was Booth's costumes, the stage and an audience.

One afternoon I got a note from Larkyns to meet him at the Merchant-street restaurant. I went up, and there he had Booth caged in the little dining-room where we always dined. I felt a great strain on my nerves when I was introduced to Booth. I thought Larkyns should have had a little more regard for me than to have brushed me up against our intended victim. Nothing on earth ever fazed Larkyns, but with me it was quite different.

I felt ill at ease, and when Booth turned his big eyes on me I wondered if he was reading the secret.

"Harry," said Booth suddenly, "what's this talk in the papers about my intention to give the public a new version of Hamlet? I saw it only yesterday in the *Post.*"

"I wrote it," replied Larkyns, as he filled his glass. "You know there has been a lot of talk that you had played Hamlet so often that you had fallen into a rut and could only play the one version. Of course, I know better, and I casually mentioned the fact that during your stay here you would demonstrate the folly of the one-rut idea by giving the public a new version. Of course it would be no trouble for you to do that. It would demonstrate your versatility and be a great treat."

Booth's face wore a clouded look and then he laughed.

"I suppose you would have the management advertise a complete change of Hamlet every night, and the actor who could present Hamlet in the most characters would knock the persimmons, eh?"

After considerable good-natured chaff between the two, we finished the dinner, which Booth seemed to relish, and in a joking way said that he would give the public a different version of Hamlet on Saturday night and have a line on the bills to that effect.

EDWIN BOOTH IN A BRAND-NEW HAMLET.
BY SPECIAL REQUEST.

Booth joked of the matter about the hotel until it began to be talked of through the city, and like most theatrical rumors spread with amazing rapidity, which played exactly into Larkyns' hand and put him in the highest spirits.

I even had to agree to sleep alone so that in my troubled dreams the plot might not escape. Well the night at last arrived. Booth was wearing off the drugged effects of Harry's dinner in a deep slumber at the hotel, his valet was properly drunk in a Clay-street saloon and all was well.

We got the key to the Hamlet wardrobe out of the valet's pocket, and at 7:45 Johnson was arrayed as the melancholy Dane at the California Theater. The place was packed and the sign "standing room only" was up. At 8 o'clock

I put the finishing touches on Johnson's wig and bade him brace up. He was pale and nervous as almost any one would be under the circumstances. He had two parts to play, Hamlet and Booth. I gave him a few words of encouragement and a small nip of brandy and turned him loose.

He strode on the stage, faced the footlights, and then what a roar of welcome went up. He bowed with studied dignity and the noise subsiding he began to speak his lines.

In a few seconds he had recovered his composure, and it seemed that it was indeed Booth who stood before the audience.

Presently the old playgoers who watched every move began to whisper among themselves and exchange comments.

Yes, indeed, he was giving the public a new version. George Bromley liked it; Colonel Cremony didn't like it so well; Scott Sutten declined to express an opinion; Joe Goodman was very reserved, and George Barnes fell to wrangling with Peter Robertson about the inflection he gave certain lines; Colonel John McComb of the dear old *Alta* was just a trifle restless.

Presently the place became noisy with discussion, and in the midst of it Hamlet stopped short and turned a full, reproachful look upon the pit.

A silence fell over that portion of the house, and the critics fell several inches in their seats. The withering, silent reproof that blazed from Johnson's eyes seemed like a command from Olympus. The gallery broke into applause at the discomposure of its natural enemies, and the rest of the house took it up.

"Great work. Oh, wasn't that a daisy play of his?" I turned, and it was Larkyns talking over my shoulder.

When the curtain dropped on the first act there was a look of complete triumph in Johnson's eyes. He felt that he had won the attention of the great audience, and the applause was water to his parched dramatic soul that had never quenched its thirst with such a delicious draught before.

Near the end of the fourth act I was arranging things in the dressing-room when I was conscious of a presence. Looking up I saw something that caused me to stagger. There stood Booth, the real Booth, in plain clothes. He simply fixed a look of astonishment on me and we both stared at each other; then in walked Larkyns, who for once in his life seemed at a loss for words.

Presently Johnson came off the stage and joined the group. Such a quartet of speechless and astonished people I never saw in my life.

Each man seemed to think that it was somebody else's turn to speak. Finally Booth, with a slight bow to Johnson, said: "You seem weary with your exertions. If you will hand me your costume I will play the last act."

Johnson somewhat nervously took off "the trappings and the suits of woe"[4] and Booth began to put them on. We all mechanically assisted him. After he was arrayed in the garb of Hamlet we deemed it prudent to withdraw from the dressing-room, and melted away as it were without the formality of excusing ourselves. Booth never seemed to notice our disappearance. He played the last act as he never played it before, and the house was in a roar of approval.

While he was bowing to the repeated calls of the audience poor Johnson sat there half clad and the picture of disconsolation. He was about to slink home when Booth extended his hand and with a pleasant smile said he had noticed a portion of his acting and was highly pleased with it. Then he shook hands with all of us and we had a hearty laugh and Booth got in a good humor and we all slipped off after the play to the little obscure Merchant-street restaurant and made a night of it.

All enjoyed it except Johnson, who seemed utterly miserable. When we separated, Booth invited him to become a member of his company, but he never showed up, and about two weeks later died in the Home for the Inebriate.

As for the performance, the papers praised it without stint, and not one of the critics ever knew of the imposition, as we all swore secrecy and maintained it so long that I hope the dead members of the quartet will this day forgive me for breaking the vow of silence.

→━*San Francisco Morning Call,* October 20, 1895, p. 13

---

4. *Hamlet* 1.2.86.

A Heart Flush

Thomas Fitch
Of the Los Angeles Bar

Thomas Fitch (1838–1923) was an eloquent and opportunistic personality known in the Old West as the "Silver Tongued Orator of the Pacific." He settled in Nevada in 1863, just as the Comstock boom was getting under way, and served as Nevada's representative to Congress from 1869 to 1871. In 1877 Fitch moved to Prescott, Arizona, to open a law practice, and he remained in Arizona until 1885. His life was eventful, and he associated with many eminent figures of his time and place. With the exception of the names, which the author's editorial note at the beginning acknowledges have been changed, the major elements of the central incident and the ludicrously convoluted legal logic about jurisdiction and punishment can be found in the record of the actual case of "Ex Parte William Janes."[1] It is less certain that all events in the tale occurred to the same person, and essentially in the way they are narrated herein. Because this story's text was found without identification in an archive, the details of its publication and date are unknown, but Fitch retold this story several times over the years. Versions of it can be found in the edited collection of his 1903 memoirs, *Western Carpetbagger,* and in the "By-the-Bye" column of the *Nevada Mining News* for August 22, 1908.[2]

⋯

[Ed. Note.—This is said to be a true story of the West of a few decades ago. The names used, however, are fictitious. The central figure of the story has been dead for many years.]

As if he were materialized out of the cover of a dime novel, Jack Billings

---

1. *Reports of Decisions of the Supreme Court of the State of Nevada,* vols. 1 and 2 (1877), 270–73.
2. Fitch, *Western Carpetbagger,* ed. Eric N. Moody, 62–65; *Nevada Mining News,* August 22, 1908, p. 19.

entered my law office in Arizona one spring morning in the late seventies.[3] From broad-brimmed sombrero to fringed buckskin breeches, he was attired in the classic costume of the bad man of the frontier. He was in the custody of a United States marshal, accused by him of stopping a stagecoach and robbing the United States mail. He came to employ me for his defense.

Jack was a peculiar character. He was at once a brave man and a braggart. He never feared a foe or shirked a contest. He would, in the language of the frontier, "have fought a rattlesnake and given him the first [bite]." But when in his cups he was a liar who would have put Falstaff and Mendez Pinto to shame.[4] He would claim to have committed all the highway robberies and homicides ever perpetrated between Alaska and Mexico. Yet, when sober, he was disinclined to talk about himself, and would tell the truth, and, drunk or sober, his hand would never close upon a tainted dollar.

Jack had a penchant for finding and burying the bones of pioneers who had been slain by Apache Indians. He started, accompanied by his hired man—for he owned a small ranch well stocked with cattle, or rather his Mexican wife owned them—one Sunday morning to find the bones of Colonel Snively, of Texas, who had been killed years before on Antelope mountain. The pair carried grain sacks in which to place the bones, and were mounted on chestnut sorrel horses.

That night the stagecoach was robbed by two masked men mounted on chestnut sorrel horses and carrying grain sacks in which they deposited the stolen mail and the contents of the express box. The robbers rode away rapidly in the direction of Antelope mountain.

The search of Jack and his companion for Colonel Snively's bones proved unsuccessful. They returned to Jack's ranch. Jack went the next morning to the mining town close by, and proceeded to drown his disappointment at the bar of the Tanglefoot saloon. By noon he was royally drunk, and when news arrived of the robbery of the stage he at once claimed that he was the robber.

On the strength of these admissions and the circumstantial evidence, he was arrested. A night in jail sobered him, and the next morning he came, in charge of an officer, to consult me.

His examination before the committing magistrate was set for that after-

---

3. The details of time and place are consonant with Fitch's biography.

4. Falstaff is the engaging but cowardly braggart in Shakespeare's plays about Henry IV and Henry V and also *The Merry Wives of Windsor*. Fernão (or Ferdinand) Mendes Pinto was a sixteenth-century Portuguese adventurer who was the first European to visit Japan. The book he wrote about his seemingly incredible but basically true adventures was widely disbelieved and unfairly earned him the reputation of being the "Prince of Liars." His name was given further notoriety by the English playwright William Congreve, who in *Love for Love* (1695) linked the name to bragging and lying.

noon, and while we were awaiting the arrival of the hour he gave me a sketch of his life and career.

"That thar district attorney has it in for me, Jedge," said he, "because I helped to defeat him for re-election. You will hear some pretty hard things about me, and I want you to be at yourself. I won't have time to explain everything in the court room, and mebbe you'd better ask me now about anything you want to know."

"They say, Jack," said I, "that you have killed eleven men."

"The hounds," said he, springing to his feet and pacing the floor. "That's just the way they lie about a good man, Jedge. It's only nine—not countin Injins. And of cose I don't count those Yankees my bullets may have hit when I was in Price's army.[5] But outside of that I never removed anybody that I didn't just have to shoot up, and I was always justified by the law. Once they came near getting me, I was convicted and sentenced to be hung, but I had no right to be, bekase the Lord and good luck and Governor Nye[6] was on my side. Early in 1864 I gin up sojerin with Pap Price, and hired out as a driver on the overland, and so drifted into Nevady territory.

"Dan O'Rourke, who tended bar at the Teamster's Retreat in Virginia City, hated me on account of a girl—well, never mind about that. She married afterwards a better man than I am, and I don't shy no stones at a woman no how.

"Dan kept a-sayin' nasty things about me all over town, and one day he allowed that if I didn't come and get down on my knees afore him and eat out of his hand he'd appint my funeral and the corpse would be ready.

"Well, I wasn't allowin' no man to make invidious remarks about me without callin' on him for an explanation. So that night I went over to the Teamster's Retreat, where Dan was tendin' bar. There was about a dozen of his crowd seated around the tables, and, when I entered, some one cried: 'Here comes that bloody A.P.A.' Now, I wan't no sich thing, and I didn't then even know what those letters meant.[7] I jest walked up to the bar, and in a quiet and gentlemanly tone I sez to Dan, sez I, 'Mr. O'Rourke, what have you got agin me? Why do you say mean things about me to your friends?' With that he called me a name, or rather called my mother a name which no man with ginger in him ever hears without resentin'. Then I leaned over and swatted

5. Probably the confederate army commanded by Major General Sterling "Paw" (or "Pap") Price (1809–1867). Much of his fighting took place in the vicinity of Arkansas, Mississippi, and southern Missouri.

6. James W. Nye, governor of the Nevada Territory, interim governor of Nevada after it became a state, and later senator from Nevada.

7. Slang for "American Park ape" (or animal)—an insult of the time.

him across his vile mouth. He reached under the counter and pulled out a six
shooter, and leveled it at me, and tried to cock it. He seemed like not to know
it was a self-cocker, and while he was foolin' with it, I got out my own gun and
let him have it. He dropped on the floor and I went out. His friends never
tried to stop me. There wouldn't have been so many of them by five if they
had. They crawled under the tables.

"I went to the sheriff's office and gin myself up. The grand jury was in session. The gang of which O'Rourke had been a member was a power in politics. They packed both a grand and a petty jury on me. I had no money to
hire a lawyer, and the jedge appinted a young cuss to defend me. I never found
any fault with him. He did the best he could, but I have a mighty poor opinion of the jedge that admitted him to practice law.

"When the trial came on I had no witnesses, and there were nine men
who swore that I went up to the bar and, without sayin' a word, shot O'Rourke
through the heart and then ran out.

"The jury convicted me, and the jedge sentenced me to be hung, or, at
least, he thought he did.

"While I was layin' in jail regretting that some Yank had not picked me off
when I was skirmishin' with Pap Price, Governor Nye came to see me. 'Billings,' sez he, 'I have a letter from a friend in Saint Joe, who tells me that when
you was on a raid there you stood between him and death and turned away
the muzzles of the guns that were leveled at him, and risked your own life in
doin' it.' 'I remember it, Governor,' said I, 'I couldn't do no less. The kid was
unarmed and wasn't doin' nothin' but beseechin' us not to take away his
mother's team.'

"'Tell me your story, Billings,' said the governor. 'Tell me the exact truth
about how you came to shoot O'Rourke.'

"I did so. When I got through the governor said: 'Billings, I believe you,
and you shan't be hung. It won't do for me to pardon you now, for if I did I
would turn all O'Rourke's friends—and there are a lot of them—against my
legislative ticket. You know, I suppose, that I was governor of the territory of
Nevada and am acting as governor of the state for only a short time until the
newly elected governor can be sworn in. But I'll tell you what I'll do. I will
commute your sentence to life imprisonment, and send you to the Carson
penitentiary. And before I go out of office, I'll issue you a pardon to take effect three months after.[8] The senatorial election will come off in the meantime, and I will either be elected or defeated. In the meantime you keep your
own counsel about the pardon.'

8. Fitch misremembered; it was six months.

"I agreed to this, of course. The governor was as good as his word, and I was imprisoned in the state penitentiary.

"Governor Nye, God bless him, was elected to the Senate, and when the three months was up I pulled the pardon and gave it to the warden, who was Lieutenant Governor Jim Slingerland. He had taken quite a notion to me. 'Billings,' says he, 'I have some doubts about the legality of this, but I'll let you go, if you'll give me your word that if anybody makes a row about this you'll come back here until the matter is settled.'

"I agreed, of course, and the next day I let out and went over to California and got a job as foreman on a cattle ranch in Strawberry valley.

"I got a letter from the warden about a month afterwards, saying that the attorney general was making a row with him about letting me go, and would I please come back. Back I went. The friends of O'Rourke had got busy with the attorney general, and he had me haled before the supreme court on a writ of habeas corpus. That court held that under the state government the pardoning power was lodged in a board of pardons, consistin' of the governor, the chief justice, and the attorney general, and that the governor alone had no power to pardon. They held that when Governor Nye issued my pardon he was acting governor of the state, and not governor of the territory, and the pardon was no good. They held that when he commuted my sentence to life imprisonment he was governor of the territory, and as such might have pardoned me, but had no power under the organic act to commute my sentence, and that I was therefore illegally in the custody of the warden of the penitentiary.

"The warden congratulated me, and then the attorney general said to the court that the law provided that when a man was illegally in the custody of one officer and it appeared that some other officer was entitled to him, the court would not release him, but would order him delivered to the custody of the proper officer. He said that it was the duty of the court to order me into the custody of the sheriff of Storey county, to have the original sentence of death carried out.

"The court so ordered, and back I went to Virginia City, and into the condemned cell in the jail there. Jo Clark, the new sheriff, didn't relish the job of hanging me. He looked up the sentence as it was written on the records, and found that it read that on a day certain I was to be hung, but didn't specify whether I was to be hung by my neck, or my heels, or my arms, and didn't say that I was to be hung until I was dead.

"'I'm not going to choke this man to death on this yere sentence,' said the sheriff. 'If the court will fix a date for hangin' him, I'll swing him up for a while by the seat of his breeches, and then let him go.'

"Well, O'Rourke's friends was disgusted. They got after the district attorney, and he made a motion before the district court of the state, which had succeeded the territorial court, to have the sentence amended. The district court heard the motion and examined the record. The district attorney was launchin' out into a speech in favor of amendin' my sentence, and O'Rourke's friends, who was a-crowdin' of the court room, was chucklin' and grinnin' when the court stopped the lawyer. 'It is useless,' said the court, 'to take up my time arguin' this yere fool motion. I have no jurisdiction to amend the sentence. There is grave doubt about the power of a court to amend a sentence after the term has lapsed, and there is no doubt about its lack of power to amend a sentence after the court that rendered it has lapsed. There is no territorial court any more. I have no power or jurisdiction to correct its error, if error it was. Call the next case.'

"Then I arose. 'Jedge,' said I, 'if they are all through with this yere damn foolishness, can I go back to my job on the ranch?'

"The Jedge said I could go. And I did. Before I could get out of town, O'Rourke's second cousin, Pat Moriarty, said he was goin' to shoot me on sight, and sent me word to heel myself,[9] which I did. Pat filled his skin full of bad whisky. He loaded a double-barreled shot-gun with slugs. He came twice to the lodging-house where I was stoppin', and he skeered the poor woman who kept the house nigh on to death. When I kem home she told me. I thought I might as well have it out, and I started down B street. Right in the middle of the street, opposite Donovan's saloon, was Moriarty a-waitin' for me. He fired one barrel at me, and the slugs whistled over me, but not one touched me. Before he could get his gun up to his shoulder for a second shot I got out my pistol and dropped him. They carried him off to the hospital. He lived a week before he passed in his checks. His friends gave him a great funeral. I was in the jail, in the sheriff's office when it passed by. I was sorry for him, and I sent $100 that I had saved up, to his widow. But what could I have done? It wasn't my fault that I had to kill him to save my own life, was it?

"The way I got out of that scrape was peculiar. The grand jury indicted me for murder. The court was busy, and it was nigh on to two months that I staid in jail awaitin' trial. In the meantime one of the doctors that attended on Moriarty at the trial died and the other went insane. Both of the nurses who attended him at the hospital and put him in the coffin had left the state. Of all the crowd who attended his funeral not one had seen the face of the corpse, and, to make a long story short, after three adjournments and three days' delay hunting testimony, the district attorney could not prove that Moriarty was dead.

9. In other words, "arm myself."

"My lawyer got up. 'There is no proof here of a "corpus delickedeye,"'[10] said he. 'I ask your Honor to order the discharge of the jury and the dismissal of the case.'

"'Motion granted,' said the jedge.

"'This is the second time Mr. Billings has been before me. I advise him to go back to the cattle ranch in California, where he was working, before he has any more trouble.'

"'Thank you, Jedge,' says I. 'I'll go. The stage leaves at daylight to-morrow for Strawberry valley, and I'll be aboard of it.'

"Johnny Brannigan, who was O'Rourke's first cousin, heard what I said, and just before daylight, while I was settin' in front of the store at the Oasis saloon about half asleep, Brannigan rushed in. 'You won't get off this time,' said he; and with that he shoved a dragoon pistol into me and fired. I fell over on my back on the floor, dyin', as I thought and he thought, and he stood there grinnin' at me and a-cussin' of me. That riled me. I rallied all my strength and sprang to me feet. He dropped his gun, and ran like a cur into a little card room in the rear of the office, went inside and braced himself agin' the door. I picked up his pistol, followed him, broke in the panel of the door with my left fist, and felt it strike agin' his body. Then I put the muzzle of his own pistol in the hole and fired two shots. Then I fell down, and they carried me to the hospital. They told me afterwards that Brannigan was plumb dead when they shoved the door in.

"I hated to get out, but I either had to or else kill about all of the Irishmen in Virginia City, so I went over to Sierra county, California, and the sheriff gave me a job as deputy. A week afterwards the Downieville stage was robbed by three men who got the express box which had $25,000 in it. Wells, Fargo, & Company offered $1,000 each for the capture of the robbers, dead or alive, and $5,000 for the recovery of the treasure. I took my Henry rifle that night, and journeyed as far as the place where the stage had been stopped. At daylight I picked up their trail and followed it up the mountain. In them days I was as keen on a track, whether of man or bar, as any Injin. Towards sunset I came in sight of three men settin' around a camp fire in front of a small cave. It was dead easy. I crept up on 'em and called on 'em to drop their arms, and surrender, and go down the trail in single file in front of me. If they had done so I would have marched them into Downieville and never hurt them. But the fools made a fight on me, and before they could get their guns up I dropped them one at a time. I got the treasure which was in the cave. I piked it down the trail to the road. That was the hardest part of the job, for it weighed over 100 pounds. I waited until the stage came along. There was

---

10. "Corpus delicti": legal Latin for the corpse of the victim in a murder case.

only one passenger. We left him in charge of the team, and the driver, the guard, and I went up the trail and carried the three bodies down, one at a time, and loaded 'em on the stage.

"I delivered the goods at the express office. The next day Wells, Fargo, & Company paid me $8,000 in a draft on San Francisco.

"By this time, Jedge, I was plum tired of killin' people. I kem down to Arizony, bought the Rodriguez ranch with 300 head of cattle, and with the exception of answerin' to the call of the sheriff to make up a posse to capture the gang that robbed the Valley bank, I have lived a quiet life ever since. One of the robbers was killed in making the capture. They say the bullet that killed him fitted my gun. Mebbe so, anyway he was due to be killed."

"That only makes eight, Jack," said I, "who was the ninth man? Wasn't he the Spaniard whose heart they said you cut out after you killed him? How was it about that?"

"Jedge," said Jack, "I will tell you about that. I did that to save human life. You see Jose Gonzales and his four cousins—them Mexicans are all cousins or something—had put up a job to rob my ranch house of the gold I took out at Antelope Hill. Jose's woman gave the job away to my wife Carmelita, who was her cousin. I heard as how the five of them was gathered at Miguel Sevrada's saloon at McKenburg, half a mile away, waitin' for nightfall, when they intended to make a raid on me.

"I threw my sack of gold nuggets down the well where Carmelita could get it in case anything happened to me. Then I started for McKenburg to have it out with the villains.

"Jose saw me comin', and he knew what he might expect. He was leaning agin a post in front of the saloon. He got out his gun. I treated him dead squar. I gin him the first shot. But he was that skeert that he never came anigh me. Then I dropped him. He was plumb dead when I got up to him. I knew I had either to kill those four cousins or to skeer them out of the country. Jose's heart wa'nt no use to him, was it? So I opened him with my bowie and took it out. I took it in my left hand, and, with my pistol in my right hand, I kicked open the front door of the saloon, and said to the four cousins, 'I have this one heart to draw to, and I aim to make it a heart flush[11] before mornin'. I shall begin drawin' to it in about ten minutes. The back door of this saloon leads into the corral where your cayuses[12] are. Get on them and keep going south until you get over the Mexican line.'

---

11. A grim pun on the poker term *flush*, or five cards in the same suit—hearts in this case.
12. Western vernacular for horses or ponies.

"And they did, Jedge. My humane scheme saved those four lives. Did any of the fellers that say hard things about me ever save four lives?"

Jack was discharged because the stage robbery was committed in an adjoining country where the magistrate had no jurisdiction, and before he could be again arrested the real robbers were discovered with their booty on them.

⟶In the private collection of the family of Sylvia Crowell Stoddard

The Loco Weed

Sam P. Davis

It was a hot afternoon on the eastern slope of the Sierras. There was no fleck of clouds in the blue sky, and the sun like a great ball of gold shed its mellow glow over the rocks and pines and green meadows of a Nevada landscape. About half way up the mountain slope, in a little hollow of but a few acres in extent, where the crystal springs gushed from under the overhanging rocks and the grass grew luxuriantly, a band of horses fed. A few yards above them under the shade of a spreading cedar were two men, lazily enjoying their pipes. It was a hazy, sleepy day for both man and beast; the balmy, pine-scented air had its somnolent effect upon everything. The men dozed in the shade, the watch dog had not moved for an hour, and half of the hundred horses in the meadow lay prone upon the ground. Suddenly the dog lifted his head from between his paws and started to his feet as both men nervously rose to a sitting posture. There was a commotion in the band below. Several of the horses began to perform the most unaccountable antics. Some rushed madly over the ground, snorting in terror, and others, apparently seized with an uncontrollable impulse, rose with their forefeet high in air and walked as if they were trying to ascend a pair of invisible stairs. It was not long before the whole band became affected. While some seemed driven to terror and madness, others were overtaken with a delirium of ecstasy and reeled about as if intoxicated with some newfound delight. Neither of the two men attempted to interfere with the antics of the animals, and the dog, that rushed in among the band, barking vociferously, soon received a kick in the side and was glad to get back in the shade. The two watchers did not interfere for the simple fact that they knew exactly what was the matter with the horses. They had eaten the loco weed and were now under its influence. While the effects of this peculiar plant are well known to the herdsmen of the sagebrush, no antidote for its extraordinary effects has ever been discovered.

216

A scientific investigation of the matter never seems to have occurred to anybody engaged in the business of horse breeding. So the loco weed is left to grow unmolested on the plains without any effort at eradication. The men in question were not even able to distinguish the plant when they saw it.

After the sun went down they spread their blankets upon the ground and prepared to turn in for the night. A few paces back of the tree was a canvas tent and the various paraphernalia of a herdsman's outfit, but the air was so still and warm that its shelter was not necessary.

"Bill," said the elder, "I guess we better let the horses shift for themselves; we can't do anything for them."

"No," said the other, "they're all locoed, and things will have to run their course."

Even as they spoke there was a fresh commotion among the band and the animals went thundering past the camp like the mad whirl of a tornado. They passed about a hundred yards from the spot and swept up the hill, their hoofs beating the rocks and underbrush. Some dashed their brains out against the heavy bounders, and their terrible death cry rang out upon the night, and others sank helpless in a network of tangled vines and retarding masses of manzanita. As they plunged away in the darkness their frantic snorts of rage and terror sounded shrilly above the din and turmoil of mad-dened hoof beats. The sounds grew fainter and fainter and died away in the distance. The herders did not stir from their camp-fire; they merely sat down on their blankets and lit their pipes for a good smoke. They did not own the horses, but merely herded them on a monthly salary, and nobody is ever blamed when the horses browse upon the loco weed.

"Have you seen any white sage growing around here, Bill?"

"Lots of it," said the other; "just beyond the spring."

The one who had first spoken started out on a tour of investigation and soon came back with a little bunch of the plant in his hand. This he placed in a pot half filled with water and hung it over the fire. He did not notice as he stirred the decoction that a little leaf which he had picked in the semi-darkness was mingled with the rest.

"Are you making some white sage tea, Jack?"

"Yes, I've got an idea I need a little, for I'm feelin' feverish for the last few days."

"When I'm feelin' that way I fall back on whisky. Here, pour a little whisky in that brew and you've got something you can depend on."

But Jack pushed the flask away, having a preference under the circumstances for his sage tea. In a few minutes it had boiled sufficiently, and after pouring it off in a tin cup to cool, he took a good draught of it.

"What sort of stuff was there in this cup?"

"Nothin' that I know of."

"Kind of a queer taste about it," and as he spoke he made a wry face. Presently he threw the remainder of the decoction away with a gesture of disgust, but a moment later he burst into a laugh and began dancing an impromptu jig on a little beaten spot of ground alongside the campfire.

"If ye feel that way, I guess I'll jine ye."

Bill walked back to the tent, and after rummaging about in it, brought out a fiddle with three strings, from which he immediately proceeded to extract the opening bars of a plantation jig. After getting about a third of the melody into circulation he paused a moment, bent his ear over the instrument with a thoughtful air, and failing to recall the balance of the tune, proceeded to repeat the bars already played. The player was not what might be called a violinist, he was merely a fiddler, and an exceedingly poor one. His weakness for the instrument was proverbial in the camps of the mountains, and he sometimes played for dances in the vicinity of Sheridan and Wolf Creek, but the memory of man does not recall a time when he was ever invited to play if a violinist of ordinary capacity could be secured. Two dollars a night and a pint of Indian whisky had been the top limit of his remuneration even in the heyday of his musical greatness. Indeed, knowledge of the divine art possessed by this wandering disciple of Orpheus had been held in such contempt by the mountaineers that after one of his efforts in furnishing music for a shakedown cotillion, payment for his services had frequently been refused, while a request to leave the camp and take his fiddle with him had been augmented by suggestive display of firearms of various calibers. But Bill was not of a sensitive nature; he was well aware of his musical deficiencies and accepted these harsh criticisms of his art with becoming humility and forbearance. When he saw his companion dancing merrily by the campfire to the discordant music of his jig there crept into his being a sensation of delight he had never before experienced. His unconquerable weakness for sawing on a violin had subjected him to much rough language, profanity and misfortune, but here was a man dancing with a most extraordinary vim to the music of his wretched fiddle, and that, too, as if he really enjoyed it. Bill had never been so supremely happy before in all his checkered existence. The absence of the bass string made no difference to him, and when the adjoining string snapped with a loud report, it did not in the slightest degree interrupt the flow of his musical ecstasy.

When an hour had passed the dancing figure by the fireside was still in motion, and the fact began slowly to penetrate the brain of the elated musician that something extraordinary had taken possession of his friend.

"Wonder if Jack's got locoed?" he said to himself as he threw some more wood upon the fire. Locoed or not locoed, he felt sure of the proposition that he was alone with a man who would dance to his fiddling as long as the instrument held out, and he did not propose foolishly to cast aside any of the advantages of the situation.

*   *   *   *   *

After the peculiar taste of the fever brew had passed from Jack's mouth he became aware of a strange mental and physical exhilaration. There was no longer a heavy feeling to his feet, stiffened with mountain tramps, and his brain, sluggish, commonplace and unpoetical, seemed kindled with the fire of new thought. Suddenly he became aware of a group of shining domes, gleaming through the interstices of the rocks and trees, and his ears caught the strains of delicious music. Pressing forward into the open space he heard the murmur of a hundred fountains, which flung their glittering lances into the moonlight. A flood of light streaming from the entrance of a palace invited him to come on, and a few moments later he found himself in the center of a vast hall, the dome of which seemed jeweled with ten thousand lamps. In the center upon a draped platform were two orchestras, and their music never ceased. The strains of the waltz which died in the hands of one band of musicians found life again in the instruments of the other, and the two were in such perfect accord that the tread of the melody from one orchestra to the other could be detected by the eye only, as he saw the instruments lowered in one group after the relief had lifted theirs.

As the bewildered herder was being jostled along amid a throng of enraptured dancers, a thousand or more of whom were whirling through the hall, one of them, a young woman, whose beauty caused his sluggish blood to bubble in his veins, approached him with outstretched hands, and with a look of invitation from the black depth of her eyes that sent a shiver of ecstasy through his frame, she fell into his arms and the two melted into the stream of revelry. Never had mortal ear listened to such enslaving melody, and the swaying revelers seemed to revolve about the musicians as the swiftly flying spokes of a wheel whirl round the axle. Presently the music seemed to lift itself into a higher vantage ground, from which point it might trample and destroy. The leader moved among his musicians, smiting the air with his baton like a swordsman engaging with an adversary, the foam flying from his lips and his face purple with excitement. Then the feet of the frenzied throng coursed over the floor with an uncontrollable speed, and the herdsman, pressing his panting companion to his breast, felt himself drifting before the gusts of music borne along without any effort of his own, intoxicated with passion and seemingly like on the verge of a trance.

Suddenly a wail from the orchestra sent a shudder through the swaying mass of pleasure-seekers. In the struggle of the instruments for supremacy the searching note of the leader's violin seemed like a voice from some charnel-vault. The note pierced the herdsman's soul like a knife thrust, but his companion, swaying in the rhythmic swing of the waltz, only drew closer to him with a smile that seemed an anodyne for the music's stab. Again the low, searching wail fluttered into the melody, only this time it was longer on the wing, and before the herdsman had recovered from the sensation that it gave him—whether of pain or pleasure he could no longer tell—the note had returned. It seemed to hover around the outer edge of the music, as if trying to find an opening, and then became the key note about which everything circled. When it had finally asserted its supremacy the rest of the instruments seemed struggling to climb to its level, and the effect, while it entranced all, caused every one to turn towards the spot with something of a shudder. The sight, extraordinary as it was, did not cause a single foot to pause. The leader was a skeleton, waving his bony arm aloft, and from the frames of his hundred musicians the flesh was dropping piecemeal. The music rose to higher key, and grew more subtle and entrancing, but the limbs of the dancers, wearied to exhaustion, could not find a moment's rest, and the mad dance circled around the fleshless players as a whirlpool around its vortex. It was then that Jack saw that the costly dresses of the revelers who jostled against him were rotting on their bodies, and through the rents of these tattered habiliments he saw the coarse, red flesh of the foul and motley groups. The lights grew dimmer and a cold wind swept through the palace. As they reeled past a flickering chandelier he looked at the face of his companion. She was growing old in his very arms, and had already become a wrinkled, withered crone. He tried to tear himself from her embrace, but she only clung to him the closer, and still the music wailed forth its seductive measures as the crowd of dancers, all growing old before his eyes, circled with lessening speed about the orchestra like a wheel losing its momentum. One by one the lights faded along with the last notes of the waltz, the walls of the palace showed crumbling gaps here and there, and along with a chill wind, the gray and muffled light of dawn crept in upon the scene. With the death throes of the music he disengaged his arms and saw that the face of his companion was stamped with the marks not only of age but vice and misery as well. Her once brown masses of shining hair lay in gray, disheveled tangles over her shoulders, and little was left of her raiment but a few greasy rags. As he waved her from him with an exclamation of disgust, she uttered an obscene oath and bounded upon him like a beast of prey.

*   *   *   *   *

It was after midnight when Bill wearied of scraping his fiddle for his companion to dance by, but it is hardly probable that he would have desisted from his musical exercise had not the last string been broken. There were no more strings to be had except at Tim Short's store in Glenbrook, at least twelve miles away, and with a sigh he laid his instrument aside. As he did so the man who had been shuffling jigs by the campfire with such extraordinary and tireless energy for several hours paused in his exercise a moment, and then with a yell of rage bounded upon the exhausted fiddler.

"Say, Jack, what's the matter? Take your hands off my throat. I say, Jack, let go. Don't you know me? Say, I'm Bill, your partner. Say, you cursed fool, let go of my—"

These were the last words the poor fellow, pinned to the ground, could utter. The weight of a heavy knee was on his chest, and the clutch upon his throat tightened like a vise. With his tongue protruding from his mouth and his eyes starting from their sockets, he died there alongside the smoldering campfire.

Next day some prospectors found the stiffened body, having been attracted to the spot by the howling of a dog, that lay with his nose muzzled in his master's breast. A few yards away was a man who had dashed his brains out against the granite bowlder.

At the inquest held in Genoa a physician noted the strange circumstance that every vein in this man's body showed as darkly through the skin as if it had been traced with India ink.

⇒*Nevada Magazine* 1:3 (October 1899): 166–70

The Mystery of the Savage Sump

Samuel Davis

This story is a peculiar combination of a fictitious literary hoax about a financial hoax and a realistic exposé. Davis created a new literary hoax by embellishing an earlier one by De Quille, but the tale's thinly disguised attack on the Silver King, U.S. Senator James G. Fair (1831–1894), one of the Comstock's richest but most avaricious and unscrupulous mine owners, which includes the charge that he was a murderer, was justified by fact.

⋙═ ═⋘

It was more than twenty years ago that Virginia City, Nevada, first wrestled with what was known as "The Mystery of the Savage Sump."

The sump of the Savage mine is an excavation at the foot of the incline where the hot water of the mine collects in volume, and from whence it is pumped into the Sutro tunnel, steaming, scalding hot.[1] The Sutro tunnel strikes the great Comstock ledge 1,750 feet below the surface, and is the drain pipe through which all the water in the Comstock mines is discharged. It runs through the boxes in the tunnel nearly five miles before it reaches the lower mouth of the tunnel and from thence finds its way into the Carson River. The sump is more than three thousand feet below the surface, and when this point was reached it marked the limit of man's ability to pierce the depths of the earth on the Comstock ledge.

---

1. Although the Comstock Lode is located in arid country, the mines encountered such huge quantities of underground water that enormous pumps had to be imported from Cornwall and operated constantly to keep the tunnels from flooding. Virginia City, moreover, was sited on thermally active ground. Air temperatures of 125–30 degrees Fahrenheit were common, and heat increased with depth. At the 2,000 foot level, the temperature rose to 160 degrees; at 3,000 feet, to 170 degrees. The water from lower levels was literally scalding.

The water came in so fast that the big pumps had to be kept constantly at work to prevent the flooding of the lower levels.

One morning the miners who came off the three-o'clock shift reported the finding of the body of a man in the sump. It was a horrible, shapeless thing, with the flesh cooked in the hot water and the features unrecognizable. The body, what was left of it, was exposed in the morgue for more than a week, but not identified. Several thousand men were working in the mines at the time, but the roll of the Miners' Union and the tally sheet of the Savage mine showed no one missing.

Besides this it was noticed that the corpse had on fine boots with high heels. It also had on remnants of clothes, and portions of a broadcloth coat were fished up from the sump. It could not have been a miner, and those who had charge of the incline leading to the sump were positive that no such man had ever gone down. There was but one way of reaching it, and that was by riding down on a sort of cage known as the "giraffe," let down and pulled up by a cable worked by machinery running in the hoisting works above ground.

The men who were employed in the responsible positions about the mine were all of the most trustworthy character, and had been employed there for years. No one could enter the mine without a permit from the superintendent, and even then no visitor ever went into the lower levels, where the hot water dripped from the rocks and the heat was sometimes as high as 140 degrees in places where the half-naked men worked with cold water playing from a hose on their bodies.

If it were murder, who could possibly be implicated? The authorities and the newspapers and the officers of the Miners' Union and the superintendents of the mines investigated the mystery on separate lines, and after a year of probing it was as much a mystery as on the day the body was discovered floating about, swollen and distorted, in the foul and steaming waters of the sump.

As the years passed the incident was well-nigh forgotten, but now, at this remote time, I am able to furnish the world with a complete solution.

If the reader will take the pains to look over the files of the San Francisco papers during the latter part of 1869 and the spring of '70, some of the most violent fluctuations that ever occurred in the mining stock-market will be noticed. One and the same narration tells the story of the death of the unknown man found in the Savage sump and the rise and fall of mining stock at the time mentioned. In the fall of '69 a San Francisco stock speculator was spending a few weeks at Lake Tahoe, the summer resort in the Sierra Nevada Mountains, which lies partly in Nevada and partly in California.

Wishing to be out of the way of the world as much as possible, he engaged quarters at a little secluded place on the Nevada side of the lake, known as Carnelian Bay. It was a cheap and out-of-the-way place, and not over a dozen guests were there at a time, but the fishing was excellent and the surroundings pleasant. The tourist's name was William Meeker, and he had lost a large fortune in the whirl of stock speculations on California Street.

One morning, while fishing about a mile from the hotel, he noticed that his boat began slowly turning, and in a few minutes described a complete circle in the water. Some chips and debris were collected about the boat and they seemed to stay there. He studied the situation carefully and reached the conclusion that there was a subterranean outlet which caused the eddy.

He was a man of quick action, and that night he carved the initials W. M. on a piece of pine, and next morning rigged up a weight at the end of a line and, fastening the stick to the weight, rowed out and lowered it into the water where his boat had been affected by the currents. It went down in about a hundred feet of water and then something began bearing it down. There was a succession of tugs and the line began spinning over the edge of the boat with rapidly increasing speed. Then the line caught in the boat and snapped with the strain. This made it clear to him that the water was surging through an outlet in the lake bottom. That night he settled his bill and started for San Francisco.

He took but one man into his confidence and that was Colonel Clair, one of the heaviest and most unscrupulous operators in the market and a member of the biggest firm on the street.[2] They figured for more than a week with maps and surveys and reached the conclusion that the water making its exit from the lake was finding its outlet in the lower levels of the Comstock mines.[3]

They pored over statistical tables showing how the lake had been, on an average, at least one foot higher before the mines in Virginia City had encountered water in the lower levels, and to them the mystery of the fall in the water of the lake was explained.

It was decided to send a man into the Savage to watch for the piece of pine with Meeker's initials on. But why trust it to a third party? Meeker himself went to Virginia City, and on a letter of recommendation from Colonel Clair was given work in the Savage and placed at the foot of the incline as a station tender.

He had not been long at his post when the little piece of wood with the initials W. M. came up on the surface of the waters of the sump, and his

2. A thinly disguised portrait of James Fair.

3. This part of the story was very likely suggested by Dan De Quille's famous 1876 hoax, "Eyeless Fish That Live in Hot Water" (included herein), which speculated that the source of the mines' water was a subterranean lake or reservoir and noted that the mines were lower than all bodies of water nearby. Some investors were alarmed by what they thought was the story's implication that Lake Tahoe was the source of the water, but De Quille's fame as a hoaxer, and the consensus of the Comstock that the hoax was innocent, laid the fears to rest.

heart gave a great bound of joy. That night he was flying to San Francisco on a fast train, and next morning was closeted with Colonel Clair, the mining operator and millionaire.

The plan these two men fixed on was the boldest ever conceived in the annals of stock speculation. It was nothing less than a method by which the hole in the bottom of Tahoe might be stopped by a mechanical contrivance and then opened and closed at will. By this means the mines might be cleared of water or flooded, to suit the convenience of the two operators, and this condition, having its influence on the stock-market, would make millions of money for the men who had conceived the bold design.

Before the week was over, Meeker, backed with the money of Colonel Clair, was back at Lake Tahoe. He ordered a large flatboat built, ostensibly for fishing purposes. It was completed in a couple of weeks and fitted with a good cabin, and here he took up his abode. From then on a lot of mysterious consignments reached Tahoe for Meeker, and he received them on his flatboat at Tahoe City and moved the boat from place to place by the aid of a small steam-launch.

To all intents and purposes it was an angler's craft, the mere pastime of a man who had the money at his disposal to catch Tahoe trout in his own way.

It proved really a simple matter to stop the hole in the lake. Careful investigation showed it to be nearly circular and about four feet across. The dimensions of the hole being known approximately was sufficient. The butt of a log about five feet in diameter was given a conical shape, and bolts were sunk into the end, to which a heavy chain was attached. This was connected with a windlass and let down through the "well" in the bottom of the boat. The well was enclosed in the rough-board house built on the boat, and on a calm day, when the water was still, Clair and Meeker could see a long distance into the depths of the water, by the aid of a large mirror and the sunlight which came in through a hole in the roof of the house, reflected down the well.

Then came the grand test, when they let down the big plug. Slowly it was lowered until it caught in the suction and the chain showed the enormous strain. Then down, deeper and deeper it went in the mighty current, taking the handles of the windlass from the hands of the men and sending it whirling. It revolved like a buzz-saw for a few seconds, and then came to a standstill. It was evident that the plug had settled into the hole as far as it would go, and that the pressure of the water was keeping it there. The deflected light thrown down by the mirror showed that such was the case.

Could the plug be lifted back? The fate of their plot depended on the answer. The two men threw their weight on the handles of the windlass, but they could not budge it an inch. That night they bored holes in the windlass shaft and inserted long crowbars. With this improved leverage they succeeded with comparatively little trouble in drawing the plug out of the hole and lifting it beyond the influence of the suction. Several times they lowered and raised it again. That night Colonel Clair was on his way to San Francisco, leaving Meeker to guard the boat.

During the next ten days brokers who watched the market noticed that the firm of Goodman & Crowley was buying Savage in any lots offered. There was nothing special in the way of developments in the mine, and those who had become tired of holding Savage began to unload on a rising market. Presently the brokers who had the handling of the deal were active bidders on the stock. The tall form of Joe Goodman was soon noticeable in the center of a gesticulating crowd, bidding up Savage.[4] The price rose gradually, and still he stood calm and serene, as was his wont, and taking in all the Savage offered.

"Five thousand at twenty-six, buyer thirty."

Goodman took them, and ten thousand more at the same figure.

A little man rose and flung twenty thousand shares at Goodman. He took them without blinking.

There was a pause and the swirl of speculation seemed for a moment to have lost its momentum.

Thirty-five thousand shares inside a minute, and snapped up by one man, was not a usual thing. They waited to see what the calm, blue-eyed man would do, as if he would dare bid higher. Then his voice rang out:

"Twenty-seven for twenty-five thousand shares, buyer thirty."

In an instant the cry of "sold" was shouted at him from all sides of the Board room.

"Take 'em all," he cried, "and will give twenty-eight for fifty thousand more."

Not a sale was offered at those figures. Something was on. The brokers scented a big deal in Savage, and no one dared take his offer.

The session closed and in a few minutes the street was a scene of extraordinary excitement. The wires were hot between San Francisco and Virginia City with cipher dispatches, but no one could report anything extraordinary in Savage. There was no development, and the water in the lower levels required the full working capacity of the big Cornish pumps to hold it in control.

Goodman was a commission broker and evidently not speculating on his own hook, and Colonel Clair's brokers were selling Savage—but in mighty small lots.

Colonel Clair was moving about the street in front of the Exchange building, deprecating the idea of a rise in stocks not based on actual merit.

4. The mention of Goodman lends the appearance of realism to this fictitious tale. Goodman was a well-known former Comstock publisher and, later, a sometime San Francisco stockbroker, as well as a friend of Davis's.

"Me son,"[5] he said to one of the curbstone brokers, "there can never be anything in buying Savage until the water is out of the lower levels."

Within a week the water was nearly all out of the Savage, and also out of the adjoining mines, and stocks began to soar. The pumps all along the big lead were slowing down, and the word went out that the water had been conquered at last and now the big bonanzas were going to be uncovered. Virginia City was happy, and the Stock Exchange in San Francisco was a whirl of speculation.

Then Colonel Clair began shorting everything right in the midst of the flurry. He had sold and realized a cool million, and was now a bear.[6] It seemed odd that this should be the case when the pumps had drained the lower levels almost dry and no water was coming in. Then unexpectedly the waters came into the lower levels in a great flood and caught the miners napping with the pumps barely moving. There was a crash in stocks when the news reached Pine Street, San Francisco, and everything went by the board. Colonel Clair cleaned up another million.

"I didn't think it could be permanent," he said.

Then came a series of rises and breaks in the market and Colonel Clair always "hit them just right." No man seemed so shrewd as he, and so the deals went on and his wealth accumulated. William Meeker had but to raise or lower the plug in Lake Tahoe according to advices.

One night, as Meeker was raising the plug with the big windlass, he became aware of a figure behind him. It was Colonel Clair, who had reached the spot by a boat.

"How is she working?"

"Never better."

"I have your share deposited in the Nevada Bank, and it is now over two million."

Meeker smiled and his heart bounded when he heard those words.

"How big the moon looks over yonder," exclaimed the Colonel.

Meeker turned his head, and a heavy iron bar crushed in his skull. Colonel Clair tied a weight to the body and lowered it into the depths. Down and down it slowly sank, and then the swirl sucked it into the hole and it was gone. Colonel Clair lowered the plug.

The Black Cat, December 1901; Duncan Emrich, ed.,
Comstock Bonanza, 281–87

---

5. Another tie to Fair, an Irishman, who often addressed men as "me son."

6. A bear, in stock market terminology, is one who sells "short," that is, sells stock (usually that he does not currently possess) at less than the going price, in expectation that the stock will soon drop in value, and that he will be able to acquire what he needs for an even lower price.

The Conversion of Champagne Liz

Sam Davis

The editor found this story in manuscript form in the private collection of the family of Sylvia Crowell Stoddard and gratefully acknowledges permission from the Crowell family and the late Sylvia Stoddard to publish it for the first time. It exists in three slightly different typescript versions, all undated. The editor has collated them into the present form.

⋆⇒◯ ◯⇐⋆

No one ever seemed able to fix the date when Champagne Liz acquired her bibulous appellation, or who christened her. She was a true daughter of the vine, however, and Omar must have had some such person in mind when he wrote of

The cyprus-slender minister of wine.[1]

She drifted into Virginia City when the old Comstock was awhirl and brought her name with her, and those who knew her earlier say that she answered to it and lived up to it in Butte City, Montana, and back of that the chroniclers make no mention.

The marked characteristic of the woman was her fondness for the best brands of champagne and when in the periods of her financial reverses she lacked the money to buy her favorite tipple, she slaked her thirst with cold water and said nothing.

She had strange moods and did strange things and was entirely unlike other people. In person she was worth describing. Tall and slender, with a tread like a panther and a sort of free unfettered carriage that would attract a second look from any man that had a drop of red blood in his veins.

---

1. Edward FitzGerald, *The Rubáiyát of Omar Khayyám*, stanza 41.

228

Her eyes were blue or gray as she happened to feel, or the way you looked into them, and her hair was gold today and a burnished copper tomorrow.

You never could tell where you would meet Liz next. She might be in the most fashionable church gorgeously arrayed and radiant in a new Easter hat, singing the hymns and anthems with a fine voice and deep aspect of piety, and a few days later she might be holding down a ringside seat at a prize fight: betting her money recklessly as she stood up on her tiptoes hurling her challenges across the ring and daring anybody in sight to cover her odds of ten to seven on the favorite.

She dealt faro and roulette and played poker with men until the gray dawn crept in, and cruised about town at all hours of the night. Yet if any one had chosen to insinuate that there was anything wrong about Champagne Liz, he never would have realized exactly what he said until he had come out of his enforced trance in some hospital.

But a woman's reputation in those days merely meant that she was true to some man with whom she had decided to live, and so it was with Liz.

In the memorable days of the Old Ledge[2] there was no rule of desert chivalry so well established and observed as the protection thrown about a mistress. Married women had the protection of the law, which in many instances was no protection at all. It might as well have been a spider's web as far as it served as a shield against the social marauder, but the "honor of the Ledge" was a different thing entirely, and hedged a man's mistress like a wall of steel. No epithet of the camp was so blistering in its rugged vernacular as that applied to a human vermin who attempted to scale this wall.

So it was that Liz spent the best years of her life in this environment, the best years of her youth, which to most of us might have been wasted years, that levied their remorseless toll on her health and beauty. But she lived for the joy of living and the pleasure she took in spending money with her friends, which were many. She was the life of the gay midnight suppers, and she sang and danced and flooded the pathway of existence with wine and flowers.

She was quick at repartee and her tongue had the sharp thrust of a flame; but she never made the thrust without repenting and begging forgiveness.

She seemed to love every human being. She nursed the sick and helped the poor, and I have seen her stop some poor devil in the street, who was down and out of luck and hungry, and loading him into a café, order a course dinner and a bottle of wine and go on her way happy that she had lifted a load of care from someone's shoulders.

---

2. A ledge is a vein of ore. In the early days of the Comstock Lode, before the incredibly rich Big Bonanza was discovered deep underground, the original silver discoveries of the 1860s were in what was later called the "old ledge," the parts of the vein nearest the surface.

But the Comstock had its period of feverish money-making and swift decline. Like all great mining camps the time came when the bats began to nest in the hoisting works and the inert machinery was mantled with creeping vines.

Liz, like any other human bubble, went out with the tide. She cracked her last bottle of wine and was gone.

Next she was part of the gay life of Treasure Hill[3] when the great camp was a blaze of money-making, but her figure had lost its classic curves, and her girlish beauty had begun to show the tread of the years and the tan of the desert sun.

She struggled along against the remorseless current of Fate, the ground slipping from under her feet gradually, and when it was soon over, Liz, once the petted and pampered favorite of the Comstock, and now ——.

One dislikes to record what she was after that for she always had so many "good streaks" in her that it seemed better to remember her virtues than her frailties.

Her conversion to religion was probably the strangest thing of all her checkered career.

She had attended a funeral, and after listening to some kindly word of charity for the erring she seemed determined to struggle up to a higher plane, and made an attempt to do so, but the footing was insecure and she fell back again.

She realized that she might never be anything but a derelict, and one night as she sat watching a roulette wheel whirling in front of her, she figured out that life after all was merely a chance. She likened herself to the ball that coursed round the circle and fell where it might; but always fell somewhere.

She bowed her head, weeping, and the tears trickled through her slim fingers.

"Cheer up, Liz," called out the dealer, "your word's good for a play here any time."

She lifted her head, remarking quietly, "A dollar on the red." It won and she was back in the game forgetting everything else and she toyed with varying fortune until her face was flushed with the excitement of the play and she was gathering in her winnings in stacks. When she had beaten the game a hundred, she ordered a bottle of wine and was back in the gambler's paradise.

Presently three men came into the resort who were taking up a subscription to collect funds with which to build a church. In the rush of putting Treasure Hill on the map the church had been overlooked.

They approached her, feeling that she might be in a generous mood just at

3. Treasure Hill was located in White Pine County, in eastern Nevada. Extremely rich ores were discovered there in 1868, as the Comstock mines were in temporary decline, and towns with populations of six and ten thousand sprang up suddenly. Treasure Hill's ores, however, were rich only near the surface; when they ran out suddenly, the mines closed and the towns were abandoned.

that time, for they knew her characteristics, and no one ever heard of her refusing aid for anything.

"Yes, I'm in for a church for Treasure Hill. I'll tell you people what I'll do. I'll put this hundred on the ten and roll the game for the Lord. Don't you think that if the Lord really wants a church in Treasure Hill He will help the ball to fall in the right place?"

She placed the five twenties on the ten and nodded to the dealer. It seemed a pretty long chance. The odds against a single number winning were thirty-five to one, but then again if the number won it paid thirty-five times.

"Is this perfectly satisfactory to you gentlemen?" she asked without looking up.

The money was there on the number, the ball was circling about on its mission of chance and there seemed no help for it. The church people did not exactly like to abet gambling but they seemed fairly in for it. Withal they were thinking, in a quiet way, that possibly the ball might stray into the right compartment.

The dealer had given the wheel a very vigorous impetus and in a few seconds the crowd in the room had gathered about the table and there was a tense silence relieved only by the whirring and gradually diminishing sound of the ball as it sped on its lagging journey.

It dropped finally into the little compartmented wheel which runs in the opposite direction from the big one, but it bounded back again, and the clicking of the ball as it skipped back and forth, as if searching for the right place, told that the end was near. The circle of men and women narrowed as they pressed in closer that they might see the finish, and Champagne Liz raised her thin hand aloft as a signal that it was all over when the ball, with a final click, rested in the No. 10 compartment.

There was shouting and clapping of hands, and a woman whose face told the sad story of a tragic past, said to a man at her elbow that she had "prayed hard" that the church might win.

A good many hardened sports who had never even thought of a place of public worship, to say nothing of ever having entered one, slid over to the bar and drank deeply and often to celebrate the victory of the church over the gambling table.

"I believe if a feller could git in with the Lord he could just break all these thievin' games."

"That game must have been run on the level that trip for I was watchin' the dealer's foot and if he'd monkeyed with the machinery I was ready to soak him."

While such comments were flying about the dealer was counting out the money that the game had lost and stacking up the gold in hundred dollar piles; Champagne Liz sat there motionless, never looking at her coin. Her gaze seemed to have wandered off into some unknown depths and she was only roused from her reverie when the dealer pushed the gold across the board to her and said, "Wake up, Liz."

The woman looked down at the money and then turning to the three men who had asked her to help the church, remarked quietly, "Take it. It is all yours."

"Liz comes through all right," said an admiring sport.

The dealer, with an accommodating spirit, loaned her a canvas sack and, filling it with the money, she passed it over to the church people.

"Here, take it. The Lord wanted you to have it or else that ball would never have won on the ten. I want to come to your church, and when it's built if you don't let me pray in it once in a while"—she paused as if about to make her contribution contingent on being allowed that privilege—but seemed to change her mind and added, "I guess there are no strings to it." This act seemed in marked contrast to some world-famous contributors to religion, who, as soon as they got into the public prints, bring up the rear of their ostentatious charities with onerous conditions.

"Of course, Liz. You will always be welcome."

"I thought churches were only for good people," was the reply. "I have been a wayward girl most all of my life but from this on I will try hard to be a Christian."

As she spoke, a colored waiter touched her on the arm with a tray on which was a bottle of champagne and some glasses. She turned toward the wine with a shudder.

"This is on the house," said the waiter.

"Take it away, Jake. I'm through with that cursed stuff. Not another drop. Take it away, I say."

To the citizens of Treasure Hill the fact that the leading house in the place had lost $3500 to the Church, so to speak, was regarded as about the richest joke of the season, but Champagne Liz looked upon it from an entirely different viewpoint. It was to her mind a manifestation of some higher power. It was as if Omnipotence had held up a warning finger to her. She could look at it in no other way. Viewed from any standpoint it was perfectly clear to her mind that some mysterious power was taking an interest in her welfare. She figured that she was the fallen sparrow being lifted from the ground.[4]

She had gone the world's pace and drunk full of the cup of life. Reviewing her past she felt the beatings of a repentant heart and was willing to make atonement.

That night word reached her that an old miner who had done her some

---

4. See Matthew 10:29.

act of kindness in the past was sick in his cabin a couple of miles away, and she determined to seek his bedside and pull him through his troubles.

It was a wild night for even a man to brave the elements and her friends tried to dissuade her from her mission. But she would listen to nothing, and with some medicine and a basket of provisions she set out in the falling snow.

"Only a couple of miles away and Bill sick," she said in answer to their entreaties. "I can make it easily."

It was easy enough at first but the snow got heavier and the rising wind bent it into drifts which obstructed her path. Then the tempest seemed to come from every quarter and when she got beyond the lights of the camp, she wandered about aimlessly, the storm beating down upon her frail figure, and again and again she stumbled into the drifts.

Then she heard a sound that sent the chill deeper into her frame. It was the wail of the coyote floating over the waste. It seemed but the ghost of a sound at first but it was joined by others until it swelled into a chorus of approaching savage voices. Stricken with an overwhelming terror, her brave heart almost stopped its beatings as she floundered on.

Presently they came on in full cry. One must hear a pack of the scavengers of the desert going up and down the diapason of their calls to realize what it means. Mere words can convey no adequate idea of the weirdness and terror of this uncanny language of the wilds.

They gathered about her now in numbers, and she felt that the time had come for her to die. She could see nothing in the darkness, but their yelps and barks came in a narrowing circle. Suddenly a shaft of moonlight shot from a rift in the clouds and for an instant she saw the mouth of a tunnel but a few yards away. The light had passed but she got her bearings in an instant and by a quick dash reached the tunnel. She felt safe enough now. The tunnel sheltered her from the blast and she put her hands against its rocky sides and enjoyed the additional warmth her retreat gave her.

The coyotes snarled at the entrance but did not come in. Soon it was evident that they were gathering more of their kind for a charge. They gave the desert call and it was answered, and when the answers came floating in on the wings of the storm from distant places, she knew that before morning she would have to fight for her life.

She gathered rocks and threw them at the pack and wondered why she had been so reckless as to leave Treasure Hill without matches. A fire would have saved her life. There was one chance left; her revolver. The very man she had gone forth to assist had given it to her with her initials engraved on the handle.

For a while the coyotes contented themselves with snarling and yelping at the entrance of the tunnel but soon the added clamor told Liz that reinforcements had arrived.

They became bolder as the pack swelled in numbers and rocks thrown in the darkness were but an insufficient defense.

As they came in she retreated. It finally occurred to her that they had scented the provisions in her basket and she cast the sop to them.

But this seemed to only whet their appetites and as they advanced with a rush her pistol cracked again and again until the cartridges were exhausted. It checked them for a few minutes but they came on again and she sank to her knees in prayer.

The leader leaped upon her and his jaws closed on her throat. In a moment the others were tearing her to pieces.

Next morning a searching party took the trail to find her but the storm had obliterated the tracks and the snow had drifted over the mouth of the tunnel, completely hiding it.

* * * * *

The seasons came and went and the mysterious disappearance of Champagne Liz ceased to be discussed in Treasure Hill.

Fortunately, the church she helped to found had a pastor who was thoughtful enough, and strong enough morally, to give her the benefit of a memorial service.

Treasure Hill had enjoyed a season of riotous opulence and was now nearing the end. The tunnels which had found such abundance of wealth in the mountain suddenly reached barren ground and in a few weeks the exodus began. Some sturdy souls hung on, loath to give up, and they fought the uphill battle of trying to make those barren rocks give up dividends.

Chad Connelly said that he would not close his saloon until the year went out, and he hung on at a loss. He vowed that his would be the last place to go.

It was New Year's night and he was sitting alone in his resort watching the clock crawling toward the midnight hour.

The winter's blast was throbbing against the frail walls of the building and the shrieking wind dominated everything. Suddenly the door flew open and a man bent, as if under a load, staggered in.

"It's a wild night on Treasure Hill," said the newcomer, and he added with a sinking voice, "and Mulligan's busted."[5]

In these few words he had told the story of his ruin.

The last bunch of stock he owned in the Hill had been sold by the broker in San Francisco and he got word that afternoon.

"Me partner's comin' behind and he has a sack of bones wid him. I wouldn't

5. The line was, for a time, a popular expression in Nevada mining communities used to indicate an abrupt onset of bad luck that doomed whatever enterprise one had been pursuing.

stay to pack such truck. He found it in the old tunnel." Inside half an hour another man carrying a sack on his shoulder came in and the gust of wind that followed him hurled him half way across the room.

"I was locatin' the old tunnel where General Kittrell used to own a claim and we found a skeleton of somebody and some coyote bones alongside."

As he spoke he emptied the contents of the sack on the table. Some bones rattled out; a skull; a pocket-book; and a six-shooter. The barkeeper picked up the weapon and looked at the initials on the pearl handle.

"Champagne Liz," he said in an undertone. The other two bent over the weapon and corroborated the statement.

"Here's a pocket-book," said Mulligan.

They opened it and found a five dollar gold piece and a faded scrap of paper.

"I've one bottle of wine left. Let's drink to her as the year goes out." The barkeeper bent behind the bar and fished up the last bottle of champagne in Treasure Hill.

"Crack 'er," was the response, and as he popped the cork the clock began clanging the hour of midnight.

"Isn't Liz payin' for this drink?"

"That's so," said the barkeeper. "Liz must be in."

They lifted the skull on the bar and filled three glasses. The rest of the wine the barkeeper poured into the fleshless jaws of Champagne Liz and then they all drank in silence. Dropping the gold piece in the till, he entered it on the book and Treasure Hill was a thing of the past.

"Here's something else," said Mulligan, as he unfolded the scrap of paper. It was in the handwriting of Champagne Liz.

> Said a woman's soul to a woman's heart,
> "I'll live forever, but dust thou art.
> For despite the fires that today doth burn,
> Tomorrow you die and to dust return."
> And the heart replied to the soul and said,
> "Though alive today and tomorrow dead,
> My day of life is worth to me
> Your endless years of eternity.
> For I'll laugh and love and sin and say,
> 'What shall it matter? The soul will pay.'"

➻In the private collection of the family of Sylvia Crowell Stoddard

Memoirs

Introduction

A surprisingly large segment of Sagebrush literature consists of memoirs, and these are far from being the least accomplished or least significant works by their authors. The samples collected herein are too few to adequately represent the extent of the memoirs, but they can convey a just impression of their character, historical and biographical importance, and stylistic power. Composition of them began early and lasted a long time, peaking in the late nineteenth and early twentieth centuries, but continuing with some vigor into the 1930s.

Because of Mark Twain's popularity, he is a favorite topic of Sagebrush memoirists. As much as we know about Twain today, much of value remains to be found in the memoirs about him, which have been greatly neglected. Alf Doten's recollection of early Nevada journalism helps fill in blanks about some Sagebrush authors as well as reinforces the standard account by Steve Gillis of the "robbery" of Twain that took place on the road between Virginia City and Gold Hill and that Twain sourly recalls in chapter 79 of *Roughing It*, but Doten adds new details and perspectives on the event. His information about Twain in Como is new.

Two accounts of Twain's December 1863 meeting with Artemus Ward illustrate both the value of memoirs and a problem with them. After twenty-five years, can anyone accurately recollect entire conversations? Yet, classical Greek and Roman historians often rendered conversations at which they were not present, nor even proximate to in time, and few subsequent readers have doubted that their accounts were of at least some value. One would like to believe Twain's narrative of his breakfast meeting; after all, he was there. On the other hand, Twain was notorious for "improving" episodes from his life. There was a dinner meeting that Twain and Ward both attended, and De Quille and Joe Goodman were both there also. Were there two meals in the same week at which the humorists met, or just one? If one, why the discrepancies? If two, why did Twain mention only one? At any rate, De Quille's 1888 account, despite the differences from Twain's—and De Quille's own second memoir in 1893—parallels Mark Twain's 1867 reminiscence, and De Quille adds believable and potentially useful information. Indeed, a problem with only one memoir being a source is that one person's memory is likely to be selective, overemphasizing some things and temporarily forgetting or entirely omitting others. We may never know exactly what was said when the two humorists dined with each other, but having more sources to choose from is almost certainly better than relying on just one.

While some memoirs must be partially discounted, others may be highly reliable. The account of the origin of Twain's Hopkins massacre hoax, for instance, is made more valuable by Joe Goodman's excellent memory and his penchant for truthfulness, as is his narrative of how Twain's humor backfired. This experience was a lesson Twain had to learn more than once. Similarly, the account of Conrad Wiegand's suicide, probably told by Joe Goodman, and nowhere else told in such detail, is not flattering to Twain. Although Goodman and Twain were close friends, this may be Goodman's way of setting his own conscience at rest—and in Twain's lifetime—for having played a regretted part in the good man's ordeal.

"Geological Reminiscences" is a valuable record of what Nevadan tycoons and men of influence liked to remember. At an informal table, they were momentarily equal, each contributing some cherished memory, usually partaking of rough and not always kind humor. The "gods," when not superhuman, were just human.

Most Sagebrush authors had a streak of sentimentality. In "My French Friend" Daggett's very likely describes real-life events, but fictionalizes them to convey the essential truth of the situations. Daggett describes an admirable man who nevertheless ends as a loser, but a loser who dies with grace. Such things happen, even though details differ from case to case. And as the story of Wiegand shows, good men do not always die with grace. Daggett and Goodman appear to have been haunted by recollections of poignant tragedies they witnessed.

No representation of Sagebrush literature would be complete without the inclusion of some andecdotes of Jim Townsend. Townsend was a legend in his own time, and newspapers all over Nevada and California eagerly seized and passed around any anecdote about his lies. To put it paradoxically, the truth was that Townsend was a genius at lying.

Nevada was notorious for its wide-open gambling, but the biggest gamble was the stock market. The memoir of how the stock market operated in those days of minimal regulation, and how stocks shot up and then plummeted, fueled only by speculation, can be read humorously today, but the laughter might be heartier without the recent experiences of Enron and the internet scandals. If these memoirs teach us nothing else, it is how little essential things change.

A Reminiscence of Artemus Ward

Mark Twain

Although he was a visiting Yankee from Maine, and not a Sagebrusher at all, Artemus Ward did significantly enlarge Twain's understanding of how to hoax. According to Joe Goodman, Ward's advance agent, E. F. Hingston, used to introduce himself with a card that read, "Ars est celere Artem-us." This wittily modified the core Latin adage "ars est celere artem" (true art is to conceal art) to mean "true art is to hurry up Artemus." What Twain learned from Ward was not only that the greatest art conceals itself, but also how to do it in plain sight. In his later work, Twain quickly became a past master at subtly loading familiar language with multiple meanings and constructing a hoax out of a pattern of controlled ironies. The jumbled and confusing rationales of the narrator of "The Carson Fossil-Footprints" (included herein) appear to be a lineal descendant of Ward's skill at double-talk. Twain seldom used this technique, but "The Carson Fossil-Footprints" shows that it was not because he had not perfectly assimilated Ward's lessons.

⋅⇒ ⇐⋅

I had never seen him before. He brought letters of introduction from mutual friends in San Francisco, and by invitation I breakfasted with him. It was almost religion, there in the silver mines, to precede such a meal with whisky cocktails. Artemus, with the true cosmopolitan instinct, always deferred to the customs of the country he was in, and so he ordered three of those abominations. Hingston was present. I am a match for nearly every beverage you can mention except a whisky-cocktail, and therefore I said I would rather not drink one. I said it would go right to my head and confuse me so that I would be in a hopeless tangle in ten minutes. I did not want to act like a lunatic before strangers. But Artemus gently insisted, and I drank the treasonable mixture under protest, and felt all the time that I was doing a thing I might be sorry for. In a minute or two I began to imagine that my ideas were getting clouded. I waited in great anxiety for the conversation to open, with a sort of vague hope that my understanding would prove clear, after all, and my misgivings groundless.

Artemus dropped an unimportant remark or two, and then assumed a look of superhuman earnestness, and made the following astounding speech. He said:

"Now, there is one thing I ought to ask you about before I forget it. You have been here in Silverland—here in Nevada—two or three years, and, of course, your position on the daily press has made it necessary for you to go down in the mines and examine them carefully in detail, and therefore you know all about the silver-mining business. Now, what I want to get at is—is. Well, the way the deposits of ore are made, you know. For instance. Now as I understand it, the vein which contains the silver is sandwiched in between casings of granite, and runs along the ground, and sticks up like a curbstone. Well, take a vein forty feet thick, for example—or eighty, for that matter, or even a hundred—say you go down on it with a shaft—straight down, you know, or with what you call an 'incline'—maybe you go down five hundred feet, or maybe you don't go down but two hundred—anyway, you go down— and all the time this vein grows narrower, when the casings come nearer, or approach each other, as you may say, that is, when they do approach, which of course they do not always do, particularly in cases where the nature of the formation is such that they stand apart wider than they otherwise would, and which geology has failed to account for, although everything in that science goes to prove that, all things being equal, it would, if it did not, or would not, certainly if it did, and then, of course, they are. Do not you think it is?"

I said to myself, "Now I just knew how it would be—that cussed whisky-cocktail has done the business for me; I don't understand any more than a clam." And then I said aloud, "I—I—that is—if you don't mind, would you—would you say that over again? I ought—"

"O, certainly, certainly. You see I am very unfamiliar with the subject, and perhaps I don't present my case clearly, but I—"

"No, no—no, no—you state it plain enough, but that vile cocktail has muddled me a little. But I will un—I do understand, for that matter, but I would get the hang of it all the better if you went over it again—and I'll pay better attention this time."

He said, "Why, what I was after, was this." [Here he became even more fearfully impressive than ever, and emphasized each particular point by checking it off on his finger-ends.][1] "This vein, or lode, or ledge, or whatever

---

1. Brackets in the original.

you call it, runs along like a curbstone, runs along between two layers of granite, just the same as if it were a sandwich. Very well. Now, suppose you go down on that, say a thousand feet, or maybe twelve hundred (it don't really matter), before you drift; and then you start your drifts, some of them across the ledge and others along the length of it, where the sulphurets—I believe they call them sulphurets, though why they should, considering that, so far as I can see, the main dependence of a miner does not so lie as some suppose, but in which it cannot be successfully maintained, wherein the same should not continue while part and parcel of the same and not committed to either in the sense referred to, whereas under different circumstances the most inexperienced among us could not detect it if it were, or might overlook it if it did, or scorn the very idea of such a thing, even though it were palpably demonstrated as such. Am I not right?"

I said, sorrowfully, "I feel ashamed of myself, Mr. Ward. I know I ought to understand you perfectly well—but you see that infernal whisky-cocktail has got into my head, and now I cannot understand even the simplest proposition. I told you how it would be."

"Oh, don't mind it, don't mind it, the fault was my own, no doubt—though I did think I was making it clear enough for—"

"Don't say a word. Clear? Why you stated it as clear as the sun to anybody but an abject idiot, but it's that confounded cocktail that has played the mischief."

"No, now don't say that—I'll begin all over again, and—"

"Don't now—for goodness' sake don't do anything of the kind—because I tell you my head is in such a condition that I don't believe I could understand the most trifling question a man could ask me."

"Now don't you be afraid. I'll put it so plain this time that you can't help but get the hang of it. We will begin at the very beginning. (Leaning far across the table, with determined impressiveness wrought upon his every feature, and fingers prepared to keep tally of each point as enumerated—and I leaning forward with painful interest also, resolved to comprehend or perish.) "You know the vein, the ledge, the thing that contains the metal, whereby it constitutes the medium between all other forces whether of present or remote agencies so brought to bear in favor of the former against the latter, or the latter against the former, or all or both, or compromising as far as possible the relative differences existing within the radius whence culminates the several degrees of similarity as to which—."

I said, "O blame my wooden head, it ain't any use!—it ain't any use to try—I can't understand anything. The plainer you get it, the more I can't get the hang of it."

I heard a suspicious noise behind me, and turned in time to see Hingston dodging behind a newspaper and quaking with a gentle ecstasy of laughter. I looked at Ward again, and he had thrown off his dread solemnity and was laughing also. Then I saw that I had been sold—that I had been made the victim of a swindle in the way of a string of plausibly-worded sentences that didn't mean anything under the sun.

Artemus was one of the best fellows in the world, and one of the most companionable. It has been said that he was not fluent in conversation, but with the above experience in mind, I differ.

New York Sunday Mercury, July 7, 1867

Artemus Ward

His Great Definition of Genius, as Confided to Mark Twain

A Mystified Waiter
An Old Story of the Two Humorists in the Comstock

Dan De Quille

The manner in which Ward befuddled Twain with spontaneous verbal adroitness is widely known through Twain's own 1867 "A Reminiscence of Artemus Ward" (included herein), about a breakfast meeting, and another famous account, about a dinner meeting, by De Quille, entitled "Artemus Ward in Nevada" (1893). It is unlikely that Ward played the same trick on Twain twice during his short visit to Virginia City, so what is important is not the meal at which Ward revealed his technique, but the technique itself. That is the common denominator of all the Comstock accounts of the Ward-Twain meeting. This earlier memoir by De Quille has been hitherto overlooked, and while close in some parts to his better-known later piece, it contains substantial new material. De Quille was in the habit of recycling his pieces, and altering them in the process. Given that at least twenty-five years had passed since the event, there is no way to know whether this account is more or less accurate than his 1893 essay, written five years later, in terms of what Ward actually said, and whether it is more or less accurate than Twain's reminiscence. What this piece does show, however, is that De Quille as well as Twain learned Ward's technique of double-talk, even though both men seldom chose to make specific use of it.

At the time Artemus Ward was on the Pacific Coast delivering his famous comical lecture, "Babes in the Woods,"[1] he was still in good health and excellent spirits. He was an overflowing fountain of fun. Artemus was not only funny in print and on the stage, in his lectures, but also in the every-day walks of life. In ordinary conversation he was full of drolleries and queer turns of speech. The serious manner and solemn face of the speaker added to the fun of these impromptu "quaints." A stranger would gaze at the man for a moment in blank amazement, then the oddity of the thing would prove too much for him, and he would let go all holds and indulge in a good hearty laugh, Artemus in the meantime, with face more solemn than ever, gazing from face to face, as though astonished and somewhat hurt at the sudden outburst of merriment.

Artemus lectured in Virginia City, and remained on the Comstock about a week. He seemed to feel quite at home among our people. All the mines were then "booming," business of every kind was brisk, coin jingled in every pocket, and the town was at fever heat both day and night. The wild whirl of excitement that prevailed seemed to exactly suit Artemus. He fell into Comstock ways at once, and laughed and joked with all he met as familiarly as though each man had been an old-time friend.

Artemus had a favorite trick that he loved to play off, mention of which has never to my knowledge been made,[2] though it was one to which he was much addicted, and out of which he appeared to get a good deal of congenial fun. The following instance will illustrate the humorist's favorite game, which might be called the "game of mystification": One evening a big dinner was given Ward by leading citizens at the best restaurant in the town, an establishment kept by a Frenchman named Chauvelle. It was a "stag" affair, and everything was free and easy. Artemus was seated beside Mark Twain (then a reporter on the *Territorial Enterprise*), near the head of the table. Artemus cleared his throat, and turning to Mark gravely began somewhat as follows, so raising his voice as to attract the attention of all present and put a stop to general conversation:

"Ah, speaking of genius, Mr. Clemens, now, genius appears to me to be a sort of luminous quantity of the mind allied to a warm and inflammable constitution which is inherent in the man, and supersedes in him whatever constitutional tendency he may possess to permit himself to be influenced by such things as do not coincide with his preconceived notions and established convictions to the contrary, suitable though they may be to one who feels that

1. The correct title is "The Babes in the Wood."
2. Either De Quille had forgotten the use of "mystifying" double-talk in the preceding selection by Twain, or De Quille had never read the piece.

he knows his real mission in life and is not carried away by that ambiguous and disputable kind of ambition which aims merely to gain favor or elicit the applause of contemporaries; though, indeed, that may be a thing equally desirable with any other prerogative of superiority; still it is held by some that all efforts having for their object the desire of being praised spring solely from a noble and disinterested generosity which is not understood by those whose selfishness has contracted their understandings. The soul of man—

"But, Mr. Clemens, what do you think of my definition of genius? Does it not hit the nail squarely on the head?"

"I don't know that I exactly understand you," said Mark. "I somehow didn't grasp the meaning of what you said—didn't catch the point, you know."

"No!" cried Artemus, elevating his eyebrows and gazing at Mark with a countenance expressive, not only of the profoundest astonishment, but also some quivering traces and shifting shades of pity. "Did not grasp my meaning? Well, that is strange," and he again gazed earnestly and pityingly into Mark's face—"However," cried Artemus, seeming again to cheer up—"however, I will put it more plainly." Artemus then proceeded in a grave and impressive tone to discourse about as follows: "Genius, Mr. Clemens, does not appear to me to consist or rest merely in sensibility to that degree of beauty which is perceived by all, but to reside in the possession of an illuminating quality which is inherent and which checks in the person possessing it whatever tendency he may have, owing to a warm and inflammable constitution, to permit himself to be influenced by preconceived opinions in regard to common objects, which opinions and convictions are common property and are possessed by mankind at large; whereas, in viewing the same objects there is an inherent illuminating power the possession of which causes luminous ideas to dart like meteors across the intellectual firmament, and which, I say, is not at all understood by those detractors who are constitutionally incapable of seeing those beauties, which all objects in nature display to the eye of the person of a warm and inflammable nature, and in whose self-luminous mind arise ideas that are by no means confined to the material which conception furnishes, but may be equally employed about all the subjects of our knowledge. The—

"But I must already have made it plain to you, Mr. Clemens?"

"I am almost ashamed to say it," drawled Mark, "but, to tell you the truth, I failed to follow you and was not able to get your exact meaning. I will admit, however, that what you say appears reasonable enough, and you speak in a very convincing tone of voice; but somehow I fail to grasp your notion or idea of genius."

"Indeed! Well, that is strange!" cried Artemus, and for half a minute he gazed at Mark with a face in which impatience, astonishment and compassion were strangely mingled. Then, heaving a sigh, he said: "Well, perhaps I was not sufficiently explicit. What I wished to say was simply that genius is a sort of illuminating quality of the mind inherent in those of constitutionally inflammable natures and whose conceptions are not of that ambiguous and disputable kind which may be said always to result where mere ambition or love of gain is the incentive and the applause of contemporaries is sought with the—"

"Hold on, Artemus," interrupted Mark; "it is useless for you to repeat your definition. The wine, or the brandy, or the whisky, or the beer, or some other thing has gone to my head. Tell it to me some other time; or better still, write it down for me and I'll study it at my leisure."

"Good!" cried Artemus, his face beaming with delight. "I'll give it to you to-morrow in black and white. I have been much misunderstood in this matter, and it is important that I should set myself right; also, that there should be a true definition of genius for reference—a—a something—that is, something to which students could refer, you know."

Turning then to a waiter, Artemus said: "Pierre, have you some good Burgundy wine?"

"Yes, sure; ze genuine, veritable Burgundy."

"Well," said Artemus, impressively, "if your Burgundy is pure, old and good you may bring me a bottle of the vintage of the year—the year. But, let me see; your Madeira is—you have Madeira?"

"Plenta—abundance, sare!"

"Well, as the Burgundy is so fine and the Madeira abundant, not to speak of the Canary, which I suppose is also of the best quality, for I know your judgment is sound in regard to all such matters, and that you are perfectly honest in your recommendation of your wines and not inclined to take advantage in these matters like some waiters, particularly in sherry and Port, which I have often found abominable. Why, knowing you will do what is right, you may bring me in a bottle. So go now, Pierre."

"Yes, sare," and away rushes the waiter.

In about half a minute Pierre comes running back looking much confused and says: "I beg pardon, sare, but it did slip my mind zee particulier wine you have order."

"O, well, don't distress yourself, Pierre," says Artemus, good-naturedly. "There is plenty of time, but of course if I had expected you to fetch me the Canary instead of the Burgundy I would have said so; only it so happened that you mentioned the Madeira, or I did, which is much the same, though at the moment I may also have said something about sherry and port, yet it does not matter; therefore bring in a bottle at once."

"Yes, sare," and starting back the waiter halts after going a short distance.

He plucks at his mustache, gazes down at the floor, then up at the ceiling, and finally turns and comes back.

"I am bien mortifie—ver macho vex," says the waiter; "bute again I have forget zee particulier wine zat Monsieur have order."

"We don't want any more wine, waiter," cries Mark. Then, whispering to Artemus, he says: "It's you that's drunk. I could no more make out what kind of wine you ordered than could the waiter. It was as bad as your definition of genius. That definition would harrow the soul of Bacon, Locke, Blair, Dr. Johnson, Addison[3] and all the other logicians, metaphysicians and moral philosophers that have ever lived. Let us go home. You're boozy, or I am—or may be we're both fuddled."

"Not I; of that I'm positively sure," said Artemus. "And as for what I said about genius I am sure nothing could be plainer than that it consists in an inherent susceptibility to those impressions which objects—"

"Here, now, for God's sake!" cried Mark; "if you go at that again you'll drive me mad!"

The general burst of laughter which followed this feeling and half angry protest made it plain to Mark that Artemus had been set to work on him with malice aforethought, and that most of those present were in the plot and had been amused witnesses of the scene.

Mark was in no amiable mood the remainder of the evening, and told several that such a thing "might be thought smart by some," but he failed to see where the fun came in.

San Francisco Examiner, February 26, 1888, p. 11

---

3. This list of seventeenth- and eighteenth-century British writers, if accurate, may be of interest for the light it casts on Twain's reading. If not accurate, then it is certainly of interest for the light it casts on De Quille's reading.

[Memories of *Enterprise* Writers]

Arthur McEwen

When Virginia City's *Territorial Enterprise* suspended publication early in January 1893, the *San Francisco Examiner* ran five memoirs of it in its January 24 issue. This selection is extracted from McEwen's contribution, "Heroic Days on the Comstock." In 1971, Oscar Lewis collected and republished all five memoirs, plus one more that appeared three weeks later, under the title *The Life and Times of the Virginia City Territorial Enterprise*.

→══ ══←

. . . Of this life of audacious gayety and gambling the *Enterprise* was the mirror, and a participant. It was a Comstocker to the backbone. Money poured into its safe and the owners of that safe were gentlemen who knew how to spend its contents for their own delectation and the good of the town. Joseph T. Goodman, the principal proprietor and controlling editor, was a young man of distinct gifts. A poet of imagination, a scholar, a dramatic critic, a playwright and a writer of leaders that had the charm of entire freedom from every restriction save his own judgment of what ought not to be said. Everything from his pen possessed the literary quality. Original, forcible, confident, mocking and alive with the impulses of an abounding and generous youth, the *Enterprise* was to Goodman a safety-valve for his ideas rather than a daily burden of responsibility. He hired Rollin M. Daggett to do the editorial drudgery—Daggett, famous then for scissors and seven-up,[1] and since Congressman and Minister to Hawaii. To Daggett was left the solemn duty of writing or stealing the necessary, the perfunctory editorials, while Editor Goodman was off criticizing the show, and banqueting the actors

1. Editors often scissored out items they liked from other newspapers for use in their own. Seven-up was a popular card game.

251

afterwards, or constructing a poem, or sharing in the easy converse of the Washoe Club. But if Editor Goodman became seized of an idea that needed expression, if somebody must be roasted, a corrupt Judge driven from the bench, the Republican party ordered to adopt or abandon a policy, Editor Goodman attended to the agreeable function himself. There never has been a paper like this *Enterprise* on the Coast since and never can be again—never one so entirely human, so completely the reflex of a splendid personality and a mining camp's buoyant life.

An unknown nobody of a miner over at Aurora sent in items occasionally. He had humor in him, and Goodman offered him a salary to come over and assist Dan De Quille[2] as a reporter. He came. It was Clemens—Mark Twain.

Than Goodman and Clemens no men could be more unlike outwardly. The first was handsome, gallant, self-reliant but not self-conscious, vehement of speech and swift in action. (He called out the silver-tongued Tom Fitch, then an editor, and shattered his knee with a pistol-ball, for instance, in return for an unpleasant article that appeared in the course of a controversy.) Clemens was sloth-like in movement, had an intolerable drawl, and punished those who offended him by long-drawn sneering speech. But the two were alike at bottom in one thing—both were genuine, and had the quality of brain that enables one man to understand another of opposite temperament and manner. They soon became friends.

Not many people liked Mark Twain, if one may judge by the tone of deprecation in which he is spoken of on the Comstock to this day. But go to any small place from which a celebrated man has sprung and the same phenomenon appears. It is the villager's way of impressing upon the stranger the villager's superior, intimate knowledge of the great man. They say that Mark was mean—that he would join in the revels and not pay his share, and so on. Those who knew him well, who had the requisite intelligence to be more than surface companions, tell a different story. His salary was not large, and he sent a good part of it back to Missouri, where it was needed, instead of "spending it like a man" on his own pleasures. In brief, Mr. Clemens, while he enjoyed the rough-and-tumble, devil-may-care Comstock life wasn't carried away by it. He knew there was a world outside. The first work that showed the stuff of which he was made was done on the *Enterprise*.

Mark, being a man of sense, never neglected his interests. The fact that to know a particular man might at some time be advantageous did not deter Mr. Clemens from making his acquaintance. He and the Episcopal clergyman became friends, and while the clergyman probably did not consider Sam

2. McEwen, like many of De Quille's friends, misspelled his pen name as "de Quille." It is corrected here, as throughout the present volume.

a devout Christian, at least he regarded him as a promising young man whose leanings were in the right direction. Now, the printers knew that to steal the shade of Mr. Clemens' lamp caused him to burn with a slow fury. So they stole it as often as they could for the pleasure of hearing him swear—an art in which he excelled. One evening at dusk he climbed to the deserted local room and found the shade gone. Thereupon he began to drag himself around in a leisurely but intense circle, as was his wont on such occasions, uttering oaths and calling down heaven's vengeance on the purloiners. While thus breathing maledictions he passed the door and beheld the Episcopal minister standing therein transfixed with horror.

Mark paused not in his slow walk, but had the grace to drawl out in low ferocity this (expurgated) excuse:

"I know you're shocked to hear me, Mr. Brown.[3] It stands to reason you are. I know this ain't language fit for a Christian man to utter nor for a Christian man to hear, but if I could only lay my hands on the —— — —— —— —— —— —— —— who stole my shade, I'd show you what I'd do to him, for the benefit of printers to all time. You don't know printers, Mr. Brown; you don't know them. A Christian man like you naturally can't come in contact with them, but I give you my word they're the —— — —— — —— —— that a body ever had anything to do with."

From that time on Mark Twain's seat was not high in the synagogue.

The local department of the *Enterprise,* for which Mark Twain and Dan De Quille were responsible, was as unlike the local department of a city newspaper of the present as the town and time were unlike the San Francisco of to-day. The indifference to "news" was noble—none the less so because it was so blissfully unconscious. They were about equally good in the sort of invention required for such efforts, and Dan very often did the better work. But the one had reach and ambition; the other lived for the moment. Dan De Quille remains still on the old lode, outlasting the *Enterprise.* He is not soured at his fate, and no man has heard him utter a word of envy of his more fortunate co-worker of the past. Indeed, no man ever knew Dan De Quille to say or do a mean thing. A bright-minded, sweet-spirited, loyal and unaffected old philosopher he, with a love for the lode and a faith in it that neither years nor disappointment can quench.

But I didn't set out to write of all the men who made the *Enterprise* the unique paper that it was—a paper with a soul in it. That soul departed when in 1874 Mr. Goodman sold it to Senator Sharon[4] and came away to become

3. A fictitious name for the Reverend Franklin S. Rising, the rector of Virginia City's St. Paul's Protestant Episcopal Church.

4. William Sharon was an imaginative, wealthy, powerful, but ruthless mine owner.

a Californian, with other than journalistic ambitions. For some years its pres-
tige and the talents of Judge Goodwin kept it up, but in 1880 he, too, departed, and since then the fate of the *Enterprise* has been the fate of the
camp—to dwindle.

Not for what it has been during recent years, but for what it was when the
paper and they were young does the death of the *Enterprise* give old
Comstockers a shock. It revives memories.

The belated tragedy brings it home to them that they are growing old—
and that's the deuce.

–➻Extracted from *San Francisco Examiner,* January 24, 1893

My French Friend

Rollin M. Daggett

It is a matter of some doubt whether this item is more accurately characterized as a memoir or a story. In its original publication, it appeared as one in a series of "True Tales of the Old West"; although Daggett probably added touches for dramatic effect, there is no reason to doubt that it recounts what was a painful memory for Daggett.

⊷⩷⩸ ⩷⩸⊶

I.

Although my mining experience dates back to a period when the mountain trails were new and dim, and unexplored bars and gulches of the gold fields of California were plentiful and inviting, my success as a gold miner was never bewildering. I could always find gold in paying quantities; that is, I never found it difficult to secure a location where I could gather from half an ounce to two ounces of gold dust per day of remarkably energetic and persistent labor; but I was not among those who were continually stumbling upon nuggets as large as a man's hand, or dropping upon pockets and crevices from which small fortunes were panned between two successive Sundays, and frequently in less time.

I was always dreaming of, and searching for, deposits of this character, where a pan of gravel, for instance, would yield a quart of fine gold, and where nuggets could be hoed from their hiding places like potatoes from a hill, and was therefore never quite satisfied with the reasonable return with which the labor of the great majority was rewarded in the early years of placer mining.

Men who have been kicked all the way down the long lane of life by scowling fortune, with scarcely a smile to sweeten their profitless years of toil, are expected to believe in a protecting and impartial Providence, through the assurance that there is no such thing as luck, and that every marked benefaction, however plainly it may seem to be the fruit of luck, is in reality but the rational result of sagacious and well-directed individual effort.

Should this assumption be correct,—should the thing we call luck be the legitimate offspring of subtle and innate deduction,—then there is a species or special quality of sagacity operating in the line of material accumulation, which is not only above and beyond the canons of human logic, but as inexplicable to those who possess it as are the gifts of Blind Tom, and other musical and mathematical wonders who from time to time have puzzled the world.

A hasty glance at the field prompts me to suggest that quite as many large fortunes have been accreted on the Pacific Coast through what seemed to be accident, stupidity, or gross violation of sound business methods, as have been amassed through well-conceived plans and intelligent management. It has been asserted that all the millions taken from the lower levels of the Comstock are due to a blast fired without orders in the Crown Point mine; and I know of at least three fortunes of over a million each accruing to the owners of mining shares, which they vainly sought to dispose of at beggarly figures on the very even of developments multiplying their values by hundreds and thousands.

Very many real estate owners in San Francisco are in affluence today because they could not sell their holdings during the great depression caused by the discovery on Fraser River,[1] and a large hotel in the city occupies a block of land which the keeper of an eating-house reluctantly took for a board bill of sixty dollars, thirty-five years ago.

A very prominent mining stock operator, now deceased, admitted that a mistake in a telegraphic cipher dispatch from Virginia City to his broker in San Francisco saved him from bankruptcy at a critical time. Had he sold the stock short, as he intended, ruin would have resulted; but the broker bought instead, and a profit of a quarter of a million followed. Another well known San Francisco stock operator, who enjoys the rental of a substantial building on Montgomery street, might relate a somewhat similar personal experience, were he so disposed.

---

1. In 1859, as California mining slumped, a discovery of gold on the Fraser River in British Columbia caused a gold rush out of the state that largely emptied San Francisco. Approximately eighteen thousand men—a sixth of the voting population of the state—crowded ships headed north, and stores, farms, and real estate were either sold for a fraction of their recent worth or abandoned entirely. The new boom did not fulfill expectations, however, and the emigrants drifted back as the state's economy was revitalized due to the discovery of silver in Nevada. It was not long before prosperity returned and property values surpassed their former levels.

A gopher hole led to the discovery of the valuable gold deposits on Shane's Flat, in Tuolumne county, and in falling over a cliff a drunken Swede brought to light one of the richest quartz veins in Amador county.

In the summer of 1852, in defiance of the advice and jeers of their neighbors, a party of inexperienced miners flumed a riffle of the North Yuba, where the shore bed-rock was bare, and there was no indication of gravel in the channel.[2] And, indeed, no gravel of consequence was found in the bed of the stream after the water had been diverted from it; but the bare crevices were studded with nuggets from one to twenty ounces in weight. There were not less than half a bushel of them; and many old residents of San Francisco will recall the exhibition of them for a few days in a Montgomery street window.

It was in that year that a party of three, including the writer, flumed about fifteen hundred feet of the South Yuba, below the mouth of Rush Creek, five or six miles from Nevada City, and about the same distance from Grass Valley. The flume was constructed by contract, by a visionary old mechanic known as "Deacon Locke," who was insane enough to erect a sawmill at the lower end of the bar, for the express and only purpose of providing the lumber required in that single undertaking. The contract called for the completion of the flume on or before the first day of August, but as the valuable months of summer were frittered away in building the mill, when the lumber needed for the flume might have been hauled down from Nevada, the waters of the river were not diverted from the bed until the first week in November, and the draining pumps had scarcely been put into motion before our beautiful aqueduct of sawed lumber was torn into fragments and carried down the stream by the Autumn floods.

It was a cruel disappointment. All the castles I had built during the summer vanished with the departing flume, and for a time I sat in the ashes of despair. Gloom was succeeded by the healthier feeling of anger. I looked around for Locke, whose puttering and procrastination had caused the disaster, and found that he had left the bar the night before. Then I stood and saw the flume go, piece by piece, until the last section disappeared; when in my wrath I threw after it into the raging waters shovels, wheelbarrows, crowbars, and every other mining appliance within reach, and started up the trail for Grass Valley, resolved to abandon a business so thoroughly at the mercy of crazy millwrights and the elements.

This resolution was inspired no less by my own misfortune than the overwhelming success of a party of drunken sailors, who the same season flumed

2. The miners diverted the river into a flume, a sort of wooden aqueduct, to allow them to prospect the bed of the river. Usually, miners hoped to find gravel, which they could pan for gold dust.

a barren looking riffle three or four hundred yards below the scene of our operations. Their short flume was a ricketty, leaky affair, patched with canvas,
and propped with slabs caught floating down the river from our mill. Their
claim was drained by the middle of September, and in the next six weeks they
took out one hundred and sixty thousand dollars, principally in nuggets, one
of which weighed thirty-three pounds.

Now, perhaps it was not good luck that gave these sailors two or three
mule-loads of gold in fluming a riffle where no reasonable man would look
for more than a color, and perhaps it was not bad luck that vitally connected
with our enterprise the only insane millwright in California; but both circumstances looked like wanton freaks of fortune at the time.

II.

Bless us! how the pen will wander in describing events connected with pioneer life in California! However, it has not gone far astray in this instance,
since it was my purpose in the beginning to say something concerning a
strange character whom I first encountered while awaiting the construction
of the flume on the South Yuba.

I occupied a log cabin on the flat skirted by our river claim, about one
hundred yards below the ferry, owned and operated by my mining partners in
conjunction with a small trading establishment, where gold dust was bought
and miners' supplies could be purchased.

Sitting in the twilight in front of my cabin door one evening in July, listening to the splashing of the waters over the riffles, and devising new invest-
ments for the quarter of a million with which I expected to leave the river
before the snow began to fall, I discovered a man coming down the flat, with
a roll of blankets strapped to his back, and carrying his hat in his hand. He
did not stop at the ferry-house, but passed on at a brisk walk until he reached
a fallen pine fifty or sixty yards back of the cabin, where he dropped his burden and began to make preparations to spend the night. After smoothing the
ground behind the tree, he unrolled and spread his blankets, and, squatting
down upon them, suddenly disappeared.

Strolling over to the wayfarer five minutes later, I found him sitting cross-
legged on his blankets, and eating from a loaf of bread, which he occasionally
moistened with draughts from a claret bottle. On discovering me he rose to
his feet, and politely returned my salutation of "Good evening."

He was a small, spare man, with bright gray eyes, and a strikingly intelligent face. He was partially bald, and his hair and cropped whiskers were
tinged with gray. He was dressed in a faded business suit, with a soft felt hat,

and shoes too frail for travel in the mountains. His hands were soft and shapely, and his whole appearance indicated that he was out of place, alone and with his blankets spread at night beside a fallen tree on the South Yuba.

No one could mistake his nationality. His face, his eyes, his gestures, his attitude in speaking, all were as French as the charming accent and amusing choice of words with which he endeavored to make himself understood in English. All that he knew of our language had been learned from books, and his vocabulary was unique and pleasing.

Finding that I could make myself understood, I invited him to the cabin, informing him that I was alone, and my lodgings embraced an extra bunk, which was entirely at his service. He accepted the invitation thankfully and without hesitation, and, gathering up his effects, followed me to the cabin.

Pointing to a vacant bunk, into which he threw his blankets, I asked him to allow me to make him a cup of coffee and serve him with a dish of cold boiled beans. But he declined to accept anything, declaring that his simple supper of bread and claret was all that he required.

"I care not to eat," he added. "I very mooch more desire to make some conversation wiz you."

As the suggestion was quite to my taste, we sat in the open doorway and talked until past midnight, and I learned much of the personal history of my guest. His name was Armand Daudet. He was born and reared in Paris, and his age was fifty-one. His father was a distinguished physician, but Armand was educated for the law. The profession did not please him, however, and after receiving his diploma he drifted into journalism. He became prominent and influential in his new vocation. He favored the early aspirations of Louis Napoleon, and assisted in securing his election to the National Assembly; but when he destroyed the republic Armand became his enemy, and was finally compelled to leave France for openly attacking the Empire. A French merchant vessel took him to San Francisco, where he landed with less than a hundred dollars. The French consul treated him with scant courtesy, and after vainly trying to find some employment for which he was fitted, he started for the mines. A fellow-countryman in Nevada City advised him to go to Sweetland's, and he was on his way thither when night overtook him at the mouth of Rush Creek.

"You must be pretty nearly out of money," I suggested.

He took from his pocket a Mexican silver dollar, and, holding it up, said with a smile: "Zis is all I have left."

"What will you do when that is gone?"

He shrugged his shoulders and pointed at the river.

"Oh, no," I replied, alarmed at the calmness with which he contemplated suicide; "you must not think of such a thing. For the lack of gold you would drown yourself in a river that is full of it. That would be ridiculous. Do you know anything about gold mining?"

"Very leetle. As I pass along I have seen some men employed in ze acquisition of gold from ze sand by means of what you denominate a rockaire. So mooch I know of mining, and no more. It is very leetle, you must say."

"Are you willing to work?"

"Am I willing? Ah, sir, I should esteem myself most happy to arduously labor wiz my hands to procure gold."

"Very well; then you shall have an opportunity. I will provide you with tools, and teach you how to mine. I shall have little to do for a month or two, and it will be a pleasure to assist you. Remain in the cabin. There are accommodations for both of us, and provisions enough to last as long as we will probably remain on the bar."

I was overwhelmed with Armand's expressions of gratitude. "You are a boy," he said, "and speak wiz ze kind impulse of youth. But I am most grateful. I am exalted wiz happiness. I could dance, I could sing, so prodigious is my joy! Yes, yes, I shall learn how to extract ze gold, and wiz stupendous assiduity you shall behold me dig ze ground! Ah, ha! I shall triumph wiz ze rockaire!"

Armand would have talked all night, so greatly was he excited at the thought of becoming a miner; but he crawled into his bunk at last, and after breakfast the next morning I started him to work at the lower end of the flat, where I knew fair wages might be realized. I placed the rocker, and after working with him for an hour or more, left him to his own resources.

As the weather was warm, I advised him to work with moderation; but he declined to rest after dinner, and toiled on ceaselessly until I dropped down in the evening to "clean up" for him. The day's work yielded him about half an ounce of gold. There should have been more, but neglect of the riffle-box had resulted in some loss.

Although his hands were blistered, Armand was surprised and delighted at this return for his labor. "Ah! Zis is grand! zis is manly! zis is noble!" he exclaimed with enthusiasm. "Zis working wiz ze hands is democratique, and I am proud to do so!"

"But how about the blisters, Armand? How do you like them?"

"Ah! I will tell you my thoughts. Ze blistaires are ze aristocratique protest against honest labor, and I will teach my hands to scorn zem!"

Notwithstanding the scorn with which Armand proposed to teach his hands to regard the blisters afflicting them, a week or more elapsed before he was able to do another full day's work. But his hands hardened in time, and for nearly two months he continued his labors, adding daily to his little store of gold. He was intelligent, good-natured and vivacious, and during the evenings we spent together his descriptions of Paris life and references to French politics were incessant and entertaining. I became very greatly attached to him, and always regretted the ridiculous occurrence which led to his abrupt departure from the bar.

As our bunks were so located that a conversation could not very well be carried on between us after retiring for the night, I had assisted Armand in making and swinging a canvas hammock for his accommodation, within five or six feet of the mattress of leaves upon which my blankets were spread. The arrangement was satisfactory to him, and he usually talked after we had bestowed ourselves for the night until silenced by my failure to respond.

One night, in a spirit of mischief, I harrowed him into a condition of nervousness by talking of snakes, centipedes, scorpions, and other venomous reptiles found in California. I told him that rattlesnakes, whose bite was death, sometimes entered cabins through defective chinking, and crawled into the bunks and hammocks of sleepers; and referred to a case which a short time before had resulted in the death of a miner at Waloupa.

Some time before daylight the next morning, I was aroused by Armand calling out in a suppressed, but terrified tone: "My friend! my friend! Are you awake?"

"Yes, I am awake. What's the matter, Armand?"

"I zink zare is a serpent in zis hammook."

"Oh, I guess not."

"Yes, but I am sure. What shall I do?"

Deeming it possible that he might not be wrong, I advised him to quietly remove his feet from the hammock, and then spring suddenly to the floor.

He attempted to follow my advice. In less than a minute there was a crash, followed by a succession of agonizing groans.

Hastily leaping from my bunk and lighting a candle, I found Armand with his head and shoulders in the broken hammock. In a wild attempt to spring to the floor, he had broken the single spike to which the head of the hammock had been fastened. The fall itself would have been severe, but on reaching the floor his head had struck a piece of hoop-iron used as a fire-hook, and the scalp was pretty badly cut.

I raised and seated him on a bench, and, seeing that he was not dangerously hurt, began cautiously to open and examine the hammock for the venomous reptile that had provoked the disaster. I found it. It was three or four loose feet of the hammock rope which accident had stretched along the side of Armand.

"Here is your snake, Armand," I said, holding up the rope. . . .

Of course, the story of Armand's mishap was too good to keep, and I told it at the ferry-house in the presence of half-a-dozen miners; and when, in the afternoon, some one in passing laughingly bawled out to him, "Crapeau,[3] how's yer snake-bite?" he knew that I had betrayed him, and straightway attempted to blow out his brains with a rusty old horse-pistol that a former occupant of the cabin had left on a shelf; but the weapon was harmless, and I had fortunately loaned my revolver three or four days before.

His sad and reproachful look at supper awoke within me a feeling of remorse, and I spent the evening at the ferry-house. When I returned, which was at rather a late hour, I found Armand asleep. At least, he did not speak, or turn to greet me even with a glance.

We ate our breakfast in silence the next morning. Then Armand rolled up his blankets, swung them over his shoulder, and stepped out of the door, where I was sitting. With tears in his eyes, he held out his hand and said:

"Adieu, my good friend. You have greatly humiliated me, but you have been kind, and I do pardon you. But I cannot remain here to be ze jest of brutal men. I did try to kill myself, but ze weapon decline to be discharge. I feel for you no resentment—nozzhing but love—but I must go. Adieu!"

I could say nothing except that I greatly regretted the pain I had thoughtlessly caused him. He made no reply, but waved his hand with a sad smile, and mounted the trail to Nevada City.

III.

As I subsequently learned, Armand proceeded to San Francisco, where, through the influence of a French friend, he secured the position of porter in a wholesale establishment on Battery street. As it was a time of the year when trade was dull, and the duties of porter were correspondingly light, at the end of the first month Armand sought the head of the house, and said to him with dignity:

"Sir, I desire to discharge myself."

"Why, what's the matter?" inquired the merchant, with surprise. "Are you overworked?"

"Ah, sir, your words confirm ze apprehension. I do very little work. I zhink you employ me from charitee, and I decline to accept ze gratitude. Sir, allow me to tender to you my very great respect." And Armand bowed himself out of the office, leaving the merchant staring at him in speechless amazement.

---

3. "Crapeau" is French for frog, and "Frog" is condescending slang for a Frenchman.

Two months later I met Armand in San Francisco. He was well dressed, and apparently in a genial frame of mind. His delight in seeing me seemed to be almost boundless. He shed tears of joy. "Ah, my friend," he said, "I have waited for zis occasion. I have eaten your bread, your beans, your bacon in ze Yuba rivaire. Tonight you must enjoy wiz me a French dinnaire."

I accepted the invitation, and at six o'clock Armand called for me in a carriage at my hotel, and we were driven to a French restaurant, where a private dining-room had been reserved for us. The table and sideboard were decorated with flowers, and the dinner was choice and elaborate, with the finest of old wines, and every appetizing accessory.

I had never seen Armand so happy. We ate, drank, chatted, and smoked until near midnight, when the same carriage in which we had been conveyed to the restaurant reappeared at the door, and Armand returned with me to my hotel, where I bade him good-night. In parting, he held my hand for a moment, as if about to say something; but with a simple "adieu" he hurriedly re-entered the carriage, and was driven off.

A paragraph in a morning paper took me to the Coroner's rooms the next day, where I saw the pale, dead face of Armand. He had been seen to leap into the water from Clay street wharf shortly after midnight, and his body was recovered an hour or two afterwards. No money was found on the person of the suicide. He had evidently spent the last of his earnings in providing a grand entertainment for his friend from the mountains, and then deliberately put an end to his life.

Poor Armand! His heart may have ached with wounds that he never showed to me.

⇒*Overland Monthly* (January 1895): 62–68

Geological Reminiscences

Senator Jones Tells How the Wolves of the Mining Lodes Played Rough Games

Anonymous

A few evenings since a group of well-known mining men were seated in the barroom of the Palace Hotel when one of them remarked that he would wager the drinks for the crowd that no one present could tell of the first mining swindle perpetrated on the Comstock.

Senator Jones[1] would never allow a betting bluff of any kind to float past him, and said immediately that he would accept the offer, and told the following:

"The first instance of a square-toed swindle in connection with mining on the Comstock was where Jim O'Riley let a contract to three miners to sink a shaft 100 feet in depth. After he had paid 20 per cent of the contract money to bind the bargain he brought a 100-foot tapeline to the miners, and stipulated that when the tapeline fell from the windlass and hung clear in the bottom of the shaft without touching he would pay the balance of the money, amounting to several thousand dollars. Shaft-sinking was pretty expensive in those days. Well, in course of time the miners called upon him for the balance of the money, and took him to the shaft where they pointed to the 100-foot tapeline hanging from the windlass to the bottom, with an inch or two of free space under the end of it. O'Riley, after complimenting them upon their work, gave them the balance of their money, and in a few hours they had disappeared.

"The next day, when O'Riley took a more careful inventory of the work, he

---

1. John Percival Jones began his career in Nevada as a mine superintendent, became wealthy, and served as a U.S. senator from 1873 to 1903.

discovered that the miners had cut twenty feet out of the tapeline, thereby making the shaft twenty feet less in depth than they had contracted for. He buckled on his six-shooter, and started out in quest of a rebate on the job; but when the story got around the ledge it raised such a laugh at his expense that he dropped the subject and relet the contract to other parties. He said that the splice where the twenty feet was cut out was made so neatly that it took him nearly an hour to locate it. A few days afterward he got a package from Sacramento containing that portion of the tapeline that was missing. They wrote to him saying that they had taken it away through an oversight, and they returned it that he might put it back where it belonged, in order to complete the sinking of the shaft with mathematical accuracy. The twenty feet of tapeline was exhibited for many years in the Delta saloon."

When Jones had finished the story Billy Foote, who had offered to bet, ordered a round of irrigation goods[2] for the entire party, and Jones, after moistening his throat, remarked: "if anybody wants to make another wager for the same amount I can tell the second operation there of the same nature." No one interrupting him he continued:

"Some of the boys had a claim up on the side of Mount Davidson when the stock excitement was pretty lively. Their claim did not prove to be of much account, and they accordingly introduced the salting process for the first time.[3] Quite a rich strike was made in the Ophir on rock that ran into the thousands. One night they extracted several sacks of ore from the Ophir shaft, and dumped it into their own prospect hole. They spread the report that they had just got into a rich formation, and quite a number of people were on the ground when the first bucket came up next morning. Of course, they pounced on the specimens and in a few minutes the rich chunks of ore were finding their way into the nearest assay offices. The result was that a forty-eight hour excitement ensued and a wild scramble for the stock, during which time the owners cleared up $15,000 or $20,000."

"Speaking of salting mines," said Lon Hamilton, "I never shall forget the time when some stock operators sent some mining experts to spy out the prospects in the Gould & Curry. A diamond drill was being run, and they wanted to know what it struck. The experts reached the Comstock looking like ordinary miners, and very readily secured a job in the mine. They considered themselves very fortunate when they were put on a level within easy reach of the diamond drill. The joke of the thing was that the insiders who were working the mine got the tip from below. They were all prepared for

---

2. That is, alcoholic beverages.
3. "Salting" was a deceitful practice of sprinkling pieces of rich ore around the surface of a valueless claim in order to make it attractive and thus hoax potential buyers.

their visitors. They systematically salted the drill, and left the key where the other fellows could find it. The natural result was that in a few days certain brokers from California were loading up with Gould & Curry in the expectation that when the drift reached the ore body they would reap a fortune.[4] But no drift ever followed that drill-hole, as it was barren rock, and in a few months the California-street sharpers who had engineered the job found themselves very beautifully dumped, and the biters proved to be the bitten."

"Do you mind the time when Captain John Kelley of the Lady Bryan had the Holy Bible salted on him?" There seemed to be a general desire to hear the anecdote, and Ben Fitch, after emptying a tumbler of red fluid, proceeded: "You see, John Kelley was working the Lady Bryan mine, down in Six-mile Canyon, and sent the drill ahead to prospect for an ore body. Meanwhile, the miners, who had a large quantity of the stock at low figures, salted the drill-hole, and as a result one morning Captain Kelley was in a very excited state of mind. He believed that he was about to make the strike of his life, and that Lady Bryan would prove to be a second Consolidated Virginia.[5] In his enthusiasm over the prospect he gave a number of his friends the tip, after which the miners had no trouble in disposing of their stock at handsome valuations. The drift was pushed to the end of the drill-hole with all possible dispatch, but no ore was found.

"During the next week the air was blue with the blasphemy that circulated around the head of John Kelley, and he feared for his life. In order to demonstrate his innocence of the charge of swindling his friends he held a sort of inquest on the defunct ore body. He made all the miners come into a room and submit to an examination. He had put a large Bible, weighing about twelve pounds, on the table in the dining-room of the company's cookhouse. Each miner when questioned was required to advance to the table and kiss the book. The scene was a very solemn one—the victims of the deal being at one end of the room and the miners at the other. Kelley meanwhile was seated at the head of the table acting as a sort of a judge. Each miner swore by the book that he had no hand whatever in the salting of the drill-holes and did not know any one else who had.

"After the entire force of the mine had made their solemn declarations to this effect and kissed the book, it began to look pretty black for John Kelley. He had expected confessions from the miners under the circumstances, and after they had testified and filed out of the room, Kelley sat at the table in a dazed condition. He then said that he was ready to swear on the same Bible

4. A "drift" is a horizontal passage branching off from a shaft in order to follow an ore vein.
5. One of the richest and most profitable mines on the Comstock.

that he had not salted the drill and that he had induced the boys to go in the deal in perfect good faith. As he pulled the book toward him, however, the cover came off and revealed to the astonished crowd not a Bible, but a big pile of leaves from a patent office report. The miners had taken the Bible out of the covers and substituted the Government literature unknown to Kelley. It became apparent to the crowd at once that men who would salt the word of God with such matter were capable of almost any atrocity in the salting line, and Kelley was absolved from further blame in the matter."

"In spite of that," said Billy Sharon, "Kelley was a pretty smooth operator, and you could always copper anything he did.[6] Whenever he was losing money hand over fist in the stock market and bleeding inwardly he would put a big diamond-pin on his shirt front, drink nothing but champagne and wear a perpetual grin upon his face, but whenever he made a hundred or two thousand on a turn he would walk up and down the street looking like a man who had been driven to desperation by bad luck, wearing an old woolen shirt and pretending to his friends that he was searching for employment. He soon got the name of the Ursa Major,[7] and every time a pump-rod broke, a shaft caved in or a fire occurred in the mines it was a good day for Kelley's stock accounts, but beyond this he was a very shrewd miner, as was pretty well demonstrated at the time Jim Fair[8] invited the experts to inspect a drift in one of his mines. The face of the drift seemed to be all in good ore, but Kelley figured out if it was such a good thing Fair wouldn't be inviting in the outsiders. He went to the surface dilating on the future prospects of the mine, but he was the only one who had sense enough to short the stock, and as he wore an old shirt and didn't indulge in a shave for several weeks afterward I figured that he must have cleared up about $200,000. The stock went down with a rush when the drift struck porphyry and the boys always said Kelley smelled it. He certainly had a great nose for porphyry."[9]

"There were no flies on Warren Sheridan as a mining operator," said Billy Wood. "At the time when the Comstock was booming and they had a man for breakfast[10] every morning Sherry was regarded as one of the smartest and smoothest quick-turn operators on the ledge. In order to be sure of inside information he accepted a situation as a miner in the Savage mine. It used to be

6. To "copper" meant to bet against something, or to give a false impression by appearing unhappy or discouraged.

7. Ursa Major, Latin for "big bear," was an erudite pun that described Kelley as a stock market bear, that is, someone inclined to bet that stocks would decline in value.

8. James Fair was known as one of the wealthiest, canniest, stingiest, and most deceitful of all the Comstock mine owners.

9. Porphyry is a purplish rock that does not contain valuable ores.

10. That is, someone had been killed overnight in a violent affray.

the custom in those days to keep news of the big ore strikes from the public, and when one was made, the mining superintendent used to send down provisions and mattresses and keep the miners imprisoned for twenty-four hours so that they could not get to the surface and give their friends the tip. When the boys dropped on this proposition they used to give orders for stock as soon as they saw the mattresses and the grub going down the shaft, but after a few of them had got badly bitten a time or two they made up their mind that this system of playing with stocks lacked the essential features of reliability, as the superintendents would occasionally send down the grub and mattresses when they struck porphyry; but Warren Sheridan, who always kept his eye pooled for the main chance, was 'laying' for something that was positive.

"He carried a little bottle of emetic in his pocket, and one night he saw a blast disclose some ore that was fairly fat with wealth. He knew that inside of five minutes, the order for mattresses would go to the surface. He accordingly took his emetic, and in a few minutes was writhing in pain and showing all the symptoms of a severe case of nausea. He begged to be taken to the surface that he might die in the bosom of his family. They sent him up on the 'quick hoist,' and the man's groans of pain would have melted the stoutest heart. He was put in an express wagon and when he got home and was carried into the house and put to bed, his wife, who was dead onto the scheme, filled the place with lamentations, and said it was another one of his heart attacks, and begged of them to get a doctor as soon as possible. She cleared the house in short order sending each man for a different doctor. As soon as the door was shut Sherry hustled on his store clothes and struck out for his broker by way of the back window, where he lined up the situation in short order. By the time the doctors got around Sherry was back in bed and calling for a lawyer to come and make his will. The order to buy reached San Francisco early in the morning and Sherry caught a few thousand shares at bedrock rates in the morning board. Sherry and his broker cleaned up about $160,000 on the deal, and when the Savage manipulators found out the big order that got in ahead of them, they recognized the fine Spencerian hand[11] of Sheridan. They laid for him to get even, and after he went back to work they jobbed some information on him and broke both him and his broker.

"One morning when he came down to his mine with his dinner bucket they advised him to go on the stage and work his death scene for the benefit of the public. Sherry stole a faint smile and walked off. He was never allowed

---

11. A mode of fancy penmanship after the manner of a handwriting style devised by P. R. Spencer that was popular in the nineteenth century. As applied here, it just means "deftly clever."

to swing a pick again in the Savage. He got so that he never could speak of the most common occurrence without using mining lingo, and once when he was at a coroner's inquest he described seeing a man fall down the Con. Virginia shaft, winding up his testimony with the remark, 'As soon as I saw him fall through the opening I knew he was a good short.' He is now down at Yuma City, Arizona, experting some new mines for Jim Brazil and H. M. Levy, and thinks he has struck another Comstock."

"Speaking of slick work in stock," said General Roberts, addressing Senator Jones, "do you remember the time I charged you $2000 for your Senatorial banquet in the Arlington House, Carson City?"

"I think I do," replied the Senator, with a slight smile.

"Did you think it was an overcharge?" continued Roberts, with a broad grin.

"I never dispute bills of that kind," said the Senator, "but my local agent informed me that he thought you got about $1500 the best of me."

"Maybe I did, temporarily," said Roberts, "but I plunked the whole wad into one of your Crown Point deals, and inside of thirty days I lost every cent of it."

"Guess the champagne is on you," said Lon Hamilton, and after the great silver advocate had divided a couple of quart bottles among the crowd somebody said that it was half-past 1 and they dispersed.

San Francisco Morning Call, October 27, 1895, p. 16

Early Journalism in Nevada

Alf Doten

Originally appearing in the September and October 1899 numbers of the *Nevada Magazine,* Doten's memoir of early Nevada journalism is particularly valuable because he kept a daily journal of Comstock events to which he could refer. A skillful writer, Doten is carefully objective as he recognizes Twain's eminence but also reports on why he was not universally popular on the Comstock.

⭲═◗ ◖═⭰

Fred H. Hart was a peculiarly brilliant and lively feature in his way. In the early seventies he began to attract attention as correspondent of the "Reese River Reveille," writing from White Pine, Belmont and contiguous localities under the nom de plume of "Van Jacquelin." His letters were spicy and interesting, and led to regular employment on that paper in 1874, and finally into partnership with John Booth, Hart editorially and Booth doing all the rest. During this period it was that Fred got up his famous little book, the "Sazerac Lying Club." He subsequently sold out his interest in the "Reveille" to Booth, and at one time made quite a popular mark as legislative reporter and outside correspondent for the "Gold Hill Daily News."

After that he was about Eureka for some time, not doing much, and finally through strong friendly influence he succeeded in getting into high position as editor of the "Territorial Enterprise" at Virginia City. There his career was remarkably brilliant as well as brief—about three months. Inspiration of some kind got into him one evening to distinguish himself editorially, and he did most effectually succeed. James G. Fair was running for United States Senator from Nevada, so Fred devoted to him one long, two-column, pungent, paragraphic editorial, headed, "Slippery Jim," ridiculing his ability or capacity as a would-be statesman, and relating sundry current anecdotes of

270

his alleged surreptitious mining methods and sly trickeries among his miners and mankind generally, both above and below ground.[1]

Next morning when John W. Mackay read the "Enterprise" he wrathfully arose and struck a bee-line for the printing office. "Look here!" roared he, shaking the paper fiercely in the face of Cohen, the bookkeeper; "What damsonofagun wrote all this infernal trash about my partner? I own half of this paper myself, and won't have Fair abused and belied in it by anybody. I've a d—— good mind to take a sledge and smash h— out of the bloody press."

By the most strenuous persuasion on the part of influential friends, John Mackay's wrath was partially appeased, and under the most stringent promises never to thus slop over again, Fred Hart's bald little scalp was allowed to remain in place. But alas, only a month later an east wind from the brewery struck him again, and under the resistless impulse he steered directly into and afoul of the Alta Mining Company—among the best patrons of the "Enterprise." Under heading of "The Alta Steal," he devoted a long-winded, viciously crotchety editorial, like that on Fair, to showing what an atrocious band of mining rascals they were—stealing the best portion of the Justice mine adjoining—worst gang of thieves ever allowed to be pirooting around outside of State Prison walls, etc.[2] There was a cloudburst, earthquake and war-dance, all in one, next morning when the Alta folks and their friends, waving aloft their gleaming machetes and tomahawks, came charging down upon the "Enterprise" office with blood in their eyes.

Poor little Fred Hart got wind of the coming cyclone, and struck out through the sagebrush across the north end of the Mount Davidson range and with great alacrity, never stopping till safe on San Francisco's beautiful shore. His journalistic ship was wrecked forever, and he drifted about, picking up little jobs of reporting by way of precarious subsistence for a few months, finally dying August 30, 1897, in the Sacramento county hospital.

Denis E. McCarthy, after disposing of his interest in the "Enterprise" in 1865, went back to San Francisco, where he was variously engaged in journalistic work until Mark Twain returned from the Sandwich Islands and commenced his famous lectures thereon. McCarthy then became his business manager, and they traveled and worked well together, Mark doing all the talking, and Denis handling all the cash proceeds.

1. Hart, though probably inspired by alcohol, was nevertheless telling the truth. Fair did have the nickname of "Slippery Jim," and he earned it through his unscrupulous deceptions of his workers and the public, his friends, and even his family.

2. Hart, again inspired by alcohol, was again probably guilty of telling the truth, not wisely but too well. Although John Mackay himself appears to have been above most of the unconscionable lying and business practices that flourished on the Comstock, the buying of judges and juries was a routine matter when the ownership of valuable mining properties was at stake.

And this is how it happened that when they were walking to Virginia one night after lecturing at Gold Hill, and the footpads held them up on the Divide, Denis obediently passed over the bag of lecture money—about $750—to the robbers, while Mark stood obediently holding his hands up in the air till they had gone through all his pockets, taking his elegant gold watch and chain, pocketknife, corkscrew and all, leaving him not even so much as a toothpick.

It had always been a time-honored custom with those road agents between the two towns, whenever they found no money in a victim's pocket, to give him a rough shake-up and a lecture, like "Left all yer money in faro bank, like a d—— fool, did ye?" or "So you're a sucker from that d—— church fair and can't give an honest footpad a chance." Then they would slew him around and kick him unmercifully, by way of parting admonition, as long as he was within reach. But on this special occasion financial circumstances were different; moreover, the masked agents were Confederate generals, addressing each other as "Beauregard," "Stonewall Jackson," "Jeff Davis," etc.; therefore, all "kicking" was courteously dispensed with on their part, or considerately left to their two victims.

Mark and Denis steered direct for the "Enterprise" office as soon as they could, where they graphically told their tale of woe, Mark grieving more over the loss of his watch and chain than anything else, being a present from his friend, Judge Sandy Baldwin, worth about $500. This reporter tried to get him to sit down and write up the full account of the aggravating episode for the morning's paper, but he declared that his nerves were "too badly stove up," so he and McCarthy hastened to put the police on the track as soon as possible.

A week later, about 9 o'clock in the evening, Mark and Denis were seated in the California stage coach in front of Wells, Fargo & Co.'s, ready to depart, when half a dozen "Enterprise" printers, with the Chief of Police, stepped forward to bid Mark good bye. Chief Birdsall politely handed him an open package containing his stolen money, watch, pocketknife, corkscrew and toothpick, saying with a genial smile and shake of the hand: "Mr. Mark Twain, my name is Jeff Davis, and in behalf of our mutual friends, Beauregard, Stonewall Jackson, and—"

"Stop right there!" drawled Mark in an indignant tone, comprehending the whole matter at once. "I don't want to hear any more. I've always regarded you fellows—I can't call you gentlemen—as good friends of mine, but I look on this thing as a derned mean, unmerited outrage. You've deliberately made me suffer more privation and inconvenience than you think or care for, and I don't like it. You may think it is a great joke, but I can't, and I don't thank you for it; go on, driver!" and he left, refusing to shake hands or bid them good bye.

McCarthy told afterward that for the first ten miles Mark was too deeply occupied with bitter reflections to speak a word, but finally he said: "Denis McCarthy, was you a party to this thing; did you know anything about it?" Denis mildly acknowledged that the boys had hinted to him a few points in the matter, but he had no idea that they would carry the joke so far. It took a whole lot of soothing talk, explanation and reasoning, but Mark never seemed to be entirely reconciled. The truth was, as far as McCarthy was concerned, they were obliged to have him in with them as an accomplice, or they could not have perpetrated the robbery without a genuine, desperate fight, for they well knew Denis McCarthy.

Some time before that, when Mark Twain was working on the "Enterprise" with Dan De Quille, in the local department,[3] those wicked printers played a similar joke on their friend, the humorous joker. They bought a clay imitation meerschaum pipe, big as a man's fist, for four bits,[4] got a tinsmith to mount it with tin in silver regulation style, finishing up with a long, cherry-wood stem and mouthpiece, the whole rig costing about two dollars, yet looking to be worth about sixty. Then they got Dan to quietly post Mark, who as quietly proceeded to smuggle a few bottles of champagne and some cigars into the office, ready for the surprise party.

Along in the evening, when it was about time for Mark to be going home, the printers came into the local room where Dan and Mark were sitting at the table, busily writing. Both tried to look surprised when the foreman, with that magnificent pipe poised between thumb and forefinger, made the presentation speech. Mark had prepared a humorous little response, which he got off in good style, thanking his admiring friends for their rich, emblematic appreciation of his humble efforts, assuring them that this noble journalistic pipe of peace should be fondly smoked through all future generations of the Twain family, in cherished memory of this auspicious event.

"Say Dan," said he, "isn't there a bottle or two of that wedding notice wine left kickin' around under the table somewhere?" Dan found it, and there was much typographical and reportorial hilarity for a short time, while the wine and cigars lasted. Then Dan carefully wrapped and tied up the pipe and Mark proudly took it home.

Next evening Mark was late in getting around to work, and when he did come he was silent and morose. Finally, however, he squared himself back in his chair, with a face on him like a salivated grave-digger, saying, "See here, Dan, I've always considered you like a friend and brother, but after that infernal snide pipe affair last night I don't know. I took it home happy, and was

---

3. Reporters "localized" when they worked gathering local news.
4. Two bits was twenty-five cents; four bits was fifty cents.

happy all night till this morning, when I unwrapped the blamed thing and was loading it for a royal smoke; then I saw what a meersham [*sic*] it was. The wine and cigars cost me sixty times more than the cussed smokestack is worth, to say nothing of my chuckle-headed speech. I met Denis McCarthy down street, and he started in to read me your glorifying account of the derned scrape, but I just turned away and left him. I fully believe he was in with the rest of 'em, and you, too. Jokes are jokes, but I don't recognize this as one. I'll be cussed if I do."

What he did with that remarkable pipe, nobody ever knew, but it was never seen or heard of afterward, and any allusion to it brought an ominous scowl to his countenance, as a sufficient warning to desist. But it was well understood by all who knew him best that although he liked practical jokes on others, he did not seem to enjoy one upon himself.

These incidents, as well as the Como episode related in last month's "Magazine,"[5] are simply illustrative of Mark Twain's peculiar journalistic

---

5. The relevant extract follows. The Twain quotation in it is from a letter of whose existence there is no other record.

"Mark Twain"—Samuel L. Clemens—worked with Dan de Quille on the local department of the Enterprise in 1862–63, having previously been a correspondent from Aurora, Esmeralda county, and his career as an established writer dates from that time. His peculiarly, original style as a genuine humorist soon brought him notoriety, but as between the two, Dan was the best and most reliable reporter, doing most of the regular routine work, while Mark filled in with humorous sketches and special reports.

Alf Doten was among the early developers of Como, or Palmyra mining district, in the nut pine range, about twenty miles south-east from Virginia, beyond the Carson river, which locality was attracting much attention by reason of the many fine looking quartz ledges discovered there. Como was a flourishing town of about six hundred inhabitants, with telegraph, express and postoffice, brewery, and of course, a newspaper, named the Como Sentinel. Alf was a prospecting miner, like most everybody else, but found time to amuse himself writing for the Sentinel, and corresponding for the Virginia Daily Union. One day he met Mark Twain, just arrived, having been sent to report upon the mining prospects and conditions of the new district, for the Enterprise, and they naturally affiliated. Mark was there about two weeks, making himself a popular favorite, writing humorous letters about scenes and incidents connected with the town, district and people, without making particular reference to the mines.

One pleasant Sunday Alf said to him: "Mark, you don't seem to get out among the mines and write 'em up. If you'll come along with me to the top of the hill, I'll point you out all the quartz ledges in the district, give you the names of the mines, and the aggravating particulars, just as good as if you tramped all around among them yourself. Splendid view, Mark; come along up and I'll give you the whole thing."

Mark's eyes twinkled genially as he quizzically responded in his peculiar drawling voice: "Say, Alf, do you know who you remind me of?"

"Well, no, Mark, I don't know as I do," replied Alf, with an inquiring smile.

"Well, you remind me of that fellow we read of in the Bible, called the devil, who took the Savior up on top of a high mountain, where he could see all over the world and offered to give him the whole thing if he would fall down and worship him. Only you aint the devil and I aint the Savior, by a blamed sight. How far do you say it is up there? Only half a mile? Well, no, thank you all the same, but I'm too derned lazy. Let's go down to the brewery."

So he made no special mention of the mines he was sent to report upon except in his last Como letter, written after he got back to Virginia—where he said:

style and disposition. As a regular daily newspaper reporter he was neither great nor intended, his true literary sphere being that of a humorous descriptive sketch or historical story writer and book maker, as since shown to the world by his exceedingly popular works. And he certainly seems far more at home taking notes and observation in Rome or Jerusalem, or among the throned halls of European royalty than he was or ever could be, writing up local items for a Nevada newspaper.

>≈From "Early Journalism of Nevada, Part II," collected from
Nevada Magazine (October 1899) and reprinted in
The Journals of Alfred Doten, 1849–1903, 3:2233–37

"This new mining town, with its romantic name is one of the best populated and most promising camps, but as to the mines, I have started out several times to inspect them, but never could get past the brewery."

Mark soon went to San Francisco, where he worked some for the Call and other papers, meeting with little advancement until he returned from the Sandwich Islands and wrote up his famous lecture thereon, delivering the same to great audiences in both California and Nevada. His grand literary and financial success dates from that time.

Alf Doten was called from Como shortly after the foregoing incident, to be local editor or reporter of the Virginia Daily Union, a morning paper which at one time outranked the Enterprise, but by mismanagement the Enterprise was allowed to overshadow it and the Union's flag went down in financial distress and rank political change. Alf had been with it about a year and a half and was then called to the Enterprise where he localized for a similar period, finally leaving it for a long engagement on the Gold Hill Daily News with which stalwart journal he remained fourteen years.

From "Early Journalism of Nevada, Part I," collected from *Nevada Magazine* (September 1899) and reprinted in *The Journals of Alfred Doten, 1849–1903*, 3:2229–31

[Jim Townsend's Lies]

James P. Kennedy

"There was never any question but that the most versatile liar that the Coast ever produced was Jim Townsend, who ran the Mono Index for years," said James P. Kennedy, the Comstock literateur in the course of talk at the Hotel Reno roof-garden last evening.[1]

"He was full of originality of expression and ready wit, and it was really a pleasure to sit down and listen to his bubbling fund of anecdote and interesting reminiscences, most of which he manufactured as he went along. You couldn't mention a place on the habitable globe that he had not visited. Some wags once figured up how many years he had spent in different localities, according to his own account. It made him over 100 years old. When these figures were presented to him, he went over them carefully and said:

"'Yes, that is about correct. But you have left out five years in St. Petersburg, when I was private secretary to the Czar; and eight years in South Africa, revising Stanley's book;[2] and four years with Peary,[3] hunting that damned North Pole.'

"'That makes you a good deal over a hundred, Jim.'

"'Yes, indeed. Bless me, how time flies.'

* * *

1. Either Kennedy synthesized this account from extant lore about Townsend or else Townsend reused good lines in different contexts. Some of Townsend's quips are reported by Richard A. Dwyer and Richard E. Lingenfelter as having been recorded by Sam Davis in a *Carson Appeal* article written probably in late October 1889. See *Lying on the Eastern Slope: James Townsend's Comic Journalism on the Mining Frontier*, 120–25.

2. It is not certain which book is being referred to, not that Townsend's claim is even true. Sir Henry Morton Stanley published several books of his travels in Africa, but *Through South Africa* (1898) best fits the context.

3. Robert Edwin Peary, an Arctic explorer, is credited with discovering the North Pole in 1909. Townsend, however, died in 1900, so either he was referring to one of Peary's earlier expeditions, or the narrator of this anecdote took some liberties, on the ground that one more preposterous claim would not make any difference to Townsend's reputation.

"Mention anything on earth, and Jim always had a story to spring. Once a friend was speaking of a hot spell of weather.

"'Hot weather? Hot weather? You don't know what hot weather is in America. Why, ten years ago, when I was correspondent for the New York World in Madrid, it was so warm there that I had to carry my mouth full of ice to keep my teeth from sweating.'

* * *

"Someone mentioned a great mathematician who could calculate eclipses and tell to a minute when a planet would reach a certain place in the heavens.

"'Didn't know the alphabet of mathematics,' replied Jim. 'My Uncle Bill was the boy that could do business with figures. Why, I recall one night I was helping him home; he was drunk to beat the band, and I took a short cut through the cemetery. He fell over a tombstone, and, hitting his head on the corner of a block of marble, was senseless for two hours. I thought for a spell he was dead; and he hadn't made his will. But he finally came to; and, do you know, that cuss had been putting in his spare time when he was insensible figuring out the weight of the corpse when it died. I tell you, boys, figures just came natural to that man.'

* * *

"Passing with a friend over the railroad trestle at Gold Hill, the friend remarked that Gold Hill didn't have any two separate areas of ten feet that were on a level, and it was probably the most carelessly thrown together town in the Union.

"Jim cast his eye over the conglomerate collection of hillocks and depressions which made up a city built on the plan of a crumpled newspaper, and replied:

"'Why, in Bodie they'd use that place for a race track.'

* * *

"In a famous mining suit tried in San Francisco the Bodie mines were in litigation, and Townsend was one of the main witnesses.

"'Did you swear yesterday, Mr. Townsend, that mining began on that claim on the 28th of September?' asked counsel for the opposition.

"'I never swore to anything of the kind,' replied the witness.

"The attorney at once produced the shorthand notes, and the stenographer read his testimony, showing that the attorney's recollection was correct.

"'Do you dispute these shorthand notes?'

"'I certainly do,' replied Jim. 'If I ever swore to that I was mistaken, and I desire to correct my testimony.'

"'Then on what date did the mining operations begin?' queried the attorney.

"'Oh, the dates are all right, but I used the wrong word when I said "mining." I meant to say "quarrying." They were lifting the gold out in blocks, sir.'

"The courtroom shook with laughter and the Judge excused the witness.

*   *   *

"There was always a crowd when Jim got on the stand. He was quite deaf, but particularly so when he wanted to spar for time to frame up an answer. On one occasion he was badgered by a lawyer whom he hated cordially and was asked if he had ever had a conversation about the case with a man named Wilson.

"'I think I did, but do I have to repeat it here?' was the reply.

"The lawyer insisted, and Townsend sparred to be excused from testifying. But the lawyer kept hammering away, and finally got the conversation from Jim as follows:

"'You see, I met Wilson the other morning in front of the Episcopal church, and he says to me—must I use his exact language?'

"'You certainly must,' was the reply of the attorney.

"'He said to me that he thought you were a long-legged, blackmailing — — —— ——. And I concurred.'

*   *   *

"Once he was talking about the fine cream he had in Bodie, even though there were no cows there.

"'How do you get the cream if you have no cows?' queried a sucker.

"'Oh, that's a scheme of my own. I buy butter from California, and then I just throw the rolls into a churn and churn it backwards.'

"'But how does that get cream?'

"'It just unwinds it and lands it back where it started. Butter is simply cream wound up.'

*   *   *

"One night at the Ormsby House at Carson City some Easterners were telling some big stories, evidently trying to impress Townsend, when the latter squared himself to come back. They had been telling about the fruit crops in Ohio.

"'Why,' said Jim, 'up in Mono county I've seen apple trees in the fall sink down in the soil with the weight of the fruit until you saw nothing but the branches, the trunks clean out of sight. This made it handy to pick the fruit, and when the trees were relieved of their weight they simply rose back to their normal position.'

*   *   *

"The conversation drifted on to the intelligence of animals.

"'Why,' said Jim, 'I knew a horse in Empire that noticed a misplaced switch, and, do you know, that intelligent animal saw a barrel of red roof-paint close by, and he dipped his tail into the barrel and rushed out and flagged the train. You bet, Nevada horses can distinguish colors all right.

"'I had a dog that used to go out every morning after the carrier had passed and bring in the San Francisco Examiner. One morning he took it in his teeth and then spat it out and refused to bring it in. I suspected something unusual and went out myself, and saw at once what was the matter. That paper had an article on the front page denouncing me as the biggest liar in America, and the dog, being rather fond of me, resented it.'

*   *   *

"This caused the Easterners to back up some. The conversation turned on great displays of nerve. They mentioned a case of a man in Kentucky who killed two opponents after his bowels had been eliminated from his anatomy with a bowie knife.

"'That's nothing,' said Jim. 'I saw a cowboy in Aurora get his entire insides cut out and strewed all over the sidewalk. The man who did it knew it would make trouble and started to run. The cowboy like a flash made his entrails into a lariat, and, throwing it 60 feet, caught the other fellow, and, pulling him back hand over hand, cut his throat from ear to ear.'

*   *   *

"Jim used to set up the whole of the Mono Index at the case himself. He never used any copy-paper. His explanation was that he wrote such a poor hand that he never could read it himself, and so he fell into the habit of setting up the matter direct from the case.

"It was at this time that the Mono Index became the funniest paper that the Coast ever produced.

"Some of the items were rather broad, but as a rule half the papers on the Coast selected a half column or so of 'Townsendisms,' and they were copied all over the Union.

"It seems a pity that the back files of this remarkable sheet could not be rescued and a compilation made of them. Such a collection would be a classic in the way of original Nevada humor."

⟿*Nevada Mining News,* August 27, 1908, p. 5

[The Origin of Twain's Hopkins Massacre Hoax]

Joseph T. Goodman

"The first piece of work by which Mark Twain gained more than a local reputation was the Hopkins massacre hoax," said Joe Goodman, formerly the moving spirit in the Virginia Enterprise, while in Reno recently. "There were several antecedent and collateral matters connected with it which have never been told, though quite as interesting as the story itself.

"As early as February, 1863, Mr. Clemens had asked my permission to sign the pen-name 'Mark Twain' to his letters from Carson City, where he was reporting the Legislature, and to occasional special articles, and he had been doing so for some months, but without producing anything particularly noteworthy, and the name had attracted no attention outside the State.

* * *

"In July of that year a man named Cornell went suddenly insane and ran amuck with an axe through the streets of Austin, out in Lander county, killing five or six persons and wounding many others. There was no telegraph then to the eastern part of the State, and the first news of the terrible tragedy was brought by the driver of the overland stage, to whom it had been passed along by the intermediate drivers. The stage arrived in Virginia City about 2 o'clock in the morning, and Mark Twain had just time to get the story and write it up in all its naked horror for that issue of the Enterprise. No other paper in Virginia City or any of the towns in the western part of the State got it.

"The atrocity of the deed rendered the account of it incredible, and none of the Nevada or California papers would copy the item. They either sneered at it as a raw attempt at deception, or censured the Enterprise for its unprincipled course in 'faking' news. It was not until some days later, when the Reese River Reveille came with full particulars of the awful event, that they discovered how their suspicion had overreached itself.

* * *

"About this time an old Frenchman named Daney discovered a wonderfully rich quartz ledge in his garden, in the Spring Valley mining district, just below Silver City. The mine was incorporated and the stock soon soared to nearly $100 a share.

"The poor old gardener didn't live to see the rocket descend, as it did within a year. In his undreamed-of affluence it became his habit to mount his mule and come daily to Virginia City, where he would fill himself and his countrymen up with cheap claret to the point of beating their breasts and chanting the 'Marseillaise,' as Frenchmen are wont to do when they get enough campeche aboard. One day he loaded up heavier than usual, and while descending the steep grade through Gold Hill on his way home, fell off his mule and broke his neck, merely exclaiming:

"'Quel dommage!' ('What a pity!')

* * *

"From the very discovery of the Comstock the San Francisco Bulletin had been unfriendly to the interests of Nevada, deprecating dealings in mining shares while pointing out the advantages of investing in Spring Valley water stock. Mark Twain, who, according to his own account, had a trunkful of the abused mining securities, resolved to deal the arch-enemy a stinging blow. He consulted me about it, and I told him to go ahead.

"So he concocted the story of old man Hopkins, whom he located in the great pine forest between Dutch Nick's and Empire City. As these were only different names for the same place, and as there wasn't a forest or even a pine tree within twenty miles of it, Mark considered that the absurdity of the location was sufficient to stamp the story as hoax.

"He went on to say that Hopkins had been largely interested in the Daney mine when the shares were at a very low figure, but being a relative of one of the editors of the Bulletin and a constant reader of that paper, he grew distrustful of his investment, sold out and put all his money into Spring Valley water stock. Almost immediately Spring Valley slumped nearly one-half in price and Daney mounted skyward. This sudden reverse of fortune drove Hopkins insane; he murdered his whole family, scalped his wife and went charging wildly into Carson City on horseback, swinging aloft the bloody scalp of the old woman.

*   *   *

"Mark and I supposed that the absurdity of detail and the extravagance of style would disclose to everyone that the whole thing was only a rough satire. But we were mistaken, as we very soon found out. The description was so graphic that it obscured the purpose of the article which appeared October 28, 1863. I was breakfasting with City Marshal Perry that morning when he read it.

"'My God!' he exclaimed, 'that was a horrible affair—that Hopkins murder!'

"'But don't you see, Jack, that it is all a fake—just a slap at the San Francisco Bulletin?' and I showed him how satirical it was and how cunningly it had been devised.

"'Well, I see it now,' he replied; 'but I never should without your explanation, and nobody else will.'

*   *   *

"And nobody else did. With their suspicion lulled by the genuineness of the Austin horror, nearly every paper in California copied the Hopkins story. Our Nevada rivals were only too ready to expose the gross imposture, as they termed it. Then came the whirlwind. In less than a week more than half of our exchanges were stopped, while angry letters poured in from journals and subscribers saying they never would exchange with or take the Enterprise again until Mark Twain was discharged from its staff.

"Poor Mark! He was the most unhappy being you ever saw. He fretted and writhed as the subscription list kept falling and the denunciatory letters continued to come, until at last he came to me one day and said:

"'Mr. Goodman, I have ruined your business, and the only reparation I can make is to resign from the Enterprise. You can never recover from this blow while I'm on the paper.'

"'Brace up, Mark,' I replied. 'We can furnish the people with news but we can't supply them with sense. Only time can do that. This flurry will pass, or, if it doesn't, I'm as responsible for it as you, and we'll weather it out together. You just go right ahead, and you'll see that we win out in the long run.'

"So Mark remained; and we not only won out as to the renewed prosperity of the Enterprise, but the story that came so near wrecking us proved to be the first positive step in his steady climb to fame."

↦*Nevada Mining News*, November 19, 1908, p. 5

[The Tragedy of Conrad Wiegand]

[Joseph T. Goodman?]

Although unsigned in the newspaper, the tragic story of Conrad Wiegand is probably the work of Joe Goodman. Its formal and judicious style is one Goodman sometimes used, and he was circumstantially situated to know the facts. Despite the lapse of time between the suicide of Conrad Wiegand, conscientious Comstock assayer, in 1880 and the publication of this piece and despite the obvious need for Goodman to do a certain amount of imaginative reconstructing of conversations, this narrative is the fullest known account of the cause of Wiegand's suicide, and there is no reason to doubt its essential veracity. As the narrator points out, Wiegand was ridiculed and held in contempt on the Comstock as a coward and weakling. The most famous expression of this attitude appears in appendix C of Mark Twain's *Roughing It* (1872).[1] Ironically, about a year before Twain completed appendix C, he began an extensive but incomplete draft of a strong praise of Wiegand.[2] Goodman, although believing Wiegand's charges of corruption were probably accurate, had ridiculed him for his quixotic and ineffectual crusades. Nevertheless, as a fair-minded and honorable man, Goodman would have respected Wiegand's integrity, whatever he thought of his crusades. Although Goodman left the Comstock in 1874, he returned occasionally—hence the reference to the hotel room—and was known to be fairly well-off—hence Wiegand's appeal to him for a substantial loan. Goodman was personally familiar with banker William Sharon and undoubtedly knew General John B. Winters as well, and his detailed account of their eventual falling out supplies valuable new information about the dishonesty of Comstock management practices as well as about the characters of Sharon and Winters. This remorseful memoir also reveals that Twain's defamatory sketch in appendix C of *Roughing It* had been protested—quite possibly by Goodman.

---

1. See also "Explanatory Notes" (760–68) in the Mark Twain Project's edition of *Roughing It*.
2. For the text and background of this piece see my " 'Assaying in Nevada': Twain's Wrong Turn in the Right Direction."

—⫶⇒ ⇐⫶—

"The most upright man I ever knew killed himself through remorse for a crime committed under the spur of circumstance," said an old Comstocker on the veranda of the Riverside Hotel, the other evening. "The story has never been told; but it is well worth telling for many reasons. There is no one left whom it can shame or injure, and I think Conrad Wiegand, if he could express his wish, would desire it told, for he was of the Montaigne stamp, anxious that men should know him better even if they esteemed him less.

"I do not believe, however, that the knowledge of his act will lessen the esteem of any one who knew him. It never has mine, and I think I represent the average sentiment of my kind. I could distinguish so clearly between the man himself and his single uncharacteristic deed, that no sense of moral outrage mingled with the sympathy I felt for him.

*　　*　　*

"I never met any one else whose purity and nobility of nature equally impressed me. I have known men who, pricked by pride, could comport themselves as loftily, and whose souls could give out as pure a lustre on the touchstone of chance occasion—freakish men, whose lethargic virtue required a strong stimulus to arouse it; but I never knew another than Conrad Wiegand in whom loftiness and purity were predominant forces, independent of all motives and surroundings and inseparable from every action of his life.

"These qualities would have distinguished him had he been only of a passive mood, content to unbonnet himself graciously to the world as it passed along. But his nature would not permit him to play the part of an indifferent bystander. Amid the pageantry of life, as it moved before him, he saw wrongs to be righted, suffering to be alleviated, high purposes to be achieved, and his soul would not let him rest while the accomplishment of any of these objects lay within his power.

*　　*　　*

"Wiegand was an assayer, one of the best on the Coast; but his business pursuits did not afford scope enough for the full volume of his impulses and energy. The superfluity expended itself in a variety of actions, some of which were eccentric to the verge of quixotry, but all alike inspired by high and unsullied motives. He went solitarily upon midnight missions, to do good wherever and however it could be done, to the extent of his means and ability; he delivered public discourses on current errors and abuses, or upon themes designed to instruct and elevate the masses; he held, at times, religious services, preaching a broad humanitarian faith intended to attract those who rebelled against the rigor of orthodox creeds; he overwhelmed the press with contributions upon every conceivable topic; and when the severity of some of his articles was modified by the prudent editors, he established a periodical of his own in which his opinions might find unrestricted expression.

*   *   *

"Such force and activity imply strong personality, and suggest the usual concomitant—egotism; but Wiegand was singularly free from that weakness, if I rightly understand it. I take egotism to be a sickly outgrowth of egoism—an obnoxious excrescence upon a wholesome trunk. A person may be superabundantly endowed with the faculty of introspection and a consciousness of individuality, which constitute egoism, and yet be devoid of that personal vanity whose tiresome exhibition render him an egotist.

"Wiegand possessed the most egoism of any man I ever met. The incessant strain of his mind, the unrelaxing nervous tension, the shock of innumerable encounters, the reaction from futile endeavor, scourged him to subjective study and made him involuntarily a lesson to himself. The problem of his being, in which there appeared to be no possibility of an equation between the large purposes and the small achievements, was constantly forced upon him, and in his baffled search for the solution he dissected his heart to pieces.

"But this intense consciousness and study of self did not betray him into egotistic display. He never alluded to himself through vanity, nor in a way to obtrude his personality upon the listener. Yet his discourse was as surcharged with self as the needle is with magnetism. But he spoke of his individuality only as a known quantity in the problem of existence, a knowledge of which furnished the only clew upon which he could rely in the maze of life's incomprehensibilities.

*   *   *

"His vagaries won the sure reward of eccentricity. The sneer of unpracticalness, the innuendo of insanity, came flippantly from men incapable of understanding either his motives or methods. It was this very incapacity, likely, that begot the scoffs. People are tolerant only of their own level and circumference. Things above or beyond them are equally objects of contempt with the things beneath them.

"If to know not what they do be still a valid plea for pardon, these ignorant scoffers must be forgiven, I suppose. It may be pardonable, moreover, in intelligent persons, who only knew Wiegand imperfectly, to have doubted the practicality and soundness of his mind, so extraordinary were some of his idiosyncrasies; but to me, who was as familiar with the structure and work-ings of his intellect as if I had anatomized it, he appeared the most practical and sane of men. Obliquity and straightness are merely matters of stand-point. Vary the angle of sight, and the oblique will become straight, the straight oblique. According to the laws that govern it, the boomerang goes as truly to its aim as the arrow. The ostensibly unpractical schemes of Wiegand became entirely practical when viewed from the conditions under which he saw them, and his apparently erratic ways, surveyed from the base of his pe-culiar mental organization, showed themselves to be the most straight-forward of courses.

"It may be urged that this peculiarity of organization should be thrown into the scale in weighing his sanity. I am not of that opinion. Exceptional facts are proportionately as authoritative with me as general ones. The laws governing the flight of comets have equal force with those that regulate the planetary systems.

* * *

"Wiegand was not ignorant of these jeers, nor altogether indifferent to them; but they provoked no resentment in him, and even the pity they ex-cited reverted upon himself. He grieved to have so failed in making himself understood that it should be possible to thus misconstrue his purposes and actions.

"But neither failure nor the certainty that every fresh effort must en-counter like scoffs could abate his zeal or cause him to deviate from the course his conscience marked out for him. He had but a single object in view—to benefit his kind. His eagerness to accomplish this rendered him in-different to everything else, and he moved onward with the exalted spirit of one who cares not, so long as victory is gained, whether his own portion be honor or martyrdom.

* * *

"For many years he held the position of assayer in the San Francisco Mint, but lost it, I believe, through exposing some crookedness in the institution. When he established his assay office at Gold Hill, he at once commanded a large and lucrative business. But he soon incurred the enmity of Sharon,[3] and the hostility in a short time proved ruinous to him, financially.

3. William Sharon, as manager of the Nevada branch of the Bank of California, the most impor-tant bank in the region, was a financier of great power. As powerful as Sharon was, he was un-scrupulously ruthless toward anyone who stood in his way. Joe Goodman destroyed his chance to be elected U.S. senator from Nevada in 1872, although he was elected to the position subsequently.

"One of the great sources of profit to the banks handling the bullion from the mines was the understamping of the value of the bars. Bars were understamped from $150 to $250, or more, each. The banks bought them at their face value, thus realizing a large profit in addition to the discount. When it is considered that the output was at times more than 100 bars a days, the enormous profit accruing to the banks from this dishonest practice will be realized. It may be possible to discriminate in some way between this usage and downright robbery, but I have failed to discover how it can be done.

"Sharon endeavored to force Wiegand to understamp bars, the same as the other assayers, but he refused to do so, declaring that no bar of bullion should ever go out of his assay office with other than its true value stamped on its face. Bear this declaration in mind. It was made at a crisis that meant wealth or poverty to him, whichever he should choose, and as he chose the latter there is no doubt it was the utterance of an honest man. But it is only another illustration of how little any one knows himself.

"Wiegand's refusal to understamp bars resulted not only in the loss of the business controlled by the Bank of California, but of such other patronage as Sharon could divert from him, and the end soon came. Wiegand was forced into bankruptcy; but I am glad to be able to add that he subsequently paid all of his indebtedness, with interest.

* * *

"It was at this period, while struggling for very existence, that his earnestness for reform impelled him to start his little periodical, 'The People's Tribune.' He couldn't afford to hire it printed, so he bought some old type and a small press, and learned how to do the composition and press work himself.

"He was unreserved and fearless in his denunciation of abuses in mining affairs; and it was his strictures on the management of the Yellow Jacket, in particular, that brought upon him the horsewhipping by General John B. Winters—Wiegand's serious account of which was turned into ridicule by Mark Twain, and is yet, in spite of repeated protests, published as an appendix to 'Roughing It.'

"Wiegand's vindication was not long delayed. The proof of all his charges, and more, came out soon afterwards when Sharon quarreled with Winters and kicked him out of the superintendency of the Yellow Jacket for getting

---

Respecting Goodman as an opponent he could neither beat nor intimidate, Sharon later made overtures to him, bought the *Territorial Enterprise* from him in 1874, and subsequently occasionally confided in him.

too thick with his (Sharon's) pretty little blonde mistress, Belle Warner. I had it from the mouth of both the principals. Sharon said to me:

"'He has played me a mean trick; a trick that no gentleman would be guilty of with a friend. But Winters isn't a gentleman. He has been nothing but a lackey, a very bootblack, to me, servilely doing my bidding, ever since he came on the Lode. And to think of his daring to treat me in that way! Damn him! I'll beggar him, and run him out of the State!'

"And Winters said to me:

"'The damned ingrate, to turn on me for such a trifle! I've lost all my self-respect by doing dirty work for him. To feed his mills, I've mixed waste rock with the Yellow Jacket ore till it would scarcely pay for crushing, when the company might have been paying dividends for years; and when he has wished to make a deal, I've smashed the engine and thrown the pieces into the sump, in order to break the price of the stock.'

"Such was mine management on the Comstock in early times. I wonder how much it has improved?

*   *   *

"Wiegand struggled along for years, his spirit unbroken and his soul holding fast to its lofty ideals. He was fortunate in his domestic relations, if in nothing else. His cultured wife was in perfect accord with him in all his aims, and his daughter was the lovely creature to be expected from such parentage. No home could be happier than theirs.

"He finally succeeded in establishing an assay office in Virginia City, making a specialty of assaying samples of ore for prospectors, and ere long had built up a fair business. In addition to this, he perfected a process for the economical manufacture of sulphate of copper—used extensively in mulling—from base ores in the course of their reduction. He was receiving a royalty for its use in several mills, and was expecting a greatly increased income from its application on an extensive scale by a company in the eastern part of the State. Under these promising circumstances, he felt justified in enlarging his assay office, to make it more complete in several respects.

"Such was the state of his affairs at the time I last saw him in Virginia City.

*   *   *

"I was in my room at the Palace Hotel one night, in the winter of 1879, when I received a card from Wiegand, on which was written: 'Would like an hour's interview with you if it can be absolutely private.'

"I shall never forget his appearance as he entered the room. The change in

him was startling. His eyes were sunken, his cheeks hollow, his carriage droop-
ing; and the beneficent, saintly look, that once lighted up his countenance
with a holy beauty, was replaced by a haggard, haunted expression befitting
only the faces of the damned.

"He did not heed my astonishment, nor the hand I eagerly extended, nor
the friendly words with which I welcomed him. Glancing anxiously about
the room, he asked, in a whisper:

" 'Are we quite alone?'

" 'Entirely so.'

" 'Is there any one in the next room?'

" 'I think not; I've heard no one.'

"He tried the door; it was locked. Then, noticing that the transom of the
hall door was open, he said he would close it, with my permission, as he
wished to stop up all possible ears.

*   *   *

"I could not conjecture what these precautions meant. Nothing suggested
itself that called for privacy, much less for the absolute secrecy upon which he
seemed intent. As I watched him during his inspection of the room, his
stealth and suspicion suddenly gave a new interpretation to his ghastly aspect. These were symptoms of insanity, I thought; the scoffers were right all
the while; I alone had been mistaken.

"When every possible precaution had been taken, he directed his attention
to me for the first time. The strain visible upon him until then, relaxed; his
manner softened; and a helpless, pleading expression came into his eyes. He
spoke in a low tone, husky with emotion.

" 'I have no right to pledge you to secrecy,' he said; 'I have no right even to
force my confession upon you. I make it to you because you have always been
so forbearing with me that I believe you will be indulgent to the last, and because I hope you may be able to assist me.'

" 'You have not misjudged my friendship, Wiegand; you can rely on my
sympathy, my secrecy, my assistance, to the extent of my power,' I replied, extending my hand to him once more.

" 'I accept your words more gratefully than I ever before received anything
in my life,' he answered; 'but withhold your hand. When you have heard
what I am about to say, you will never offer it to me again.'

" 'Always, as now, Wiegand, no matter what may have happened,' I said,
still insisting on his taking my outstretched hand.

"'Withhold it, I say!' he exclaimed, shrinking back. 'Do you wish to shake
hands with a felon?'

" 'You are jesting, Wiegand.'

" 'Would to God I were! Do I look like a jester? My crime is attested by every change you see in me, by the wreck I am.'

" 'This is hallucination, the result of overstrain, Wiegand,' I said. 'You know as well as I do that it is one of the commonest of maladies, and have failed to recognize it only because you are the sufferer yourself.'

" 'Would to God it were!' he repeated. 'But you deceive yourself. This is no phantasm, from which I shall some day awake with a buoyant sense of relief. It is natural, in your inability or reluctance to associate me with crime, that you should have recourse to the common belief in my insanity. I have thought of it myself and reckoned how securely I could entrench myself behind it, should I choose to do so, in the event of justice pursuing me. I have even become a partial convert to it; not that any action or utterance of mine appears less rational to me now than ever, but that it is a sort of madness, as the world goes, to act or think otherwise than by rote. But in this case, it is not my madness but my trespass that speaks. Will you listen to my confession?'

" 'I will listen with interest to anything you may see fit to tell me, Wiegand,' I answered.

*   *   *

" 'Thank you,' he said. 'You will remember how prosperously I thought I was getting on, the last time I spoke to you of my affairs. Well, I proceeded with the additions to my assay office. The cost far exceeded the loose estimates I had made; but that gave me no worry, until one day my bookkeeper called my attention to the fact that my bank account was overdrawn. I told him he must be mistaken, but he insisted on the correctness of his figures. I still believed him to be in error, but I was so busy with the adjustment of the machinery in my new refining department that I had no time to go over the books. I knew on how precarious a footing my credit stood, especially with the Bank of California, and that the least breath of suspicion would precipitate the avalanche. It was indispensable to my safety that I should have a balance at the bank.

" 'For some years I had been buying bullion in small quantities from prospectors, sluicemen and others, casting it into a bar whenever I had accumulated enough for that purpose, and depositing it in the bank, to be drafted against to the extent of its face value. I generally let three or four of these bars accumulate, and then sold them in San Francisco or some Eastern city, the difference of the price thus obtained more than offsetting the interest.

" 'At the time my bookkeeper told me that my account was overdrawn one of these bars was lying in the assay office. It was refined silver, not a trace of gold in it, and was worth a little over $1000. I knew that my drafts within the next few days would exceed that amount, but I was expecting money from my sulphate of copper royalties and other sources. The only question was how to bridge my credit over the interval.

"'The thought occurred to me: "This bar is to be deposited only as security; what, then, does its face value matter, since I shall redeem it in a few days?" That settled the question, in my mind. Without a thought of the culpability or consequences, I took my punches and stamped upon the bar an additional value in gold of upward of $2000.

*   *   *

"'My action was so excusable in my own sight that I had no sense of wrong-doing. But mark the revenge of violated Right, and believe that no moral law can be transgressed without bringing punishment in one shape or another. The use of my invention on a large scale in Eastern Nevada was abandoned, the mills on the Comstock that were paying me royalties shut down, the assaying business suffered a great depression. In consequence, my income fell to almost nothing. Instead of redeeming that first falsified bar, as I had intended, I was forced to falsify another and another, in order to keep up my credit and prevent detection.

"'I have now five bars in the bank, representing on their face upward of $8000 more than their actual value. Nothing but the stupidity of the bank folks has protected me thus far. They are a lot of dolts. If they had chipped a corner from any of those bars, and had it assayed, as they should have done, they would have discovered there was not a trace of gold in it.'

"'Have you any memoranda with you showing the exact value of the bars?' I asked.

"'I see your drift, but unhappily, must dispel the illusion,' he replied. 'Madness is not quite so methodical as this,' he said, drawing a memorandum book from his pocket, and reading off the number, weight, and value in gold and silver stamped upon each bar.

"'I am forced to believe you, Wiegand,' I said. 'What is to be done?'

"'Can you let me have the money to get these bars out of the bank?'

"'Unfortunately, I cannot.'

"'Do you think Senator Jones[4] could?'

"'I don't know. He is in Washington.'

"'I shall go there. He is the only other man I have any hope in appealing to.'

_____

4. John J. Jones, a former Comstock mine owner and financier and now a U.S. senator.

*   *   *

"I met Wiegand on the train a short time afterwards. He was on his way to Washington. His appearance was more spectral than human. He told me he had overcome the bitterest of his misery, the concealment of the secret from his wife. He had told her everything, and had been rewarded by the assurance of her unalterable love and sympathy.

"Senator Jones was not able to give the required assistance at once, and Wiegand applied to his relatives in Philadelphia. The necessary amount was raised, and the fatal bars were withdrawn through the agency of Drexel, Morgan & Co. and the Nevada Bank.

*   *   *

"Wiegand returned to Virginia City, but the removal of the proof did not lift the sense of guilt from his mind. He became a prey to remorse, and a few months afterwards put an end to his wretched existence by hanging himself.

"The shock and details of his suicide caused me many a sleepless night. The most noticeable thing in Wiegand's attire always was a long-knitted 'comforter,' which he wore on account of bronchial trouble. He had gone into his assay office, ascended a step-ladder, tied one end of that comforter around his neck and the other to a beam, and then thrown himself from the ladder. The knot had slipped, and he had fallen to the floor, bruising his features frightfully. But so determined was he in his purpose—poor, gentle, timid Wiegand!—that he made those horrible preparations all over again, going to his death more bravely than most heroes.

*   *   *

"Wiegand's daughter was already dead, and his wife went East shortly after his death. Only a year or two later her friends were shocked by the news that she had died there of starvation.

"Like the psalmist, I have been young and now am old; but, unlike him, I have seen the righteous forsaken and his seed begging bread."[5]

⇢*Nevada Mining News,* October 1, 1908, pp. 5–6

---

5. Psalms 37:25–26.

[The Gamble of Nevada Mining Stocks]

Anonymous

"In one respect," said the Old Comstocker, as he scanned the blackboard in the Nat C. Goodwin office yesterday,[1] "the investors in the mining stocks of Nevada today have a little more the best of it than those who tried their luck at the game 40 years ago. One important item is that the stock-buyer of today doesn't have to pay assessments: once he buys his stock, it is his for keeps. He can lay it away in a trunk, use it for wall-paper, or do anything else he pleases with it in the days of borrasca,[2] but if ever it goes up, he can realize on it. It was not so in the good old times of which I speak.

"In 1867 I had a friend who was shift-boss in the Justice mine, at the extreme south end of the Comstock. He came to me one night, and after swearing me to secrecy, informed me that a development of the utmost importance had occurred in the mine. He counseled the purchase of the stock without delay. As he was a friend of proved fidelity and a man of the strictest integrity, I made no delay about taking his advice. The very next morning, on the first board, I became an owner in Justice stock to the limit of my financial resources.

* * *

"Time went on, and there was no movement in the market for Justice. The fluctuations were slight, but, if anything, they carried the stock downward. Soon an assessment of \$5.00 a share was levied. Then I called on my friend, the shift-boss, and inquired what was up.

1. Nat C. Goodwin was a Reno stockbroker specializing in stocks in the Rawhide and Goldfield mining camps of southern Nevada. The identity of the "Old Comstocker" has not been established.
2. "Borrasca" was a Spanish term meaning "bust," the opposite of a boom.

"He told me that immediately after the strike was made the superintendent had ordered that work be suspended in that part of the mine and had bulkheaded the face of the drift, so that nobody could see the splendid ore-showing hitherto visible. 'Of course,' he added, 'it is only a question of time until that drift is opened up again and then your stock will appreciate several hundred per cent.'

"I went away and made further investigation, which revealed to me that at the time of the strike the superintendent and the dominant faction of the company had but little of the stock, and they were gathering in all they could by slow stages, in order not to elevate the market. In fact, they were manipulating it to keep it down.

*　*　*

"I was satisfied, and concluded to hang on. But something I had not counted much upon was the assessment end of the game, and it came like a douche of cold water when I picked up the Gold Hill News one day and found that another assessment of $5.00 a share had been levied on Justice.

"I paid it, of course, but it put quite a crimp in my diminished bankroll. Then, three months later, the dose was repeated. And so on, for every quarter, they levied an assessment of $5.00 a share on Justice.

"I stayed with them and came through every three months, although I had to borrow the money more than once. Finally, when I was about at the end of my financial rope, I was called East by a telegram informing me of the fatal illness of my mother, and I had to sell my Justice to get enough money to go on. I got $10 a share for it—about what it had cost me. I was out about $40 a share paid in assessments.

"I returned to my old home in New York, and was gone about six months. During that absence I forgot all about the stock market. But on my trip back to Nevada, I bought a copy of the Alta California at Ogden, and instinctively my eye fell upon the column given over to the transactions of the San Francisco stock exchange. It almost pulled me straight up in the air when I saw that Justice was selling at $60 a share.

"At every station westward where we met an east-bound train, I was the first to buy a San Francisco newspaper, and each time it recorded a big advance in the price of Justice. And within a week after my arrival on the Comstock, the stock sold for as high as $300 a share. Justice had never been so high on the Comstock since the time Judge North retired from the bench.

"I figure that the assessment cinch cost me around $210,000 that trip, not to speak of what I lost outright in the payment of assessments.

*　*　*

"When you come to think of it," continued the old man, "it's something wonderful the way investors in those stocks have stood for the assessments. And the fact that a mine, while being continually assessed, never paid a dividend, made no difference in the stock quotations.

"For instance, there is Alpha, as assessment-mill of the first water, that never in the 49 years of its existence gave back a dollar to its stockholders. It sold up to $1570 in February, 1868, dropped to $33 in September of that year, rose to $62 the following February, dropped to $11 in October, 1869, went up to $21 in March, 1870, fell to $3 in September, rose again to $21 in September of 1871 and kited to $240 the next April. By July of '73 it was selling for as low as $15, and in the following September, as high as $100. In February, 1874, it was selling for $9, in June, 1875, for $45. In the same month it fell again to $3, in May, 1876, it sold for $67, in December, for $18. During the year following, it ranged at from $5 to $23. Talk about playing 'snap-the-whip,' talk about 'bumping-the-bumps,' the stock-investor of those days had plenty of fun for his money. Being alternately thrown from the top of a sky-scraper and pulled back from earth again with a balloon is nothing to it.

* * *

"The sums realized in the aggregate from this assessment process were enormous. For instance, my pet, Justice, extracted from the shareholders the sum of $3,500,000; Sierra Nevada, close on $4,000,000; Bullion, $3,400,000; Yellow Jacket, $2,750,000; Overman, $3,250,000; Caledonia, $2,000,000; Alta, $1,400,000; Imperial, $1,250,000; Mexican, $1,400,000; Silver Hill, $1,700,000; Baltimore, $1,000,000; Utah $1,000,000; and New York about $1,000,000. There is an aggregate of $27,650,000 from 13 mines out of the 103 companies capitalized on the Comstock, out of which six only paid more in dividends than what they demanded in assessments.

"You may judge from the activity in the shares of these worthless mines, as illustrated in the case of Alpha, what a chance a man had for a big killing in a property of merit. Take Belcher, for instance, that has levied assessments amounting in the aggregate to about $2,000,000, but which has paid dividends amounting to nearly $16,000,000.

"In the spring of 1868 that stock was selling at $430 a share. The July following, it had dropped to $110. The following year it ranged from $12 to $35. In 1870 it fell to $1 a share. In January of 1871 the stock sold for $6 a share; in December for $450. The next month, the stock was selling for $6 a share, but by the following April, less than three months later, it was quoted at $1525. It sold again that year for $1.50, but went up again to $95. In 1873 it sold as low as 25 cents, soared up the same year to $113, and fell again to $1.50. The year following it sold as high as $120 a share.

"History repeats itself, in mining, as in everything else. The prospects of the Goldfield of today had their Comstock progenitors. I shall never forget one of them; for I have good cause to remember it. Its name was Eclipse, and it was an appropriate one so far as I was concerned, for it completely eclipsed me.

"For a long time after Mackay and Fair discovered the big bonanza in the Con. Virginia and California ground, but few people knew anything about it. The two partners were not interested in the stock market; they had the control of the mines, and all they cared about was to get out the rich ore, and rake off their dividends. They were absolutely indifferent as to what the public knew or thought of the property, and this very indifference fooled the public, who thought that the candid information so readily given out about developments in the property was peddled purposely to influence the market and catch a new crop of 'suckers.'

"Some 'hunch' prompted me to buy 300 shares of California at $3 a share. I held it for a long time, and then a wise friend came along and tipped me to get into Eclipse, a rank 'cat,' which was selling at $21 a share. I told him about my California and my hunch that it was going to make good, but he explained that the coming deal in Eclipse was to be a manipulated affair,[3] and that it was to come off at any moment. He pointed out that when I had cleaned up a good profit in Eclipse, I could go back into California, buy more stock than I then held, and make a still bigger profit if California should ever conclude to move upward—a thing which he very much doubted.

*   *   *

"I hearkened to the voice of temptation and fell. I bought all the Eclipse I could stagger under, and sat down to wait for the promised turn. It came, but in an unexpected direction: the stock shot downward like a thunderbolt. Then they clapped on an assessment. The brokers called for 'more mud.' I could not respond. They wiped me off the board and sent me a statement that I was $1600 in debt to them. I went to work in the California at $4 a day to pay that debt off. And I worked in the big bonanza, which was to send the stock sky-high. Before long, California stock was selling at $800 a share. That time I figure I lost $240,000 by monkeying with Eclipse."

"Maybe you didn't lose quite that much," chipped in a sympathetic-looking individual. "I was tipped to buy Mohawk for 30 cents a share in the month of January 1906. I took the tip, but sold out for $1 shortly after the San

---

3. Many Comstock offerings were manipulated by inside information, insider trading, and deceitful practices that drove stock prices up or down so that insiders could profit.

Francisco earthquake. Of course, the stock went to $20 that fall, but in my case it was simply a matter of not knowing how high it would go."

"Perhaps, you're right," said the other, "but I'll always believe I'd have held out for at least $750 a share for my California if I hadn't been stung by that deal in Eclipse."

⇒*Nevada Mining News,* May 27, 1909, pp. 5–6

Nonfiction

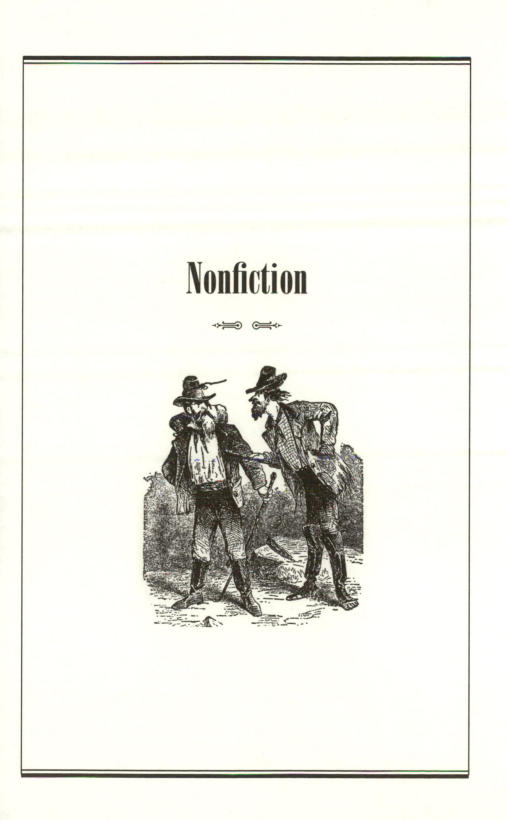

Introduction

✧⇀═◉ ◉═↽✧

Some Comstock literature comes to us as essays, informative (as opposed to personal) letters, speech manuscripts, and other kinds of writing devoted to describing or explaining something. C. C. Goodwin's panegyric "The Prospector" is an eloquent example of an idea that was popular among Sagebrush writers. The prospector was often contrasted to the miner, as later the pioneer would be contrasted to the settler: the former, heroic and the necessary forerunner of civilization, but probably fated to an anonymous death; the latter, mundane but also necessary to provide the base for the flowering and fruition of the civilization that was the next step.

Thomas Fitch's "Sage-Brush Sketches" is a good, relatively early example of how memoirs can verge over into history, providing, as it does, not just a recollection by an insider of what happened but also clear-eyed and unsentimental insight into the causes and nature of events.

Goodman's editorial essay "Cranks and Their Uses" reflects his sympathy for the bohemian, the avant-garde, the eccentric, and the reformer. Unconventional in his own thinking, he prized unconventionality in others and furthered it by his personal example and by the editorial policies he promoted.

Two essays describe the situation of the Paiute Indians at the end of the nineteenth century. Sarah Winnemucca probably adapted hers from speeches she gave around the country on behalf of her tribe. She was one of the first Indians, and most likely the first Indian woman, to go on a lecture circuit. Her animus toward Indian agents is pronounced, and probably justified. American government policy toward Indians has often been scandalously inept, even when well intentioned, and administered by self-serving bureaucrats. G. W. Pease's letter to Dan De Quille written ten years later, however, reflects a more benign state of affairs on a Paiute reservation. It is not apparent in his letter that he intends to take advantage of the Indians; on the contrary, he is perhaps atypically sympathetic to them. No effort is being made in this book to pass judgment on the matter, but only to present grist for the mill.

Fred Hart's book *The Sazerac Lying Club* is, on the face of it, a strange place to go for factual information, but that is only because the title of his book is more colorful than accurate. The book includes some excellent essays that depict the culture of Nevada in places other than the Comstock. White Pine County is on the eastern edge of the state, and Reese River is also remote from Virginia City. Nevertheless, the mobility of the population carried Nevada mores to all parts of the state. The narrative of the first Fourth of July celebration in White Pine describes a proudly patriotic community that went all-out to commemorate the holiday. It is a vivid and joyful picture. On the other hand, the absence of a reliable law enforcement system enabled ruffians and thieves to flourish—until the general population got fed up. The phenomenon of the vigilante movement was not a simple one. Some of the "best" people in a community were often involved with it, and it accomplished what the sheriff, police, courts, and juries could not or would not do. In the essays represented here, rough justice is done. It is not pretty, and it is not admirable, but it was better than the alternative. This was part of the Sagebrush ethic, a refusal to be defeated by the failure of the system.

The First Fourth in White Pine

Fred H. Hart

Fred H. Hart (?–1897) was a journalist with experience on a number of newspapers around Nevada, most signally the *Reese River Reveille*. While editing that paper, he concocted the Sazerac Lying Club, a column reporting the fictitious meetings of a group of men devoted to telling lies in an entertaining manner. He collected these columns and associated material and published *The Sazerac Lying Club* in 1878. Much of this entertaining book, which rapidly went through several printings and was widely distributed, consists of the tall tales that supposedly were floated at the meetings, and most of the rest of it is a collection of the humorous squibs that were filler items on many newspapers of the time. A good deal of this material is now dated, but also included in the book were some essays that were not lies but provided vivid and still engaging historical reports of aspects of life on Nevada's mining frontier. These essays, in addition to their intrinsic merit, also illuminate other items in this anthology.

⋯⋙◉ ◎⋘⋯

The spring of the year 1868 witnessed the inception of the great mining craze known as the "White Pine Excitement." At the time of the discovery of the then rich mines there, Austin was the nearest town to the district, and it was from that place that White Pine was first settled. The discoverers of the mines were Austin prospectors, and on making their find brought their specimens here for assay and testing. I was living in Austin when the first ore from the Hidden Treasure and the famed Eberhardt mines was brought in. It was not necessary that a person should be an expert to determine that the rock was rich. A man who had never in his life seen a silver mine, or never before handled a piece of silver ore, could tell at a glance that it was metal. It came pretty near being pure silver, some of the "horn-silver" specimens being so heavy and metallic that they could be converted into bullion by the simple process of melting in a crucible. Ever on the alert for a new camp, I had no sooner seen these specimens than I determined to go to White Pine. And to White Pine I went. It is situated 120 miles from Austin, and I made the trip on horseback in two and a half days; but there was nothing in the journey in the way of incident that could interest the reader of these pages in its relation.

The mines, which were destined afterward to make such a stir in the world, were contained in a high mountain called Treasure Hill, whose peak rises to an elevation of 9,000 feet above the level of the sea. At the foot of the western and southern slopes of this mountain lies the town of Hamilton. It was then called "the Caves," owing to numerous caves in the dolomite of which the geological formation of the locality consists—and a few ambitious miners even went so far as to call it "Cave City." The city I found, on my arrival at the Caves, consisted of three or four stone cabins, a tent in which a couple of gentlemen from Austin had started an establishment combining store, saloon, restaurant, lodging-house, post-office, and express office, a few tents used for dwellings, a number of prospectors' open-air camps, and about seventy-five inhabitants. There was also a city on the mountain, at the mines, to which the description given of Cave City is likewise applicable.

At the time of my arrival there was considerable rivalry as to which of the two camps should be the future metropolis of White Pine. The mines were marvelously rich, and the prospects were that they were extensive; and it was evident that the district was destined to receive a large population ere long—so, of course, it must have a city. The hill people based their claims for metropolitan prominence on the fact that they were "squatted right down on the top of the mines." The Cave fellows knew the city would be at the foot of the mountain, because there was not a drop of water on the hill, and no likelihood of there ever being any found in that limestone formation. Besides, it was a straight pull of three miles up the mountain to get there; and again, there was not as much room for a large city on top of the mountain as there was at its foot, where the slope gradually spread out, and ended in a level plateau. Time proved both parties to be right. Cities sprung up on both sites, and, though their existence was short, they were "lively camps" while they lasted. "The Caves" was located for a town-site, and named Hamilton, after the man who made the location. Treasure City kept its original name through the varying fortunes of White Pine, and keeps it yet—but it is only a name.

The opening of the month of July, 1868, found the rivalry described above existing in bitter intensity, and so strong was this feeling that a man who owned a town-lot in one survey hardly felt like speaking to the possessor of a similar piece of real estate in the other. The Fourth of July was approaching, and the propriety of celebrating that day in a manner befitting the patriotic founders of two great cities began to be broached. The inhabitants of each town held a public meeting, at which committees of arrangements and officers of the day were appointed, and resolutions adopted that each town would hold a celebration on its own hook, independent and entirely oblivious of even the existence of the other. Better counsels prevailed, however, when on "counting noses" it was found that there was not a sufficient number of men in each camp for two celebrations, and that the only way in which an air of respectability could be secured to the occasion was by fusing the forces and holding a joint celebration. A compromise was effected, by the terms of which Treasure City was to have the poet of the day and the chairman to preside over the literary exercises. Hamilton was to have the other offices, and the meeting and the "ball in the evening" were to be held in that town; but it was stipulated that the citizens of Hamilton were to march in procession up to Treasure City, meet the citizens of that metropolis drawn up in line to await their coming, and escort them in procession back to Hamilton.

At the meeting held in Hamilton to perfect arrangements for the celebration, it was my fortune to be appointed a member of the Committee on Flag, Music, and Ball in the Evening. It was the most difficult position with which an admiring constituency have ever honored me during the whole course of my checkered career. I may say it was a position of impossibilities—but some fellow has said nothing is impossible. It was just because there was nothing in the way of material from which to fulfill my duties as committeeman that made the position such an impossible one.

As to the flag, there was not such an article to be had nearer than Austin, and that was 120 miles distant, and the time lacked only forty-eight hours to the morning of the Glorious Fourth.

The "ball in the evening" was an easier matter than the flag, though even that was attended with many difficulties. There was a man called "Pike," who could play one tune—the "Arkansaw Traveler"—on the violin, and call a few of the simpler figures of an easy quadrille; but there was danger that he would succumb to the "spirits" of the glorious occasion before Night cast her sable mantle over the earth, and he be thus incapable of disseminating melody for the revelry. This danger was overcome by appointing a sub-committee to follow in Pike's wake during the day we celebrated, and to prevent him, even by the use of force if necessary, from imbibing more than three drinks of whisky an hour. The combined female population of the two camps numbered but two, and they both belonged in Hamilton. They could "stand in" on the round dances, and help fill out one quadrille set, and such other sets as might be formed on the floor could be "stag" dances—that is, dances in which only men take part. So the committee could see its way clear on the music, and the "ball in the evening" questions; but the flag was the poser.

Add nothing to nothing and you've got nothing, is a logical conclusion from the axiom, "Take nothing from nothing and nothing remains." There was not an American flag in the district, and the best rider in the camps could not ride to Austin to procure one and return in time for the Fourth. What would a celebration of the Fourth of July amount to without an American flag? was the question that agitated the minds of the pioneers of White Pine, and nearly drove the Committee on Flag, Music, and Ball in the Evening to hard drink. But an attempt must be made. The committee could manufacture a flag, if they could only procure material with which to build it; and the said committee passed a resolution, resolving each member thereof into a sub-committee to scour the camp for flag material. The stuff for the stars and the white stripes was easily procurable, because there was a quantity of drillings at the store, which was used for "lining" houses and making tents. We might even find some red shirts, which we could cut up for the stripes of that color; but how and where to obtain the blue for the field was the grand puzzle.

In my capacity as sub-committee on searching for flag material, I came across an aristocrat who had a quilt on his bed. This article was lined with red calico, and was confiscated forthwith, thus doing away with the necessity of calling for donations of red shirts. The evening preceding the Fourth arrived, and a thorough search of both camps by the committee had failed to discover and procure any textile fabric of a blue color; and the committee sat in solemn council, debating the propriety of making the field of the flag out of a gray shirt, and taking the chances that the vivid imagination of the be-holder might give it a blue hue, as the emblem of our liberties floated from the ninety-foot pole which the Committee on Pole had already erected and fitted with halliards. While this important matter was under discussion, a courier arrived at the council and announced that a family of Mormons had just arrived and were making camp in a little ravine below our embryo city—and there were four girls and an old woman in the outfit, too. This was glori-ous news. Four girls and an old woman could not fail to have among their aggregate possessions a blue dress, or some other garment of cerulean hue; besides, the four girls—to say nothing of the old woman—would fit in splen-didly in the "dance in the evening." The committee immediately passed a res-olution that I was the best-looking member, and instructing me to forthwith wait on the Mormon family and interview them as to their possession of "something blue," and if found, to not only make a note on't, but to purchase it instanter, without regard to cost. In pursuance of these instructions, I wended my way to the spot where the family of Saints and Saintesses were camped, which was but a short distance from the collection of huts and tents that we called "town." It was dark when I arrived there, but a big sage-brush fire was burning, which rendered surrounding objects distinct. The father of the outfit, assisted by a couple of lads, was engaged in constructing a habitation for his brood, by driving poles into the ground in a circle and enclosing them with bits of carpet, horse-blankets, and pieces of cloth; poles laid across the top of the upright poles, and covered with brush, constituted the roof. The mother and girls were at work around the camp-fire, preparing supper.

Approaching the fire, and advancing to where the old lady was kneeling in front of it, holding over it a long-handled frying-pan, in which were some slices of bacon, I raised my hat from my head, made my best bow, and said:

"Good evening, madam."

The old lady was very large, fat, and ungainly. She was so busy with her cooking that she had not noticed my presence in the camp till I addressed her as above stated. Whether it was my handsome features or my good clothes that so forcibly impressed her, I know not, but when I spoke to her she started as if somebody had called "fire!" in her ear through a fog-horn; and in attempting to get up from her knees and assume a position of dignity befitting the reception of so evidently distinguished a stranger as myself, she lost her equilibrium, and keeled over on her back at full length on the ground, while the frying-pan described an arc of a circle and landed in the brush about twenty feet behind her, in its flight shedding a shower of slices of sizzling bacon, one of which struck the oldest girl on the back of her neck, and slid down inside her dress. The girl set up a yell that would have done credit to Sitting Bull when urging his warriors on to victory with the war-whoop of his tribe, and I commenced to take up the line of a masterly retreat. I was intercepted, however, by the *pater familias,* who confronted me with an uplifted ax, and demanded to know what I had been doing to his "folks." Tremblingly I explained my mission; and while I was talking, the old woman and the girl with the hot bacon down her back recovered their composure, and the entire family gathered about me, wide-eyed and open-mouthed, and stared at me as if I was the first handsome man they had ever seen. When I had concluded, the man said:

"Mother, aint you got some blue stuff among the traps you can let this gentleman have?"

"Le's see," replied "Mother," "that thar blue gownd of Brigamette's we traded off to them Injuns would have been jest the thing. Heberine, what's gone of that blue apron of yourn?"

Heberine, who was one of the daughters, replied she had "tored up" the blue apron into strips to tie round "Orsie's" foot when he was "snake-bit that time back yander."

"Say, marm," spoke up the girl who had undergone the "moxa" operation with the bacon, "don't ye mind we brung along thet thar big blue veil of yourn, that you used to wear going to Conference to Salt Lake, so's the sun wouldn't spile your complection?"

"Sure enough! Sure enough!" exclaimed "Marm;" "whar is it?"

"Down in the bottom of the big hair-chest," answered one of the smaller girls, in a piping voice, and shrinking away as if she had said something awfully wicked, and I was an ogre who was going to eat her for it.

The entire family then "adjourned" to a hair-covered trunk that stood on the ground by the wagon in which they had made the journey from Utah to White Pine, and after the unknotting of sundry ropes and the cutting of various strips of raw-hide which bound it, the trunk was opened, its contents taken out and laid on the ground, till at last, by the light of a fagot, held by one of the boys, my expectant eyes beheld that "big blue veil."

A bargain for the purchase of the "blue stuff" was soon concluded. The old lady said she had owned the veil for a long time and did not like to part with it; she had "brung" it from the States when they first "jined the Mormons," and it was to her a souvenir of happy days gone by; but if I did not mind paying five dollars for it I could have it and welcome; and that ought not to be too high a price in a new country, where the mines were so rich that the silver was sticking right up out of the top of the ground, so she had heard.

I paid the five dollars, took the veil, and hurried back to town, and hunted up the members of the committee; and that night was put in by the Committee on Flag, Music, and Dance in the Evening, in manufacturing an American flag for the celebration of the first Fourth of July in White Pine.

While the committee were seated on the floor of my tent, sewing on the flag by the light of a number of candles, it was resolved to invite the Mormon family to be present at the literary exercises to be held on the morrow, and also at the ball in the evening; and that the committee should wait on them in a body and tender the invitation. Accordingly, early the following morning, the committee visited the camp and extended the invitation in due form.

In response, the mother said: "I'd jest as lief the gals would go, but thar aint one of them got a shoe to their foot."

This was a very embarrassing situation. The boards which composed the floor of the ball-room were unplaned and full of splinters, and it was impossible that the girls could dance on it in their bare feet, and it was not a supposable case that women's or girls' shoes could be found in the stock at the store. However, the committee said they would "look around," and if they could find suitable shoes, would buy each of the girls a pair, and the old lady said they could go up town and look for the shoes, but she wanted it understood right there that the girls were to dance only "square" dances; for round dances were against their faith, and they had not "apostatized" from the Mormons just yet, if they had come amongst the Gentiles to try and better their worldly condition.

The promise about the "square" dances was given, and the committee went back to town to seek the shoes. They succeeded in finding in the store a sufficient number of men's cowhide brogans to shoe the Mormon girls, and thus was another difficulty overcome.

The morning of the Glorious Fourth broke bright and beautiful. The day was ushered in with a salute fired from anvils, and the flag was hoisted to its place on the pole midst the shouts and cheers of the multitude—and as it floated up there, ninety feet above ground, it was a pretty respectable flag, and the beholder would never have guessed the materials of which it was composed, or that it was not a regular, Simon-pure, store flag.

At the appointed hour the male inhabitants of the future city of Hamilton formed in line of procession—two and two—and marched up the trail to Treasure City. There was not a brass band at the head of the procession, but two of the best whistlers in camp walked in front and whistled "Yankee Doodle" till the steep ascent and light atmosphere took away their breath. Arrived on the hill they were met by the citizens of Treasure City, who, after the formalities of reception were gone through with in the nearest "saloon," also fell in line, and the combined forces of the two towns marched in procession back to Hamilton.

On the return to Hamilton the literary exercises were inaugurated. They consisted of an oration by the orator of the day, a poem by the poet of the day, and the singing of patriotic songs by the congregation.

At the conclusion of the exercises, a White Pine Pioneer Society was formed, and a resolution adopted that the flag then flying from the pole outside should form a part of the Society's archives, that future generations might know the difficulties, hardships, and privations with which the pioneers of White Pine District and the founders of the city of Hamilton had been beset in their endeavors to properly celebrate the anniversary of the nation's independence.

This stage of this narrative is probably as good as any other at which to record the fate of the flag.

As times began to get lively and people poured into Hamilton, the parties owning the store where the archives of the Pioneer Society were deposited, added a lodging-house to their establishment. This department consisted of tiers of bunks ranged along the sides of a room in the rear of the store, each bunk being furnished with a coarse, straw-filled tick, two pairs of blankets, and a rude pillow. These bunks were rented out to weary travelers and hopeful pilgrims to the new mines at the reasonable rental of two dollars per night, with the privilege of a free cocktail at the bar on arising in the morning. One night an aristocratic capitalist from San Francisco put up at the lodging-house, and had the effrontery to demand a pair of sheets on his bed. The proprietor of the establishment was almost struck dumb with amaze at this outrageous request; but then the man was a capitalist, and was from San Francisco, and it might be against the interest of the mining resources of the district for him to become offended. He might get mad and go back to San Francisco without having purchased a mine. The landlord had no sheets, and there were, in all probability, none to be had in the camp; but he was equal to the emergency. He went to the archives of the Society of White Pine Pioneers, and took there from its only archive—to wit, the flag—and tore it in half and spread the two pieces on the bed to be occupied by the high-toned capitalist. The dismembered flag of our country did duty as bed sheets for many months afterward, and the particular bunk in which they were laid was kept in reserve for the occupancy of San Francisco capitalists, who were charged half a dollar extra for its use, because it had sheets on it. The last that I saw of the starry emblem which had thus been prostituted to such base uses, a couple of Shoshone squaws were wearing each a piece of it over their shoulders for a shawl.

Before entering on a description of the "ball in the evening," it is necessary, in order to aid the reader to the better understanding of some of the incidents connected therewith, which I am about to attempt to describe, that descriptive mention be made of the "hall" in which this social event was held. The said hall was an incomplete house, one of those mushroom board houses such as are usually constructed in new camps. It was intended to be used as a store, and was in dimensions about 40 x 20. The floor was laid on posts set in the ground, and as the ground sloped off abruptly from the front to the rear of the lot, the back part of the building was some six feet above the ground, while at the front it was but a step from the floor to the ground. Only the sides of the building were up, the ends and roof not yet being completed, so that it merely consisted of a floor and two board-sides. It was intended that the building should be ceiled and lined with cloth, and the material for this purpose had all been sewed together into one large piece. This canopy was spread over the top of the two standing sides, making a roof, and the end surplus was dropped down over the rear opening, making a rear wall, the front of the building being left open on account of lack of material. Pike, fiddle in hand, was seated on a little three-legged stool in the rear end of the hall, next to the unsubstantial and deceptive wall. His guard had kept him tolerably sober, and he fiddled away at the "Arkansaw Traveler" and called the figures with an energy worthy of the day that was being celebrated. There was a large attendance at the ball, the Mormon girls and their brogans being on hand, and taking part in all the square dances. The costumes of the men were not full-dress, being principally gray shirts, overalls, and "stogie" boots; but everybody seemed to enjoy the occasion, till an unforeseen and calamitous incident cast a pall of gloom over the festivities, and broke up the affair. The watch of Pike had been relaxed, and during the intervals between the dances he visited the tent next door. The constant worship at the shrine of Bacchus unsettled the musician's nerves and unsteadied his brain. The dancers were in the midst of a quadrille, when suddenly the music grew faint in sound, and the "calls" ceased. The fiddler had suddenly and mysteriously disappeared. Wonder and curiosity were depicted on every face in the ball-room, but the overturned stool, which had been the orchestra stand, and notes of the "Arkansaw Traveler" welling up faintly from the rear of the building, told the awful tale. Pike, in an effort to put some artistic variations, had leaned back against the treacherous cloth wall, lost his equilibrium, and dropped out of sight through the wall to the ground below. A number of men rushed out to the rear of the house to recover the orchestra, but when they got to him he was just passing into a peaceful sleep, his right hand spasmodically working the fiddle-bow, which lay across his left shoulder, and the expiring notes of the "Arkansaw Traveler" dying on the air. All efforts to arouse him were fruitless, and as he was the only man in the camp who could fiddle, the "ball in the evening" was at an end.

Shortly after the Fourth of July, 1868, the big rush to White Pine set in, and from that time till the autumn of 1869, all was excitement in the new district. Town lots, which could have been bought during July, 1868, for merely nominal sums, were valued in September of that year high in the thousands, many selling as high as $25,000 a lot 25 x 100. The mines were panning out big, and money was the most plentiful article to be seen in the two cities. Buildings went up in a night, streets were laid out, banks and express offices established, stores opened with immense stocks of goods; the streets were blocked with freight teams and crowded with people; and it was exultingly proclaimed on every hand that "forty-nine" had come again, and the old flush days of California were about to be repeated. The Fourth of July of 1869, compared with that anniversary of the year preceding, was like the transformation scene in a spectacular play in a theater, or, better, a veritable fairy tale. Where the handful of coarsely-clothed prospectors had marched in procession the year before, now marched a grand pageant—military companies, a fire department, with handsome and costly and beautifully-decorated engines and hose carriages; a car of state, containing bright-faced and gaily-attired girls, representing the various States in the Union; brass bands, streamers, brightness, and beauty; and where but one short year before had waved the solitary home-made flag, the starry emblem now kissed the breeze from a hundred staffs. The line of the procession of the year before, over a mere trail through the brush, with a few poor tents and cabins only marking the site of the town, was now a broad street, with handsome two and three-story structures of brick and stone, built compactly on each side. A thousand women and children gazed on the procession from the upper windows of stately structures; and at the "ball in the evening" there were hundreds of richly dressed and jeweled women, in contrast to the two Gentile women and the four Mormon girls in their homespun dresses and charity brogans, that had graced with their presence the "ball in the evening" of the Fourth of July a short twelvemonth before.

White Pine went down almost as rapidly as it came up. The mines petered and the bubble bursted. To-day, Hamilton and Treasure City are both insignificant and nearly depopulated camps; the few who remain in them have clung on, hoping on, hoping ever, for a strike in the mines that shall bring a return of something like the good old times of the early days. Their hopes will in all probability never be realized; though both places have a reasonable prospect that sufficient mineral wealth will be developed in the deep workings which for several years have been energetically pushed in Treasure Hill, to make them prosperous small mining camps. But they will never again see the rush, the excitement, the money, the wild speculation, and the rapid gain and loss of fortunes that characterized their career for a year succeeding the "First Fourth in White Pine."

⇒*The Sazerac Lying Club* (1878), 128–37

Under the Gallows

Fred H. Hart

In the course of the journey during which the incident detailed under the head "Not Worth Killing" transpired,[1] I arrived at a mining camp known as East Bannock, sometimes called "Grasshopper Creek." I reached the edge of the town at night, when all the lights were extinguished; and, knowing it to be what was called a "vigilante town," I did not care to enter it during the night. It might not be healthy for a stranger to be caught prowling around East Bannock at night, and he might experience considerable difficulty in convincing any of the watchful inhabitants who might be abroad of the honesty of his intentions. I therefore concluded to camp at the outskirts of the town that night, and enter it in the morning. I accordingly spread my blanket on the ground, lay down, and was soon sleeping the sleep of the tired.

When I opened my eyes in the morning, the first object they encountered was a gallows. I did not know it was a gallows at first, but was soon enlightened as to the true nature of the beast. The night preceding had been very dark, and when I made my camp I did not notice the instrument of execution of the death penalty, and had laid my blankets directly under the cross-beam, and between the uprights, and there I had slept. There was a small piece of rope dangling from the center of the cross-beam; but still it did not strike me that the machine was a gallows. I lay there in my blankets, looking up at it, and wondering what it could be, until at last the sun began to mount in the heavens, and I arose. As I looked about me, I observed, a short distance to the right, what appeared to be a small cemetery—a row of head-boards and small grave-like mounds, situated on a little knoll. The first thought was that it must be the town-cemetery, and I wondered that a town of the size of East

---

1. A section of Fred Hart's *The Sazerac Lying Club* consists of historical accounts under the general title of "Frontier Sketches." This allusion is to a trip described in the sketch called "Not Worth Killing," pp. 118–28.

Bannock should, at its age, (it was then probably four or five years old) have so small a graveyard. In new mining camps, about the first work of public utility performed is to lay out a graveyard, and there is almost invariably some public-spirited citizen who contracts to provide occupants for it. In most mining camps, a graveyard can boast at least twenty graves before it is six months old, the majority of the occupants being obstinate men who thought they had a better title to a town-lot or a mining claim than the man who had established the precedence of *his* claim with a bullet, or men who had unfortunately held the opinion that they were better fighters and surer shots than the individuals who had convinced them of their error with a six-shooter. However, I walked over to the cemetery, and approaching the first headboard, read thereon the name, "Henry Plummer," and the date of the aforesaid Plummer's death.

The whole thing was now plain to me—this was the private graveyard of the East Bannock Vigilantes.

The story of the execution of Henry Plummer and his band of "road agents" was familiar to me then. I had heard it in Nevada, and at intervals, at different places all along, during my journey to Montana. It is not very fresh in my memory now, as I have forgotten some matters of detail; but the story substantially is about as follows:

Plummer had been City Marshal and a prominent local politician of Nevada City, California; but, if my memory serves me, killed a man there, and escaped to the then Territory of Nevada. He did not linger long in the sage-brush, however, for fear of arrest by the California authorities, but made his way "up north," as the section now comprising Montana and Idaho was then by a general term designated. There had been some placer-mining discoveries in British Columbia, and it was to that country that he first went; but as other mines were found to the eastward, in what is now Montana and Idaho, Plummer followed the "rushes" till he at last brought up in Bannock, under which designation a large section of the eastern portion of the present Territory of Montana was then known. I am not familiar with much of his career during the earlier portion of his residence in Bannock, except generally that it was a wild and desperate one.

The Territory of Idaho was formed and divided off into counties, and county governments organized. Each county covered a large area; for the country was new, and the population small and scattered. Of one of these counties—the one in which East Bannock was situated—(it is now in Montana) Plummer was chosen sheriff. He had married, and apparently reformed, and abandoned the life of a desperado, and was looked upon as a good citizen for a new country. He was known to be a determined, and was thought to be a brave man; and having had some experience in a police capacity, was deemed just the man for the position.

The country was infested with cut-throats and highwaymen, jocularly called "road agents." These "agents" stopped the stages and robbed and murdered passengers, killed men on the trails and roads for pure wantonness, and committed murder, robbery, and outrage on every hand, and with the utmost impunity; and not an arrest was made, or an effort put forth to bring one of them to justice. Every man was his own law, and his pistol the only peace officer to which he could look for protection. The agents were banded together, and usually went in gangs, and no man was safe from them, even in the towns. They would enter a camp, and after filling themselves with liquor, would "take the town"; that is, they would be masters of the situation, do as they pleased, and maltreat and abuse peaceably disposed persons as their humor moved them. In short, they ruled the country, and had everything their own way, apparently safe from all danger of arrest or punishment.

This state of things would not last forever. The patience of the law-abiding and peaceable men of the country was exhausted, and a Vigilance Committee was quietly and secretly formed. At first they made no move to visit punishment upon any of the suspected or notoriously bad characters, but quietly busied themselves, each man acting as a detective, in posting themselves as to the ramifications of the road agents' organization, finding out their haunts and learning their mode of operations. During the course of these investigations it was learned, and the discovery created the utmost surprise among the Vigilantes, that Henry Plummer, the Sheriff of the county, was the head and front of the road agents' organization. He personally took no part in their exploits, but knew all their plans, and received a certain share of their spoils. He posted them when there was gold dust on the stages, and when he learned that a man or a party of men were traveling with large sums of money or batches of dust, he informed the agents as to the route taken, and consulted with them as to the best method of accomplishing the robbery and disposing of the victims. Besides this, he protected them from arrest, and aided them to get out of the country if the facts implicating them were so plain and glaring that his failure to arrest them if they stayed would tend to betray his connection with the gangs.

A watch was put on Plummer, and the Committee satisfied themselves that he saw there was no chance for a mistake about his connection with the road agents; and on a certain night, which had been agreed on, he was arrested. Plummer had not dreamed that he was suspected, and the arrest was a complete surprise to him. He blustered considerably at first; but when he saw that the Committee had indisputable evidence of his guilt, he "weakened," and offered to tell all he knew. This offer was rejected, as enough was known to show that he was undeserving of mercy. He was placed under a strong guard that night, and a detachment of the Committee proceeded to arrest others of the road agents.

If I remember the circumstances aright, several of the gang were Mexicans, who, learning that a vigilance committee had been formed and was after the road agents, took refuge in a stone cabin situated on the outskirts of the town of East Bannock. This cabin was visited by a detachment of the Committee, who demanded the surrender of the occupants. The Mexicans made answer by firing a volley on the Vigilantes, without, however, hitting any of them. The Vigilantes then set fire to the cabin, and when at last the heat grew so intense that they could no longer remain inside, they made a rush on the party of Vigilantes, but were all shot down before they could do any mischief. Thus one portion of the gang was disposed of.

In the meantime, another party of the Vigilantes had arrested several Americans who were known to have been active participants in the robberies, murders, and outrages; and others who were suspected managed to effect their escape. I do not remember the exact number arrested, but it was somewhere between six and ten.

In the days of vigilance committees in California, it used to be the custom, before executing the law of Judge Lynch, to give the accused a sort of trial, at which he was allowed to bring forward any evidence tending to establish his innocence which he might be able to procure. But this plan was not pursued in Bannock, and never in Montana, that I am aware of.

When the Committee had arrested all the known road agents they could find, a gallows was erected just outside the town of East Bannock, a resolution condemning the men to death having previously been passed, and the prisoners were conducted to the place of execution, and there hung by twos and threes, with the exception of Plummer, who, on account of his former prominence as a politician and county officer, was granted the courtesy of an execution all to himself.

It is stated that when Plummer became satisfied that the Vigilance Committee were determined to hang him, he cried like a child, and begged piteously for his life, but all in vain. There had been too many men murdered and mutilated, and life and property had been rendered too insecure for mercy to be shown to the man who, while holding an office of public trust, and one created to give protection to the people, had aided and countenanced the murderers and robbers. The hour of vengeance had come, and the people had arisen in their might to demonstrate to the ruffians and cut-throats that their sway was at an end; that they would no longer be allowed to ride rough-shod over peaceable and law-abiding men; and even while Plummer, with the rope around his neck, was pleading, and begging, and promising, the box on which he stood was pulled out from under his feet, and in a moment he was strangling and dangling at the end of the rope.[2]

The gallows on which these men were hung was the same under which I had camped the night I arrived at East Bannock, and the little mounds with the boards at their head on the knoll at one side were their graves.

The formation of the Bannock Vigilance Committee was, I believe, the foundation of the great Vigilance Committee which in short time extended in its ramifications over the entire Territory of Montana, which was soon afterward created. Springing out of the necessity for self-preservation, and starting off with the performance of a necessary act, it at last grew to be a curse, where at first it was a blessing. Bad men, to keep suspicion away from themselves, joined the Vigilance Committee, which came to be an oathbound organization of the strictest secrecy. There were good men also in its membership, nearly every merchant and business man in the Territory joining it; and it was even hinted that United States Marshals and Judges, Sheriffs, Constables, and District Attorneys were enrolled on its muster. It soon, however, fell into the control of the villains and adventurers, many of whom, for plunder, or to gratify malice and revenge, made accusations against innocent men—and to be accused before the Vigilantes was equivalent to being condemned. Sentence was passed in secret, and the accused was given no opportunity to be heard in defense, but the officers of the organization on whom devolved the duty of executing the sentence immediately proceeded to put it into execution. The unwarned wretch was surprised at night in his cabin, or on a road or trail, or even late at night in the streets of the towns, by a body of masked men, by whom he was overpowered, gagged, blindfolded, bound, and carried to the tree used as an engine of execution. There one end of a rope was tied around his neck, the other thrown over a limb of the tree, the victim hauled up and the rope made fast, a placard on which was written the crime for which he was executed being generally pinned to his breast. Murder was not the only crime for which men were executed. Horse or cattle-stealing, passing bogus gold-dust, or highway robbery, also met the punishment of death. But in the late days of the Vigilance Committee the mere suspicion or accusation of these crimes was sufficient to hang a man.

I remember hearing a story—in fact, it was generally current in Montana

2. Despite striking parallels between this account of the career, capture in Montana by vigilantes, and death of Plummer, and the similar account of the career, capture, and death of Slade in chapters 10 and 11 of Mark Twain's *Roughing It*, Plummer and Slade were both historical individuals and the similarities were coincidental.

at one time—that the Vigilantes seized and hung a boy on suspicion of having stolen some work cattle, and while he was dangling from the rope the missing cattle, which had strayed, walked into the corral in which the boy was hanging.

Some of these Vigilantes themselves at last met with their just deserts at the end of a rope, pulled on by their fellow members of the Committee. There was one of these who went by the name of "Frenchy." He was a thief, a murderer, and a villain; but he gained admission to membership in the Vigilance Committee, which for several years he used as a cloak for his crimes. He was known as a Californian, and many members being from the Eastern States, Frenchy was relied on to furnish information concerning the antecedents of such Californians as came under the ban of the Committee; and it was afterward suspected that he gave evidence against men of whom he had never before heard or had never before seen, simply that he might appear to be well posted. If he took a dislike to or held a grudge against a man, he denounced him to the Committee as having been a horse-thief in California or Nevada; if a man refused to be blackmailed by him, he lodged an information against him before the Vigilance Committee, charging him with some crime, and in most cases the charge was equivalent to conviction, and resulted in execution. In some instances, all that was necessary to bring the executioners of the Vigilantes down on a man was that he should have money. In such cases the "stranglers," as they were called, would pounce on him at night, or follow him out into the country when he started on a journey, overpower him and hang him, take away his money or live-stock, and then report to headquarters with a trumped-up charge against him, and aver that they found it necessary to hang him to prevent his escape. Frenchy was particularly at home in this class of cases, acting the part of a detective to find out men who were going to travel with long sacks of gold-dust. At last Frenchy began to be suspected by the more respectable members of the Vigilance Committee, and a watch was set on his actions; and it was not very long till he was caught. One dark night, Frenchy fell in company with an old man from one of the outside mining camps, who was known to possess considerable money. The Vigilante spy and informer soon placed himself on friendly terms with the stranger, and the two visited the saloons and dance-houses, and dissipated until the old man became intoxicated. Frenchy then inveigled him into a dark street, and knocked him senseless, and proceeded to rifle his pockets. The pair had been followed during the night by a party of Vigilantes; and while Frenchy was engaged in robbing the old man, they rushed in on him, and captured, bound, and gagged him before he could make a move or utter a cry.

It was always swift work with the Vigilantes. After they had once suspected Frenchy, many things about him became plain, and facts were obtained showing his villainy; and now that he was caught in the very act, no
time was lost in executing vengeance on him. He was conducted through
out-of-the-way streets and over lonely trails to the execution tree in Dry
Gulch, on the outskirts of the city, and was there given a short shrift and a
long rope. I heard, several years afterward, that during the preparations for
execution Frenchy got the gag out of his mouth, and screamed out that he
was a Californian, and implored any Californians who might be in the party
to help or save him, for the sake of geography, as it were. But if there were in
the party any gentlemen from the Golden State, they said not a word in his
behalf, nor attempted to put forth a hand to save him. And next morning the
people of the good city of Helena beheld the body of the late Frenchy dangling from a tree, and on his breast a placard bearing the words:

> ## A MURDERER AND A THIEF!
> Swore Away Men's Lives

⇒ *The Sazerac Lying Club* (1878), 137–42

Hoist by His Own Petard

Fred H. Hart

As the story goes, another prominent member of the Execution Band of the Montana Vigilantes also met his death at the hands of his former comrades. He had helped at the execution of so many that hanging men grew to be a passion with him; and it was said that he only knew happiness when he was pulling a rope over a limb, with a man fastened to the other end by the neck. Finally, this fellow gave offense to some of the other Vigilantes, and a party of them talked the matter over, and decided to hang him. He knew too much about some of them, or had failed to divide some plunder fairly, or they had come to dislike him. I don't know the exact reason for his execution, only that they strung him up, and that there was a sort of grim humor to the story.

The party were at Fort Benton, the head of navigation of the Missouri River, which was quite a busy little city in those days, on account of the travel and freight from the East; and numerous steamers which plied the river from St. Louis, St. Joe, and Omaha, tied up and unloaded their cargoes there, for transshipment by mule and ox-teams to various points in the Territory. Fort Benton is situated on a sand-flat on the bank of the river, a regular desert waste, and the view on all sides, as far as the eye can reach, is nothing but sand, without a tree or shrub to relieve the barrenness and desolation. This fact gave rise to some difficulty in the hanging of the doomed Vigilante; and the stranglers, in their dilemma, went to him and requested him to devise a plan for hanging himself. The matter was worked in this wise. Hunting up the victim and taking him aside, one of them said to him: "We have got a fellow we want to string up, and don't know how to manage it, as there's not a tree, or anything big enough to hang a man on, growing within miles of this place. How would you manage it?"

"Manage it!" exclaimed the unconscious victim, "you just leave that to me, and I'll fix you up the loveliest contrivance that ever raised a man off the ground. Leave it to me, will you?"

The party consented to leave the construction of the "lovely contrivance" to their candidate for a noose, and he proceeded to business at once. Procuring three stout poles and some baling-rope, and a stouter rope for a noose, he packed them on a horse, and mounting his own horse he drove the pack-horse before him, and rode out on the plain to a point secure from observation from the town. Here he unpacked his gallows material, and with the baling-rope tied the three poles together fast at one end, and setting the other ends on the ground, spread them out in the form of a tripod. He then made a running noose with the other piece of rope, and fastened it to the top of the tripod, hanging inside of the poles. This done, he returned to town to hunt up his friends and invite them out to an inspection of his ingenious work.

It did not take long, and having got them together, he said:

"Come on, boys, and go out and look at her; she's just the sweetest thing in that line you ever laid eyes on."

In response to this polite invitation, the "boys" mounted their horses and rode out to view the "sweet thing," the victim accompanying them.

They had intended to hang him at night; but such a splendid opportunity for the work was now presented that they concluded to take advantage of it; and as they rode along they communicated with each other by whispers, and a plan was agreed on to hang their man before they returned to town. The gallows was handy, and they had him secure and safe from observation, and it seemed like tempting Providence to let this chance slip and take the chances of something happening before night to put him on his guard, so that he might get away.

Arrived at the tripod, the party dismounted, and after they had viewed it a few moments, the leader asked its architect how it worked.

"Easiest thing in the world," replied the victim of misplaced confidence; "you see, you walk your man in under here (pointing to the space under the noose); slip this thing over his head (pointing to the noose); then three of us each pick up one of these poles and shift its end inwards towards the center, and that raises the height of the machine, and draws the noose tight, and your man has nothing to stand on. Did you ever see anything smoother than that?"

"Suppose *you* get under, and let's see how it works," said the leader.

"Me get under it! What for? It's the simplest thing in the world, and a baby could understand it."

"*Get under there!*" exclaimed the leader, in a stern tone, drawing and cocking a six-shooter, and pointing it in the victim's face.

Simultaneously the other men drew their pistols, covered the fated wretch, and said, "*Get under there!*"

The face of the gallows-builder turned pale, and his limbs began to quake with fear.

"Oh, boys! You don't mean it. You're only joshing me, I know; but those pistols look wicked, and make me nervous. Put up your guns and go back to town and take a drink with me, and we'll fetch that fellow out here to-night and give him a lively send-off."

The only reply was the nearer approach of the muzzles of the six-shooters to his head, and the words: "*Get under there!*"

The poor devil begged, cried, and implored, but to no purpose; and at the very point of the pistols which surrounded him on every hand, he was forced inside the tripod and the noose slipped over his head, and he was duly hung in strict accordance with his own directions for the hanging of the other fellow. There he was left hanging, and a few days subsequently, after the carrion birds had made several hearty meals from it, his body was discovered by some men from Fort Benton, who cut it down and buried it.

The Sazerac Lying Club (1878), 143–44

Sage-Brush Sketches

Thomas Fitch

Despite the perhaps overdone rhetorical character of its writing, this hard-hitting essay, the first of a series of three the *Argonaut* published in 1878, is an excellent account of the state of affairs in early Nevada. It does not exaggerate the corruption, bad judgment, and venality that was rife in the territory and the state during its early years. In a condensed but comprehensive form, Fitch supplies a valuable context not only for many of the pieces in this collection but also for Mark Twain's *Roughing It* and even for *The Gilded Age*.

⋯⟊⟎ ⟐⟫⋯

The "flush times" of the Southwest and the days of "forty-nine" furnish no parallel to the history of Nevada during her Territorial career. Like California, in that the report of rich mineral discoveries, with their glittering promises of sudden wealth, allured the industrious, the adventurous, the unsettled, the hopeful, along with the desperate, the vile, the fugitive, and the pariah to her sterile mountains, Nevada was yet unlike California, in that capital, daring the presence of its hereditary foes, crossed the Sierra hot on the trail of the pioneer, and lavishly sowed itself in the hope of multiplied harvests. It was not only those who had successively journeyed to Gold Lake, Kern River, Fraser River, and Gold Bluff,[1] who had successively followed every shining phantom that the cupidity of speculators or the credibility of adventurers danced before their eyes, that thronged in unsifted masses the roads to the new Dorado, for the accumulated capital of San Francisco caught the infectious "Washoe fever," and its owners, becoming satisfied of the existence of great wealth under the arid slopes of Mount Davidson, poured treasure

---

1. Sites in California and British Columbia where gold had been found.

upon them more freely and more potently than Hannibal of old poured vinegar in his efforts to melt the Alps.

Then came the era of flush times and loose morals. "Wild cats" were created with a fecundity never equaled by their feline prototypes; and the most prosperous owners of wild cats were not those who located granite and called it quartz; who held up mica and pronounced it gold; who, seizing on hornblende, looked through the spectacles of speculation and denominated it sulpherets;[2] but they were those who, succeeding in establishing some sort of jumping claim to a mine of known value, incorporated their fighting titles ten deep, and went to develop—not their mine, but their lawsuit. A bar more learned, more active, and perhaps more unscrupulous, than any metropolitan capital contained, flocked in the streets and huddled in the attics of Virginia City. Money was plentiful, moral restraints were loosened or altogether untied, society was a chaos. Unprincipled men were ready to violate, for a consideration, the oath of a witness or the solemn obligations of a juror. An attorney who had his wits about him knew that he would probably be called upon to encounter at every step a mine of perjured witnesses, or a masked battery of purchased jurors, or a bribed judge. He who relied merely upon the equity and strong presentation of his cause leaned often upon a broken reed. He who depended solely upon legal precedents was guided by a compass from which the magnetic current of integrity had departed, and which veered to the four corners of space. Nevada was a whirl of excitement, a chaos of corruption, a very hades of dishonesty; and yet cases involving millions were weekly decided by the courts—and such courts!

Nevada was organized as a territory in the spring of 1861. The framework of our National Territorial system, then as now, provided that the executive and judicial officers of a Territory should be appointed by the President of the United States, and, then as now, a practice prevailed—a practice pernicious in theory, and resulting disastrously in practice—of not appointing such officers from among the residents of a Territory, but of sending men from distant communities to fill them. If there was ever a time when the President of the United States should have selected officers, and especially judicial officers, with extremest care, it was when the community called Nevada was begotten by labor and enterprise out of weird deserts and barren hills, and thrown suddenly into the lap of dazzling affluence. If there was ever a time when a President was poorly prepared to exercise such care, it was when the Territorial offices of Nevada were chosen. The President was un-

2. Silver often occurred blended with sulphur in a bluish or blackish ore; hornblende was bluish green or black rock that had no silver in it.

used to public life, and he was elected by a party then strange to political dominion. With the cloud of war settling rapidly over every speck of light upon the shortening horizon, with the air full of mighty threats of battle, and the Presidential presence filled with petty clamors for office, there was neither time nor opportunity to properly consider the condition of remote territories. Most feebly were the wants of Nevada portrayed, or the necessities of Nevada understood, by those who represented California at Washington. Those Senators and Representatives to whom a President might ordinarily have looked for advice were of opposite political faith, and were far more diligent in securing supposed party advantages by permitting the President to make mistakes, than in serving a remote people by helping him to make wise selections. Interested advisers, on the other hand, wishing to serve a party friend, or get rid of a party rival, were plentiful, and so the East sent to Nevada her lazzaroni, and not her laborers, her pettifoggers and not her jurists, her weak men rather than her best men, and with the people of Nevada it was Hobson's choice—these or none.

What could be expected of briefless barristers and broken-down politicians, unable to make a living or gain public confidence at home, shipped off, as England used to send her rusty spinsters around the Cape of Good Hope—for India and a market? What could be expected of such men, placed in positions supposed to be trifling, but suddenly discovered to be of the gravest importance and the most weighty responsibility? It was because of their Territorial judges that the people of Nevada accepted the responsibilities of Statehood—perhaps somewhat prematurely. "Anything to get out of the judicial deadfall" was the popular thought, and after the people had escaped from Judge Log to Judge Stork,[3] from gay to grave, from draw-poker to a quartz-mill—after they had forced from the bench a Judge who would not try causes at all, to find his place supplied by a Judge who was bought by both litigants, and was protected out of the country by an armed guard of the party in whose favor he finally decided—at last they reluctantly, but almost unanimously, shouldered the cost of self-government, and the State of Nevada was born into the American family.

Argonaut 2:6 (February 16, 1878): 10

---

3. An allusion to one of Aesop's fables, in which frogs were persuaded to transfer their veneration from an inert log in their pond to a stork, which gobbled them up; in other words, to go from bad to worse.

The Prospector

C. C. Goodwin

This generation has brought into existence a new order of men. They are not appreciated now, but by and by some thoughtful artist will catch the full significance of their lives, and on canvas, imperishable as marble, will fix their enduring picture. They were the birth of 1849, and their numbers grow less and less with each receding year. On this coast they are called "prospectors." So far they have received little respect in comparison with their merits, because the sappers and miners of civilization are seldom appreciated in their day. We met one a few days since. He introduced himself to us in these words:

"Stranger, let me tell you; don't be carried away with Colorado, because I was there long before the excitement. There are some good leads, but the country is overestimated. The same is true of Arizona, of Montana, and Idaho. I have seen them all. When the Comstock was discovered I went there, and taking in the country, determined to find a better one, and I have not been idle since; I have not found it, but I certainly think I will this summer. I know the place, know it well, and no one else does. I am going there now. See, yonder are my horses; they are good for the trip, and I am only waiting for a little ammunition. I shall start to-morrow, and before the turn of the summer, you will hear from me."

For twenty years his home has been the desert; he has not known a pleasure; as the desert commenced to put on the robes of civilization he has retreated deeper into the wilds, while his eyes have ever been strained towards the heights where a fortune lay, until they have taken on an unnatural brightness. He has struggled until hardship has become his second nature. He can not sleep in a comfortable bed in a comfortable house; he must have the desert for his pillow, where the winds, as they sweep over him, have voices which forever whisper to him of the golden mountains which he is to find. So he has toiled while all the early hopes of his early life have gone out. So he will toil, until some morning, as the rising sun lights up the bold brow of the desert, he will say to himself, "I was weary last night; I am not yet rested; I will sleep a little longer this morning," and so he will sink into the sleep which shall be dreamless.

Looked at one way, there could not be a more profitless life; looked at another way, we realize that because of him, because he was civilization's advance guard, pleasant homes have been made possible in the desert; temples have been upreared to Justice, law, and learning; careful men have been enabled to amass fortunes, and new fields have been opened to enterprise. But not many realize these facts. By most people the prospector is looked upon as little better than the tramp.

But in the days to come, when the hills are all explored and fair homes light all the West, some inspired pen will picture the race of prospectors as the men who, bidding adieu to youth and all the softer comforts of life, went out into the wilds, and with unrequited toil, laid the first foundations of the States which illume the West with a splendor all their own.

⇒*Nevada Monthly* 1:6 (August 1880): 303 [*Salt Lake Tribune*, n.d.].

The Pah-Utes

Sarah Winnemucca

Sarah Winnemucca (1844?–1891) was the daughter of Chief Winnemucca of the Paiutes and the granddaughter of Chief Truckee. Unusually well educated, she served for a time as an interpreter for the army and later traveled around the country, especially to Boston and San Francisco, giving lectures on behalf of her people, who were being taken advantage of by unscrupulous Indian agents. It is possible that this article was adapted from one of her lectures. It was followed, in 1883, by the publication of her book, *Life among the Piutes*. She and her book have received much attention in recent years, but critics are divided over whether to consider her ethnoautobiography as shaped by her self-aggrandizement or as outspokenly courageous on behalf of her people and a valuable source of information. In the 1890s, Dan De Quille wrote "Pahnenit," a novella that, though largely the work of his own imagination, nevertheless was inspired by his new sympathy with the Paiutes and touches on some of the legends Sarah Winnemucca recounts.

⊷⚬⚬⊶

Our home is at the sink of Humboldt River, by the Carson Mountains. My father and I were both born there, about four miles from the railroad. My Indian name is So-mit-tone, meaning Shell-flower. I was educated at the St. Mary's Convent in San Jose.

On our mountains there are many pine trees. We gather the nuts for the winter. This was our principal food, which our women commenced to gather about the middle of August. Our men used to hunt, and after that, our women go into the valleys to gather different kinds of seeds. The men go to fish along the Humboldt and Truckee rivers. They dry game of all kinds, and lay it up for the winter. Later in the fall the men hunt rabbits. The furs are afterwards woven into blankets, called rabbits'-fur blankets. In the winter they all get together to locate their lodges, and all their supplies are collected and put into one place. They remain there about six months, having merry-making, eating and drinking, and getting married; and they give themselves up to great enjoyment until the spring opens. Then they go to the fishing-grounds; and when the roots begin to grow, the women dig them up. The name of this root in Indian is called *yah–bah,* and tastes like carrots. They boil them, like potatoes, and use them in soups, and also dry them. Another root is called *camas* root—a little root that looks like chestnuts; and *kouse* root, which tastes a little like hard bread. In early days, when white people came among us, they used to eat our food, and compare it with theirs. The same toil was gone through with every year, to lay up the winter supplies; and in those days they always seemed to have plenty of food, and plenty of furs to keep them warm in the winter time.

Now you must not suppose that my people are weak or uncourageous. They are not what you call "slouches." There are the Utes and the Pah-Utes. We helped the Bannocks and the Umatillas in the war, because we were kindred of theirs. They are our cousins; therefore we helped them. Now you say, Why did they make war? I will tell you: Your white men are too greedy. They [the Indians] had a little prairie, called the Camas Prairie, about fifty miles long by twenty wide. They wanted it because it supplied them with roots, and prevented them from starving. The white man wanted it, because the roots were good for his cattle, and could make milk and beef and hides and tallow; so he tried to rob them of these lands. They did not like this, and because he despised them, and would give them no redress, they killed him.[1] But the cattle alone were not the cause of this war. The agents were worse than the cattle: what the cattle left the agents took. The agents buy their places for so much, and mean to make their money out of the poor Indians.

During my great-grandfather's time there was a tribe of Indians lived in our country, called Side-okahs, which means man-eaters, or cannibals. They were not very large in numbers. They used to seek to kill us; and when they caught us they would have a grand feast. In this way they lived for a number of years, until my people made war with them. Then we had war, and they fought too, but they did not kill many of us. They fought with bows and arrows, just the same as we did. They seemed to fear nothing; would even sport with and catch the arrows directed to them, which flew past. They could jump us and catch the arrows as they would pass over their heads, showing great agility. We fought them for a long time, until their number was quite

---

1. The Northern Paiutes, to which the Humboldt River band belonged, generally went out of their way to be friendly to whites. The few armed conflicts—"wars"—with settlers in which they were involved, such as the one described here, tended to be based either on misunderstandings or on provocations by whites.

small. They used to trap us, by digging pit-falls in the ground and wells in the paths. We were so afraid of them that we used to crawl at night; and sometimes our people would fall into these places after dark. When we had fought them some time, they saw that we were getting the best of them. Then they made canoes out of the tule grasses, and floated out on the Humboldt Lake; and they lived on the lake for a short time, but had to leave it again for the land. We kept pushing them out; then they went into a great cave. They did not remain there long, on account of lack of water. They then went into the *tule* marshes, but my people surrounded the *tules,* and set them on fire, and when they saw they were getting killed, they ran back into the cave. There they remained, and my people watched them when they would come out to get water, and then kill them. Then, to make quick work of it, they went to work packing wood, and piled it up in front of the mouth of the cave; and as fast as my people filled the mouth of the cave, they pulled it inside, and of course the cave was very soon filled; and then they [the Pah-Utes] set fire to the outside. In that way my people killed all these cannibals, smothered in the cave. Then we owned all their land, which was called the Side-okahs' land by other Indians, and it lay along the Humboldt River in Nevada.[2]

After the Side-okahs were exterminated we lived peaceably, now and then only having a little fight with other tribes—no tribes being allowed to settle among us. If they came on very important business they could stay a while; or if they came for a visit, they would be entertained by feasts and plays and dancing: amusing them all the time they were with us. They always brought presents to our chiefs, and they [the chiefs] gave them presents to take back; but they were never allowed to settle with us or marry with us, each tribe maintaining its own individuality very pronounced; every nation speaking a different language.

Our language is not a written one, but oral; neither have we any signs to convey information to distant parties—only verbal messages sent by our warriors traveling on foot; as they could go over rough ground, rocks, and places that ponies could not, and they could endure more. If our relations were sick at a distance we would signal to the others by a fire on the highest top of the mountain. Three times during the night in the same place is a signal for sickness. For moving, our signal would be several fires all in a row, in the same direction we were to move. Fires of that description were peaceable ones; but we had, also, war-signals of fire. In olden times, the way we used to make fire was with two sticks, both made of sage brush. One had a hole in the middle, and was about six inches long by two or three in diameter. This was laid

---

2. This story is told in less detail in chapter 4 of her book, *Life among the Piutes.*

down on dried grass, rotten wood, and such materials. Another stick was sharpened at the end like a top. This was put into the hole, and rubbed between the hands, causing a friction which ignited the materials, and we had a fire. We never had flint, nor knew its uses until the white man came to us. Signal fires for war are made in the day-time. A man takes a torch longer than his arm, made of sage brush bark, lighted at the end. He runs towards our encampment, and warns us that the enemy is coming, by making quick fires as he comes towards us, lighting the sage brush as he comes. Then when he gets in sight of the camp he halloos, gives a war-whoop, and runs three times around the encampment, and halts in front of the chief's lodge. The warriors by this time are all ready to fight the enemy with their quivers and arrows. He then relates what he saw at a distance. In those early times we always had scouts and spies out, so that we would not be surprised by our enemies.

The traditions of our people are handed down from father to son. The chief is considered to be the most learned, and the leader of the tribe. The doctor, however, is thought to have more inspiration. He is supposed to be in communion with spirits; and we call him "doctor," as you white people call your medicine-man; and the word is not taken from the English language, as may be supposed, but purely Indian. We do not call him a medicine-man, because he does not dose us, as your doctors do, and therefore we call him "doctor." He cures the sick by laying on of hands, and prayers and incantations and heavenly songs. He infuses new life into the patient, and performs most wonderful feats of skill in his practice. It is one of the most solemn ceremonies of our tribe. He clothes himself in the skins of young, innocent animals, such as the fawn; and decorates himself with plumage of harmless birds, such as the dove and humming-bird and little birds of the forest—no such things as hawks' feathers, eagles', or birds of prey. His clothing is emblematic of innocence. If he cannot cure the sick person, he tells him that the spirits of his relations hover around and await his departure. Then they pray and sing around his death-bed, and wait for the spirit to take its flight; and then, after the spirit leaves the body, they make merry, because he is beyond care, and they suppose in heaven. They believe there is only joy in that place; that sorrow is before and not after death; that when the soul departs, it goes to peace and happiness, and leaves all its misery behind.

The warrior is the reverse of the doctor. The warrior wears eagles' feathers during the battle. He wears the claws of an eagle around his neck and head. The eagle is our national bird; the Americans taking that emblematic notion from the Indians in the early days of their nation. Some braves that have ridden in the battle front, and have only been engaged once or twice, wear the claws of a grizzly bear, to show they have been in battle; the same as the medal that was given to my brother Natchez for saving three men's lives, showing his bravery.

I will now speak about the chief. His rank is inherited from father to son, the oldest son being the chief by law. If he is dead, the one next to him becomes chief; or, if there are no sons, the next male relative; but never a woman. The custom of having more wives than one arose from the capture of other tribes during war. If the women were pretty, the chief claimed them— but only one wife. The first married is claimed as legal and head of the rest, and is acknowledged in public as the chief's wife. The others are not called wives, but merely assistants—*pe-nut-to-no-dequa*, in Indian. The heirs of the first wife, and she herself, take precedence over the others. The chief, as also the head of every family, is supposed to teach his children the traditions of the tribe. At times of leisure in the evening, and at twilight, these traditions are related around the camp-fires to eager listeners. No note of time is taken, and no record of ages is known. Once in a while, when the spirit moves the chief, he arises and speaks in a loud voice to his people. At those times, all work must cease. If a woman is cooking a meal, it must be left undone. All fold their hands, incline their heads, and listen to what he has to say; and then, when he is through, they go on again with their work, as left before he commenced to speak. Before every event, the chief gets up first in the morning, and the people are warned to get ready. If it is for a fishing excursion, or to hunt deer, or for any other excursion, he tells them to get ready—all that are to go. The old women and children stay behind in the lodges, while the young married women and daughters accompany their relations, to carry the game which is caught by the braves.

These excursions sometimes last ten days, the people remaining wherever night overtakes them. When through, they return to their lodges, having great rejoicing; and divide their game with the poor and aged and sick—no payment ever being required for such attention. Their belief is to have what they can enjoy on earth, and share it with each other, as they cannot carry anything out of this world. When they die possessed of horses and other goods, their wearing apparel is given to the poor, and some portion of it is buried with them. Horses are generally killed, for they think the dead man will not have any further use for them; and this is considered the last token of honor and respect that can be shown on this earth to the memory of the dead. The way that my people mourn for their dead is by cutting their hair close to their heads, and laying it on the body of the dead to decorate it. The hair of his wife and that of his children, braided and ornamented with beads, is laid upon the dead man's breast; and if the wife refuses to part with her hair to thus honor her husband, she becomes the object of pity and scorn, laughed at, spit upon, and abused by the whole tribe. Thus they seldom refuse to part with their hair. The doctor also contributes ornaments from his person, and is not allowed to doctor any other sick person for some time, until he again gets into favor by some prophecy or inspiration supposed to come from the spirits. These are old traditions. Nowadays he knows his value. He will not attend a patient unless he is paid, as white folks pay their doctors. Thus we follow your customs as our association grows with you. Our doctor now charges a fee of five dollars, or as the case may be, as white folks do.

Indian girls are not allowed to mingle freely with the braves; never go out walking or riding with them; nor have they anything to say to each other. Even in courting, the same strictness is observed. A young brave takes a notion to marry a young girl, but cannot do so until he has been declined. The woman removes from the rest of the family to a small wickiup, or lodge, where she remains one month by herself, abstaining from flesh, and living only on seeds or berries. She must be very industrious during that time, going out every morning at daybreak to gather wood and logs, which she arrays in five different piles. This labor is repeated at noon and at sundown. Every five days she is acknowledged by the other women and men to be a young lady ready to marry, and at these times the wood is set on fire, she jumping over the piles while they are burning. Eating, drinking, and dancing are indulged in every fifth day. Then at the end of the month she returns to her father, casting away all her old clothing, and appearing before her parents in new robes made of buckskin.

The ceremony of courtship is as follows: The brave seeks the place where the Indian maiden is at rest. If she discovers him, she gets up and goes away. He never follows her, but comes again the following night, and so on indefinitely. Then when her parents give consent to their marriage, she is given a feast, at which he is invited to partake. At no other time is he allowed to eat with the family. The ceremony of marriage is very simple. The lady passes the brave some food in a dish. He takes it and sets it down; then they are considered man and wife. They remove to a lodge by themselves if able; if not, they remain in their father's lodge. When the first child is born, they go by themselves and work for others, remaining that way one month. They do not eat meat of any kind during this period, and bathe every five days. After that they return to their old home again. Deformed children among this people are almost unknown.

Cooking is performed in willow baskets woven so tight as to hold water. A fire is built, and small stones are thrown into it. When hot, these are dropped into the basket that contains the water, causing it to boil, when the meal is stirred in, and hot rocks [are] continually thrown in until the mush is cooked. Meat for stews and soup is cooked in the same manner. In early times meat was generally eaten this way, and the use of salt was not known until after the advent of the white man.

Virtue was a quality whose absence was punished by death—either by burning alive or stoning to death. My people are not so severe in these later days. The ceremony of marriage is not so strictly carried out as in olden times. They take a woman now without much ado, as white people do, and leave them oftener than of old. One of the latest evidences of civilization is divorce—an indulgence taken advantage of to abandon an old wife and secure a young one. They argue that it is better for them to do so than to leave their young women for the temptation of the white man.

In 1867 I was interpreter for my people; but even then they had nothing. The game has been all killed, except for a few rabbits. The pine trees have all been destroyed, so that we can get no more nuts. The cattle have trampled out the grass in our little valleys, and we can dig no more roots. If the white people leave us, to go over the mountains to California, as some people tell us, we must go over the mountains with them too, or else starve. If we cannot get wild game, we must take tame game, like cows or steers; the same as the white people would do if they had nothing to eat, and nothing to feed their wives and little ones with.

When we were shivering and starving, the soldiers were our best friends. They gave us their cast-off clothing, and they gave us rations. When I left the convent and went back among my people, it was funny to see the men and women dressed in soldiers' overcoats and pants. They thought it was the grandest kind of dress. Then the agent promised us provisions and clothes for the winter; but he lied. He knew he lied when he said it. That winter our children were shivering, while he was amassing money by selling the things which the government voted for us. This is how your civilization treats us. Are we to be blamed for thinking that you care for us like the snake in the grass? When I carried the dispatches for the soldiers, they promised Sarah money. Did she ever get it? or did she get any thanks for doing this? None: nobody said "thank you" to poor Sarah. I was greatly deceived when I came to San Francisco to get money and help for my starving people. I thought my own people would help. I call the Methodists my own people. They preached and they prayed, but they did nothing else for my poor, hungry, shivering people. I know something about sermons myself, and can preach a better sermon than any of their ministers. The soldiers are much better than the ministers. The Indian is like my white brother: Emperor Norton:[3] he likes epaulets.

3. Emperor Norton was a locally well known, colorful, and indigent eccentric, indulged by amused San Franciscans, who proclaimed himself an emperor and was fond of dressing in gaudy cast-off uniforms.

Once the Indians possessed all this beautiful country; now they have none. Then they lived happily, and prayed to the Great Spirit. But the white man came, with his cursed whisky and selfishness and greed, and drove out the poor Indian, because he was more numerous and better armed and knew more knowledge. I see very well that all my race will die out. In a few short years there will be none left—no, not one Indian in the whole of America. I dare say the white man is better in some respects; but he is a bigger rascal, too. He steals and lies more than an Indian does. I hope some other race will come and drive him out, and kill him, like he has done to us. Then I will say the Great Spirit is just, and that it is all right.

⇒*Californian* 6:33 (September 1882): 252–56

Cranks and Their Uses

[Joseph T. Goodman]

The authorship of Joe Goodman is inferred from the fact that this essay appeared as an editorial in the *San Franciscan*, the literary journal that Goodman founded in 1884 and for six months edited largely by himself.

·⇒ ⇐·

A woman passed along Kearny street, one afternoon this week, who attracted a great deal of attention. People did not turn and look after her because she was very beautiful, famous for her genius, notorious for her misdeeds, or because she was doing anything unusual. She was just walking along on the proper side of the pavement, like the rest of the people. Her face was far from handsome, and not by any means bright. She was past the age when men compete for the favor of her attention. Yet this unknown, middle-aged, commonplace woman drew as much notice as if she had been a great actress or a great criminal.

She wore trowsers.

A skirt came down to within a foot of her gaiters, but enough of the masculine garment was visible to let everybody know that it was there. Wherefore everybody turned, looked astonished, and then smiled or laughed. This ridiculous conspicuousness was the price the woman paid for her practical protest against the inconveniences and follies of the prevailing style of her sex's attire. Probably the gratification of a love of distinction, got no matter how, was her reward. Possibly the woman had an earnest purpose, and was willing to suffer ridicule for its sake. But whatever her motive for making herself ludicrous, she deserves well of the world for being one of the noble army of cranks, who serve civilization by keeping up a guerilla war upon it. Cranks are the salt of the earth. They are question-marks set up against established institutions. They put the accepted under examination, and stir up the stagnant waters of received opinion. The people who let one idea, big or little, get into their heads and run away with them, are not sensible people; but the world is not suffering from a lack of sensible people—it has too many of them. It is the fellow whose sense of proportion is out of order that is most wanted. The sensible man sees multitudes of evils around him, all tightly rooted in the soil of custom, and, as each impresses him as being as bad as the other, and all needing uprooting alike, he sighs in despair and gives up the idea of attempting to tear up any. Sensible men don't turn reformers. But the crank has a narrower vision than his level-headed fellow-citizen. Some one of the myriad evils tolerated by society catches his eye and excites his generous indignation. The longer he looks at it the bigger it gets, until at last he can see none of the other evils. His anger at it grows in the same distorted proportion, and he falls at the evil tooth and nail, and screams until often the world, indifferent to the whole plantation of familiar evils, has its curiosity excited and pauses to have a look at the particular evil about which the crank is making such a noise. It sees that the noise is not raised over nothing, but that the crank is angry about a thing that ought not to be in the way, and very often it lends him a helping hand. When it does, up comes the evil, and the crank's existence is justified. He has not lived and howled in vain.

All reformers are cranks—at first. When they are men of superior mind, and their one idea is a big one which they succeed in getting the world to accept, we call them benefactors a century or so after their death, and raise statues to them. Had we lived when they did we should have laughed at them, and perhaps have helped to starve them or stone them to death. The great cranks, however, are not very plentiful. They are fewer than the centuries. When one is given to the world he turns the electric light of his intellect upon the evil which has roused him into being, and continues to blaze upon it from the battery of his writings long after he is gone, and earnest men are attracted toward it like moths to a flame. When their numbers are great enough the evil is uprooted, however big it may be.

But we should not despise the day of small things in the matter of cranks, any more than in other directions. It is good to abolish little evils as well as big ones. Even the woman in breeches who strode along Kearny street making a guy of herself, makes the world better for being in it. Nobody will deny that a great deal of good money and good health are wasted on dress by women—not as much as in the days of those sainted dames, our grandmothers, but still far too much. The woman in trowsers, while she excited our laughter by her comical but undoubtedly comfortable and healthful costume, drew the attention of hundreds during her stroll to this important fact. Of course no lady seeing the superior healthfulness of such a dress, went home straightway resolved to discard skirts henceforward forever and become herself a spectacle. But quite possibly many a sensible woman, unthinkingly following the fashion, bethought her that her stays were too tight and that the weight of drygoods depending from her hips was too great, and, so reminded, loosened one and reduced the other.

Tolerate the cranks. Let us remember that male and female created He them, and that He knew what He was about when He did it.

→═*San Franciscan* 1:3 (March 1, 1884): 9

[A Paiute Reservation]

G. W. Pease

This letter originated in response to an inquiry by Dan De Quille, who at that time was writing weekly columns for C. C. Goodwin's *Salt Lake Daily Tribune*. In 1890–1891, De Quille had written a series of columns about Wovokah, a Paiute prophet who considered himself a messiah and who introduced the "ghost dance," which quickly spread among the Indians of the Great Plains. The import of the dance mutated, and some Indians became convinced that they were about to recover all they had lost to the whites and that the dance would make them invincible to bullets. De Quille's articles, written at a time when Nevada whites were anxious about the Indians, were responsible journalism. They described Wovokah as a false messiah who had confused Indian and Christian beliefs, but who himself was not advocating violence and was not dangerous. De Quille probably initiated his request at this time because he was apparently composing the novella that, when completed between 1893 and 1895, became "Pahnenit." Wovokah is mentioned briefly in it, and De Quille also takes liberties therein with some Indian legends. Granville Winchester Pease, who enjoyed a good reputation for his clerical and writing skills, at the time of his letter was the issue clerk and assistant farmer for the Walker River Indian Reservation and was stationed at Schurz, the railroad station for the reservation. He left the reservation in 1893 and died a year later.

Schurz, March 1892

Dan De Quille
Virginia City
Nevada

Dear Sir

In reply to yours of 9th inst I furnish herewith such general information with reference to the Indians of this Reservation in particular, and the Pah Ute tribe in general as I have had time to prepare, this being one of the busy periods of the year with me when my quarterly returns must go forward without delay. I regret that I have not had time to study my diction more closely, and to arrange matters in better order.

A census of the Indians is taken every year, during the month of July. That for 1891, or rather the Government fiscal year 1892, which commences July 1st showed a population of 515 on the Walker River Reservation with the following classification:

Males over 21 years of age		131
Males under " " " "		115
Females over 18 " " "		161
Females under 18" " "		108
	Total	515
Males with one wife		101
Males with plurality of wives		7
Males not married		141
Females married		114
Females not married		152
	Total	515

I have no copy of the census of the preceding year, but knew that it did not exceed 465. From this you can judge of the natural increase. It is the policy, in fact a strict injunction of the Government to Indian Agents to keep a record of births and deaths. But it is a difficult task to do so correctly, especially with the Pah Utes, as they are very loath to give any account of births, and far more so of deaths. To report births and deaths is a part of the duty of the Indian Police—of which we have five—four of whom draw a salary of $10.00 per month, while the Chief or Captain of Police and Interpreter is paid $15.00 per month. All are furnished with rations by the Government. Notwithstanding it is a misdemeanor in not reporting births and deaths, even our most reliable police always have some cunning device in readiness as an excuse. This renders one's own observation as reliable as anything else, and possibly more so. "Pah" means water. Pah Ute.—Indians living near water or lakes. Names are usually given to children according to some peculiar trait of character manifested by them. For instance, Pah-wich—Pah-po-nan-na, and Pah-cu-tus all signify that the children were partial in some manner to water. Names are often given to children for traits of character that would not be very elegant language to publish, while some of the names are quite musical. Que-si-va—Nu-ne-na and Se-wu-sa are the Indian names of three very pretty Pah Ute girls. O-pen-no is the name of the Chief of this band of Pah Utes. He-cu-lu-nar is the Indian name of one who bears the English name of Carl Schurz, and resembles the original Carl very much in features and general proportions.[1] All the Indians with the exception of adhering to the blanket or robe, whether in summer or winter, and handkerchiefs instead of bonnets, dress in citizens' clothing, and present about as genteel an appearance as country people in general. Very few are living in frame or wood houses. I know of but four such houses on the entire reservation. The majority live in huts or wick-e-ups built of poles and covered with tules, while some are living in houses constructed of poles set in the ground parallel to each other, about six inches apart, and the spaces filled in with willows, and roofed with tule; and a few are living in canvas tents. Within these rude abodes they live and breed, (not as fast I am sorry to say as the Irish, and would that God the gift would give me to reverse the order) but about as fast as the general average of people. Tribal names, like those given to children, have a specific meaning. The Pah Utes of Pyramid Lake and Carson Sink are called "Que-we-wy's" meaning those who live principally on fish; while those of Walker River Reservation are called "Ho-gi-wy's" denoting those who live principally upon the products of the soil. The Indians of this Reservation as their name denotes, are, I think, in advance of those of Pyramid Lake in agricultural pursuits, having according to recent estimates furnished to Government about 2000 acres under cultivation, from which was raised the past season, and a large portion shipped to market, 62,000 lbs. of wheat, 15,000 lbs. of barley, 5,000 lbs of potatoes and 400 tons of hay, besides quite a liberal amount of garden vegetables, such as melons, onions, cucumbers, etc., of which they are passionately fond, while a few, a very few, are raising poultry; but the temptation to eat is so strong that the increase is hardly perceptible, and but little of garden products [were] ever sent to market.

1. Carl Schurz (1829–1906), the German immigrant also mentioned in "The Typographical Howitzer" who became a general, political figure, and editor.

Of their legends and traditions, I have obtained but little information, of which as a general rule they are chary about giving; and my official relation to them renders it impudent on my part to question them too closely, suspicion being a prominent feature in the character of all Indians. Those mentioned in your letter to me are probably as reliable as any as far as they go. It is very seldom that a Pah Ute will attempt to kill a coyote, their general belief being that the coyote is the spirit of their relatives who have died, and his barking their conversation to them from the spirit land.

Doctoring is invariably done by singing and howling, and mostly at night. This is for the purpose of driving away the evil spirit. Mysterious emblems are also used in the tent of the sick, such as eagle feathers tied to a stick, in which certain notches and various other devices have been made. I have heard it said, but cannot vouch for it, that if a Doctor loses three patients in succession, he forfeits his own life to the relatives and friends of the one[s] he doctored. I have often wondered if this would not be an excellent custom to adopt among our own M.D.'s. To avoid this extreme penalty, the Pah Ute doctor invariably takes down his sign and retires forever from the business immediately after losing the second patient; another excellent custom that others might profit by. Immediately after death, and often before life is fully extinct, the body is taken in a hurried and secret manner to some secluded spot, usually some cave or cleft in the rocks and deposited. This may account in a great measure for human remains that have been found in secluded places in the vicinity of Virginia and Gold Hill. It was formerly the universal custom, and is so to a great extent at the present time, to burn the wick-e-up in which one had died; but Government is trying to suppress this superstition.

Marriage is simply a business contract, and is usually made with the parents of the bride, the consideration being as a general rule, a stipulated amount of household provisions, the groom going to live at the residence of the bride. This gives the newly married couple a continuous Mother-in-law who makes as much mischief as Mothers-in-law do in general. But affection, a genuine love for some other than the one selected, often plays havoc with the contracting parties, and a trip to Gretna Green is sometimes taken by those who have "Two heads with but a single thought, two hearts that beat as one."[2] Jealousy is as common among the Pah Utes as with any other people. One suicide from jealousy has been committed since I came here. In reality it is a second Medea. Our Jason, like the original, is a mighty hero, and is our Chief of Police and Government Interpreter. Our Medea was Annie, his

2. Gretna Green is a Scottish village on the English border that was notorious for the ease and quickness with which marriage ceremonies could be performed.

wife, who became jealous of his other wife, who lives near the sink of Carson; and with her husband's pistol, like the original Medea, first attempted to take the lives of her two children; but failing in this, sent a bullet through her own heart, dying almost instantly, a broken-hearted, wretched mother.[3] Polygamy is only permitted by Government on reservation to those who had a plurality of wives prior to the issuing of the order, and two arrests have been made for a violation of the order since I came here.

A large number of horses are as much an indication of wealth with the Indians, as an extensive area of land with the whites, and are frequently used as a medium of exchange in business transactions. Government rations are issued weekly to the old and blind, there being about one hundred and fifty on the issue rolls, and very nearly equally divided in numbers between Pyramid Lake, and this reservation. There are at Pyramid, in round numbers,   500

At Walker River	500
Total on reservation	1000
Estimate of those not living on reservation	500
Grand Total	1500

From the above, you will readily see that but ten per cent of the entire population are supported at Government expense, and that but partially; and with the exception of a few annuity goods, ninety per cent are self supporting. If we confine ourselves to reservations where nearly all of the old, blind and infirm reside, we have 15 per cent partially supported, and 85 per cent self sustaining. Where, oh! where is "Europe's higher order of civilization"? It has cost more to support imported paupers, maintain Police Courts, and suppress imported riots, than all the Indian wars and annuity goods since 1492. Government is quite lavish in its expenditures in establishing and maintaining educational institutions for the benefit of the Indians, and of our own State in particular.

The school at the agency, or what is the same, at Pyramid Lake, is a boarding school, and is under the very excellent management of Miss Hummel of Virginia City as Teacher, and Miss Felnagle as Matron, and has an average attendance of more than forty pupils. Another Indian School is maintained at Wadsworth and is under the management of Miss Evans. The average of attendance at this school I am unable to give, but know that it is fair. Our school

---

3. In Greek mythology, Medea, jealously enraged that Jason—the adventurer whom, out of love, she had helped to acquire the golden fleece—now wished to marry another, murdered her own children.

at Walker River is a day school, with Mrs. Nelson Hammond as Teacher, and Miss Sarah Pursel as Matron, and has had an average attendance during the present quarter, now near its close, of 35. Two meals a day during the five days of each week that school is in session are served. Considering all the surroundings; the home influence; it is really surprising that so much educational progress has been made, there being many pupils in all the schools I have mentioned that read, write and speak the English language quite fluently. All the Indian Schools of the state are under the general supervision of U.S. Indian Agent, C. C. Warner, with the exception of the Stewart Institute at Carson City, which is under the general supervision of W. D. C. Gibson, formerly Indian Agent for this state. A hurried visit to the Institute recently convinced me that it was well and ably conducted.

Of the Messiah craze, had not the newspapers of the land given the matter so much notoriety, but little would ever have been known of it. I have conversed with Jack Wilson the Prophet or Messiah. Have heard him talk to his own people in their language, and had his language translated to me. Have conversed with Army Officers and delegates from the Smithsonian Institute who have been sent to investigate, and this is the summary of the whole matter. Jack Wilson is an Indian farmer living in Mason Valley and not on the reservation as many suppose. He is quite intelligent for an Indian, and speaks English very well, having lived among the whites for years. His ideas of Christianity have evidently been obtained from stories told to him by Sabbath school children, and listening to worship around the family altar, and the vaporings of some itinerant preacher through the open windows of a country school house. He believes in beauty, industry, temperance and morality, and urges it upon his people. Does enlightened Christianity do anything more? He has a vague idea of the second coming of Christ and believes in it, and imagines that the Pah Utes are to be the chosen people. Does this vary in any essential particular from that of the Christians and the Jews? He has a vague idea of Apostolic succession, and believes he is one of them. Does not the Greek Church, the Catholic Church, and the Puseyite wing of the Church of England believe the same thing?[4] Nearly all the Gods of which we have any knowledge are the creations of man; and Robert G. Ingersoll contends that a noble God is the noblest creation of man.[5] If such is the case why not give this Indian, this Pah Ute, the same show in the God Factories of the world that are enjoyed by others, or do they fear competition?

4. Under the influence of Edward B. Pusey (1800–1882), a wing of the High Anglican Church inclined even more toward Roman Catholic tradition, practice, and dogma.
5. Robert Green Ingersoll (1833–1899), a controversial American lecturer whose attacks on organized religion earned him the enmity of the religious public and the admiration of skeptics.

Relative to the Indian war of 1860 I think, and the battle that took place near where Wadsworth now stands, very few know the true cause that led to it. My information is this, and in fact much that I have written comes from Mr. James O. Gregory, now of Wadsworth, but the Farmer in Charge of this Reservation when I first came here, a gentleman whose word can be strictly relied upon, and one whose knowledge of the Pah Ute Indians is probably superior to that of any other white man in the state, having lived among them since 1858. Two men named Wilson had taken up ranches on the Truckee River near Wadsworth. One day a young Indian with his squaw came to their cabin. They fell upon the Indian, beat him unmercifully, forced from him his squaw whom they retained for immoral purposes. In retaliation the Indian accompanied by some of his friends returned in a day or two to recover his squaw, and administer justice to the Wilsons. In the mean time a stranger had arrived at Wilson's camp whose name I could never learn, and was unintentionally shot, while the Wilsons escaped. News spread that the Indians had started on the war path, and were going to exterminate the whites. A little army was organized by Maj. Ormsby, and the battle near the present site of Wadsworth was the result. The Indians did not want to fight, and would never have done so had they not been forced. They knew every move that was being made from the time the whites left Carson, Virginia and other places. They urged Mr. Gregory to go away, telling him they did not want to harm him in the least, but feared some of their warriors might mistake him for one of the enemy. Chief Winnemucca with some of the leading men of the tribe went out to hold a council with Maj. Ormsby and his officers. While doing so, some of the young warriors from lack of discretion, or for a little mischief, fired a few shots at random in the air. This was interpreted by the whites as an attack, and the fire returned, which soon became general on both sides. The result of that battle is well known to all early settlers. The whole matter was nothing but a series of mistakes and blunders from the first.[6]

In conclusion, friend Dan, I will say to you that what I have written is, I fully believe, in all essential points truthful and correct. If there is anything of benefit to you in the preparation of your article you are entirely welcome. But I fear I have gone to such an extant, and written so much, you will think I am

6. Pease does not have the details quite correct. The Indians attacked Williams' Station because two young Indian women had been kidnapped by the station keepers. In the attempt by the whites to punish the Indians, seventy-six whites, including Major William M. Ormsby, were killed, and only twenty-nine escaped. Another American expedition against the Indians was launched a few days later that broke the Indian force, killing 160. Pease, however, is correct in his assessment that the conflict was provoked by whites and was characterized by tragic misunderstandings and blunders.

trying to write your article for you, and may become angry thereat. To appease your wrath and partially compensate you for a perusal of this, if you and friend [Alfred] Doten have the cheek, the moral courage to call on Matt Kyle, he may be able to liquidate[7] the whole business. To still farther atone, I send by Wells Fargo & Co. a package containing two little souvenirs of Indian handicraft. One of them is for you, the other for Doten. There is a void in one of them. In your research into Indian affairs, if you penetrate sufficiently deep, you may be able to fill the place I have left vacant. Would be pleased to hear from you at any time, and to receive a few copies of the article you are about to write, when published.

Your friend

G. W. Pease

⇒From the collection of the North Baker Research Library,
California Historical Society, San Francisco

---

7. Probably a pun about drinking, that is, "liquidate" by means of whisky.

Letters

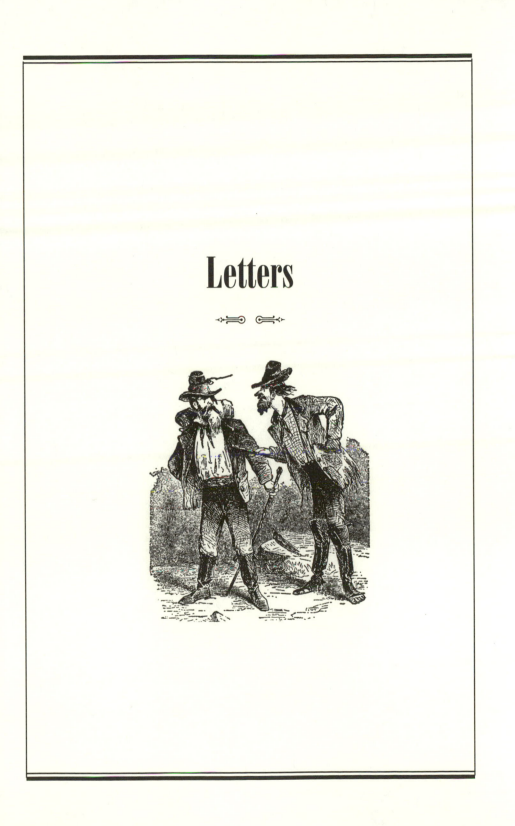

Introduction

⊷⇌ ⇋⊶

The five letters in this section tell us a good deal about Nevada and the Sagebrush mentality. Twain's 1863 letter captures the high spirits and optimism that were characteristic not just of youth but of the situation on the Comstock when it was young. Less than a year later, Twain left in a disgruntled mood, and his brief visit in 1866 also ended in a fit of pique. But his 1905 letter of forty years later is typical of Sagebrusher recollections. It is not just his youth he laments, but a place where youthful excitement reigned— where even the murderers and scoundrels added spice to life. This letter is a prose counterpart to Joe Goodman's poem "Virginia City."

A distinction between the early and later years of Nevada settlement is made poignantly by two Daggett letters. In *The Gilded Age* (1874) and "Corn Pone Opinions" (1901) Mark Twain observed how character can be corrupted by prospects of gain; Daggett bitterly experienced the process in operation. The shortness of his stay in Congress was probably the result of political and financial pressure put upon Nevadans by railroad interests, which Daggett had attacked vociferously in Washington. He could bear defeat by enemies but not betrayal by friends.

The perhaps unmailed draft of C. C. Goodwin's letter is full of Sagebrush spirit. Goodwin's letter is refreshing in its directness and in its scorn and challenge. Sagebrushers had a talent for plain speaking.

Mark Twain to His Mother and Sister

Steamboat Springs,
August 19, [1863]

My Dear Mother & Sister

Ma, you have given my vanity a deadly thrust. Behold, I am prone to boast of having the widest reputation as a local editor, of any man on the Pacific coast, & you gravely come forward & tell me "if I work hard & attend closely to my business, I ~~e~~ may *aspire* to a place on a big San Francisco daily, some day." There's a comment on human vanity for you! Why, blast it, I was under the impression that I could get such a situation as that any time I asked for it. But I don't want it. No paper in the United States can afford to pay me what my place on the "Enterprise" is worth. If I were not naturally a lazy, idle, good for nothing vagabond, I could make it pay me $20,000 a year. But I don't suppose I shall ever be any account. I lead an easy life, though, & I don't care a cent whether school keeps or not. Everybody knows me, & I fare like a prince wherever I go, be it on this side of the mountains or the other. And I am proud to say I am the most conceited ass in the Territory.

You think the picture looks old? Well, I can't help it—in reality I am not as old as I was when I was eighteen.

I took a desperate cold more than a week ago, & I seduced Wilson (a Missouri boy, reporter of the Daily Union,) from his labors, & we went over to Lake Bigler. But I failed to cure my cold. I found the "Lake House" crowded with the wealth & fashion of Virginia, & I ~~had to~~ could not resist the temptation to take a hand in all the fun going. Those Virginians—men & women both—are a stirring set, & I found if I went with them on all their eternal excursions, I should bring the consumption home with me—so I left, day before yesterday, & came back into the Territory again. A lot of them had purchased a site for a town on the Lake shore, & they gave me a lot. When you come out, I'll build you a house on it. The Lake seems more supernaturally beautiful now than ever. It is the masterpiece of the Creator.

The hotel here at the Springs is not as much crowded as usual, & I am having a very comfortable time of it. The hot, white steam puffs up out of fissures in the earth like the jets that come from a steamboat's 'scape pipes, & it makes a boiling, surging noise like a steamboat, too—hence the name. We put eggs in a hankerchief & dip them in the Springs—they "soft boil" in 2 minutes, & boil as hard as a rock in 4 minutes. These fissures extend more than a quarter of a mile, & the long line of steam columns looks very pretty. A large bath house is built over one of the Springs, & we go in it & steam ourselves as long as we can stand it, & then come out & take a cold shower bath. You get baths, board & lodging, all for $25 a week—cheaper than living in Virginia without baths.

We shall bud out into a State before many months, which will relieve Orion[1] of his office. If I have influence enough, I mean to get him nominated a candidate for some fat office under the State Government, so that you can come out and live with him. I am a pretty good hand at such things. I was a mighty heavy wire-puller at the last Legislature. I passed every bill I worked for, & on a bet, I killed a bill by three-fourths vote in the House after it had passed the Council unanimously. Oh, I tell you a reporter in the Legislature can swing more votes than any member of the body. We'll have rare times the coming session, & in the State convention.

Yrs aff
Mark

⇝Mark Twain's Letters (1988), 1:263–65

---

1. Orion Clemens (1825–1897), the brother of Mark Twain, was secretary of Nevada Territory at this time. By the time Nevada became a state, in late 1864, Twain had lost his influence in Nevada and was residing in California. Orion did not succeed in becoming part of the state government.

Rollin Daggett to C. C. Goodwin, January 21, 1894

Hollymount is the Daggett estate described in the opening paragraph of his story "Looking Down upon the Suisun Marsh Tules." This letter and the one written on March 6 were sent to his old friend C. C. Goodwin, now the owner and publisher of the *Salt Lake City Daily Tribune*. The identification of Goodwin as the recipient of this letter was determined by the details of the book the letter describes, Goodwin's *The Wedge of Gold*.

Daggett's scorn of prissy literary standards was not just theoretical; he and Joe Goodman had refused $10,000 for the rights to their play *The Psychoscope*, because they believed the purchaser wanted to excise or tame the play's boldly realistic scenes set in a brothel. Daggett's enthusiasm for the connection between metal and culture was not unusual in Nevada, whose economy depended on mining.

⌖

"Hollymount," Vacaville
Jany 21, 1894

My Dear Charley:

Your book came promptly to hand; also, your letter two or three days after. It is a charming little story, interspersed with lofty bits of rhetoric and enlivening situations. "Jordan" is a splendid character, and the chapter relating to his first experience with the Texas school-ma'm is a gem. It has become popular to admire novels utterly barren of dramatic interest, and with no incident more thrilling than the artistic painting of the agony of a wife on discovering that her husband has a doubt respecting the parentage of the Pentateuch, or that her eighteen-year-old son was caught smoking a cheroot behind the barn. Their characters, to suit the tastes of the potential critics of the Boston school, must be impossibly moral, absurdly sensitive, and as far removed from ordinary mortals—from the bulk of civilized mankind—as heaven is from hell. I like a novel that tells a story of vigorous and rational human action, and is something more entertaining than a rigmarole of emotions inspired by the silliest and most inconsequential of causes. You know the sort of literature I refer to. But it will have its day, and the world will turn again to well-told stories for their choice in fiction, and look for emotional bosh in separate volumes. By the "world" I mean the cultured classes, who are weak enough, as a rule, to be willing to follow a fashion in literature as in the cut of their garments.

There is a stout basis of reason in your opening chapter on the precious metals, and you did not exhaust the argument either. I discovered the truth of your position in a moment. As man is the only animal that uses tools, and as effective tools *must* be made of metal, it follows that the people who have the best tools, either for peaceful or warlike purposes, must dominate. And you are right in holding that metal-working is an essential to human advancement. Without the use of metals the social and intellectual advancement of mankind would have stopped with the cave dwellers. Utterly without metals, the Hawaiians, had they remained apart from the world, could not have progressed greatly beyond the point they had reached when Cook found them a century ago.[1] Their case came to my mind in reading your book.

I wish we could sit down together, in our old age, and pass neighborly together as well to the other side, which does not seem far to me now. But this can hardly happen. Do you recollect the old Roman, who took his son to the seaside, and showed him a host of stranded and broken wrecks? He likened them to the many who made politics their business, and warned his offspring to choose another pursuit. Well, I am one of those old hulks, except that I have landed on an Ararat of my own instead of on the seashore.[2] You know the [illegible] which I split, and I hope have avoided it. But I know you are wary of newspaper drudgery. You have been long at it, and are more industrious than the most of journalists. You would like to lie down in the shade of a tree away up in hills, and stop thinking. But you haven't the time, and may never have it. Well, perhaps it is just as well. We must all play our little parts on life's stage, and chance pregnantly arranges the cast.

Give my love to you and yours,

Ever Yours,

R. M. Daggett

⇒Daggett File, Special Collections, University of Nevada, Reno

1. Captain James Cook rediscovered Hawaii (later known as the Sandwich Islands) in January 1779 and died there a month later in a fight with Hawaiians.
2. Genesis 8:4 tells that Noah's ark came to rest on the "mountains of Ararat."

Rollin Daggett to C. C. Goodwin, March 6, [1894]

This letter appears to be Daggett's response to Goodwin's acknowledgment of his January letter. It captures the near-contradictory mixtures of sentiment and stoicism, idealism and realism, that can be found in Sagebrush authors and their literature. Daggett's disillusionment with Comstock politics probably resulted from his experience as a Republican congressman from Nevada in 1879–1881, during which time he actively battled the railroad interests, which were extremely influential in Nevada. For a similar mood of disappointment, see also Sam Davis's poem "The Gleaner." Despite his rejection of Nevada, Daggett retained close contacts with such friends from the early days of the Comstock and the *Territorial Enterprise* as Goodwin, Joe Goodman, and Mark Twain.

◦⇒ ⇐◦

My Dear Charlie:

I have yours of the 28th ultimo. Don't thank me for the pleasant and grateful thoughts your book inspires, but thank God that you have the heart to write such things as I find in it. I wish I could think as gently of the past as you do; but I can't. I had a desperate death-grapple before I gave up the ghost politically in Nevada, and had the mortification of seeing life-long friends turn their faces against me because it was not to their interests to be just. Every pledge was openly and shamelessly violated, and I was virtually driven from the State because I refused to betray the people I was elected to serve. And the people—well, they stood by with downcast faces and saw it done. Voltaire, or some one else, says every man in this world must be either a hammer or an anvil. In other words, he must either hammer or be hammered. This is only partly true. There is another factor in the hammering business. It is the shrieking and protesting bar of steel—heated in the hell of persecution

354

until it is softened beyond the power of resistance—that is beaten all out of shape, or burnt up in the forge. I have been that other factor. As I could not be hammered into the desired form, I was hacked, and punched, and drawn out, and finally half burnt to cinder. And that is the reason why I cannot look as pleasantly at the past as you do, unless I go back among the dead, and that is where your book takes one, and I can feel as you feel in dealing with the characters you bring on the stage. To hell with some of the living! My tenderest thoughts of the Comstock go back to the dead.

I had a birthday last month—the 22d.[1] I tried to pass it by in silence, but the family wouldn't allow it. They kicked up the devil in a quiet way, and hallowed the evening with a Dutch lunch—caviar, sour herring, limburger, onions, beer, etc. They knew I liked such Godless grub. I drank five bottles of beer to forget that I was growing old, and had a disordered stomach the next day. You and I never ought to grow old. It's a burning shame to saddle one with the infirmities of years, while our hearts are kicking up their heels in perpetual boyhood. Life is a blasted fraud. We are always reaching out for something we can never *quite* reach—for something we cannot get a good grasp on. If we ever do reach it and get hold of it, it will be just as the undertaker is beginning to look over his stock for a casket that will fit us. For eight years I have been fixing me up a home in the hills overlooking Vaca Valley. It is beginning to be a dream of loveliness. It is a lovely eyrie among the clouds. The vines and trees are now bearing their fruit. The stone terraces are being covered with moss, and the leaves of the cherry trees in front of the house are nestling against the window shutters of the second story. Everything around the place is wearing the softening touch of age—everything around it begins to look like *home*—something that I have never had before since I was a boy. And now that I have it, now that it has been shaped to my liking, I shall sit grey-headed among the vines I have planted, and hobble with a cane under the shadow of the trees. And the family—all but my wife will soon have taken up their separate burdens in life, "leaving all things for the stranger," and I shall probably spend but little time where I expected to spend it all.—But what am I grumbling about? I am not an exception. The most of us get what we want only when too old to enjoy it.

J. T. Goodman is in San Francisco.—The love of me and mine to you and yours.

Ever Yours,   R. M. Daggett

⇀Daggett File, Special Collections, University of Nevada, Reno

1. Daggett was seventy-three years old on this birthday.

Mark Twain to Robert L. Fulton, May 24, 1904

Twain's letter declining an invitation to attend a reunion in California was first published in Albert B. Paine's biography. The bracketed material is Paine's introduction to the letter, which was subsequently precisely dated by the Mark Twain Project. The list of names beginning with Goodman is of those who were close to Twain in his western years. The list of names beginning with Sam Brown is of notorious murderers who provided good copy for reporters such as Twain had been.

⤛══ ══⤜

["A number of more or less notable things happened in this, Mark Twain's seventieth year [1905]. There was some kind of a reunion going on in California, and he was variously invited to attend. Robert Fulton, of Nevada, was appointed a committee of one to invite him to Reno for a great celebration which was to be held there. Clemens replied that he remembered, as if it were but yesterday, when he had disembarked from the Overland stage in front of the Ormsby Hotel, in Carson City, and told how he would like to accept the invitation."]

If I were a few years younger I would accept it, and promptly, and I would go. I would let somebody else do the oration, but as for me I would talk—just talk. I would renew my youth; and talk—and talk—and talk—and have the time of my life! I would march the unforgotten and unforgetable antiques by, and name their names, and give them reverent hail and farewell as they passed—Goodman, McCarthy, Gillis, Curry, Baldwin, Winters, Howard, Nye, Stewart, Neely Johnson, Hal Clayton, North, Root—and my brother, upon whom be peace!—and then the desperadoes, who made life a joy, and the "slaughter-house," a precious possession: Sam Brown, Farmer Pete [Peel], Bill Mayfield, Six-fingered Jake, Jack Williams, and the rest of the crimson discipleship, and so on, and so on. Believe me, I would start a resurrection, it would do you more good to look at than the next one will, if you go on the way you are going now.

Those were the days!—those old ones. They will come no more; youth will come no more. They were so full to the brim with the wine of life; there have been no other like them. It chokes me up to think of them. Would you like me to come out there and cry? It would not beseem my white head.

Good-by. I drink to you all. Have a good time—and take an old man's blessing.

➤Albert Bigelow Paine, *Mark Twain: A Biography* (1912), 1247

C. C. Goodwin to G. H. Babcock

June 27, 1907

G. H. Babcock
  Denver, Colo.
Dear Sir:—

Your febrile effort of recent date reached us yesterday, and before answering it in print I wish to congratulate you on your command of English. It is seldom that a man of your calibre reaches the paretic stage after 60 or 70 years of use of mind and body and can kid himself into the belief that he is still the bulldozing official in a railroad office kicking out cub reporters.

You state in your letter that upon your return to Denver you were made aware of the purport of my telegram to Adams for the first time. This is entirely untrue, as I told you exactly what was said in my wire to him. After every effort to locate you in Goldfield, while you were zigzagging from the dives to the gutters, he wired me asking if you were really sick, and if not, just what was the matter. In confidence and in an entirely friendly way I told him very plainly that you were drunk—that you had been drunk for five or six weeks. I also in accordance with his request told of your financial condition and asked if there was any suggestion he cared to give. I did this in a pitying spirit and only with a desire to help you.

I understand from your letter that you had a complication of diseases here, and I am sorry I mistook them for intoxication. Perhaps, however, I was led into that belief by the statement of your physician, who told me you had the delirium tremens.

Now, my dear sir, I care nothing whatever for your threats. I share with you the feeling that I would a great deal rather meet you and tell you what I think than to write it, and I am equally sorry with you that I should ever have been troubled with your affairs. I have had more or less experience with men who waited until they were married and in the sere and yellow leaf to sow their wild oats, but I must confess that of those with whom I have come in contact from the time I was a Police Court reporter at fifteen years of age to the present day, I have never before had any dealings with anyone who came so close to the limit as you. It is more in a spirit of pity than of anger that I answer your Bacchanalian effusion, and I hope—more for the sake of those that are dependent upon you, than yourself—that you will in the future refrain from intruding upon me or mine when one of your periodical orgies gets the better of you.

C. C. Goodwin file, Special Collections,
University of Nevada, Reno

Poetry

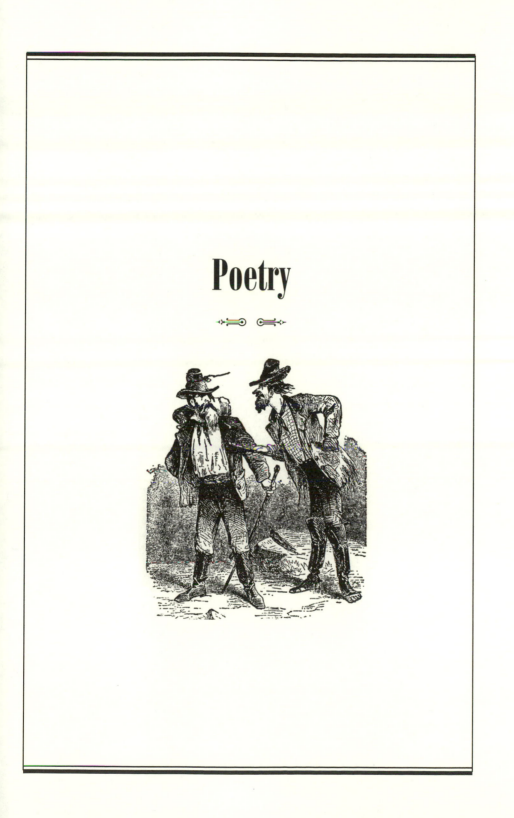

Introduction

Surprisingly, perhaps, for men in a rough environment, Sagebrushers took poetry seriously. There were no Nevada poets who approached the best American poets of the century, Walt Whitman and Emily Dickinson. But there were no poets elsewhere in America who approached them, either. If we scale down the competition to the next level of poetry, there are some Sagebrush poets worthy to be remembered. Three, at least, deserve some consideration: Joe Goodman, Rollin Daggett, and Sam Davis.

Joe Goodman and Rollin Daggett were friendly competitors for the reputation of being the best poet on the Comstock, and partisans of both men were known to argue earnestly about their champion's merits. Both men were periodically invited to compose poems for public holidays and celebrations. Today most such poems appear to be somewhat artificial in their straining for effect and their deliberate loftiness. But both men were capable of achieving poetic elegance with familiar themes. Daggett's "My New Year's Guests" is a heartfelt elegy for heroes who built the West, but are now passing from memory—a recurrent motif in the writings of old Sagebrushers. His very popular "The Oak and the Vine" is another sentimental poem that escapes mawkishness by its honesty. Having lost his own wife, Daggett spoke from experience.

Goodman's "Virginia City" is now a standard poem to cite when recalling the old Comstock: an elegy for a lost place, a lost youth, and a lost age. In its acceptance of the bleak truth that time is uncaring and unsparing, the poem ends with tragic honesty. His other three poems collected here are characteristic of the man in their straightforward, virile language, their rejection of religious cant, and their moral Stoicism. The title of "Sursum Corda," Latin for "lift up your hearts," is taken from the mass; the poem therefore can be seen as replacing a Christian rationale with a humanistic one. The final lines of

363

"The Two Sermons" and the untitled poem are particularly powerful in their brutal plainspokenness.

The poems of Sam Davis reflect the man's multifacetedness; he could be humorous, sentimental, ironic, or tragic. What they have in common is the skill of their composer. "The Lure of the Sagebrush," written in response to criticism of Nevada for its harsh landscape and sparse vegetation, inverts those criticisms and turns them into reasons for praise. Similarly, but in a jocular mood, Davis reduces to a logical absurdity the then popular campaign for pasteurization; it is a good thing applied to milk, but its virtue ends there. "The Campaign Debt" and the untitled poem about the Mrs. Warren of Carson City derive from Davis's long experience with Nevada politics but are in fact wryly ironic reflections on the human comedy. The Bible regards with wonder "the way of a man with a maid," but Davis admiringly acknowledges the truth of the reverse proposition. The value of these poems is not exhausted by these paraphrases; there is more to be found in them.

Active and popular though he was, Davis in his later years recognized somberly the unfairness of life, the evanescent quality of its boons, and the inevitability of disenchanting death. The last three poems of his in this collection are products of these years. "The Storm" shows the same grim influence of naturalism on his thinking as does his short story "The Loco Weed." A note on the manuscript for "The Gleaner" (also known as "The Gleaners") by his daughter, Mrs. Ethel Wait, describes it as the last thing Davis wrote. Like his friend Joe Goodman, at the end Davis spoke plainly and without illusion.

The pages on which most of these poems were found in various files and archives seldom indicated a date of composition, a date and place of publication, or even if the poem had been published. No claim is being made that all the poems of these authors have been located and collected. Other fine poems are undoubtedly still unrecovered.

The Oak and the Vine

Rollin M. Daggett

This poem achieved instant popularity and was republished widely across the country. Charles Follen Adams imitated it in the also popular "Der Oak und der Vine," a pseudo-German vernacular version published under his literary pseudonym Yawcob Strauss.

A graceful oak, with branches broad and bold,
   Lived in a forest, gray with years and dim,
And from its roots, with many a circling fold,
   A tender vine crept to its topmost limb,
And slyly nestled there. What could it mean,
Its tendrils toying with those locks of green?

Low at its feet the oak first saw the vine,
   Crouching for shelter from an April shower,
And when it reached around the heart to twine,
   It clasped and loved it more from hour to hour;
Nearer and dearer with each rising sun,
Until the surpliced seasons made them one.

An autumn evening, as the sun went down,
   While thunder-fingers swept the stormy lyre,
Its branches bent beneath the whirlwind's frown,
   And touched the lightning's dreadful tongue of fire.
The storm passed on: the strong oak bowed its head,
For, looking down, it saw the vine was dead.

In time its tendrils loosened, and the cold
    Breath of November threw its pallid spell
O'er leaf and blossom, turning them to gold,
    And to the earth the vine, long lifeless, fell;—
But, winding round the oak, the scars were shown
Thenceforth, of where the tender vine had grown.

Thus, in the paths of life,—no matter where—
    In castle or in cottage we will find
Strong men who in their hearts will always bear
    The cureless wound of where some vine has twined.
Is there beyond, where endless daylight breaks,
A balm for earthly wound, and heart that aches?

⤙N.d., n.p. (published in *Argonaut*, October 20, 1877, p. 2)

My New Year's Guests

Rollin Daggett

Although this is one of Daggett's best poems, there does not appear to be a definitive form for it. It has been published as a long poem without stanza breaks, in variously broken stanzas, and in four-line stanzas, with a concluding couplet. The latter form has been adopted here on the basis of readability.

✦══ ══✦

(Scene: a chamber in Virginia City,—one of the pictures on the wall being the reduced photographs of over five hundred California Pioneers of 1849. Time, midnight, December 31st—1881.)

The wind comes cold from the Southward, with incense of fir and pine,
And the flying clouds grow darker as they halt and fall in line.
The valleys that reach the deserts, the mountains that greet the clouds,
Lie bare in the arms of Winter, which the prudish night enshrouds.

The leafless sage on the hillside, the willows low down the stream,
And the sentry rocks above us, have faded all as a dream.
The fall of the stamp[1] grows fainter; the voices of night sink low;
And, spelled from labor, the miner toils home through the drifting snow.

As I sit alone in my chamber this last of the dying year,
Dim shades of the past surround me, and faint through the storm I hear
Old tales of the castles builded, under shelving rock and pine,
Of the bearded men and stalwart I greeted in forty nine;[2]

---

1. Stamping mills crushed large pieces of ore into small pieces that could be processed more efficiently.
2. Eighteen forty-nine is when the California Gold Rush began, and Daggett was part of it.

The giants with hopes audacious; the giants of iron limb;
The giants who journeyed westward when the trails were new and dim;
The giants who felled the forests, made pathways o'er the snows,
And planted the vine and fig-tree where the manzanita grows;

Who swept down the mountain gorges, and painted their endless night
With their cabins, rudely fashioned, and their camp-fires' ruddy light;
Who builded great towns and cities, who swung back the Golden Gate,
And hewed from a mighty ashlar the form of a sovereign State;

Who came like a flood of waters to a thirsty desert plain,
And where there had been no reapers, grew valleys of golden grain.
Nor wonder that this strange music sweeps in from the silent past,
And comes with this storm this evening, and blends its strains with the
    blast;

Nor wonder that through the darkness should enter a spectral throng,
And gather around my table with the old-time smile and song;
For there on the wall before me, in a frame of gilt and brown,
With a chain of years suspended, old faces are looking down;

Five hundred all grouped together—five hundred old pioneers;—
Now list as I raise the taper and trace the steps of the years.
Behold this face near the center; we met ere his locks were gray;
His purse like his heart was open; he struggles for bread to-day.

To this one the fates were cruel; but he bore his burden well,
And the willow bends in sorrow by the wayside where he fell.
Great losses and grief crazed this one; great riches turned this one's head;
And a faithless wife wrecked this one—he lives, but were better dead.

Now closer the light on this face; 'twas wrinkled when we were young;
His torch drew our footsteps westward; his name is on every tongue;
Rich was he in lands and kindness, but the human deluge came,
And left him at last with nothing but death and a deathless fame.

'Twas a kindly hand that grouped them—these faces of other years—
The rich and the poor together—the hopes and the smiles and the tears
Of some of the fearless hundreds, who went like the knights of old,
The banner of empire bearing, to the land of blue and gold.

For years have I watched these shadows, as others I know have done;
As death touched their lips with silence, I have draped them one by one,

Till, seen where the dark-plumed Angel has mingled them here and there,
The brows I have flecked with sable the living cloud everywhere.[3]

Darker and darker and darker these shadows will yearly grow,
As, changing, the seasons bring us the bud and the falling snow;
And soon—let me not invoke it!—the final prayer will be said,
And strangers will write the record: "The last of the group is dead."

And then—but why stand here gazing? A gathering storm in my eyes
Is mocking the weeping tempest that billows the midnight skies;
And, stranger still—is it fancy?—are my senses dazed and weak?
The shadowy lips are moving as if they would ope and speak;

And I seem to hear low whispers, and catch the echo of strains
That rose from the golden gulches and followed the moving trains.
The scent of the sage and desert, the path o'er the rocky height,
The shallow graves by the road-side—all, all have come back to-night;

And the mildewed years, like stubble, I trample under my feet,
And drink again at the fountain when the wine of life was sweet;
And I stand once more exalted where the white pine meets the skies,
And dream in the winding canyon where early the twilight dies.

Now the eyes look down in sadness. The pulse of the year beats low;
The storm has been awed to silence; the muffled hands of the snow,
Like the noiseless feet of mourners, are spreading a pallid sheet
O'er the breast of dead December and glazing the shroud with sleet.

Hark! the bells are chiming midnight; the storm bends its list'ning ear,
While the moon looks through the cloud rifts and blesses the new-born
    year.
And now the faces are smiling. What augury can it be?
No matter; the hours in passing will fashion the years for me.

Bar closely the curtained windows; shut the light from every pane,
While, free from the world's intrusion and curious eyes profane,
I take from its leathern casket a dinted old cup of tin
More precious to me than silver, and blessing the draught within,

3. An alternate line exists in the version of the poem published in the *Quarterly of the Society of California Pioneers* 5 (n.d.): 200–201: "The brows I have flecked with sable crowd the living everywhere."

I drink alone and in silence to the "Builders of the West,"
"Long life to the hearts still beating, and peace to the hearts at rest."

⇒Based on handwritten and corrected copy in Daggett file,
California State Library, Sacramento

Untitled

Joseph T. Goodman

With lids shut tight to repel the light
That had seldom revealed a welcome sight,
And skinny lips set close to repress
Her scorn of life and its worthlessness;
With wasted features and silvered hair
And the ugly brands of work and care;
She seemed to have gone from the world to protest
And defy its spite by her perfect rest.

A life of sacrifice only—a lot
Where, forgetting herself, she was all forgot;
Where affection, duty, motherhood made
Their loyal offerings unrepaid
And her humble faith in a love divine
Never met with an answering sign;
A lot with guerdon and joy so small
It were better she never had lived at all.

N.d., Goodman file, Bancroft Library,
University of California, Berkeley

The Two Sermons

Joseph T. Goodman

The minister mumbled that God was good;
That His ways, if rightly understood,
Were the lovingest, the best of ways,
And deserving of endless thanks and praise;
That toil and pain and care and woe
Were the kindly means employed below
By the Holy One, in his boundless love,
To fit the soul for its home above.

But the silent lips of the dead impeached
Every word that the preacher preached:
"Look on this form," they seemed to say,
"This poor, worn wreckage of misused clay,
And see if in all the unsightly clod
You can find a sign of a loving God!
Preach on; it is still your stock in trade
But I am through with the masquerade."

N.d., Goodman file, Bancroft Library,
University of California, Berkeley

Sursum Corda

Joseph T. Goodman

Why should we fret, and strive to hold
   Our course along an ordered way,
When in the mazes manifold
   At last our feet must go astray?

The earth's first born as straitly walked,
   But went amiss; then others came
And in like manner wrongly stalked;
   And we in turn shall do the same.

Somewhere, while I sit here at rest,
   Swift trains are plunging on their way,
A dove is brooding on her nest,
   The lion roaming for his prey.

How will it matter, at the last,
   What fate befalls the rushing train?
Whether the lion feed or fast?
   Or if the dove shall brood in vain?

It will not matter; but the soul
   Has yet this choice in the game:
The end may be beyond control
   But we can keep the lofty aim.

N.d., Goodman file, Bancroft Library,
University of California, Berkeley

Virginia City

Joseph T. Goodman

In youth, when I did love, did love
(To quote the sexton's homely ditty)
I lived six thousand feet above
Sea level, in Virginia City;
The site was bleak, the houses small,
The narrow streets unpaved and slanting.
But now it seems to me of all
The spots on earth the most enchanting.

Let Art with all its cunning strive,
Let Nature lavish all her splendor,
One touch of sentiment will give
A charm more beautiful and tender;
And so that town, howe'er uncouth
To others who have chanced to go there,
Enshrines the ashes of my youth,
And there is Fairyland, or nowhere.

Who tends its marts, who treads its ways,
Are mysteries beyond my guessing;
To me the forms of other days
Are still about its centers pressing:
I know that loving lips are cold
And true hearts stilled—ah, more the pity!
But in my fancy they yet hold
Their empire in Virginia City.

Unhallowed flames have swept away
The structures in which I delighted,

The streets are grass-grown, and decay
Has left the sunny slopes benighted—
But not for me: for my dimmed sight
The town is always like the olden,
As to the captive Israelite
Shone aye Jerusalem the Golden.

I would not wish to see it now,
I choose to know it as I then did
With glorious light upon its brow
And all its features bright and splendid;
Nor would I like that it should see
Me, gray and stooped, a mark for pity.
And learn that time had dealt with me
As hard as with Virginia City.

⇾N.d., multiple MS[1]

1. The Goodman file in the Bancroft Library of the University of California, Berkeley, has a type-script—possibly an early draft of the poem—with an alternate ending beginning with a variant fourth stanza followed by fifth and sixth stanzas that differ from the fifth stanza that ends this version of the poem.

Unhallowed flames have swept away
 The structures in which I delighted,
The streets are grassgrown, and decay
 Has left the thoroughfares benighted—
But unto me, upon its height
 The town is always like the olden,
As to the captive Israelite
 Appeared Jerusalem the Golden.

A point there is in all our fates
 Of best achievement and endeavor,
Where all of being culminates
 In one high ride, then ~~sinks~~ ebbs forever;
And, as life sluggishly recedes,
 We gaze back with a tearful yearning
Across the stagnant slime and reeds
 To that bright spot that marked the turning.

So I look back. And, if this life
 Is not the end-all and the be-all,
If when we've done with earthly strife
 There be a Paradise or Sheol,
Or any other named abode
 Which we may gain through love or pity,
Grant me a heavenly Comstock Lode,
 A spiritual Virginia City.

The Pasteurized Kiss

Sam Davis

The latest scientific fad,
 Which seems to me outrageous,
Puts microbe germs on ruby lips,
 And makes a kiss contagious.

It hardly seems the proper thing,
 To put love on half ration,
Or take the soul from out the kiss,
 By filtered osculation.

I learned to know the gentler sex,
 E'er I was one and twenty,
And when it came to kissing games,
 We liked 'em good and plenty.

All kinds of people played the same,
 Married, widowed, misses,
But no one thought of asking them,
 To sterilize their kisses.

Although I'm not prepared to say—
 "To fear I am a stranger"
But certainly an added charm
 Goes with the spice of danger.

So when I come to Mary's lips,
 Or Lucy's, Flo's, or Nancy's,
I might pause and reflect a while,
 Then—straightway take the chances.

I do not pine for lips that reek,
  With antiseptic lotion,
Nor would I journey far to seek,
  A Pasteurized devotion.

⟿N.d., MS in the private collection of the
family of Sylvia Crowell Stoddard

The Campaign Debt

Sam Davis

Once when on a campaign trip I met a dainty maid,
Who for a job political solicited my aid.
And in the conversation she led me to infer,
She'd like a stenographic stint at a hundred dollars per.
In compensation for a boost this maiden did agree,
To fall upon my willing neck in payment for her fee.
Lured by her gauzy promise I got the girl the place,
And all the other candidates were hustled from the race.
But after she copped the job and salted down some dough,
She didn't seem to me the same seductive little Flo.
And when she ambled down the street, in gay attire you bet,
She lost all recollection of that little campaign debt.
I met her once at eventide, and told her I felt sore,
That she had been so mortal slow in settling that score.
She looked me squarely in the face, with eye that never swerved.
"A pact political is never religiously observed.
You told the voters you would send monopoly to grass,
But ever since election you have ridden on a pass."[1]

* * *

I never got the principal from that designing maid.
But installments on the interest have occasionally been paid.

N.d., MS in the private collection of the
family of Sylvia Crowell Stoddard

1. Railroads, which often exercised monopoly powers in the regions they traversed, gave free
passes to influential supporters.

[The Mrs. Warren of Carson City]

Sam Davis

This poem exists in at least three versions, all untitled. The editor proposes this version as combining the best features of all of them and has supplied the bracketed title.

⌁⌁⌁

Her figure was perfect, her face was exquisite
When first she blew in to pay Carson a visit.
She had been but a couple of weeks in the city
When she copped a fat job as a clerk of Committee.
Her bonnets were dreams, clothes perfect in fitting
Whether standing or walking, reclining or sitting.
Whether dancing or flirting, receiving or feeding,
Her manners were always the height of good breeding.
The kids in the lower house simply adored her
And the senators most deferential toward her.
But 'twas covertly whispered when half through the session
That the lady had known "Mrs. Warren's Profession."[1]
Of course 'twasn't sure and not positively certain
Of her present or past, and none lifted the curtain.
If a bill needed help, you'd certainly find it
Moved better along with this lady behind it.
Slow, adipose members who long loved to linger
Would jump like gazelles at the crook of her finger.

1. The title character of *Mrs. Warren's Profession* (1894), a play by George Bernard Shaw, is a prostitute.

379

Her conduct was seldom with levity laden;
She posed as a prim Puritanical maiden.

Her figure was perfect, her face was exquisite
When first she blew in to pay Carson a visit.
Now mention her name and there's scoff and derision
And she's gone from our gaze like a beautiful vision.

   N.d., no title—edited for spelling, grammar, and punctuation
  from original version on a scrap of paper in the private collection
      of the family of Sylvia Crowell Stoddard

The Storm

Sam Davis

There is a whisper in the evening air,
The solemn pine trees tremble and are still,
    And then a moan, as when from out its lair
Some wild beast springs to tread the tangled hill,
And now the restless forest feels the thrill
    That is the shivering courier of the snow,
    And like some giant sobbing out its woe,
It pours its fitful grieving in mine ear,
The stars are hidden. Lo! the storm is here.

A dull, gray sky, just creeping from the night,
A shattered cabin in the drifting light.
    A prostrate pine tree, twisted by the blast,
    A dead man in the snow. The storm has passed.

⇒*Overland Monthly* (September 1892): 298

The Lure of the Sagebrush

Sam Davis

Like Joe Goodman's "Virginia City," Davis's "The Lure of the Sagebrush" appears not to have a single, definitive source but has been reprinted countless times, especially in Nevada. The bracketed introduction to it by Thomas Brown, for one of its printings, also explains its great popularity.

⊷⩵ ⩵⊷

[By Thomas P. Brown, Publicity Manager, Western Pacific Railroad, San Francisco, California

Every prospector, every lover of the West, who knows its plains and its deserts, pays homage to the gray-green sagebrush that dots the landscape and often forms its principal vegetation. Of the many varieties, the best known is the common or bitter sage, botanically termed the artemisia tridentata which is Nevada's chosen state flower. With its silver, wedge-shaped leaves, it has a unique beauty that is accentuated by moonlight. Its aromatic fragrance gives a tang to the air that is especially exhilarating after a rain.

The sagebrush exemplifies the tenacity of life. Ever courageous, it scorns the ravages of heat; it digs in the more deeply when winds blast it away; it reincarnates in the Spring though covered by snowdrifts through the winter.

To the roving Indian it offers seeds for food and leaves for medicine; to hungry sheep it affords forage; to the prospector, firewood. As Rev. Brewster Adams of Reno has said: "It is the great mother of the desert—sheltering, protecting, feeding and fighting for its own against the elements." Truly, the sagebrush is the immortelle of the West.

Of the friendly sagebrush, Sam P. Davis, Nevada's noted journalist of two decades ago, has written the following lines:]

Have you ever scented the sagebrush
    That mantles Nevada's plain?
If not, you have lived but half your life;
    And that half in vain.

No matter where the place or clime
    That your wandering footsteps stray,
You will sigh as you think of her velvet fields
    And their fragrance of leveled hay.

You will loiter awhile in other lands,
    When something seems to call,
And the lure of the sagebrush brings you back
    And holds you within its thrall.

You may tread the halls of pleasure,
    Where the lamps of folly shine,
'Mid the sobbing of sensuous music,
    And the flow of forbidden wine;

But when the revel is over
    And the dancers turn to go,
You will long for a draught of her crystal streams
    That spring from her peaks of snow.

You will sigh for a sight of the beetling crags,
    Where the Storm King holds his sway,
Where the sinking sun, with its brush of gold,
    Tells the tale of a dying day—

And when you die you will want a grave
    Where the Washoe zephyr[1] blows,
With the green of the sagebrush above your head,
    What need to plant the rose?

꜠June 16, 1904, MS in the private collection of the
family of Sylvia Crowell Stoddard

---

1. Washoe County was famous for strong winds, which residents humorously called "zephyrs."

The Gleaner

Sam Davis

I watched the gleaners rake the field
　　After the ripening sheaves were stored,
Toiling the while in the noonday sun,
　　As they garnered their meager hoard.

And when they called on the autumn winds
　　To help them winnow the golden wheat,
The chaff went out to be scattered wide,
　　While the grain fell at their feet.

I wandered over the field of life,
　　Following after the harvest done;
While in the stubble I sought for friends,
　　And gathered them one by one.

And after the crowning autumn years
　　The field of friendship I culled once more.
And, as I gathered the winnowed grain,
　　I grieved at the scanty store.

The winds of adversity swept the chaff,
　　And, as it littered the desert sand,
I gathered the wheat from about my feet
　　And held it all in my hollowed hand.

N.d., MS in the private collection of the
family of Sylvia Crowell Stoddard

Bibliography

Adams, Eva B. "Joseph T. Goodman—the Man Who Made Mark Twain." M.A. thesis, Columbia University, 1936.

Berkove, Lawrence I. "'Assaying in Nevada': Twain's Wrong Turn in the Right Direction." *American Literary Realism* 27:3 (Spring 1995): 64–79.

———. *Dan De Quille*. Boise State University Western Writers Series No. 136. Boise, Idaho: Boise State University Press, 1999.

———. *Ethical Records of Twain and His Circle of Sagebrush Journalists*. Quarry Farm Papers No. 5. Elmira, N.Y.: Elmira College Center for Mark Twain Studies, 1994.

———. "Joe Goodman, in His Own Write." *Nevada Magazine* 61:1 (January/February 2001): 16–19.

———. "Nevada Influences on Mark Twain." In *A Companion to Mark Twain*, edited by Peter Messent and Louis J. Budd, 157–71. Oxford and Malden, Mass.: Blackwell, 2006.

———. "The Sagebrush School Revived." In *A Companion to the Regional Literatures of America*, edited by Charles Crow, 324–43. Oxford and Malden, Mass.: Blackwell, 2003.

———. "Samuel Post Davis." In *Dictionary of Literary Biography, Vol. 202: Nineteenth-Century American Fiction Writers*, edited by Kent P. Ljungquist, 92–99. Detroit: Gale Research, 1999.

Branch, Edgar Marquess. *The Literary Apprenticeship of Mark Twain*. 1950. Reprint. New York: Russell and Russell, 1966.

Cummins, Ella Sterling. *The Story of the Files*. San Francisco: World's Fair Commission of California, 1893.

Daggett, Rollin M. *Braxton's Bar*. New York: G. W. Carleton, 1882.

Daggett, Rollin M., and Joseph T. Goodman. *The Psychoscope*. Edited with an introduction by Lawrence I. Berkove. Charleston, S.C.: Mark Twain Journal, 2006.

Davis, Sam. *The Prince of Timbuctoo*. In *The Old West in the Old World: Lost Plays by Bret Harte and Sam Davis,* edited by Lawrence I. Berkove and Gary Scharnhorst. Albuquerque: University of New Mexico Press, 2006.

————. *Short Stories*. San Francisco: Golden Era, 1886.

De Quille, Dan [William Wright]. "Artemus Ward in Nevada." 1893. Reprinted in *Dan De Quille, the Washoe Giant,* edited by Richard A. Dwyer and Richard E. Lingenfelter, 219–24. Reno: University of Nevada Press, 1990.

————. *The Big Bonanza: An Authentic Account of the Discovery, History, and Working of the World-Renowned Comstock Lode of Nevada*. 1876. Reprint. New York: Knopf, 1947.

————. *Dives and Lazarus*. Edited with an introduction by Lawrence I. Berkove. Ann Arbor: Ardis, 1988.

————. *The Fighting Horse of the Stanislaus: Stories and Essays by Dan De Quille*. Edited with an introduction by Lawrence I. Berkove. Iowa City: University of Iowa Press, 1990.

————. *The Gnomes of the Dead Rivers*. Edited with an introduction by Lawrence I. Berkove. Sparks, Nev.: Falcon Hill, 1990.

————. "Pahnenit, Prince of the Land of Lakes." Edited with an introduction by Lawrence I. Berkove. *Nevada Historical Society Quarterly* 31:2 (Summer 1988): 79–118.

————. *The Sorceress of Attu*. Edited with an introduction by Lawrence I. Berkove. Dearborn: University of Michigan–Dearborn, 1994.

Doten, Alfred. *The Journals of Alfred Doten, 1849–1903*. 3 vols. Edited by Walter Van Tilburg Clark. Reno: University of Nevada Press, 1973.

Dwyer, Richard A., and Richard E. Lingenfelter, eds. *Lying on the Eastern Slope: James Townsend's Comic Journalism on the Mining Frontier*. Miami: Florida International University Press, 1984.

Emerson, Everett. "A Send-Off for Joe Goodman: Mark Twain's 'The Carson Fossil-Footprints.'" *Resources for American Literary Study* 10 (Spring 1980): 71–78.

Emrich, Duncan, ed. *Comstock Bonanza*. New York: Vanguard, 1950.

Fitch, Thomas. *Western Carpetbagger*. 1903–1904. Reprint. Edited with an introduction by Eric N. Moody. Reno: University of Nevada Press, 1978.

Gally, James W. *Sand, and Big Jack Small*. 1880. Reprinted in *Comstock Bonanza,* ed. Duncan Emrich. New York: Vanguard, 1950.

Gillis, William R. *Gold Rush Days with Mark Twain*. Introduction by Cyril Clemens. New York: Boni, 1930.

Goodman, Joseph T. "Artemus Ward on the Comstock Lode." 1892. Reprint. In *Heroes, Badmen, and Honest Miners: Joe Goodman's Tales of the Comstock Lode,* edited by Phillip I. Earl, 21–26. Reno: Great Basin Press, 1977.

————. *"An Irregular Correspondent": The European Travel Letters of Mark Twain's*

Editor and Friend Joe Goodman. [1870.] Edited with an introduction by Lawrence I. Berkove. *Mark Twain Journal* 35:2 (Fall 1997): 1–44.

———. "The TRUMPET Comes to Pickeye!" Number Four of Six California Tales. [San Francisco:] Book Club of California, 1939.

Goodwin, C. C. *As I Remember Them.* Salt Lake City: Salt Lake Commercial Club, 1913.

———. *The Comstock Club.* Salt Lake City: Tribune Job Printing Co., 1891.

———. *The Wedge of Gold.* Salt Lake City: Tribune Job Printing Co., 1893.

Hart, Fred H. *The Sazerac Lying Club.* 5th ed. San Francisco: Samuel Carson, 1878.

Hopkins, Sarah Winnemucca. *Life among the Piutes: Their Wrongs and Claims.* 1883. Reprint. Reno: University of Nevada Press, 1994.

Lewis, Oscar, ed. *The Life and Times of the Virginia City Territorial Enterprise.* Ashland, Ore.: Lewis Osborne, 1971.

Paine, Albert Bigelow. *Mark Twain: A Biography.* 2 vols. New York: Harper and Bros., 1912.

Stoddard, Sylvia Crowell, ed. *Sam Knew Them When.* Reno: Great Basin Press, 1996.

Twain, Mark. *Early Tales & Sketches, Volume 1: 1851–1864.* Edited by Edgar Marquess Branch, Robert H. Hirst, and Harriet Elinor Smith. Berkeley: University of California Press, 1979.

———. *Mark Twain's Letters, Volume 1: 1853–1866.* Edited by Edgar Marquess Branch, Michael B. Frank, and Kenneth Sanderson. Berkeley: University of California Press, 1988.

———. *Roughing It.* 1872. Reprint. Edited by Harriet Elinor Smith and Edgar Marquess Branch. Berkeley: University of California Press, 1993.

Weisenburger, Francis Phelps. *Idol of the West: The Fabulous Career of Rollin Mallory Daggett.* Syracuse, N.Y.: Syracuse University Press, 1965.

Zanjani, Sally. *Sarah Winnemucca.* Lincoln: University of Nebraska Press, 2001.

Index of Authors

Index of Titles

About the Editor

Lawrence I. Berkove is Professor Emeritus of English at the University of Michigan–Dearborn and the author or editor of eleven other books, including *A Prescription for Adversity: The Moral Art of Ambrose Bierce* and *The Best Short Stories of Mark Twain*.